The House of Commons
seven hundred years of British tradition

The House of Commons
seven hundred years of British tradition

Edited by Robert Smith & John S Moore

This publication has been made possible by the generosity of Manorial Auctioneers Limited

The House of Commons
seven hundred years of British tradition

Published by Smith's Peerage Limited, Heron Place, 3 George Street, London W1H 6AD

ISBN 0 9524229 2 1

British Library Cataloguing in Publication Data. A catalogue record for this book is available from the British Library; Great Britain – History – early medieval to present (R Smith and J S Moore, joint Eds).

This book originated at a Conference held by the Manorial Society of Great Britain at Oriel College, Oxford, in September 1994. *The House of Commons, seven hundred years of British tradition,* is the second in a series of three books about the British Constitution. *The House of Lords, a thousand years of British tradition,* was published in November 1994; and *The Monarchy, fifteen hundred years of British tradition,* will be published in autumn 1996.

Typeset and printed by Staples Printers Rochester Limited, Neptune Close, Medway City Estate, Frindsbury, Rochester Kent ME2 4LT England

London 1996

LIST OF SUBSCRIBERS

THE PEERAGE

The Lord Alexander of Weedon QC
The Earl of Annandale and Hartfell
The Lord Biddulph
The Viscount Brookeborough DL
The Lord Carnock
The Lord Carter
The Lord Chalfont OBE MC PC
The Earl of Clarendon
The Lord Clark of Kempston PC
The Lord Clifford of Chudleigh
The Viscount Cobham
The Viscount Cross
The Lord De Ramsey DL
The Lord Gray of Contin PC DL
The Lord Hanson Kt
The Earl of Iddesleigh DL
The Earl of Illchester
The Lord Kissin of Camden
The Lord Macfarlane of Bearsden DL
The Lord Martonmere
The Lord Menuhin OM KBE
The Lord Mostyn MC
The Lord Nelson of Stafford
The Duke of Northumberland
The Lord O'Neill TD
The Lord Peyton of Yeovil
The Lord Prentice
The Lord Rayner Kt
The Earl of Shannon
The Earl of Shrewsbury and Talbot DL
The Lord Skelmersdale
The Lord Sudeley FSA
The Viscount Tonypandy PC
The Lord Waddington GCVO DL QC
The Lord Wakeham PC
The Lord Walker MBE PC
The Earl of Wemyss KT LLD
Lt Col The Lord Wigram MC

THE COMMONS

Ronnie Campbell MP
Sir Patrick Cormack MP
Quentin Davies MP
Nirj Deva DL MP
Llin Golding MP
The Rt Hon Sir Edward Heath KG MBE MP
The Rt Hon Michael Heseltine PC MP
Jane Kennedy MP
Bill Michie MP
Andrew Mitchell MP
Sir David Mitchell DL MP
William O'Brien MP
The Rt Hon Sir Geoffrey Pattie MP
Geoffrey Robinson MP
The Rt Hon Sir Nicholas Scott KBE MP
The Rt Hon John D Taylor MP

THE FEUDAL BARONS

Stuart Crane, Baron of Cluny
Charles Eugster, Baron of Callan
D G Jenks-Handford, Baron of Clanmaurice
David Hodge, Baron of Cavan
P J Hurlstone, Baron of Carlingford
Bruce King-Siem, Baron of Morgallion
Peter Liddle, Baron of Gilsland
Dr H I Lockett, Baron of Castleknock
Hermann Meyer, Baron of Newry
John Mulvihill, Baron of Roscommon
David Person, Baron of Garrycastle
Michel Pilette, Baron of Kinnear
Lady Previn, Baroness of Tirrerill
Trevor Prider, Baron of Ballintober
General Stephen Shadix, Baron of Orior
Daniel Sharpe, Baron of Twynehame
Paul Sleigh, Baron of Carbury
Maurice Taylor, Baron of Portlethen
Gordon Teall, Baron of Huntly
Melody Urquhart, Baroness of Eye and Leyny
Kimberly Baroness Von Der Trenck
Douglas Wagland, Baron of Pitcruivie
M C J Whitby, Baron of Ballycowen
Robert Williamson, Baron of Ballumbie

THE MANORIAL LORDS

Jacqueline Albright, Lady of Ireby
Gerald Andrews, Lord of Grayrigg
Anthony Appleton, Lord of Great Baddow
J M Armitage, Lady of Knockaline
Bhupendra Arora, Lord of Grittenham
D A W Ashdown, Lord of Waterhead
Richard Ayearst, Lord of Bothamshall
Arnold Baker, Lord of Barton
Sir Robert Balchin
Miriam Batts, Lady of Birch and Lyth
Hermann Erwin Beck, Lord of Great Hallingbury
Daniel Beirne, Lord of Downholme
Jacques Bichsel, Lord of Hackford
William Bowmore, Lord of Heywood Hall
George Braden, Lord of Carrigaline
Gueorgui Briling, Lord of Cropwell Bishop
Valerie Bull, Lady of Thoby
Clifford Buxton, Lord of Tibenham Hastings and Tibenham Bishops
Brian Callan, Lord of Athlone
G B Campbell
Peter Chancellor, Lord of West Hartford
Murray Chapman
Peter Chapman OBE, Lord of Dodford
M L Clarke, Lord of Carlton
Timothy Clark, Lord of Soham
Mervyn Cole, Lord of Knowstone
Jack Connolly, Lord of Cheam and Cuddington
Robert Coombes, Lord of St Winnow
Roy Cooper, Lord of West Bretton
Arnold Davis, Lord of Barnham Broom
Bernard Davis, Lord of Castelmai
Jacqueline de Fonseca, Lady of Purse Caundle
Douglas Densmore, Lord of Stratford St Andrew
Elsie Downer, Lady of Crouch
Barry Drury, Lord of Wiveton
Ruth Drury
C H W Dunning Gribble, Lord of Marnhull
John Dyhouse, Lord of Woodford Halse
N Elnagy, Lord of Wicklewood
Anthony Farnath, Lord of Woodcote
N J Fisher
S G Flavell Matts, Lord of Mountsorrel
Andrew Forster, Lord of Mynchens
David Garrison, Lord of Byng
Jack Garside, Lord of Sulby

A N Georgiou, Lord of Blisworth
K K Gibson-Wynes, Lord of Bottitors
P N G Gilbert, Lord of Cantley
J Gillies Shields, Lord of Melbourne
Christopher Golding, Lord of Kempshott
John Gommes, Lord of Elm
John Grant, Lord of Walton Wood
Richard Grayson, Lord of Mursley
Gillian Green, Lady of Alverton and St Buryan
Jacqueline Harris, Lady of Caldwell
Col P W Herring OBE, Lord of Berewyk Hall
James Hilton, Lord of Lytham
J A Holland, Lord of Boyland
Charles Holloway, Lord of Seavington Dennis
Paul Hooley, Lord of Hoole
Niall Horan
John Hornchurch, Lord of Hornchurch Hall
Geoffrey Horne, Lord of Wakes Colne
Brian Hornsby, Lord of Hornsby
Cecil R Humphery-Smith FSA
Peter Jennings, Lord of Thremhall Priory
Roy Jennings, Lord of Minterne
W H Joseph, Lord of Stormy
Siegfried Joussineau, Lord of Diss
Steven Kellner, Lord of Blencogo
A C Kirby, Lord of Stockwith
E P Kirby, Lady of West Coatham
Nicholas Kittrie, Lord of Croughton
William Kulesh, Lord of Brampton
Ernst de Kuthy, Lord of Worminghall
Peter Lake, Lord of Hoe Benham
Frederick Lambert, Lord of Tockington
Cyril Lane, Lord of Shrewsbury's Fee
E C Lashbrooke, Lord of Duston
J E Laurie, Lord of Boylands
Raymond Lescott, Lord of Tilstock
Alan Littlewood, Lord of Wharton
Mrs Duncan Livesey
Ambassador John Loeb, Lord of Brinsley
Stefan Lohr, Lord of Benham Lovell
John Longford-Lewis, Lord of More Malherbe and Cotley
J V Machin, Lord of Gateford
Sadie Marks, Lady of Shovelstrode
R D McCracken, Lord of Crofton and Whinnow
Patrick McKenna, Lord of Ashridge
John Montgomery, Lord of Thirlwall and Brunstock
A J Moore, Lord of Hardwick

F L Morgan, Lord of Kenfig
M E Mottram, Lord of Chatteris Nunns
Richard Nokes, Lord of Middleton Cheney
David Nugent, Lord of Castletown Delvin
Dr D E Olliff
E P Pain, Lord of Lubenham
Michael Pendred, Lord of Frithsden
Antonio Mas-Perez, Lord of Elkesley
D Pilgrim JP, Lord of West Anstey
P F Poeliejoe-Zewald, Lord of St Aylotts and Beckenham
Charles Poole, Lord of Upton Warren
Michael Pritchard, Lord of Brighstone
Gerald Rand, Lord of Lynford
Raymond Rayner, Lord of Chepstow, St Arvans, and Chilworth
Leslie Retford, Lord of Pleshey
Ken Richards-Greene
Mark Tudor Roberts, Lord of Merrion
Hans Roesner, Lord of Mautby
L H Rosan, Lord of Haverhill
R Rozario, Lord of Ditton
V Rubinstein MBE, Lord of Garford
Terence Rutter, Lord of Ling Hall
Leslie Ryder, Lord of Tixall
Iaria Sandro, Lord of Tillingdon
Leslie Sayer DSM, Lord of Bures at the Mount
Jerome Schooler, Lord of Lurgashall
T Van Schoonbeek, Lord of Lambrigg
Louis-Marc Servien, Lord of Quendon
Barry Sewell, Lord of Hardingham and Flockthorpe
Christopher Shadix, Lord of Dardistown
John Shazell, Lord of Didcot
Timothy Shorland, Lord of Hempton and Northwick
Leslie Spears, Lord of Mayfield and Hormead Redwells
Major Mark Steele, Lord of Hassenbrook
John Stedman, Lord of Irthington
Lt Col Howard Steers, Lord of High Hoyland
Robert Steventon, Lord of Thistleton
Gunter Streib, Lord of Westhall
John Szepietowski, Lord of Ingestre
Nicholas Taurovsky, Lord of Westerfield
B J F Theobald-Hicks, Lord of Danbury and Bretton
Peter Trapp, Lord of Ulpha
Major H B Trevor-Cox, Lord of East Winterslow
F J Turner, Lord of Calthorpe
Pier Felice degli Uberti, Lord of Benham Valence
A E Vidler, Lord of Lanhadron
Arthur Waine, Lord of Horley and Hornton

Frederick Wardle, Lord of Wardle
Edgar Wayman, Lord of Downham
Dr Archibald Weems McFadden, Lord of Deopham
Thomas Wharton, Lord of Kirby Stephen
Gordon Whitehead, Lord of Cockshutt
Robert Williams, Lord of Allerby
R J Woodberry, Lord of Prittlewell
Denis Woodfield, Lord of Hamptonet
Clifford Worthing
Michael McManus
Nicholas Steward
Scott Toberman

Contents

Notes on Contributors, page ii

Picture Captions, page v

Foreword: The Rt Hon Betty Boothroyd MP, Speaker of the House of Commons, page xi

Preface: Robert Smith, Publisher, page xii

Introduction: John S Moore, Co-Editor, page 1

1. *Origins of the Commons, Magna Carta to 1307,* D A Carpenter, page 26

2. *The Later Middle Ages,* Simon Payling, page 48

3. *The House of Commons, 1528–1603,* Jennifer Loach, page 70

4. *James I, Civil War, and Restoration, 1603–1660,* Kevin Sharpe, page 83

5. *The Glorious Revolution and the Hanoverian Succession, 1660–1734,* W A Speck, page 100

6. *The Rotten Borough Commons, 1734–1832,* Jeremy Black, page 109

7. *The Victorian Commons, 1832–1884,* Valerie Cromwell, page 118

8. *Universal Suffrage: The Modern House,* Michael Fry, page 132

9. *Layman's guide to the European Union and the British Parliament,* L W Gormley, page 143

10. *Life of an MP,* Michael Stephen MP, page 150

11. *Parliament and the Press,* Edward Pearce, page 161

12. *The Parliament of Scotland, 1296–1707,* Adam Bruce, page 173

Notes on Contributors

Professor Jeremy Black, PhD, FRHistS, (chapter 6) is Professor of Modern History at the University of Exeter. Educated at Queen's College, Cambridge, he graduated with a starred first-class degree. He was subsequently at St John's and Merton Colleges, Oxford, and has been at Durham from 1980 to 1994. He is a member of the Councils of the Royal Historical Society and the British Records Association. His 18 books include *Sir Robert Walpole and the nature of Eighteenth-Century Politics* (London, 1990), *Culloden and the 'Forty-Five* (Stroud, 1990), *War for America* (Stroud, 1991), *Pitt the Elder* (Cambridge, 1992) and *The Politics of Britain, 1688-1800* (Manchester, 1993).

The Hon Adam Bruce, (chapter 12) read History at Balliol College, Oxford, where he was President of the Union. He then returned to study Law at Edinburgh University and now works for a firm of solicitors in Edinburgh. He contributed a chapter on the Scottish nobility to the *House of Lords: a thousand years of British Tradition*.

Dr David Carpenter, FRHistS, (chapter 1) is a leading authority on English medieval history. His publications include *The Battles of Lewes and Evesham* (Keele, 1987), *The Minority of Henry III* (London, 1990) and numerous articles in books and learned journals. He was educated at Westminster School and Christ Church College, Oxford. He has held lectureships at Christ Church and St Hilda's Colleges, Oxford, at the University of Aberdeen, and at Queen Mary College, London. He is now a Reader in Medieval History at King's College, London.

Valerie Cromwell, MA, FRHistS, (chapter 7) has been Director of the History of Parliament since 1991. She is currently a Vice-President of the Royal Historical Society and a Senior Research Fellow of the Institute of Historical Research, University of London. She was Fellow in History at Newnham College, Cambridge, before moving to the University of Sussex where she was Lecturer and later Reader in History. She was Secretary-General of the International Commission for the History of Representative and Parliamentary Institutions, 1975-85, and since then one of its Vice-Presidents. She has written numerous articles on nineteenth- and twentieth-century British administrative and political history as well as *Revolution or Evolution: British Government in the Nineteenth Century* (London, 1977).

Mr Michael Fry, MA, (chapter 8) is a Research Fellow at the University of Strathclyde. He has been a visiting fellow at the Aldo Moro Foundation in Rome and at Brown University, Providence, Rhode Island. He was Chairman of the Adam Smith Bicentenary in 1990. He is the author of *Patronage and Principle: a political history of modern Scotland* (Aberdeen, 1987), *Adam Smith's Legacy* (London, 1992), and *The Dundas Despotism* (Edinburgh, 1993), and co-editor, with Professor Stewart J. Brown, of *Scotland in the Age of the Disruption* (Edinburgh, 1993).

Professor Laurence Gormley, Ll D, (chapter 9) is Professor of European Law at the Rijksuniversiteit, Groningen, Netherlands; he is also a Professor at the

College of Europe and Visiting Professor at the University of Bremen and at University College, London. A barrister, he is a graduate of the Universities of Oxford and London and received his Ll D from the University of Utrecht. He is a partner with the Amsterdam and Rotterdam law firm, Houthoff, and is a former Official of the Commission of the European Communities. He has written extensively on European Law, and his works include major contributions to Vol 52 of *Halsbury's Laws of England* (London, 4th edn, 1986).

The late Dr Jennifer Loach, D Phil, FRHistS, (chapter 3) was educated at King Edward VI School for Girls, Birmingham, and St Hilda's College, Oxford. She was successively Moberly Senior Scholar of St Hugh's College, Oxford, and Research Fellow (1969-74), Lecturer (1970-4) and Tutorial Fellow of Somerville College, Oxford. With Robert Tittler she edited *The Mid-Tudor Polity* (London, 1980); her other works included *Parliament and the Crown in the Reign of Mary Tudor* (Oxford, 1986), *Parliament under the Tudors* (Oxford, 1991), *A Mid-Tudor Crisis?* (London, 1992) and *Protector Somerset: a reassessment* (Oxford, 1994). At the time of her death she had nearly finished a biography of Edward VI, which will be completed by Dr Penry Williams.

Mr John S. Moore, FSA, FRHistS, (General Editor; Introduction) was educated at Brighton Technical College and the Institute of Historical Research, London. He was awarded the Alexander Prize of the Royal Historical Society and the John Nichols Local History Prize of Leicester University. Since 1968 he has been Lecturer in Economic History at Bristol University. His main research interests are in the economic and social history of medieval and early modern England; his books include *Laughton: a study in the evolution of the Wealden landscape* (Leicester, 1964), *The Goods and Chattels of Our Forefathers* (Chichester, 1976) and *Domesday Book: Gloucestershire* (Chichester, 1981), and he has also written articles in *Anglo-Norman Studies, Economic History Review, English Historical Review* and other historical and linguistic journals. He is now writing a book on the population of Tudor England, and has been invited by the British Academy to edit two volumes in their series, *Records of Social and Economic History*.

Dr Simon Payling, D Phil, FRHistS, (chapter 2) is a graduate of Southampton and Oxford universities. He was a Junior Research Fellow and British Academy Postdoctoral Research Fellow at Balliol College, Oxford. He now works for the History of Parliament Trust. His publications include *Political Society in Lancastrian England* (Oxford, 1991) and several articles on late-medieval landed society.

Edward Pearce, MA, (chapter 11) writes for a number of newspapers including the *Evening Standard*, the *Daily Mail* and *The Independent*. He has been a regular member of the Radio 4 programme 'The Moral Maze' since it began in 1990. Educated at Darlington Grammar School and St Peter's College, Oxford, after working at Transport House and contesting a parliamentary seat for Labour, he taught for a while in the North East before entering journalism in 1975. A leader-writer with the *Daily Express,* 1977-79, he became Commons sketch-writer and leader-writer on the *Daily Telegraph,* 1979-87, columnist with iv

the *Sunday Times,* 1987-90, and the *Guardian,* 1990-95. He has written seven books from *The Senate of Lilliput* (London, 1983) to *Macchiavelli's Children* (London, 1993), and is now writing *Winning Near the Goal,* a study of men who narrowly failed to become Prime Minister. He is married with one daughter and lives in Buckinghamshire.

Professor Kevin Sharpe, D Phil, FRHistS (chapter 4) is Professor of History in the School of Research and Graduate Studies at the University of Southampton. Among his books are *The Personal Rule of Charles I* (New Haven (USA), 1992), *Politics and Ideas in Early Stuart England* (London, 1989), *Criticism and Compliment: The Politics of Literature in the England of Charles I* (Cambridge, 1987), and he has edited, with Peter Lake, *Culture and Politics in Early Stuart England* (London, 1994). He has held Visiting Fellowships at the Institute of Advanced Study, Princeton, at Stanford Humanities Center, and the Humanities Research Centre, Canberra. He is currently working on the culture of authority in early modern England.

Robert Smith, BA, (Preface) read history at Nottingham University and graduated as BA in 1969. He is the Chairman of the Manorial Society of Great Britain and Publisher of Smith's Peerage Ltd. *The Peerage, Baronetage and Feudal Title Holders* in four volumes is in the process of research for publication in 1998. He edited and published *Domesday, 900 Years of England's Norman Heritage* (joint editor with H R Loyn) for the Public Record Office (1986); *Royal Armada, 400 Years* for the National Maritime Museum (1988); and *Against the Odds, the 50th Anniversary of the Battle of Britain* for the Royal Air Force Museum (1990). He jointly edited and published *The House of Lords, a thousand years of British tradition* in 1994, and edits and publishes the Manorial Society Bulletin.

Professor W A Speck, D Phil (Oxon), FRHistS, (chapter 5) was educated at the Queen's College, Oxford. He subsequently taught at the universities of Exeter, Newcastle upon Tyne, Hull and Leeds, where he is currently Professor of Modern History. He is the author of *Tory and Whig: The struggle in the constituencies, 1701-1715* (London, 1970), *Stability and Strife: England, 1714-1760* (London, 1977), *The Butcher: The Duke of Cumberland and the suppression of the Forty-Five* (Oxford, 1981), *Society and Literature in England, 1700-1760* (Dublin (Eire), 1983), *Reluctant Revolutionaries: Englishmen and the Revolution of 1688* (Oxford, 1988), *A Concise History of Britain, 1707-1975* (Cambridge, 1993), and *The Birth of Britain: A New Nation, 1700-1710* (Oxford, 1994).

Michael Stephen, MP, (chapter 10) has been MP for Shoreham, Sussex, since April 1992 and is Vice-Chairman of the Conservative Home Affairs Committee. He was called to the Bar by the Inner Temple in 1966, and then joined the British Army, serving as Lieutenant in the Life Guards from 1966 to 1970. Having won a Harkness Fellowship to the United States in 1970, he was awarded the degree of Master of Laws by Stanford University, and did postgraduate research in International Law at Harvard. He served as Assistant Legal Adviser to the United Kingdom Delegation to the United Nations, and on returning to London practised as a barrister. He is a member of the Royal Institute of International Affairs.

Picture Captions

A: An imaginary Tudor representation of a Parliament in the reign of Edward I. The difficulties of the last years of King John and those during much of the reign of Henry III, culminating in the Barons' War of the 1260s, brought a new idea to the 13th century – and central to the rest of parliamentary history: that a king's need for taxation could only be granted by Parliament. Edward also opened up Parliament to petitions, meeting a very real social need. *Wriothesley MS, Royal Library, Windsor, quire B, by Gracious Permission of Her Majesty The Queen.* See David Carpenter, page 26.

B: The deposition of Richard II in 1399 in favour of his cousin, Henry Bolingbroke, Duke of Lancaster (immediately to the right of the Throne in the tall brown hat). This picture depicts "the Duke of Lancaster and the other dukes and lords spiritual and temporal and the people of the realm in great numbers", assembled in Westminster Hall "in the place solemnly prepared for holding Parliament". Richard II was a prisoner. The Archbishop of York declared the Throne vacant in Latin and in English, and the question was put (through by whom is not known) "to the estates and people there present". Then "each for himself and all in common, together with the people, unanimously and of one accord accepted it. . . It was then publicly expounded" that an act should be passed, confirming the deposition, and the Duke of Lancaster, now as Henry IV, issued writs for a Parliament. *British Museum, Harleian MS, 1319, fol 57.* See Simon Payling, page 48.

C: Thomas Wolsey, Cardinal Archbishop of York, Papal Legate, and Chancellor – Henry VIII's most trusted servant for the first 20 years of his reign. By careful use of royal power and patronage, Wolsey became the great manager of the Commons, whose fall and death in 1529 Henry would live to regret. He was succeeded by his own secretary, Thomas Cromwell, who "showed the King what he might do", and made Henry "Emperor in his own kingdom". Although Cromwell himself had fallen, by 1542, the King had Parliament pass an act which enabled him, and his successors, to legislate without Parliament. Fortunately, the minority of Edward VI caused this act to be repealed almost at once, on Henry's death, by the Council who had most to fear from an "absolute monarch". *Courtesy National Portrait Gallery, London.* See Simon Payling, page 48.

D: The Parliament at Blackfriars, London, in April 1523, from a MS made for Thomas Wriothesley, Garter King of Arms. Henry VIII is crowned, carrying the dove sceptre, with the Royal Arms, encircled by the Garter, above his head. Properly speaking, the Houses of Parliament are not two, but three, and this picture is a good example of this fact. The King sits with his ministers and judges, to the right in the picture, Cardinal Wolsey and Archbishop Warham (both depicted by their arms). On the carpet, decorated with fleurs de Lys, are the peers holding the swords of state and the white wand of office, just as they are borne today at a State Opening. In the centre are the Woolsacks, upon which sit the senior judges. On the right are the peers, headed by the Duke of Norfolk, and the left the bishops and abbots. In the foreground are the Commons, called, as we would say today, to the Bar of the Lords. The King's ministers and judges formed the third "house" of Parliament, as they still do. Judges may be summoned to Parliament without being peers of the realm, although this has not happened since 1888. Until that date, Lords of Appeal were summoned to Parliament as royal counsel and ceased to be called once they had retired as appellate judges. Sir Thomas Moore, Henry VIII's Chancellor, sat in Parliament, but was not a peer. The third House is that area from the Woolsack to the Throne. *Wriothesley MS, Royal Library, Windsor, quire P, by Gracious Permission of Her Majesty The Queen.* See Simon Payling, page 48.

E: William Cecil, Lord Burleigh, Queen Elizabeth I's chief minister. Burleigh was of minor gentry stock who made his family's fortune in government service. Like Wolsey and Cromwell under Elizabeth's father Henry VIII, Burleigh was a great manager of the Commons. In general, the Commons seems to have seen its relationship with the Crown and the Crown's ministers very much as a meeting of shareholders sees itself in relation to the chairman and board of a company – devoted to the same purposes. . . but occasionally disagreeing about how best to achieve them. Note that Lord Burleigh is wearing the collar of the Order of the Garter, of which there are only 24 knights plus the Sovereign, the highest order of chivalry in the kingdom of England and the oldest in the kingdom of Great Britain (Order founded in 1346). By the 19th century, even the Garter had become a "bauble" to be dispensed on the recommendation of prime ministers, so far had the Crown fallen under the tutelage of the Commons. Clement Attlee "returned" the Order to George VI in 1946, and it is now once again in the Sovereign's personal gift. Burleigh's eldest son, Thomas, is ancestor to the present Marquess of Exeter and his second son, Robert, ancestor to the present Marquess of Salisbury. The Cecils have provided servants of the State for the last four centuries. The third Marquess of Salisbury was the last peer to be prime minster from the House of Lords in the 1890s, except for the three-week technicality of the Earl of Home, who was prime minister from 1963 to 1964, and renounced his peerage to become Sir Alec Douglas Home which enabled him to be elected to the House of Commons. *Courtesy National Portrait Gallery, London.* See Jennifer Loach, page 70.

F: Charles I: although he lost his head as well as the Throne, he is perhaps the King who has made it possible for Britain still to have a Monarchy in the last decade of the last century of the second millenium. He has come down to us as a romantic hero, but he was impossible to deal with. Parliament thought that it had reached an accommodation with him on the conclusion of the first Civil War in 1646, but no sooner done than the King left his comfortable confinement in the Isle of Wight and raised a new army. His word could not be trusted, though it has to be said that the Parliament and its New Model Army by this time comprised a pretty appalling group of men. Those whose hearts had been with the King and their heads with the Parliament in the 1640s, found both intellect and emotion with the Monarchy by the end of the 1650s. Charles defended himself with the utmost eloquence and courage in 1649 at his trial in Westminster Hall, a place where he and his ancestors had been wont not only to have their say, but to have their way; and he died bravely on a cold January morning outside his own palace in Whitehall. The Monarchy and the Commons were both caught up in a set of traditional customs which were strained at the edges but not broken, leaving the Crown unable to govern and the Commons, rather like modern critics of the health service, irritated at the deficiencies and grumbling at the costs. *Courtesy National Portrait Gallery, London.* See Kevin Sharpe, page 83.

G: Oliver Cromwell, Charles I's brilliant adversary. He was a natural military tactician and ruler. In another age, he might well have become the King's chief minister as Thomas Wolsey and Robert Cecil had done in the previous century. He was a Norfolk squire and came late to Parliament. If the Commons, as Marxist historians suggest, was determined to take the reins of power from the beginning of the 17th century, it is extraordinary how willing the House was to surrender them to Lord Protector Cromwell after 1650. Perhaps revolutions are always like this – commissars always begin life as opponents of authority. But Cromwell's problems were a mirror-image of those of the King, whose execution "cruel necessity" had imposed upon him: how to pay for the expanding role of government. He died trying to square this circle in 1658, and was succeeded as Lord Protector by his son, Richard, who resigned in 1659. Edward Hyde might have been the unseen guiding hand of the Declaration of Breda in 1660, but it was Charles I's son and namesake who saw the importance of compromise, signed it, and returned to the Throne as Charles II. No *ne plus ultra* in this Monarch, which has been the downfall of European monarchies since the beginning of the last century. He was restored with most of his father's powers which he handed on to his brother. *Courtesy National Portrait Gallery, London.* See Kevin Sharpe, page 83.

H: Sir George Hayter's picture of the reformed House of Commons in 1833. The great Reform Act of 1832 did little, in fact, to make the Commons more democratic, but it met a need. The second Reform Act of 1867 and the Representation of the People Act, 1885, did far more towards "universal suffrage", although women could not vote until 1918. Except for the room and the large windows behind the Speaker's chair, the arrangement of the Commons has changed only slightly. The Mace lies between the dispatch boxes, and the lawyers take their notes; government and opposition face one another, and those who cannot find a seat stand in the foreground, just as they still do. It has always struck me as absurd that continental parliaments are circular – indeed, the European Parliament is also circular – based on the Roman senate. The Roman senate was packed with aristocrats, while the plebeian consul was a nominee of the aristocratic oligarchy. French presidents and German chancellors can still fill their parliaments with nominees. I dare say that there is not a modern British prime minister who has not wished to nominate members of the Commons. Fortunately, they cannot. The arrangement of the House also means that political rivals can "eye-ball" one another. Opposition members can actually look a minister in the face and have him or her look back in their face – not the back of their heads. It is hard to have a row with some one whose face you cannot see unless they turn round to you, or across a wide expanse. *Courtesy National Portrait Gallery, London.* See Valerie Cromwell, page 118.

I: Thomas Osborne: possibly among the first of the commoners who had his own following in the Commons yet could count, not only on the support, but on the affection of the monarchs he served. He came to the fore in the 1670s when the King was still a serious contender for sovereignty, as demonstrated by the virtual disappearance of Parliament during the 1680s. He was created Earl of Danby, Marquess of Carmarthen, and Duke of Leeds by grateful monarchs. *Courtesy National Portrait Gallery, London.* See W A Speck, page 100.

J: James II has long been seen by some historians as the last of our kings to have absolutist pretensions. He and his brother, Charles II, who died in 1685, seriously attempted to rig the electoral system. James had failed in this by the autumn of 1688 on the curious business of the seven bishops. Although he had called a Parliament on his accession in 1685, he almost immediately prorogued it, and dissolved it in 1687, never to call another. The bishops refused to give orders for Anglican priests to read from their pulpits the King's Declaration of Indulgence, effectively giving civil rights to Roman Catholics. It is hard for us to understand why anyone would wish to discriminate against Roman Catholics, although, in some respects, Ulster is still stuck in this mind-set. James II's own judges ruled against him in the case of the bishops, and the moment the hand-picked King's Bench defied the King, there was an outburst of "protestant" indignation. But what had really happened in the case of the seven bishops is that the law had been interpreted as being above even the King in whose name it was administered. This was not the first time the judges had found against a king, but it was the last time it mattered. In the hands of a contemporary, some one like Louis XIV of France, things may have turned out differently in Britain, but James II took fright and, by December 1688, had fled his kingdom. *Courtesy National Portrait Gallery, London.* See W A Speck, page 100.

K: Sir Robert Walpole, first British prime minister from 1721 to 1742. If Margaret Thatcher were still in office today, she would have another four years to serve before she caught up with Walpole's span of power. His administration has routinely been described as deeply corrupt, but concern about corruption in these years arose not because the Commons was peculiarly corrupt under the later Stuarts and early Hanoverians, but because contemporaries were particularly concerned about it. It has taken 250 years for historians to arrive at this view. Current opinions of the present

Tory administration of John Major may be that his administration is corrupt, but it may not be seen as being worse than the standards of the late 20th century in 250 years' time. The late Chairman of the Chinese Communist party, Mao-tse Deng, is supposed to have replied to the question, what do you think of the impact of the French Revolution? by saying, "too soon to tell." History seems to demonstrate that contemporaries – especially political opponents – are not the best judges of such matters, and memories are short. Most people under the age of 30 will never have heard of John Stonehouse MP, Postmaster General in a Labour Cabinet in the 1960s, who, in the 1970s, to elude the police, faked his own suicide. *Courtesy National Portrait Gallery, London.* See W A Speck, page 100.

L: Philip Stanhope, fourth Earl of Chesterfield, from whose published correspondence we learn so much of 18th century politics and personalities. At a time when the modern role of Parliament is being questioned, and may be fundamentally revised as a consequence of devolution within Britain, and both federalism and constitutional-legal changes within Europe, it is possible to look back and note that even in an earlier glorious era doubts had been raised about the value and function of the Commons. *Courtesy National Portrait Gallery, London.* See Jeremy Black, page 109.

M: William Pitt the Elder, subsequently Earl of Chatham, whose administration presided over the "Year of Victories" (1759) against the French in the Seven Years' War. Parliament, in guaranteeing the National Debt by appropriating taxation, enabled Britain to compete successfully with the growing military strength of the other European powers and was crucial to the global power of the British state: there was no collapse of naval finances comparable to that which affected France, *Courtesy National Portrait Gallery, London.* See Jeremy Black, page 109.

N: Edmund Burke wrote to his politically aware constituents at Bristol in 1774 that an MP should be guided by "the general good. . . he owes you, not his industry only, but his judgement; and he betrays you, not serves you, if he sacrifices it to your opinion." Burke favoured freer trade with Ireland, whereas Bristol did not, and he came bottom of the poll at the next election and lost the seat. It has always seemed to me that MPs should not be delegates, for as delegates they are likely to represent only a small cabal of party activists in a constituency. Much better that MPs set out their stalls at each general election and let the voters decide. *Courtesy National Portrait Gallery, London.* See Jeremy Black, page 109.

O: Charles, second Earl Grey, who introduced the first Reform Bill which passed in 1832, in the teeth of massive opposition. It is now generally accepted that at no point in the period 1815 to 1918 did Britain experience democracy. More importantly, Britain did not and has not experienced any type of violent political revolution such as have almost all continental states in either the 19th or 20th centuries. Some explanation of these apparently antipathetic phenomena must be found in the functioning and responsiveness of Parliament to active external political forces. *Courtesy National Portrait Gallery, London.* See Valerie Cromwell, page 118.

Captions by Robert Smith

Foreword

The Rt Hon Betty Boothroyd MP, Speaker of the House of Commons

This book is the second in a series of three which aims to throw new light on the history of the Crown in Parliament, the core of the British constitution. In the first volume, on the House of Lords, Lord Mackay, the Lord Chancellor, rightly remarked that the upper chamber is "a dignified part of the British Parliament". The House over which I have the honour to preside, the Commons, may perhaps be seen as the less dignified.

This would be a superficial view. As David Carpenter and Simon Payling particularly say, when speaking of the Middle Ages, the Commons was where the Crown laid out its financial needs to which Parliament responded. Normally, the Commons responded favourably to calls for taxation.

It is only much later, in the 17th century, as Jennifer Loach and Kevin Sharpe record, after the Commons had established its own identity, that real disagreements about the Crown's policy and the Crown's requests for taxation brought demands for serious redress of grievances. Eventually, this led to the Civil War and, as W A Speck shows, the Crown learned the lesson that successful management of the Commons was necessary to good government.

After the Glorious Revolution of 1688–9, Parliament became the dominant component of the constitution, and by the 1730s, as Jeremy Black notes, the Commons had come to dominate Parliament.

By the 19th century, the "unreformed" Commons had become dangerously unrepresentative of a population growing in numbers and affluence. This brought demands for parliamentary reform, the fulfilment of which would take up much of the last century, and indeed would continue into this century until votes for all women were achieved in 1928, as Valerie Cromell and Michael Fry demonstrate.

In the last 30 years, Parliament has had to make decisions about Britain's future in Europe and, consequently, decisions about its own hard-won sovereignty. It is hardly surprising, therefore, that debate on this subject, in the arc of television lights, is sometimes agitated when taken in conjunction with the things members of the Commons have discussed for more than 700 years: the voting of taxation and appropriation of the proceeds.

One of my predecessors, Sir John Finch, was held down in the Speaker's Chair while the Commons forced through the Petition of Right in 1628, and the Speaker's job, as intermediary between Crown and Commons – the representatives of the people – has never been easy. I welcome this book, therefore, as an insight into the past, present, and future of the House of Commons.

Preface

MY OLD head of department, Professor Ron Fryer, told all his undergraduates in his annual inaugural lecture that if we actually read our history books, we would discover that there is nothing new, that no modern politician, or political pundit, or anyone else had thought of anything that had not been thought of by some one else already. I do not think that any of us paid much attention to this statement, and if we had we probably would not have believed it. Like many an undergraduate then, as now, we thought everything was new and that everything in the world could be changed for the better if only there were the will. This sentiment was particularly prevalent in 1966, when I went to Nottingham University. Certain truths and certain goods were absolute and moral, and truth and good were inextricably linked.

I did not start *reading* history until long after supposedly reading it at Nottingham, and it took some time for Professor Fryer's inaugural wisdom to dawn on me that there *was* nothing new. He might have added that truth and good were not linked, and that truth itself, in the words of Rahel Levin, "is relative, and time is nothing but the condition in which truth exists, develops, functions, survives. Every organism known to us is confined within this context: each man in his times." To take an example from my Swinging Sixties: free love was new and an absolute truth. Free love was certainly not new and almost within living memory had been advocated by H G Wells in one of his many contributions to the defunct *Pall Mall* magazine in the 1890s. As for being an absolute truth (the word "right" was much used then interchangeably), what sensible person would subscribe to that theory today with the Aids tragedy all around us?

In drawing an outline for a history of the House of Commons, this book will suggest that every political expedient has already been thought of, and that every political truth today, if not an untruth once, was deemed unworthy at some time in the past, quite often recent past. This is not to say that politicians are fundamentally dishonest. I do not believe that they are. Perhaps they are optimistic, but it seems to me that optimism must be one of the principal qualities in any politician who wants to stay the course. We expect too much of politicians and possibly they are to blame for this, to some extent, themselves. MPs want the best for the majority of their constituents, if only to please them and get re-elected, but what is best? Here, we return to "the will", for there is more than one route to achieve the "greater good", and not all politicians can agree on it. Nor can they, or we, agree on what is good.

Perhaps the nearest we can get to certainty is "death and taxes". None of us can do anything about death, but taxes are what we pay, to paraphrase the stone-carved words on the US Treasury Building, to live in a civilized society. (It has always struck me that there is something disingenuous about this American statement if it has to be cut into stone.) Taxes are what we elect our MPs to raise and then to spend on us, and here we have reached the heart of the State, and I use State instead of government lest I become confused with Conservative or Labour government.

The State is an agglomeration of rules, enforced by an executive, which pays for this enforcement by the gathering and spending of taxes for a majority of those members of a society – at least in this country today – who live by the rules. Essentially, the power we give to the State, by electing the House of Commons, is the power to strike at offenders against the rules. Law and an executive to enforce it are the critical elements of the State – indeed, of every state since the beginning of written history. The great 19th century lawyer, Sir William Anson, defined four types of sanction: physical, religious, moral, and political, or Law proper. He illustrated the physical sanction by describing an incident where one man forces another man to sign a document against his will; the wrath of God forms the religious sanction; the "golden glow" for conduct that receives public approbation is the moral sanction. The political sanction incorporates, in one way or another, at least two of the previous three: the adult must keep ever in his or her mind the knowledge that an offence against the rules will be visited by the State, or the community in its political character, which has taken to itself the right to maintain order, and to punish the offender by such process and in such ways as the State may provide.

Originally, an English or Scottish king ruled on disputes, made laws, led his people to war, collected customary taxes. As the State grew in complexity and population, so a king's ability to discharge these functions became impossible and passed into the hands of ministers and judges. In this growing complexity, a king needed more money to discharge his (or his minister's) functions than customary taxes allowed and he turned to the community for their agreement to grant new money. Eventually, the community – represented by the baronage at first – required a wider consent, and representatives of counties and towns were summoned to Parliament. As the representatives of by far the most populous group in the country and also as the ones who were going to have to justify (and in many instances collect) the taxes they voted, the burgesses and knights of the shire began to bring petitions to Parliament for the King's attention. To a wise king, they became a sounding-board for embryonic public opinion. Soon the representatives of the community, the Commons, established that no tax could be imposed except by its consent, and instead of leaving new laws, agreed in Parliament, to promulgation by the King and his Council, MPs became the drafters of laws they themselves had decided upon. The King's legislative power sank to a formal right to assent or dissent from a law submitted to him, and this today to a merely formal expression of assent. Statutes still commence: "Be it enacted by the Queen's most excellent Majesty, by and with the advice and consent of the Lords Spiritual and Temporal, and Commons, in this present Parliament assembled, and by the authority of the same..." But all legislative and executive power rests with a government which can command a majority in the House of Commons. The Queen has nothing to do with it, nor the Lords Spiritual and Temporal above what the Commons will allow them. It may also be worth mentioning, though it is little more than a technicality today, that, unlike most other Western democracies, sovereignty does not vest in the people. There is no "We the People" about British constitutional arrangements. Sovereignty vests in the "Crown in Parliament", not in the Queen, or the Lords, or the Commons, though the Commons is the most important, but in all three in this constitutional expression; notwithstanding the European Union, for the 1973 Act of Accession is no different from a road traffic act: the Crown in Parliament can repeal it.

Some dates will be useful: by 1340, although the King is still supreme, he can lay no new tax without the consent of the House of Commons; by the reign of Henry VI (1422-61), the Commons drafts the laws its members want enacting (this is when a parliamentary draft comes to be known as a bill, and when the Royal Assent is given it becomes an act or statute); in 1641, the King's power to create new courts of law is abolished; in 1689, the King's power to ignore the law (suspending and dispensing power) is abolished; the last king to be effectively the chief of the executive is William III who died in 1702; the last royal veto occurs in 1707 and was exercised by Queen Anne; the last king to lead his troops into battle is George II at Dettingen, Germany, in 1743, and there were special reasons for this. The king had the right, as the Queen still does, in the paraphrased words of Walter Bagehot, to be informed, to encourage, and to warn, but in every essential, the Queen's views, if she has any, can be ignored and her powers can be exercised only on the advice of ministers. (We shall deal extensively with the powers of the Queen and especially the myth of the Royal Prerogative, in *The Monarchy, fifteen hundred years of British tradition,* to be published later this year).

The State in which we live today is collective, in that there is hardly any sphere of daily living in which the State has not made rules for our observance. Until quite recently (ie the last 200 years), the rules were fairly simple: there were laws against murder, treason, and theft, rules to enforce the payment of taxes, poor relief, and that kind of thing. Essentially, provided there was no rule against doing something, it was legal to do it. Whereas, until roughly 1830, the rules were based largely on Common Law and acts of Parliament were on the whole simply declaratory of customs and conventions which had evolved naturally; after this date and onwards, the State has increasingly intervened in the lives of the people. Among the first such important interventions were the factory and public health acts of the 1840s. There have been many subsequent acts dealing with these matters and myriads of others which go into every aspect of daily life, so that the State now runs everything from the health service to Stonehenge, as Mr Simon Jenkins puts it in his persuasive book, *The Tory Nationalization of Britain.* Perhaps the only omission from this excellent read is that almost certainly under any other government nothing much would have been different in its effects. Indeed, this paragraph is not intended as any kind of critique of the kinds of governments we have had since 1945. There is no advanced Western country whose rules and regulations have not followed a similar course in the last 50 years. This book tries only to recount some facts and, where appropriate, to synthesize them in their period.

But in this context, it is not surprising that political parties in the Western democracies increasingly speak of personal choice, while trying to legislate for it, which is to say that such legislation tends to circumscribe personal choice by saying what personal choice should be. This is true whether one votes Conservative, or Republican, or French or Spanish Socialist, or German Christian Democrat. Political parties, particularly those in opposition, say they want to change this and advance ways in which this might be done. In Britain, this has recently taken the form of proposals to devolve powers to a Scottish and Welsh assembly, perhaps even English regional assemblies; to claims that proportional representation is a fairer way of electing the House of Commons. All political parties claim that education is the key to solving our political and economic difficulties, but no sooner is a party in office than it is counterclaimed that educational standards are slipping and much evidence is adduced to demonstrate the case. In fact, there is nothing new about proportional representation: Mr Courtenay put it firmly on the agenda in the 1880s and Mr Gladstone (ironically, a Liberal) rejected it, as indeed Mr Asquith's Liberal government was determinedly against women's suffrage, introducing the "Cat and Mouse Act", and presided over the force-feeding of suffragette prisoners. Winston Churchill proposed the devolution of powers to Welsh and Scottish assemblies in the early years of the 20th century. In 1885, a parliamentary commission reported that unless Britain reformed its education system then the country stood in grave danger of being overtaken by Germany and the United States. In 1923, the Institution of Mechanical Engineers bemoaned the declining educational achievements of applicants for its practical course. These examples could be multiplied many times over, and seem to stem, in the democracies, from a belief on the part of the people that government can do anything, with which government, to judge from the legislation, seems wholeheartedly to agree. Governments cannot do everything, and often should do nothing.

"To a modern House of Commons, it is almost enough that a practice has prevailed for a long time to create an impression that such a practice must need examination and revision. But the step is a long one from the time when the State first enforces custom vigorously and constantly, to the time when it takes upon itself without fear or hesitation (the task) to recast or alter custom." These sentences could have been written yesterday. In fact, they were written by Sir William Anson in 1886. If this reminds you of the Poll Tax or the Dangerous Dogs Act, I rest my case. This is not to make a judgment against the Conservative government, merely to reflect the fact that the Conservatives have been in power for the last 16 years. The Poll Tax is a very good example, though, of Sir William's opinion, and it is one of the few such examples that brought an instant and almighty protest, and brought down a prime minister. The Dangerous Dogs Act is an example of the thousands of pieces of legislation that seem a good idea at the time, most of which go unnoticed, until we suddenly wake up to discover that instead of being able to do anything the law does not say is illegal, we can only do things that the law says are legal, and then only in prescribed ways.

I wonder if it is an accident that Britain made its greatest economic strides in the 18th and early 19th centuries when there was a kind of chaos. Is there perhaps a similar kind of chaos which enables the economies of the Far East Pacific Rim to burgeon? This is not to propose hanging people for stealing sheep or sending children back up chimneys or taking protective devices off dangerous machinery, but are we over-governed with our silliest whims catered for and, if we are, have we not ourselves to blame for this? Take three examples of what the State can now do for us. A woman bought a coffee from a McDonalds' drive-in, placed the beaker between her legs, drove off spilling the coffee in her lap, sued the company for making the coffee too hot because it burned her, and got judgment. A travel company was sued because Tunisian waiters pinched two female tourists' bottoms, and lawyers *took on* on such a case. Finally, one London borough, sharing a street down the middle with another, has one parking time on its side, while the time on the other side is two hours different. Motorists might reasonably look at the sign on one side, which says 6.30pm, find no space there, and park on the other side and not think to look at another sign,which says 8.30pm. This is done in the name of road safety, but I can only draw the conclusion that the borough with the later time expects to collect a crop of fines from people who are to all intents and purposes tricked. Are we living in so perfectly regulated a society that we are actually living in a perfectly regulated madhouse, and just do not know it? I suspect that in this country, Western Europe, and North America we are, and we have built the madhouse ourselves for our own incarceration.

An annexe to the madhouse has been added in recent years, and it appears to be peculiar to the Western democracies, or the First World. It is the development of an underclass. It is too disparate and its members too individualistic to be called a sub-State, but it does have certain cohesive factors, and it may yet become a sub-State. It is curious that increasingly affluent societies have thrown up a minority (but a growing minority) of people disadvantaged economically and educationally, many of them from birth. The response of the modern State is to legislate in a variety of ways: for example, in criminal law, policing, the giving or taking away of benefits, and similar social legislation. But no amount of legislation seems to make any impression. In the United States, there are whole areas of large cities: Washington, New York, Los Angeles, to name only three, which are police no-go areas. The American experience may differ somewhat from the British and European in that it may divide more on racial lines, but the fault lines, however caused, are clearly visible. Perhaps we should not be surprised. After all, if white-collar criminals can be acquitted of multimillion-pound fraud, or their trials be stopped, what kind of example is that? If an under-age boy can steal cars, mug old people, abscond from council care with apparent impunity, what kind of example is that? Add in that an increasing number of children are leaving school barely literate and numerate, and it becomes evident that such children, already denied a stake in the benefits of society, will hold the State and its rules in contempt.

The payment of benefits and their administration, the search for benefit fraud, the fraud itself, the growing population of jails, the boot camps, the police, the social workers, and everything else in the social security and home offices budgets have to be paid for. The State pays for this by ever-increasing taxes on the industrious, or by taking away their benefits: for instance, by reducing their mortgage interest relief, or by charging them for old age care over a certain (low) asset value, presently £3,000, care which people thought they had paid for already. In 1955, a husband and wife with two children, on average earnings, paid no direct tax. Today the same family pays 24% of its income in taxes: national insurance and income tax. The figure and dates are roughly the same in the United States. Additionally, there are the *quasi*-taxes for which none of us votes at a general election: traffic fines, fines of £5,000 and even prison promised to traders who make the mistake of selling in pounds and ounces. No matter that the small business minister may say that traders will not be unfairly penalized, while the new system becomes embedded, the treasury needs to raise money, and you can be sure that weights and measures officers throughout the land have been briefed accordingly, for the billions now raised in one fine or another does not go to the local authority, or even to the local police – it goes direct to the treasury.

Society is often described as a pyramid and this is undoubtedly a good description of society in the high Middle Ages. It was better described recently as being shaped more like an onion. At the rooty bottom are the underclass and at the top are the rich who have their own ways of ignoring the rules. The most succulent part of the onion is the vast middle class. They are easy prey: they are on pay as you earn, so their employers can collect the taxes for the State; they own houses and cars, so they are simply found by police and tax officials. The State knows that the underclass has no money, while the rich form too small a group from which to raise significant sums, even if the rich declared all their income, which they do not, usually for perfectly legal reasons. But there is this ocean of middle class folk, ripe for tallaging and criminalizing with proliferating fines "for their own good". A new, rich area for fines will be the identity card. Home office and treasury officials want ID cards for different reasons. The home office wants them because they are seen to be a response to public opinion, the same reason as politicians felt they had to encourage the pernicious neighbourhood watch scheme. The treasury wants them because of the crop of fines it can collect if you are caught not carrying yours. Imagine being stopped on the way to the shops by a policeman and being asked for your ID. Unlike a driver's licence or your car insurance papers, which you can take to the police station within seven days, because the officer has noted your registration number, he will have to take *you* to the police station until your identity is established. You will, of course, be fined for not carrying your card because it is too good an opportunity for the Treasury to miss. Worse still, imagine being stopped by a nosey parker member of the neighbourhood watch, or by a special constable, or some one with whom you have quarrelled in one of these organizations. The Home Guard was disbanded before the end of the Second World War, not because it was a silly force – politicians knew that, although it had propaganda qualities. It was disbanded because of the anger it engendered among the general public who were constantly being asked for their ID papers, often by people who knew perfectly well who they were. Lord Goddard said as much in 1954 when his inquiry recommended the abolition of ID cards. Nothing has changed since then.

It is already apparent, from changed attitudes to the police, that lumps of this middle of the onion are bruised and will rot. Thirty years go, most people only spoke to a policeman to ask the time. Today most of us have been stopped by the police about our cars, or have called the police in a futile attempt to catch a burglar, or report a theft, or at least we know people who have had brushes with the police on these everyday matters. If "real criminals", like child hooligans and business fraudsters, go unpunished, and formerly law-abiding people are criminalized, is it not likely that the middle class will eventually hold the law in contempt? Sections of the middle class seem already to be alienated. In Britain and the West, are we witnessing the beginnings of the end of the Nation State?

But the Nation State is also being undermined by something with implications that can only be guessed at. We are on the edge of an age which, *pace* my opening comments, is truly new, which the "political nation" does not address meaningfully, and of which it has little or no understanding. Not even the media, except specialist publications, have understood it, although journalists have been among the first to employ it. It is computer technology, especially the Internet. The American government's reaction to the potential was as predictable as it was feeble. It was to offer a free Clipper Chip to all users. This would have guaranteed complete privacy and security of all computer communication, except from the US government. Never mind the Inland Revenue Service, for which some kind of specious right could have been argued for the invasion of privacy, the National Parks Department could have read your E-Mail and all your electronic correspondence. The programmers and manufacturers immediately saw this for what it was and they refused to use the system. Instead, they have developed encryption programmes which, on one estimate, would take government experts many years to decipher. The State would probably like to read our ordinary post, but, sadly for its officials, Western mail systems were born in the 19th century when personal liberty was something the people still prized highly.

The Internet puts us on the threshold of the Virtual State. Those people at the sharp end of Internet development forecast that within years only, everyone with a terminal will be able to bank offshore, move funds around without tax officials knowing how much and from where to where, and buy goods and services completely without let or hindrance. If government tries to clamp down on the City of London, the City will simply decamp offshore, and another source of such corporate revenue as there remains will dry up. Of course, certain things, like tankers of oil, or freighters loaded with cars, will be traceable and taxable; but when more than 50% of gross national product is in the form of intellectual property (services), its income cannot be taxed because it cannot be traced. It is even possible that offshore NatWest and offshore Namoura will simply establish a Virtual State monetary unit. National currencies will still be needed, but to nothing like the extent they are today. With diminishing interest in national currencies, the Nation State, some say, will atrophy and even die. Perhaps worse than this is that the State could transform itself into a Police State, like the Soviet Union or the South American dictatorships in their death throes. Borders can be closed. Internal borders can be established. Its geography would make Britain very easy to close physically. There were banning orders against subjects of the Crown entering mainland Britain from Ulster. Perfectly reasonable, people might think, but it is not hard to see the possibility of such orders being extended to other "offences" in the interest of "the national good", and large numbers of people might well be persuaded of their virtue.

We have been told not only by a home secretary that innocent people need not fear ID cards, but by members of audiences on such television programmes as Question Time and, of course, at Tory party conferences. Felix Dzherzinsky, father of what became the KGB, used precisely the same argument in 1918 against the better judgment of men like Nikolai Bukharin when the new Soviet Union instituted the internal secret police, the Cheka. Bukharin was shot with millions of other men and women during the Stalin purges of the 1930s. I do not attribute fault to Parliament for these matters, although, as the pinnacle of the "political nation" – a term much used in the following chapters – might members not have cautioned us against the speed with which we expect our demands to be acted upon? Should they not address middle class alienation and particularly the ramifications of the Internet? I know many members of Parliament, and they are men and women of good will and high intelligence. I am unsure, unlike Edward Pearce, whether the media can influence our votes, but I am sure that the media can influence politicians. Dogs have been biting people for as long as anyone can remember, and a good deal before that; but that law was made because the media made the discovery that dogs do bite people from time to time, and publicized the fact. Dogs are a bit like Rwanda, or Somalia: they exist as tragedies when the media tells us they exist, and then governments "do something". As soon as they drop off the news list, we forget about them, but the tragedy continues – just as we now have our own "mini-drama trials" as dogs and their owners await appeal after appeal before sentence of death is carried out, and owners do not even have visiting rights.

The issues facing politicians today are as profound as the first Reform Act, as profound as the Norman Conquest. My fear is not that we shall elect a government so wicked as to have a secret Police State agenda. My fear is that it might happen by slow accident. The greatest strength of the House of Commons, once it had established itself by the end of the 17th century, was its facility to respond to change without a collapse of the State or without turning to dictatorship. Whether it can rise to that challenge in the coming years only history will tell.

My thanks to John Moore, who has co-edited this book with me, and to Sheila Pearson and Christine McGeoch, respectively for their unstinting administration and indexing.

Robert Smith,
Publisher, London,
March 1996

John S Moore

Introduction

THIS volume presents the papers given at the Annual Conference of the Manorial Society of Great Britain held at Oriel College, Oxford, in September 1994, with a few exceptions. Robert Smith and I are most grateful to Dr Simon Payling of the History of Parliament Trust for providing, at very short notice, chapter 2 on the House of Commons in the later Middle Ages. We are also grateful to Professor Laurence Gormley for stepping-in with a chapter on the relations between the House of Commons and the European Union. Finally, it is a matter of very great regret to the editors, as to everyone who knew her, to have to record the death of Dr Jennifer Loach, who read her chapter 3 to the conference only a week after leaving hospital, and delivered the typed version to us a few weeks before her much lamented death.

This volume is the second in a series of three on the constituent elements of the Crown in Parliament, the core of the British Constitution: the first, on the House of Lords, was published in 1994,[1] and it is hoped to publish the third, on the Monarchy, later this year. The House of Commons as it now exists is, subject to some overriding controls from the European Assembly and the European Court (see chapter 9), now the dominant partner in the British legislature: by a long-standing constitutional convention the Crown automatically signifies the Royal Assent to all bills sent from both Houses of Parliament. Since the Parliament Act of 1911, the House of Lords cannot delay or reject money bills and can only amend or reject parts of bills sent up from the Commons for a limited period. Effectively, the House of Lords is now only a revising chamber, admittedly very useful, for the detailed scrutiny of bills sent up from the Commons where the overcrowded parliamentary timetable often prevents adequate discussion of all clauses, a function which was already assuming great importance as early as the later 18th century.[2] Thus their revising power was already singled out by Lord Hardwicke in the 1750s as the essential counterpart to a House of Commons already overbusy:

> Our statute books are increased to such an enormous size that they confound every man who is obliged to look into them ... now ... almost every new law is first drawn up and passed in the other House, so that we have little else to do ... but to read over and consent to the new laws they have made: nay, some of them are sent up so late that we have hardly time to read them over ... the other House by their being so numerous, and by their being destitute of the advice and assistance of the judges, are too apt to pass laws which are either unnecessary or ridiculous, and almost every law they pass stands in need of some new law for explaining and amending it ... it is high time for this House to ... resolve to put a stop to it, by resolving not to pass any Bill ... that comes from the other House unless it comes up so early in the session as to leave us sufficient time to take the advice and assistance of the judges upon it, and to consider every clause of it maturely.[3]

Thus the present dominance of the House of Commons is a relatively recent phenomenon; the power of the House of Lords was much greater before 1911, while the ruling power of the Crown was of ever-greater importance as one moves back through the centuries before 1800 (chapters 4-6). In and before the 16th century, the Crown was more important than either Lords or Commons (chapters 2-4), and Parliament itself only came into existence in the 13th century (chapter 1); of its constituent parts, the Lords were older than the Commons, for the early Parliaments consisted only of "lords", whose consultative and advisory powers had their origin in the Anglo-Saxon *witan* and the Anglo-Norman "great council.[4] Even after the county knights and burgesses were summoned to the 1265 Parliament, there were still parliaments consisting only of barons and knights, in 1275, 1290, 1294, and 1297.[5] For most of the Middle Ages, the monarch was the ruler, supported by a civil service increasing in size and efficiency which derived its power almost entirely from the Royal Prerogative, and only to a very limited extent from powers conveyed by statutory authority. It was by very gradual degrees that the Commons come to "represent" the nation in any real sense, and then mainly at the behest of the Crown which found "popular consent" to taxation essential in the constant search for royal solvency, as Dr Carpenter shows in chapter 1. (The House of Lords has never claimed to represent directly anyone except its members.) As with so much of British history, evolution appears more important than revolution: a main theme of this book is the long process of change in the balance between Crown, Lords, and Commons in the Constitution.

The word "represent" immediately raises a host of questions and assumptions, often inaccurate ones. The British, or even English, Parliament is not, as has often been claimed, the "Mother of Parliaments" in the sense of being the representative national assembly in Europe with the longest continuous history; that distinction belongs to the Icelandic *althing,* which was set up in 929-30 and, apart from a few breaks, has met annually ever since.[6] The word "representative" is not synonymous with "democratically elected" as in modern British, West European, and North American usage; indeed, before the 1920s, even in a formal sense, the House of Commons was not democratically elected, since universal manhood suffrage came only in 1918 and all adult women had to wait till 1928 to get the vote, although from 1832 onwards the House of Commons was representing an increasing proportion of the adult male population (see Table 2 below). Indeed, one of the contributors points out that real democracy came only in 1945, the first election at which all but three parliamentary seats were contested.[7] In fact, "representation" does not automatically or necessarily imply any electoral process, democratic or otherwise. Being naturally immodest, I cite myself as an example: as timetables and admissions officer I "represent" my university department on various committees as a result of appointment by my head of department; I "represent" my department as safety adviser as a nominee of my head of department, but I act under the authority of the university safety officer; on the other hand I "represent" my faculty on the senior common room committee by election and outside the university I am Chairman of a local history society, also by election. Thus, even now, representation may result as much from selection by higher authority as from election by one's peers.

We need, therefore, to be clear in our own minds, and in our writing, whether we in fact mean "appointed" [or "selected"] representation rather than "elected" representation: in present-day usage, one tends to assume that all "representatives" are "elected" in free elections by secret ballot, but these are assumptions which are often invalid. In Britain, the secret ballot for national and local government elections was established as recently as 1872 (interestingly, its centenary passed almost unnoticed in 1972); in more corrupt regimes, such as British trade union elections, the use of the secret ballot had to be enforced, again by acts of Parliament, in 1980, 1982, and 1983. In many areas even of Europe before the collapse of the Soviet Empire in the late 1980s, and in many areas of Afro-Asia and Latin America to this day, elections remain open to abuse by force, fraud, and corruption. Many totalitarian regimes, past and present, wishing to present the ostensible appearance of "free" elections, did or do operate a halfway house where elections do indeed take place, but the choice is confined to those candidates on an official list: in fact, this procedure combines elements of both the "selected" and the "elected" systems of representation. Democracy is, in fact, a fragile flower as well as a plant of recent growth.

Before the Second Reform Act of 1867, in Britain most adult males of the lower middle class were not enfranchised, and not until the Third Reform Act of 1883 were most working-class adult males able to vote. Before 1832, the electorate numbered less than about a fifth of the adult male population (see Table 2 below), although the electorate was larger than is sometimes thought; in chapter 5 Professor Speck argues that about 1720 perhaps a quarter of all adult mates could vote.[8] But, since the way they cast their vote was known to all and increasingly recorded in "poll books" from the late 17th century onwards, most of which were printed, their vote was open to the threat of coercion and the promise of bribery.[9] It is, therefore, widely assumed that the electorate generally voted as their landlords or employers dictated, or sold their vote to the highest bidder. Again, this is an assumption that sometimes can be shown not to be true. In the Gloucestershire election of 1710, local loyalties clearly counted, since in the south of the county, for which a poll book still exists, most of the electorate cast one vote for John Symes Berkeley, the head of the well respected, but not very wealthy or powerful Berkeley family of Stoke Gifford, even though there was a considerable difference in the pattern of voting for the other candidates.[10] The electorate even in the period of the "unreformed" Commons should not be assumed to be simple-minded sheep, blindly following their aristocratic shepherds.

Even before 1832, the electorate was growing in size, partly as a result of the two periods of prolonged population-increase, the first from the mid-15th century to the mid-17th century, the second from the late 17th century to the present day. In round numbers, the total population of England rose from about 1.5 million in 1450 to about 2 million in 1500 and perhaps to 3 million in 1555. After a sharp fall between 1556 and 1561, growth resumed, passing 4 million in 1596 and 5 million in 1636, but from 1656 to 1686, the population fell and it did not again exceed 5 million until 1701. Thereafter, growth was at an ever more rapid rate: the population doubled to 10 million in 1816 and doubled again to 20 million in 1866, after which the rate of growth slowed; 40 million was not achieved until after 1931; in 1991 the population of England and Wales was about 50 million.[11] But the proportion of the total adult male population able to vote was also growing in these four centuries, especially before 1640, for two main reasons. The first was the expansion of the urban sector of the population, partly a result of economic development,[12] but partly a result of a deliberate government policy, notably under the Tudors and early Stuarts, of expanding the municipal sector, and perhaps also the urban electorate (though the expansion of the urban electorate was often a result, whether intended or not, of the expansion of the number of boroughs).[13] Thus the number of borough constituencies rose throughout the period from the 1450s to 1679, while the number of English county constituencies hardly altered before 1832, the chief additions being Monmouthshire in 1542, Cheshire in 1543, and Durham in 1673. From 1603, there were four MPs representing the universities of Oxford and Cambridge, and from 1801 one MP representing Trinity College, Dublin: these have been included with the borough MPs. As Table 1 shows, the percentage of borough MPs in the House of Commons was always high, and only slightly increased over time, from 70% in 1421 to 82% in 1707, before the Union with Scotland, falling back to 78% in 1708, falling a little further to 72% after the Union with Ireland, and to 62% after the 1832 Reform Act. Again, this figure is delusive: increasingly between the 15th and the 19th centuries, borough seats were being taken over by the rural gentry or their professional associates, especially lawyers, who increasingly did not reside in the constituencies they represented. What is also noteworthy is the reversal after the second Reform Act of the trend for the House of Commons to be dominated by borough MPs; the period 1832-67 saw the largest number of borough seats ever (405). From 1885 to 1922, there were more county seats than borough seats, and since 1922 county seats have never composed less than 45% of all Commons seats. Despite the urbanization of modern Britain – in 1851 half the British population lived in towns and the proportion has now risen to about 90% – the balance between county and borough seats has been affected by the suburbanization of much of the landscape during the 19th and even more the 20th centuries and by the desire of electoral managers and legislators to create constituencies of roughly equal size with a reasonably balanced social composition. As a result, the equivalence of "county" seats with rural areas and "borough" seats with urban areas has partly broken down: in my own home area, for example, the South Gloucestershire constituency, nominally rural, contains the old market towns of Chipping Sodbury and Thornbury, the expanding new town of Yate and part of the "North Bristol Fringe" built-up area. In such regions, the distinction is already being blurred and it seems likely that the trend will continue.

The number of county MPs did not greatly increase before 1832, since the number of English county constituencies only slightly increased in that period, with the addition of Monmouthshire, Cheshire, and Durham, as already noted, and the only other additions were 12 Welsh county MPs after the Act of Union in 1536 (the Welsh MPs, however, first appeared in the Commons in 1542) and 30 Scottish county MPs after the Act of Union in 1707.[14] But the appearance of constancy is delusive if it is taken to imply that an unchanging number of English rural MPs represented an unchanging number of English rural constituents. The property qualification of the rural electorate remained unchanged from 1430, when it was fixed at a freehold worth 40 shillings a year, to 1832, yet because of inflation, which was prevalent especially from the 1480s to the 1640s, again from the 1690s to the 1720s, and from the 1750s until after the Napoleonic wars, the real value of 40 shillings had declined very greatly in 400 years. A building craftsman's daily wage had risen eightfold between the 1420s (6d a day) and the 1830s (4s a day); 40 shillings could buy about 40 bushels of wheat in 1430 and about five and a half bushels in 1832.[15] Hence the unchanged monetary value of the freeholders' property qualification ought to have expanded the rural electorate very greatly, and Derek Hirst has argued cogently that even freeholders with only four to five acres each could by the early 17th century have been worth 40s a year, while many uncertainties about tenure (annuities, leaseholds, and copyholds for lives all counted as freeholds) and the general absence of official lists of electors still further enlarged the electorate.[16] Indeed, even in 1430

> many ordinary wage-earners, at 2d per day, would have earned over 40s per annum. At its inception, then, the new rubric was not an especially rigorous economic test. It was progressively undermined by the rapid inflation of the 16th and 17th centuries, to the extent that the value requirement must have become virtually meaningless.[17]

After the Restoration, this expansion of the electorate was perhaps partly offset by the increasing concentration of land in the hands of fewer but larger owners,[18] leading some historians in the past to talk of the "disappearance of the small landowner".[19] Tenurial changes, such as the conversion of copyholds and leaseholds for lives into leaseholds for terms of years (which conduced to better estate management, more advanced farming, and therefore higher profits and higher rents) would also reduce the number of voters. On the other hand, some estate owners with political ambitions were by the 1690s creating new "freehold" interests to swell the number of votes they controlled, a process which continued for much of the 18th century.[20] Thus there is no reasonable doubt that the rural electorate was increasing in absolute numbers before 1640, and was probably also increasing between 1690 and 1832.

We can add to these rural freeholders the electors in the growing number of boroughs with MPs. While many smaller boroughs before 1832 were indeed "rotten", controlled by their landlord either directly or through his henchmen on the corporation, the larger boroughs, with a franchise comprising all burgesses or freemen, sometimes all residents or even all those liable for "scot and lot", often had large electorates and a vigorous political life; they needed to be wooed, as Burke wooed Bristol in 1774. In town and country, the electorate was further augmented by the inclusion, from 1665, of the lower (mainly parish) clergy who had been disfranchised since 1340, when their representatives had been transferred from the House of Commons to the Lower House of Convocation. Combining estimates for the rural freeholders and the urban electors, the total size of the electorate can be roughly estimated, and compared with estimates of the total number of adult males in the English population up to 1832; from 1833 onwards, much more precise statistics for the size of the electorate and the age distribution are available. All these figures are given in Table 2, which shows that the absolute size of the electorate was increasing over time, though the proportion of the adult male population enfranchised changed radically only in quite widely separated periods. The first great period of change was between the mid-15th century and the eve of the Civil War, during which the electorate by comparison with the adult population tripled from 5% to 15%. Although the estimates at the beginning and end of that period are open to doubt, neither is likely to be so imprecise as to obscure seriously the degree of overall change revealed by this comparison. What still remains unclear, however, until more research has been done, is when in the intervening period the main move towards this increased enfranchisement occurred: Hirst concluded that the growing importance of Parliament in the early Stuart period made it probable that this was the period when the expansion of the electorate mainly took place, but this is no more than a subjective expression of probability.

From 1640 to 1754, however, the electorate as a proportion of the adult male population fluctuated only within quite narrow limits (13.5 to 19.3%, if we exclude Holmes' over-estimate: 1722 (c) in Table 2 (below). From 1754 to the 1820s, in fact, this proportion fell by a third, from 19.3% to between 11.5 and 12.9%; effectively, the widening of the franchise in 1832 did no more than restore the relative proportion of the electorate to the adult male population to the position of 1722. Thus the number of electors had not kept up with the growth of population in the 18th and earlier 19th centuries. The next period of change was between 1832 and 1868: the 1832 Reform Act increased the number of electors by half, from 12.9% of adult males to 19.4%; the second Reform Act of 1867 further raised the proportion of adult males able to vote to 34.7%, and the third Reform Act of 1886 increased it to 58.8%. Finally, all adult men got the vote in 1918, together with women over 30, and the remaining women eventually achieved the suffragettes' goal in 1928.

Genuine representation of the people by the House of Commons only occurred, even in theory, in the 20th century, aptly termed by some "the age of the common man". As so often in history, theory and practice are not identical. The "single (non-transferable) vote" coupled with the "first past the post" system can, and often does, lead in large constituencies to a large minority of the electorate not being represented by a MP of their choice, and in many elections the winning candidate is elected by less than 50% of those voting, let alone 50% of the electorate able to vote. In the country as a whole, in only two general elections since 1918 (1931 and 1935) has the party which won the election received a majority of the votes cast, though the Conservatives in 1955 and 1959, and the Labour party in 1966, came near to doing so.[21] Before the present century, it is clear that in no sense was representation in Parliament democratic, since before 1918 most women, and before 1886 a majority of men, had no direct say in the election of their local MP. (I say "most women" before 1918 because it is one of the oddities of the 1832 Reform Act that the minority of women who had the right to vote up till then lost it). Is the system of democratic government a farce, as fascists of both left and right have contended, or is it justifiable as the least bad and most effective system of government yet devised? When one looks at the non-democratic alternatives in action during the past century – Mussolini's Italy, Hitler's Germany, Franco's Spain, above all Stalin's Russia, to go no further than Europe – "Western democracy" begins to look more attractive as a practical system of government. In the 1980s and early 1990s, I was often forced to defend Mrs Thatcher against assertions by some of my students that she was a "fascist". That the lady was strong-minded, perhaps even authoritarian, was hardly in doubt, but fascist she was not: she could have been removed from office by a general election had she not lost the support of her own party; indeed, she lost the support of her party precisely because it was widely supposed that she would lose the next general election. By contrast, military defeat in a long, exhausting, and destructive world war was necessary to remove Hitler and Mussolini, while economic disaster and a failed coup were required to bring about the downfall of Soviet Russia.

But, in the main, this book is concerned with the past and the present rather than the future. In what sense were the knights of the shire and the burgesses representatives of their communities in Parliament? We know that probably in the earlier 13th century, and certainly in 1254, the knights of the shires were "elected" (probably "chosen" may be a better English translation) in the county courts, but by whom? The normal suitors of the country court, officials such as hundred-reeves and other local personages, or some specially convoked assembly? We simply do not know, because our sources are silent on the matter. What the sources do tell us is that the kings, Henry III and Edward I, deem the knights and burgesses so chosen to be representative of their community, by royal command. They are deemed able to assist in doing justice – to this day Parliament is correctly styled the "High Court of Parliament" – and to consent to the levying of taxation on behalf of their counties and towns, and thus Edward I quoted the Roman law maxim "What touches all must be approved by all" in the writ summoning archbishops and other prelates to Parliament in 1295.[22] The 13th century knights of the shire and burgesses hence represent their communities before a royal assembly primarily for the dual purposes of doing justice and providing the monarch with money, in exactly the same way that, two centuries earlier, we are told that the villages of Anglo-Norman England were represented by the priest, the reeve, and six villagers at sessions of the Domesday survey, probably also held in county courts, where they gave evidence about illegal land claims (doing justice) and provided a check on the accuracy of economic and fiscal information ("whether more could be had than is being had?"):

> Here follows the inquest of lands as the King's barons made it, to wit, by the oaths of the sheriff of the shire and of all the barons and their Frenchmen and of the whole hundred, *of the priest, the reeve and six villagers of each village* (my emphasis).[23]

No serious scholar, not even the Victorians at their most Whiggish, has ever suggested that these "villagers" were democratically elected representatives of their villages; these "jurors", where they can be identified, in the East Midlands, appear to be the more substantial members of the local community, thegns, knights, and substantial freemen.[24]

The period after the Norman Conquest saw a large fall in the numbers of "freemen" and "sokemen" who had comprised just over one-third (36.9%) of the entire English rural population in 1086, according to the Domesday survey, which records that the decline began after 1066; in Cambridgeshire, for example, there were nearly 900 sokemen in 1066 but only 177 in 1086; at Benfleet (Essex) a freeman with about 60 acres of land in 1066 "had been made one of the villagers" in 1086.[25] The decline continued in the following two and a half centuries: the ordinary peasant tenant of a Manor, the villager (in Latin *villanus,* "man of the village", translating the Old English *tunesman*), who was of free status as late as the reign of Henry I (1100-35), had become by the 13th century a person of unfree condition, a serf or villein in Norman-French. The change in terminology was significant, for "serf" was the Norman-French derivative from, and equivalent of, the Latin *servus,* "slave". Various reasons have been suggested for this change: the development of the Common Law, the desire of royal officials to reduce the number of free suitors to the central royal law courts at Westminster, the increasing "reception" of Roman Law, one of the maxims of which was the rigid division between free and unfree (*aut liber aut servus omnis est*, which medieval English lawyers were able to mistranslate as "every man is either free or unfree" because slavery proper had disappeared from England by 1135). Other reasons include the rise of inflation which put pressure on landlords, population-growth which converted labour shortages into labour surpluses, and combined to stimulate a changeover from the leasing of demesnes to direct farming of demesnes for the lords' benefit, and enhanced the value of labour services owed by the villagers to their lords.[26] An analysis of peasants who held more than just a cottage in six Midland counties in 1279 showed that the freemen constituted just over a third of the total (35.6%), a proportion that would certainly have been far lower in the more heavily manorialized western and southern counties.[27] With the removal of most free peasants from royal courts, including the county courts where rural MPs were elected, the freemen who remained would have been the knights and the substantial freemen already being called "franklins" and soon to be called "yeomen". It was, therefore, not surprising that the Good Parliament of 1376 petitioned the Crown that electors should be "only the better sort of people of the shire", and perhaps not too surprising that the Crown still insisted on election "by the common assent of the whole county".[28]

For the times were "a-changing": England was probably over-populated by 1300 and the number of its people were falling after the great famine of 1315-17 even before the Black Death of 1348-50, the Children's Plague of 1361, and later outbreaks of plague reduced English population from a peak of perhaps more than five million to no more than 1.5 million in the mid-15th century. The results are well known; disrespect for an effete ruling class slow to recognize new conditions, which was encapsulated in John Ball's famous couplet,

> When Adam delved and Eve span,
> who was then the gentleman?

refusal to render labour services, rent strikes, widespread rural discontent culminating in the Peasants' Revolt of 1381.[29] Although the revolt itself was put down, the stresses and strains which it exemplified could not be suppressed: the clock could not be put back to what the nobility and gentry regarded as the "good old days" of the 13th century. The more adaptable and go-ahead landlords faced up to reality sooner than the rest, but the result was inevitable: tenants who were refused lighter money rents, the abolition of labour services, and, above all, free tenure and free status simply "voted with their feet" and removed themselves to the estates of more flexible and accommodating landlords.[30] This great expansion in the numbers of freemen/freeholders able to attend the county courts and vote helps to explain the attempt to restrict elections to "the better sort of people" in 1376 and why in 1430 the franchise was limited to the 40-shilling freeholder. As we have already seen, that limit did not exclude many poor men of free condition. In the towns also, where even in normal times, population levels could only be maintained by continued immigration, the new circumstances forced concessions out of urban oligarchies. The great advantage and opportunity which towns had offered in the High Middle Ages, summed-up in Professor Postan's phrase describing the towns as "little islands of freedom in a feudal sea", protecting all unfree rural immigrants into a town who could stay there unclaimed by their manorial lords for a year and a day, no longer seemed so attractive an option in the later Middle Ages when freedom returned to the fields and woods of the countryside. Again, it seems that electorates were being widened in many instances, though not all. The larger and more enterprising towns tended to have wider franchises, comprising, in ascending order of magnitude, all burgesses, all freemen, all paying "scot and lot", and finally all residents ("all" in this context, of course, generally meant of the male sex only).

Given the increasing awkwardness of the electorate in the eyes of the ruling class, the "political nation" as some historians have termed it, and given also that, as again already noted, inflation after the 1480s eroded the real value of 40 shillings and thus enlarged the number of potential voters, how are we to explain the rise of Parliament, including the House of Commons? How are we to explain the astonishing rise in size of the House of Commons from a total which never exceeded 302 between 1295 and 1515, but had risen by more than 50% to 452 by 1563, to 530 by 1679 and to a peak of 551 in 1689 before falling to 513 on the eve of Union with Scotland in 1707 (see Table 1)? More, how are we to explain the astonishing rise in the power of the House of Commons from a body called at the Crown's behest, which was apparently only required to assent to the Crown's wishes, in the 13th century, to a body thought so useful by the Crown in the 16th century that Henry VIII stated that "we stand in no such high estate as when we are in Parliament", and then used it to legislate the Papacy out of existence, to a body which in the 17th century successfully asserted its right of obtaining "redress before supply" and by the 18th century effectively controlled government? I have earlier stressed that the representative role of the early MPs was very much an example of what I have previously defined as "appointed" or "selected" representation, in which the role was ascribed to the MPs by the Crown rather than being implicit in the process by which they were appointed. In other words, here is yet another example of what has been called, without conscious irony, "self-government at the King's command". Other answers to the questions I have posed, somewhat rhetorically perhaps, are to be found in the chapters of the contributors.

The first, and initially most important, aspect is that of royal financial needs. Medieval and early modern rulers, not only in England but also in Europe, were perpetually short of money: Philip II, the first European ruler of a great non-European empire, beneficiary of the riches of Mexico and Peru, nevertheless "went bankrupt" (was forced to repudiate his debts) four times during his reign. Although, after the Norman Conquest, the kings of England were extremely wealthy, owning nearly one-fifth of the landed wealth of the kingdom, the royal share had shrunk to 4% on the eve of the Dissolution of the Monasteries (1536-40).[31] To adapt Francis Bacon's adage about Henry VII, "considerations of power" had overcome "considerations of plenty": the need to ensure a place in Heaven by pious donations, to reward friends, to attract new supporters, and to conciliate enemies meant that most royal land had been granted to sections of the landed nobility between the 11th and the 13th centuries, so that by 1300 the King was seriously short of money even in peacetime. Any long war, especially overseas or in the Celtic borderlands, revealed the Crown's financial straits. Moreover, war itself was becoming more expensive: plate armour was replacing chain-mail; armour was being extended to horses, which were therefore becoming larger, stronger, and more costly; offensive armies and defensive garrisons were becoming larger and increasingly comprised reliable men-at-arms serving for pay rather than less reliable contingents fulfilling feudal obligations of knight-service; new technology (always expensive) was being introduced (the replacement of wooden castles by stone castles, the evolution of larger, "Edwardian" stone castles, new siege-weapons, the longbow, artillery); campaigns which had once lasted for a few months in the summer now continued for years at a time.[32] It was hardly surprising, therefore, that the 13th century was fertile in new forms of taxation such as the carucage (a tax on ploughteams, first levied in 1220), the tax on moveables (first levied in 1225, developing into the lay subsidy later known as tenths and fifteenths by the end of the century) and the tax on overseas trade (customs), a permanent tax from 1275 but one anticipated by a unique experiment of 1203-4 under King John.[33] When Edward I found himself fighting a war on three fronts (France, Wales, and Scotland), and even more when his grandson Edward III embroiled himself in what became the Hundred Years' War, it was necessary to turn to Parliament which was deemed the only fit body to assent to taxation on behalf of the whole community of the realm. As Dr Carpenter makes clear in chapter 1, the old claim of the baronage assembled in a great council to "represent" their under-tenants (because of the mutual vertical links of feudal lordship) and to assent to taxation on their behalf was becoming stale by the 13th century, as was the nobility's parallel claim to "own" all the property of their unfree tenants. This latter claim, developed by lawyers in the age of Glanvill and Bracton largely, one suspects, to generate legal fees, was abandoned as soon as the Crown began to tax the property of all peasants, free and villein alike. The essential weakness of the baronial position had been exposed, and the Crown turned to look for other and better representatives of the community. The baronage itself, the old greater tenants-in-chief of the Crown, were becoming attenuated by escheat and forfeiture, by female descent, and by the growth of a class of large landholders who were not great tenants-in-chief. A new aristocracy, the parliamentary peerage, was to emerge in the later Middle Ages, while the barons, never more than a few hundred in number, were a small fraction of the landed nobility as a whole, who were to be numbered in thousands: 3,300 c. 1300, 4,300 c. 1400, 8,000 in 1524.[34] The English towns were also growing in numbers, in wealth, and in population, partly because of their freedom from feudal control and interference, partly because of the growth of trade, internal and external, partly because of the growth of specialized industries, partly because of government and baronial policies ever since the Norman Conquest which had seen the "planting" of new towns as a useful means of pacifying first the English, then the Angevins and especially the Gascons, and of pacifying and civilizing the Welsh and Irish.[35] Because most big towns were or became royal boroughs, outside the control of the baronage, it was impossible for the baronage even to pretend that they could represent the towns.

The financial needs of the Crown were not, however, the only reason why Parliament was repeatedly summoned or why, after 1325, the House of Commons was regarded as an integral and essential part of Parliament. The Great Council continued to meet as an assembly of nobles called to advise the Crown until the reign of Henry VII, but Parliament had become the legislative body which represented the community of the realm: the House of Commons also had for most of the Middle Ages an important judicial function as a channel through which petitions for redress could pass to the Crown. Eventually, this role was to decline, just as the judicial role of the Great Council had passed in the 12th century to the more specialized *Curia Regis* and in the 13th century to the still more differentiated Common Law courts of King's Bench, dealing mainly with criminal matters, and Common Pleas, dealing with civil disputes.[36] A parallel development had seen the move of the great administrative and financial departments of the Chancery and the Exchequer "out of court" (splitting off from the Royal Household and developing as separate bureaucratic units normally located at Westminster).[37] But until Chancery began, in the 14th and 15th centuries, to develop an equity jurisdiction alongside its administrative function as the registry of the King's written orders (the Charter, Patent, Close, and Fine rolls in particular), there was no other means (apart from direct petitions to the Crown or to the Council, which could always be intercepted or censored by royal officials) by which the Royal Prerogative could be invoked to provide redress of grievances falling outside the remedies offered by Common Law, which was slow to change. As Dr Carpenter has emphasized in chapter 1, ever since Magna Carta in 1215, the localities had been raising problems in the hope that the Crown would provide a solution, so that parliaments, however constituted, increasingly provided one way in which such requests from the country could reach the centre of government. In the medium term, therefore, and in particular from the late 13th century to the early 15th century, the House of Commons assumed considerable importance as a means of obtaining redress in matters of equity. Eventually, the rise of the "equity side" of Chancery, followed in the 16th and 17th centuries by the development, firstly, of the prerogative courts of Star Chamber and Requests and, secondly, of the Exchequer as an equity court, reduced the significance of this aspect of the House of Commons' work to insignificance.[38]

Nonetheless, the combination of royal financial needs, the desires of many petitioners for justice which was not available from existing Common Law courts, and the political desirability of having a two-way channel of communication between the centre and the regions, ensured the continuance and survival of the English Parliament and the House of Commons. Parliament did not shrink to being just a law court, as the French *parlements* did by the 16th century; the House of Commons did not become a servile and sycophantic representative body voting taxes on royal demand, as was true of the Spanish *cortes*; neither did it wither away as the French Estates-General did by 1614, so that when it was necessary to convene the Estates-General at the start of the French Revolution in 1789, archivists and officials had to be set to work to discover how the Estates had been summoned and how they operated.[39] If there was a "myth of Parliament" which was eventually incorporated into the "Whig interpretation of history", it came about partly, as Professor Sharpe shows in chapter 4, because contemporary Englishmen *were* increasingly aware that representative assemblies almost everywhere else in Europe were declining into impotence. Indeed, if the absolutist pretensions of the Stuarts (and also of Oliver Cromwell) had not been checked, the English Parliament would almost certainly have gone the same way. Why, then, was the English experience so different?

The reason almost certainly does not lie in any so-called "Lancastrian constitutional experiment" which gave a greater share in government to Parliament in general or the House of Commons in particular: that, in Dr Payling's words, "may be to project the constitutional preoccupations of the 17th century into an age in which they had no place" (chapter 2). As Dr Payling shows, it is difficult to discern the political role of the Commons because we have extremely little evidence of the expressed thoughts or the underlying reasons of 15th century MPs. Certainly, the continuing importance of MPs was made clear as early as the 1320s when the treatise called *Modus Tenendi Parliamentum* asserted that they

> represent the whole community of the realm [hence] two knights who come to Parliament for the shire have a greater voice in the granting and denying [of taxation] than the greatest earl in England.[40]

The continuing desire of the Crown to fight foreign wars right down to the close of the Hundred Years' War, the corollary of the Crown's continuing need for tax revenues since it was less and less able "to live of its own", and the increased emphasis on indirect taxation in the form of customs duties, all militated to highlight the role of the Commons. The yield from normal direct taxation on moveables, the tenths and fifteenths, fell by two-thirds between the 1290s and the 1330s, when assessments were fixed; thereafter, until the new Tudor subsidy of the 1520s, they could only change in a downwards direction, if privilege and patronage secured reduction or exemption for particular places. Customs revenue also more than halved between the 1360s and the 1450s, and any possibility of radical change, had it been envisaged, would have been wrecked by the great population decline between the 1320s and the 1450s and the stagnant or falling rental income of most landlords. The landlords, indeed, made the situation worse by effectively shifting the bulk of direct taxation onto the poorer classes and refusing a permanent tax on land properly assessed. In general, in any case, the Commons assented to most grants of taxation until well into the 16th century.

But the involvement of the Commons in assenting to taxes and helping to provide answers to petitions (themselves addressed more and more frequently to the Commons as such rather than to the Crown), even in approving the Royal Assent to petitions sent direct to the King, led to the eventual development of legislation proper, so that by 1489 all valid legislation required the consent of the Commons. It would be entirely wrong to see Parliament and King as rivals rather than, still, very unequal partners in government; but the later Middle Ages had witnessed the growth of the sense of corporate identity and *esprit de corps,* the establishment of the office of Speaker, the increasing regard in which the Commons was held by the population at large (evidenced by the apparent widescale participation in elections before the 1430 act establishing the 40 shilling freehold qualification), more frequent parliaments in which there were more MPs being returned who had served in previous parliaments. The influence of the House of Lords on the late medieval Commons was very considerable, which, given patronage, retaining, and other aspects of "bastard feudalism" is hardly surprising, yet it would be difficult to argue that such influence was less than it was in the 18th century, when the Commons included 20% of peers' sons and peers' nominees at the start of the century and 60% at the end of the century, and yet the Lords was already clearly no longer the dominant part of the legislature.[41] The growing power of the Commons reflected the growing power of the gentry which the knights of the shire both represented and in fact comprised, and the power of the gentry, in the Commons as in the country at large, was strengthened when they began in the 15th century to take over the representation of boroughs in the Commons.

All the trends I have mentioned in the previous paragraph continued and intensified in the one and a half centuries before the outbreak of the Civil War in 1642. The Crown's financial needs expanded as a result of royal extravagance – the openly competitive display at the Field of the Cloth of Gold in 1519, the rebuilding, expanding or new building of royal palaces[42] – and wars, with France and Scotland in particular, which required the expansion of the Royal Navy and the building of many coastal forts designed to accommodate, and to withstand, artillery.[43] These needs, together with the absolute need (or what appeared to Henry VIII and to most of his subjects to be absolute need) for a male heir, combined to produce the abolition in 1534 of the authority in England of a pope who was unable or unwilling to grant the King an annulment of his marriage, and the dissolution of the monasteries between 1536 and 1540. Since the Crown and its advisers, notably Thomas Cromwell, deemed it advantageous to assert that these royal policies had "popular" support (by which they did not mean the support of the people at large, but that of the "political nation" who were represented in and by Parliament) all the policies were embodied in acts of Parliament to which the Crown "graciously assented". Since even the windfall of monastic and later chantry properties was insufficient to meet royal expenditure, the Crown increasingly needed more taxation revenues; before the end of the 16th century, taxes in peacetime were a normal occurrence. Since the grant of taxes was normally a matter for Parliament (although the Tudors and early Stuarts occasionally resorted to benevolences and forced loans or anticipations to make ends meet) Parliament, therefore, met more frequently, and this must have increased the sense of corporate identity of the Commons, especially since this sense would be reinforced by the fact that these more frequent meetings would mean more members serving for several parliaments. Still, the Crown clearly did not regard the more frequent meetings of Parliament which it had engendered as dangerous to its interests, although these meetings increasingly did entail efficient management of the Commons by senior ministers and Privy Councillors. Some MPs, though not many, were royal nominees, sitting for seats controlled by the duchy of Lancaster. Although the Elizabethan House of Commons was raising more grievances as time went on, it did not push matters to extremes, and avoided confrontation even on serious grievances such as monopolies, as Dr Loach shows in chapter 3. Partly, this may have been because of increasing reverence for the ageing and much loved Queen, partly because of a sense of gratitude to a dynasty which had kept England aloof from entanglement in most of the wars which engulfed the continent. But it was certainly not because of the weakness of the Commons: the expansion in the number of borough constituencies under the Tudors and early Stuarts was mainly in response to demands by the county gentry for more seats which the Crown was unwilling to oppose. Having made all due allowance for changes, the Commons was still very traditional in its attitudes:

> the main concerns of its members were local and personal rather than
> political and neither electors nor members saw it as a major forum for
> political or social or religious change.[44]

These words, among the last that Jennifer Loach wrote before her untimely death, are a considered judgment worthy of "deep thought and much discussion".

If, therefore, it could be argued that there was relatively little change between, say, 1504 and 1603, it is beyond doubt that considerable change had occurred by 1714, when the last Stuart monarch died. This is not to deny, as Kevin Sharpe has demonstrated in chapter 4, that the nature of the changes that took place have been viewed from a number of often contradictory and sometimes anachronistic perspectives. What is also undeniable is that the Crown's finances were still deteriorating: by 1603, there was little Crown land left to sell; the yield from the subsidy, which had greatly improved in the 1520s, fell after the 1540s as assessments not only failed to keep pace with inflation, but were eroded by corruption: Queen Elizabeth's chief minister, Lord Burghley, was assessed for the subsidy at £133 a year when we know he was receiving over £4,000 a year. Customs revenues on foreign trade did not recover from the crisis in the Antwerp trade until the 17th century, by which the area and value of England's foreign trade was beginning to expand greatly, as it would continue to do until the present century. But expedients such as the widespread sale of offices were never tried and the excise, already adopted on the continent, was only introduced by Parliament during the Civil War as an emergency measure, and was severely pruned after the Restoration. There was little legislation before the 1640s and little change in the nature of the people who became MPs; local issues and concerns still dominated the minds of most MPs. In short, it took exceptional events, the war with Scotland, the Irish rebellion, to break the mould in which Crown and Parliament normally coexisted, more or less peacefully, coupled with a breakdown in the Crown's management of Parliament. In addition, new military developments were again making warfare more expensive and thus worsening the financial problems of government.[45] As Professor Sharpe notes, after the Civil War,

Parliament's hero, Oliver Cromwell, was to encounter precisely the same problems in dealing with the House of Commons which Charles I had confronted, and it is therefore difficult to blame only Charles' arrogance and ineptitude for the breakdown in relations with Parliament. Crown and Parliament were trapped in a relationship governed by custom and tradition which were increasingly irrelevant to new conditions; the old partnership was only to be reestablished after the Glorious Revolution of 1689 when the threat of religious divisions within English Protestantism leading to civil strife was removed by the Toleration Act and a new political culture had arisen allowing the political nation and the monarch to join in ruling the state together.

This outcome was by no means certain after the Restoration, as Professor Speck shows (chapter 5). Partly, this was because the Cromwellian regime had bequeathed to the returned Stuarts a vastly more healthy financial regime. Charles I, since he ruled without Parliament between 1629 and 1640, received no income from regular taxation, and had struggled to survive on a regular gross annual revenue of about £85,000 from the Crown estates, £50,000 to £80,000 from the Court of Wards, and £100,000 to £120,000 from the Customs. In all, with other minor sources of revenue, the King received no more than about £350,000 a year. By contrast, Charles II had between £500,000 and £600,000 from the Customs, between £110,000 and £215,000 from the Hearth Tax, offset by the falling net yield from other direct taxation (which peaked at £1,300,000 in 1664-6) and between £450,000 and £620,000 from the excise. From all sources, Charles II received a total income of about £1,500,000 a year in the 1660s, rising to more than £2 million yearly in 1685. This excludes his French pension. Given expanding foreign trade, and hence rising customs revenues, and rising living standards, hence more excise revenue, and the substitution of the Land Tax for the Hearth Tax, royal revenues grew dramatically: the total government revenue under Queen Anne rose to between £5 million and £6 million a year, and rose to more than £10 million yearly in wartime under George II.[46] In addition, the Cavalier Parliament (1661-79) at least in its early years enthusiastically cooperated with Charles II. The Crown thus had parliamentary support and also the financial resources to manage the Commons by bribing MPs, as was widely believed by contemporaries. It also had the resources, if it chose to do so, to rule without calling a parliament, as Charles II did after 1681 and James II did after 1685. The Commons was thus vulnerable not only because of its reliance on a summons by the Crown to bring it into being, but also because of the Crown's attempt to rig the electoral system, especially for borough constituencies, between 1681 and 1688. Fortunately for the House of Commons the Crown's more general power to enfranchise new constituencies was not exercised after the enfranchisement of Durham City and County in 1673 and Newark borough in 1674; after 1688, no further royal attempts were made to expand membership of the House of Commons except as a result of the unions with Scotland in 1707 and with Ireland in 1801 (see Table 1). Although the Crown (or now perhaps more accurately the Crown's chief minister) could count on 120-150 MPs as a court party, this was no more than 27% of the Georgian House which, in Professor Speck's words, "merely served to strengthen the influence of the Crown in Parliament, not its power over it". Ironically, as he concludes, "the sovereignty of the King in Parliament had finally triumphed over the sovereignty of the people".[47]

Consequently, as Professor Jeremy Black shows in chapter 6, the political nation largely controlled political life between the Glorious Revolution and the 1832 Reform Act. Many small constituencies were controlled by their landlords and contested elections were rare: only once was the Great Commoner, William Pitt the Elder, opposed at an election, in Salford in 1747; in all the other seats he occupied he was returned unopposed. Most borough seats by the 18th century now had representatives drawn from the national elite or the country gentry; the Lords, as we have already noted, had considerable direct and indirect influence in the Commons, which, together with the increasing promotion of MPs to the Lords from the reign of George III onwards, encouraged continuing good relations between the two Houses of Parliament. In the counties, where electorates were larger than in most boroughs, contested elections were rare because of the expense involved, and thus rival noble dynasties usually agreed to divide the two county seats between their candidates. But, as I have remarked, the landed classes could not take the electorate for granted: at Derby in 1722 and again in 1748 local men were successful as candidates despite the opposition of the normally dominant magnates, the Dukes of Devonshire and the Earls of Chesterfield. Local interests were deemed important by the electorate, and Edmund Burke, elected MP for Bristol in 1774, refused to support "local prejudices", and came bottom of the poll at the next election. Private, local, and personal acts occupied much of Parliament's time and attention, but since improvement, whether of urban paving, lighting, drainage, and policing, or of regional transport (turnpike roads and canals) or of agrarian improvements (mostly enclosure but also land-drainage), required statutory authority, such acts were of considerable importance in promoting the desired improvements in the country and as demonstrating Parliament's sensitivity to purely local demands. (It must be said that the concatenation of such local promotions was to provide the nation as a whole with the necessary physical infrastructure of transport facilities and advanced agriculture using its labour efficiently without which the Industrial Revolution could hardly have started, much less succeeded).

But, as Professor Black also shows, Parliament fulfilled (or appeared to fulfil) national needs. It legitimized the Glorious Revolution of 1688 and the Hanoverian Succession in 1701. It enabled England, and after 1707 Britain, to surmount the severe financial difficulties resulting from prolonged warfare with France around the world between 1689 and 1815, by raising adequate taxes and by guaranteeing the funding of the National Debt at low rates of interest, the "financial revolution".[48] Hence it was that Britain, with a third of the population of France under Louis XIV and no more than half the French population under Napoleon I, and with national wealth no higher than France's before the last quarter of the 18th century, was normally able to defeat France in war during that period; the only French success was her assistance to the American colonists. Parliament was also useful as a channel of communication between commercial interests and the government. Against these propositions it can be argued that governments could not always be sure of majorities in the House of Commons, and even when they did secure parliamentary majorities, the policies might be extremely unpopular with the public at large, such as the Cider Excise Act of 1763 which provoked such uproar that it had to be repealed three years later. And in the period between the "two-party system" of Queen Anne's reign and the resurrection of "party" in the 1780s, factiousness and political opportunism could cause severe problems for government: even the "patriot" Pitt the Elder was guilty of self-interested manoeuvrings at times of crisis in the 1740s and 1750s. Nevertheless, Parliament and constitutional government did survive the 18th century in Britain whereas representative assemblies in the Netherlands, Poland, and Sweden did not, and even the "benevolent autocracies" succumbed to the pressures unleashed by the French Revolution and Napoleon. Only in the American colonies did representative government survive. As Professor Black notes, "the alternatives were bleak. Enlightened Despotism was not only autocratic; it could also be inept and unsuccessful."[49] In the last analysis, in the years between 1790 and 1815, as in the years 1939-45, parliamentary government in Britain survived attack by a continental dictator who had otherwise removed all opposition from his path. The British system was not without its faults which were to become increasingly apparent after 1815 and finally lead to successful pressure for reform in 1832: the electorate comprised only 11.5% of adult males in 1818 and had only risen marginally to 12.9% in 1831 (see Table 2); these figures were below the level of 1690 (13.5%), and even after the first Reform Act the electorate in 1833 (19.4%) was no higher as a proportion of adult males than it had probably been in 1722. In numerical terms, however, which contemporaries probably found it easier to comprehend, the early 19th century scene appeared promising: the electorate had increased by a quarter between 1818 and 1831 and by a half as a result of the first Reform Act.

Obviously, therefore, Miss Valerie Cromwell (chapter 7) is entirely correct in asserting, "there can be no doubt that the significance of the 1832 Reform Act was largely symbolic".[50] A harsher critic might describe the first Reform Act as a Whig confidence trick; the first real advance over previous levels of the ratio of electors to adult males came in 1867 when the Conservatives, Derby and Disraeli, "dished the Whigs". The electorate nearly doubled as a proportion of adult males and more than trebled in numbers; it was not, however, until after the third Reform Act, and a further more than doubling in the numbers of electors, that more than half the adult males had the vote. Even in 1918, not all women were enfranchised, hence Valerie Cromwell again correctly states that "at no point in the period 1815-1918 did Britain experience democracy".[51] The changes in the social composition of the new

House of Commons were minimal after 1832, as were the methods of election; so long as open voting and the public recording of the votes cast remained, coercion could too easily be applied to voters. Even after the Secret Ballot Act of 1872, it took a further decade to eliminate "corrupt practices" as an everyday occurrence.[52] It is probably true to say that the biggest shock administered to Parliament in the 19th century was the accidental destruction of the bulk of both Houses by fire in 1834 and the subsequent rebuilding of the new Palace of Westminster between 1844 and 1870.

At the same time, increasing literacy, resulting first from the massive building programmes of the National and British School Societies after 1818, especially in and after the 1840s, accelerated by Forster's Education Act of 1870, and growing political awareness among the bulk of the population led to more interest in, and more pressure on, proceedings in Parliament. The recording of debates by Cobbett since 1803 and by Hansard since 1812 and the rise of parliamentary press correspondents aroused more public interest, and in turn the rise of party organizations in the constituencies after 1867 enabled the politicians to assemble public support for their proposed policies. (This, of course, only put on a formal basis what the Whigs had somewhat hypocritically done in 1831-32 to frighten the Tories into allowing Reform, and the more widespread level of local organization by the Chartists in the 1840s). Paradoxically, though, just as the House of Commons came within striking distance of being able to claim that it was "representative" of at any rate the male population, its power was being weakened increasingly by two new developments of the second half of the 19th century. The first of these was the growth of more tightly controlled party machines which more and more sapped the independence of the ordinary backbench MP, which was further eroded by the decline in the amount of Commons time devoted to the business that was of concern to them. The second new development was the rise of the collectivist state, which required more and more detailed legislation to provide its powers: this resulted in a congested parliamentary timetable in which even government bills could fail to pass all the necessary stages in time to receive the Royal Assent. In the long run, "delegated legislation" such as Statutory Instruments – the old royal proclamation under a new guise – and a longer parliamentary session would be necessary to cope, followed in the late 19th century by the use of the "guillotine" to restrict the length of debates. At the same time, Parliament's control of financial details was weakened by the appointment of the Comptroller and Auditor General, and although in theory the Public Accounts Committee was instituted to implement such control, in practice it tended to discuss the government's general financial policy. Detailed scrutiny of finance passed to a civil service department, the Treasury, which in the 20th century would become the main arbiter of decisions about government spending, symptomatic of the rise of the Civil Service as the real masters of government.[53] Further problems also tended to weaken the authority of Parliament, and these are outlined by Michael Fry in chapter 8. The second British Empire, it was once said, was acquired "in a fit of absence of mind", and was an expanding area of settlement in the 19th and earlier 20th centuries, despite what was, in the main, the disinterest of the Conservatives and the active hostility of most Liberals. But attempts to make the British Parliament into a truly imperial Parliament with representatives from what would later be called the dominions failed to come to fruition, partly because it was over-ambitious in the light of the means of communication then available, partly because a uniform tariff did not suit the interests of all the overseas territories, partly because the intellectual tide was turning against imperialism and free trade. As Michael Fry notes, attempts at federation on a smaller scale in Australia and South Africa, following the Canadian precedent, were successful in the early part of this century, but federation on a world scale was simply impractical. With the failure of Imperial Preference in the 1930s, the Empire gradually evolved into the modern Commonwealth, an association of independent countries with a common heritage from the past and some common aims in the present and perhaps the near future. A situation, in fact, redolent of the 17th-century "Three Kingdoms" united only by allegiance to the same ruler. For most British politicians, a bigger problem, and one much nearer home, was the rise of Celtic nationalism, in Wales rather more than Scotland but above all in Ireland. There, a long and unhappy historical inheritance of racial and religious intolerance, augmented by special features such as gavelkind and, as a result, a prevalence of uneconomic smallholdings occupied by a peasantry whose counterparts in England had largely disappeared by 1600, soured by the tragic accident of the "Hungry Forties", was manipulated by the Liberals for party advantage and by Irish nationalists who blamed the English ruling class for all the ills of Ireland, but failed to explain how that same ruling class of English landlords had achieved such very different economic results on opposite sides of the Irish Sea.[54] In the end, after the war of independence, Eire was granted dominion status in 1922, but the legacy of bigotry was to bedevil Northern Ireland for the rest of the 20th century. Welsh nationalism seems to have been largely a vehicle for the ambition of Lloyd George, one of the most unscrupulous politicians of modern times.

Two aspects of the present day Parliament are covered by Mr Michael Stephen, a sitting backbencher (chapter 10) and Mr Edward Pearce, a journalist covering parliamentary affairs (chapter 11): there are also many more journalists covering parliamentary *affaires*! Michael Stephen gives a good account of how to become and act as a MP, and the high standards required. But it is clear that there is little scope for independent minds on the backbenches, whose occupants are expected to troop into the division lobbies at the behest of party whips like sheep corralled by a shepherd and his dog. As in many other aspects of modern British life, integrity and the ability to think for oneself are not qualities valued by the whips. This must present a considerable dilemma to those MPs like Michael Stephen: unless they have private incomes or are totalling lacking in political ambition, they must at some point have to compromise with the party managers and the whips if they have any hopes of rising to a place in government (which in itself is not an ignoble desire). Their delicate situation, like that of royalty, is not made better by the glare of publicity directed on them by the press and the broadcasting media, whose operations are very unnecessarily intrusive. MPs are, one presumes, as much entitled to a private life as any other persons in the population. But I cannot agree with Edward Pearce that this situation is all the fault of the media, and even less of one particular section within the media. Readers must make up their own minds.

Finally, I wish to thank all the contributors for their wisdom and hard work, my wife and children for their support and forbearance while this book occupied my time and attention, and finally, my friend, co-editor, and publisher, Robert Smith, without whose efforts nothing would have come to fruition.

Footnotes to the Introduction may be found on page 182–7.

TABLE 1: CONSTITUENCIES REPRESENTED IN THE HOUSE OF COMMONS, 1295 -1995:

DATE	COUNTY MPs	BOROUGH MPs	TOTAL MPs
1295	74	228	302
1384	74	178	252
1421	74	176	250
1439-40	74	190	264
1442, 1445-6	74	194	268
1453-4 > 1463-5	74	206	280
1470-1 > 1504			
1510, 1512	74	222	296
1515	74	228	302
1536, 1539	74	238	312
1542	88	250	338
1545	88	251	339
1547, 1553	88	291	379
1554-5	88	306	394
1558	88	310	398
1559	91	314	405
1563	101	351	452
1571	91	352	443
1572	109	422	531
1584, 1586	91	377	468
1589	91	376	467
1593	90	374	464
1597	92	380	472
1601	91	376	467
1640-1	90	403	493
1660	90	417	507
1679, March	96	426	522
1679, October	95	435	530
1681	93	409	502
1685	91	434	525
1689	94	457	551
1690 > 1707	92	421	513
1708 > 1800	122	436	558
1801 > 1832	186	472	658
1832 > 1868	253	405	658
1868 > 1885	283	375	658
1885 > 1918	377	293	670
1918 > 1922	372	335	707
1922 > 1945	300	315	615
1945 > 1950	302	338	640

**TABLE 1: CONSTITUENCIES REPRESENTED IN THE HOUSE
OF COMMONS, 1295 -1995:** *(continued)*

DATE	COUNTY MPs	BOROUGH MPs	TOTAL MPs
1950 > 1955	288	337	625
1955 > 1974	295	335	630
1974 > 1983	288	347	635
1983 > 1995	333	317	650

Note:

The sign > indicates all parliaments between the dates specified.

Sources:

1295, 1384, 1421: S Roskell, L Clark, C Rawcliffe, eds, *The House of Commons, 1385-1421* (Stroud, 4 vols, 1992), I, p 41.

1439-40 > 1504: J Wedgwood, ed, *History of Parliament, ... 1439-1509* (London, 2 vols, 1936, 1938), I, pp lxxxiii-vi.

1512 > 1558: S T Bindoff, ed, *The House of Commons, 1509-1558* (London, 3 vols, 1982), I, p 4. The figures for 1512-54 include 2 MPs from Tournai (1512, 1515) and 2 MPs from Calais (1536-54). The Welsh MPs comprised 12 rural and 12 borough representatives.

1559 > 1601: P W Hasler, ed, *The House of Commons, 1558-1603* (London, 3 vols, 1981), I, pp 67, 70, 73, 77, 81, 84, 87, 90, 94, 97; English and Welsh MPs have been combined under the appropriate headings.

1640-1: D Brunton, D H Pennington, *Members of the Long Parliament* (London, 1954, repr 1968), p 2. After the election, the House of Commons voted to enfranchise seven "restored" boroughs, adding 14 MPs to make a total of 507.

1660 > 1689: B D Henning, ed, *The House of Commons, 1660-1690* (London, 3 vols, 1983), I pp 65-6, 104.

1690 > 1754: R Sedgwick, ed, *The House of Commons, 1715-1754* (London, 2 vols, 1970), I, p 1.

1754 > 1800: *Ibid,* p 1; L Namier, J Brooke, eds, *The House of Commons, 1754-1790* (London, 3 vols, 1964), I, pp 2, 10, 36-8, 41; R G Thorne, ed, *The House of Commons, 1790-1820* (London, 5 vols, 1986), I, p 4.

1801 > 1832: *Ibid,* pp 100, 102.

1832 > 1995: F W S Craig, *British Electoral Facts, 1832-1987* (Aldershot, 5th edn,

TABLE 2: THE TOTAL SIZE OF THE ELECTORATE (ENGLAND AND WALES), 1432-1992:

DATE	RURAL FREEHOLDERS	URBAN ELECTORS	TOTAL ELECTORATE	ESTIMATED ADULT MEN	ELECTORS AS % OF ADULT MEN
c. 1450 (a)	10-15,000	?2,000	12-17,000	4-500,000	?4.3
c. 1450 (b)	?17,000	?3,000	20,000	4-500,000	c. 5.0
1640	180,000	50,000	230,000	1,478,000	15.6
1690	N/A	N/A	200,000	1,476,200	13.5
1715 (a)	N/A	N/A	250,000	1,538,600	16.2
1715 (b)	160,000	101,000	261,000	1,538,600	17.0
1722 (a)	N/A	N/A	260,000	1,551,700	16.8
1722 (b)	N/A	N/A	330-340,000	1,551,700	21.6
1722 (c)	200,000	100,000	300,000	1,551,700	19.3
1754	177,000	105,000	282,000	1,697,900	16.6
1790	190,000	111,000	301,000	2,006,100	15.0
1818	190,000	123,000	313,000	2,716,300	11.5
1831	N/A	N/A	435,000	3,365,300	12.9
1833	–	–	651,500	3,365,300	19.4
1868	–	–	2,008,000	5,744,200	34.7
1886	–	–	4,377,000	7,443,300	58.8
1918	–	–	17,192,500	19,517,700	88.1
1929	–	–	25,023,000	25,023,000	100.0
1945	–	–	28,844,000	28,844,000	100.0
1955	–	–	30,791,500	30,791,500	100.0
1970	–	–	34,696,000	34,696,000	100.0
1983	–	–	37,257,000	37,257,000	100.0
1992	–	–	38,265,000	38,265,000	100.0

Sources:

Electorate:

c.1450 (a): A L Brown, *The Governance of Late Medieval England, 1271-1461* (London, 1989), p 191. I have arbitrarily assumed that burgesses numbered about one-eighth of the county electors, since medieval towns contained about 10 per cent of the population.

c.1450 (b): S Payling (below, p 00 and n 71) suggests that Brown's estimate was 'slightly conservative' and that the electorate may have amounted to 'at most, 5 per cent of the adult male population'. Since in the 17th and 18th centuries the adult males consistently formed 25-30 per cent of the total population, the adult males c.1450 would have numbered between 350,000 and 500,000 out of a total population of about 1,500,000 at most.

1640: D Hirst, *The Representative of the People? Voters and Voting in England under the Early Stuarts* (Cambridge, 1975), pp 104-5.

1690: J H Plumb, "The Growth of the Electorate in England from 1600 to 1715" (*Past and Present*, 45 (1969), p 111).

1715 (a): *Ibid;* G Holmes, *British Politics in the Age of Queen Anne* (London, 2nd edn, 1987), p 56; Holmes, "The Electorate and the National Will", p 14.

1715 (b): Sedgwick, ed, *The House of Commons, 1715-1754*, I, p 20.

1722 (a): Holmes, 'The Electorate and the National Will", p 18.

1722 (b): *Ibid*, p 23.

Electorate: (continued)

1722 (c): W A Speck (chapter 5), has argued that the estimates of 330,000 to 340,000 provided by G Holmes, "The Electorate and the National Will in the first Age of Party", in G Holmes, ed, *Politics, Religion and Society in England, 1679-1742* (London, 1986), p 23, are too high, but asserts that at least 300,000 men must have been enfranchised at a time when the total number of adult males cannot have been more than about 1,550,000 (E A Wrigley, R S Schofield, *The Population History of England, 1541-1871* (London, 1981), pp 528-9).

1754: Namier and Brooke, eds, *The House of Commons, 1754-1790,* I, p 2; M Pugh, *The Evolution of the British Electoral System, 1832-1987* (London, 1988), p 6.

1790: Thorne, ed, *The House of Commons, 1790-1820,* I, pp 4, 42.

1818: *Ibid.*

1831: H Hanham, *The Reformed Electoral System in Great Britain, 1832-1914* (London, 1971), p 35.

1832-1974: Craig, *British Electoral Facts, 1832-1987,* pp 66-71.

1992: C Rallings, M Thrasher, *Britain Votes, 5: British Parliamentary Election Results, 1988-1992* (Aldershot, 1993), p 162.

Population:

Total population for the period 1541-1871 at the nearest five-year point from E A Wrigley, R S Schofield, *The Population History of England, 1541-1871* (Cambridge, 1981, repr London, 1989), pp 208-9; estimates of adult males at the nearest quinquennial year from *ibid,* pp 528-9, for population aged 25+, adjusted for population aged over 21, and halved to allow for women. After 1871, male and (from 1918) female adult populations from B R Mitchell, P Deane, *Abstract of British Historical Statistics* (Cambridge, 1962), p 12. The voting age was lowered to 18 in 1970

1: D A Carpenter

Origins of the Commons, Magna Carta to 1307

IN NOVEMBER 1295 King Edward I assembled a Parliament at Westminster. Looking back from the 19th century, in the pages of his great *Constitutional History of England,* William Stubbs[1] considered this to have been "a model assembly ... serving as a pattern for all future assemblies of the nation". It was so because it "fixed finally" the right of shire and town representatives to attend Parliament and thus ensured the future of the House of Commons. After 1295, no assembly which did not conform to the model of 1295, Stubbs suggested, was entitled to the name and authority of Parliament.[2] Stubbs's "model parliament" (it is so named in one of those marginal headings which ease one's passage through *The Constitutional History*)[3] captured the imagination of the Victorian public. Its subsequent history has mirrored the decline and fall of the self-confident age which gave it birth: first respectful qualification;[4] then contemptuous contradiction;[5] finally, as a serious academic argument, virtual extinction.[6] Whatever the rights and wrongs of Stubbs's model, and to these we shall return, he was unquestionably right to see Parliament in general and the Commons in particular as creatures of the 13th century. It is with the development of Parliament in the 13th century that the following pages are concerned.[7]

In November 1236, King Henry III adjourned a law case to the "Parliament" which was to meet at Westminster in the following January.[8] This is the first "official" use of the term Parliament, "official" because it appears in a government record, in fact in the rolls of the Court of King's Bench. A good deal is known about the ensuing assembly. It passed legislation, confirmed Magna Carta, voted taxation, and, as we have seen, heard law cases. It was attended by the King, his councillors, and large numbers of lay and ecclesiastical magnates.[9] But, as far as is known, there were no representatives from the shires and the towns. There was, in short, no embryonic House of Commons.

After 1237, government records and monastic chronicles bestow the term "Parliament" with increasing frequency on assemblies of this kind, a usage sanctioned and reinforced by the Provisions of Oxford in 1258 which called for regular meetings of Parliament "to review the state of the realm and to deal with the common business of the realm and of the King together".[10]

In origin, the word "Parliament", in French *parlement,* in Latin *parliamentum,* simply meant "discussion", a usage which easily expanded to describe the assembly in which the discussion took place.[11] When the word first appears in England in the 1230s and 1240s, it was, up to a point, simply a new word for an old institution. From the earliest times, the kings of England had always assembled their great men to discuss the affairs of the realm. Under the Norman and Angevin kings, such gatherings had been called "councils" or "great councils" and under the Anglo-Saxons "witans".[12] In this perspective, it was the Venerable Bede who described the earliest parliamentary debate: that in the royal hall in Northumbria between King Edwin and his priests and thegns on whether to embrace Christianity.[13]

This, however, is only part of the story. The word Parliament was also used in the 13th century to describe an assembly which was changing fast and fundamentally in terms of form and function. It was not merely, therefore, the name which was new. In many ways it was the institution itself. In discussing these changes we will look first at function and then at form or structure.

Function

i] The dispensation of justice

Stubbs took it for granted that the essential purpose of Parliament was to discuss the great affairs of the realm. A totally different view was advanced by two of the most learned, irascible, and heterodox historians of the last generation, H G Richardson and G O Sayles: "We would, however, assert that parliaments are of one kind only and that, when we have stripped every nonessential away, the essence of them is the dispensing of justice by the king or by someone who in a very special sense represents the king".[14] Richardson and Sayles, in their extremist way, were wrong to stress the judicial role of Parliament to the disadvantage of everything else (the nonessentials)[15] but they were right to grasp that the dispensation of justice, largely in the form of the hearing of petitions from the King's subjects, had played a vital part in Parliament's development. By the end of the 13th century, it was central to its activities. Take the Parliament which Edward I held at Westminster between February and April 1305. Before it met, Edward called for petitions to be presented at the Parliament and set up special committees to hear them. The result was that individuals and institutions presented 133 petitions which took up four-fifths of the Parliament Roll, the official record of the Parliament's business.[16] The tract the *Modus Tenendi Parliamentum* ("How to Hold a Parliament"), written in the early 14th century, even claimed that the assembly could not be dissolved so long as any petition remained unanswered; otherwise the King would be in breach of his coronation oath to dispense justice to everyone.[17] Likewise, one reason why the reforming Ordinances of 1311 called for regular parliaments was so that petitions could be determined along with a range of other judicial business.[18] This judicial aspect of Parliament was well summarized by *Fleta,* a legal treatise written about 1300: "there [in Parliament] doubts are determined regarding judgments, new remedies are devised for wrongs newly brought to light, and there also is justice dispensed to everyone according to his deserts".[19]

By 1300, therefore, the dispensation of justice was a primary feature of Parliament's activities. This was due to developments which had taken place during the course of the century. Of course, great assemblies had always determined difficult and important law suits. What was new in the 13th century was the use of Parliament to hear petitions on a regular basis from the King's subjects. There is no indication that the first assemblies called parliaments in the 1230s, 1240s, and 1250s were used in this way. Nor indeed did the reformers in 1258 envisage such a role for the parliaments they wished to meet thrice annually. Rather, they set up a single official, the Justiciar, who was to tour the country and "do right to all persons".[20] All this changed, as J R Maddicott has shown, early in the reign of Edward I. From the late 1270s, Edward positively encouraged his subjects to present petitions to Parliament. Sixty-one were presented to the Parliament of 1278, their diverse form being testimony to the novelty of the procedure.[21] Two years later, the pressure of hearing petitions at Parliament was already prompting steps to reduce or share the burden. Edward I ordered the Chancery, Exchequer, and justices to dispose of all they could directly; only those which "be so great or are matters of grace" were to come before the King and his Council.[22]

In opening up Parliament to petitions, Edward was meeting a very real social need. During the long reign of King Henry III (1216-72) there had been a rising tide of complaint against the oppressions of royal and seignorial officials in the localities. At the same time, litigation had become far more common and far more complex. Both developments had created grievances and difficulties which only the centre could redress. Yet central government, during the same period, had become more faceless and bureaucratic. How could a person outside the charmed circle of the Court open its doors? The answer became by presenting a petition to Parliament. At first sight, the answers given to such petitions seem disappointing for few embodied final decisions. The majority were posted off to the appropriate government department; the Exchequer was ordered to investigate a grievance; the Chancery to issue a writ to enable litigation to begin.[23] Essentially, what Parliament was doing was oiling the clogged, slow-turning government machine. For most of the King's subjects this was its most important function.

ii] *Taxation and politics*

Whether Edward I took the same view is another matter. He had solicited petitions, thereby fulfilling his coronation oath to dispense justice, and strengthening his kingship after a disastrous civil war. But he did not want petitions to swamp other parliamentary business, as his filtering measures of 1280 showed. He wanted, as he said on that occasion, to be free with his Council "to attend to the great affairs of his realm and of his foreign lands".[24] Discussion of great affairs had always been one of the chief functions of national assemblies. But from the middle years of the 13th century, it gained an altogether new importance; one which gave Parliament a power and a place in the political constitution which it had never enjoyed before. This was brought about by a fact new to the 13th century and central to the rest of parliamentary history, namely the King's need for taxation which only Parliament could grant.

The kings of the 12th century had been able to fight wars without any need for general taxation. The kings of the 13th century could not. True, the revenue of Henry III, as indicated by the pipe roll of 1230, was some £24,000, much the same as the revenue of Henry I as revealed by the pipe roll of 1130.[25] Henry III, however, unlike Henry I, had no revenue from Normandy on which to draw, for the duchy had been lost to the King of France in 1204. Even worse, the real value of Henry's income had been eroded by a period of slow but steady inflation since 1180. As a result, his revenue in 1230 was worth between two and three times less than that of Henry I a hundred years before. The sources of revenue had also changed in a significant way. The proportion of easy, politically inoffensive income from Crown lands had diminished as those lands were given away to reward servants and supporters. More and more money had to come from politically sensitive exactions from individuals. It was, therefore, very difficult to increase income without giving political offence. This was John's situation. For a few years after 1209, he raised his real income substantially above the level achieved by Henry I. The result was Magna Carta, for the Great Charter was above everything an attempt to limit the money-getting activities of royal government. Mindful of the political consequences, Henry III never resorted to the methods of his father, and never achieved his levels of revenue. Edward I (1272-1307) did rather better: he was the first king to exploit the customs and make use of Italian bankers; but even Edward found that his ordinary revenues were totally inadequate to meet the cost of war on four fronts – Scotland, Wales, Flanders, and Gascony – in the 1290s. The conclusion was inescapable. To fight vigorously in war and even to live amply in peace there was no substitute for general taxation.

Such taxation could take several forms, but far the most lucrative was a percentage tax on movable property: essentially a tax on each individual's animals and corn. Thus in King John's reign, the seventh of 1207 produced £60,000; under Henry III, the fifteenth of 1225 brought in £40,000; the fortieth of 1232 £16,500; and the thirtieth of 1237 £22,500.[26] The bulk of these sums had come in within a year. Extraordinary taxation, therefore, had the power, depending on its rate, of doubling, tripling, or even quadrupling the King's ordinary annual revenue. The only trouble was that it could only be levied by "common counsel" of the realm. That principle had been asserted in chapters 12 and 14 of Magna Carta in 1215. The chapters were omitted from subsequent versions of the Charter but the principle was reaffirmed by Edward I in 1297. In any case, whatever the state of the law on the subject, the practical reality was the same. No extraordinary tax could be levied without common consent. The difficulties in collecting the taxes of 1220 and 1297, which were imposed, or so it was alleged, without such consent, sufficiently proved that.[27] For practical purposes, common consent could only be given by an assembly representative in some way of the realm. But such an assembly could refuse to give its consent or to give it only upon conditions. The great lever by which Parliament ultimately prized power from the King had arrived. There was no steady progression in the force with which it was used. The first King who went regularly to Parliament to ask for taxation was Henry III and he was answered at once by demands every bit as revolutionary as those made in the 17th century. The debates between Henry and his magnates in the parliaments between 1237 and 1258 were long and acrimonious. They covered the whole theory and practice of his kingship. In 1242, a detailed record was drawn up of the reasons why taxation was refused.[28] Parliament demanded the right to choose the King's chief ministers. Henry refused to accept such damaging inroads into the customary authority of the Crown. In these confrontations, the very nature of parliamentary assemblies was being transformed. The King needed their cooperation in a way he had never done before; the assemblies in their turn had a power they had never possessed before. They were now at the very centre of national political life. It was a position they were never to lose.

Form

Alongside these changes in function, there were related changes in Parliament's form. The King's Council emerged as its inner core. Around that core Parliament developed as an assembly of the estates of the realm with representatives of the lower clergy and, more importantly, of the counties and boroughs, being summoned to attend for the first time. The great magnates, of course, had always attended, but the basis on which they did so was quietly redefined.

i] *The king's council in parliament*

"It seemed necessary to remind readers, who are conversant with the parliaments of later days, that about the parliaments of Edward I's time there is still much to be discovered, and that should they come to the opinion that a session of the King's Council is the core and essence of every *parliamentum* ... they will not be departing very far from the path marked out by books that are already classical."[29] So F W Maitland in one of those long, leisurely sentences so characteristic of his style and the spacious age in which he lived.

Maitland's view was based on his study of the Parliament of 1305 whose roll he edited. He observed that some of the King's councillors received a special summons to Parliament; that many of the petitions were addressed to the King and his Council;[30] and that, on 21 March, after the Parliament had been in session for some three weeks, the lay and ecclesiastical magnates together with the representatives from the counties and the towns were allowed to go home, while the "bishops, earls, barons, justices, and others who are of the council" remained. Parliament thus constituted, constituted simply as the King's Council, continued in session until 7 April.[31]

Up to a point, there was nothing new about this. At great assemblies since Anglo-Saxon times, the King had always been surrounded by an inner core of councillors and ministers. What had changed in the 13th century was that the core had become larger and more formal. In the 1190s, a bench of justices had emerged at Westminster separate from the Exchequer. After 1234, there were professional judges staffing the court with the King, the Court of King's Bench. Two years later, the Council appears for the first time as a formal body with a defined and limited membership bound together by oath.[32] Much remains obscure about the history of the Council, notably its composition and the formality and regularity of its sessions. The sworn Council of 1236 had only 12 members. The revolutionary Council of 1258 had 15, nearly all of them important lay and ecclesiastical magnates. The Council under Edward I seems to have been considerably larger than this for it contained, alongside great magnates, a large official element: the Chancellor; the Keeper of the Wardrobe; the barons of the exchequer; the justices of the bench; and the justices of the court *coram rege*.[33] From this point of view, the purpose of Parliament was to assemble less "the estates" of the realm than the diverse magnates and ministers who made up the King's Council. It was that Council which was at the heart of Parliament's work.[34]

ii] *The parliamentary peerage*

Chapter 14 of Magna Carta in 1215, in defining how the King should seek the common counsel of the realm, laid down that he should summon all the greater barons individually and other tenants-in-chief by a general summons through the sheriffs. Parliament, as thus conceived, was an assembly of the tenants-in-chief of the Crown, dominated by the greatest of those tenants, the barons. By the end of the century, the King still issued individual summonses to great men to come to Parliament, but those men were no longer simply the baronial tenants-in-chief. Of the 53 magnates who received a personal summons to the Parliament of 1295, 22 were outside that category.[35] For a while, after 1295, there was a great variation in the numbers of magnates summoned to Parliament, but in the 14th century the right to a summons became the hereditary title of about 70 families.[36] A new grade had been created within the nobility: the parliamentary peerage.

This transition was painless and unnoticed, not surprisingly. Essentially, in the 13th century, as in the 12th, the King summoned his great magnates to national assemblies. In the 12th century they were nearly all baronial tenants-in-chief. In the 13th century they were not. What had changed was not the definition of the summons, but the definition of the aristocracy. In 1215, it was still possible to define the aristocracy, in Magna Carta, as baronial tenants-in-chief. A hundred years later, it was not, as the *Modus Tenendi Parliamentum* recognized when it said that earls and barons were to receive personal summonses to parliament *and also* everyone with equivalent incomes.[37] The fact was that the termination and division of baronies and the rise of nonbaronial families had made the equation of the baronage with the aristocracy increasingly meaningless.

A similar process took place with ecclesiastical tenants-in-chief, a group which embraced all the bishops and significant numbers of abbots and priors.[38] They had been entitled to a personal summons under the terms of Magna Carta. Indeed, as early as 1164, the Constitutions of Clarendon had laid down that ecclesiastics who held baronies in chief must attend judgments in the King's court along with other barons.[39] Once, however, lists of ecclesiastics receiving personal summonses survive, in the second half of the 13th century, it is clear that these summonses no longer corresponded to any precise tenurial criteria. Some of the abbots and priors summoned were not tenants-in-chief; some abbots and priors who were tenants-in-chief were not summoned. Eventually, "a class of ecclesiastical barons by writ" emerged to mirror the parliamentary peerage.[40]

iii] *Lower clergy*

The bishops and greater abbots, whether as tenants-in-chief or not, were summoned personally to Parliament. But what of the lower clergy: the deans and priors of the cathedral churches, the archdeacons and above all the parish clergy?[41] Their representatives attended Parliament in 1254 and again, in all probability, in 1268 and 1269. They were certainly summoned to the Parliament of 1295, as they were with increasing frequency to parliaments thereafter.[42] In terms of appearance, this was an important change in the structure of Parliament. It meant the attendance of 23 cathedral priors or deans, 60 archdeacons, 23 proctors chosen by the cathedral clergy, and 42 (two from each diocese) chosen by the parish clergy. By the early 14th century, Parliament was formally representative of the whole body of the English Church in a way it had never been before.

iv] *Representatives of the counties and towns: the origins of the House of Commons*

In the long run, by far the most important change in the structure of Parliament was the attendance of representatives from the counties and the towns. By the end of the 13th century, this was becoming a normal though not a universal occurrence. By then, the form of summons was fairly standard.[44] Each sheriff was to send to Parliament two knights from his county and two burgesses or citizens from his towns.[45] Since there were 37 counties, this meant 74 knights attending Parliament and, on average, about 186 townsmen, the number of towns sending representatives fluctuated from parliament to parliament, according to the decisions of individual sheriffs.[46] The knights were almost certainly elected in the county courts. They were to have "full power" from the "communities" of their counties to "do what is ordained by common counsel" about the affairs of the kingdom.[47] There was no doubt, therefore, about their representative nature. In explaining the attendance of the knights and townsmen, we shall concentrate on the former and begin by tracing the steps through which they were summoned to parliaments on a regular basis as representatives of their counties, and, although the importance of this was not that great, with a general brief rather than one requiring their participation for just some particular point.[48]

The years 1212-1213

In August 1212, King John ordered the sheriffs to come before him "with six laworthy and discreet knights" from their counties "to do what we tell them". Next year, knights from each county (we do not know how many) were again summoned before the King, this time with four men from each county, who were "to speak with us on the affairs of our kingdom".[49] There is no suggestion that either the knights or the men here were to be in any way representatives of their counties. The nature of the assemblies which they attended, if they took place, is obscure.[50] Nonetheless, these are the first known examples of the King summoning small numbers of knights (or in 1213 of men) from each of the counties of England to come before him at the same time. Moreover, the brief to the men in 1213 "to speak with us on the affairs of our kingdom" was very much a general one. Indeed, it almost implied, however misleadingly, that they were to participate in some kind of parliamentary debate.[51]

The year 1227

In 1227, by a proclamation read out in the county court, the "knights and honest men" of each county were to elect, in the county court, four knights to come before the King to explain "on behalf of all the county" (*pro toto comitatu*) grievances against the sheriffs about the implementation of Magna Carta.[52] Here, for the first time, the knights are clearly representatives of their counties, chosen by the county courts. On the other hand, their brief was a particular one, to give information about the Charter, and if they did appear at Westminster in October 1227, as bidden, they did not attend an assembly exactly like a later Parliament for, while at least eight bishops were present, the great lay magnates were conspicuously absent.[53]

The year 1254

In February 1254, the sheriffs were instructed to send before the King's Council after Easter two knights from each county, chosen by the county court "in place of all and each of the county" (*vice omnium et singulorum*) to say what tax they were prepared to grant "for everyone in the county".[54] Representatives of the lower clergy were summoned at the same time and an official record survives of the debate "in the Parliament at Westminster" where they conceded a tax only on the most stringent conditions.[55] If the knights from the counties also attended, and there is evidence that the elections did indeed take place,[56] then this was the first time they appeared at an assembly specifically called a Parliament,[57] although it was a Parliament held by the King's regents, the King himself being absent in Gascony. Apart from that, the only difference between these knights and later parliamentary representatives was that they were summoned, like the knights in 1227, for a stated specific purpose (in 1254 to grant a tax) whereas the later representatives were summoned more generally "to treat" or to "do what is ordained by common counsel" about the affairs of the realm and thus were by implication to take a fuller part in the affairs of the Parliament. This, however, may well be a distinction without a difference since, on many occasions, the business of taxation was almost certainly the main reason for the attendance of later representatives, while the knights of 1254, if, like the clerical representatives, they agreed the tax only on conditions, were already treating of the affairs of the realm at a level far above the heads of many of their later successors.

The Provisions of Oxford 1258

In August 1258, four knights from each county were ordered to bring to the King's Council in October (a time when Parliament was in session) the inquiries which they had carried out into local abuses. Some of these knights later received expenses for the time they spent "before the King's Council at Westminster in Parliament".[58] Again, as in 1254 and 1227, the knights were attending Parliament for a specific purpose. Indeed, the parallel with 1227 is close since in both cases the knights were bringing local grievances to the centre. Again that purpose may well have taken them into discussions about the great affairs of the realm. The attendance of the knights in 1258, as in 1254 and 1227, however, was still a particular expedient. It created no feeling that representatives were a necessary or normal part of Parliament. This is sufficiently proved by the way Parliament was conceived in the revolutionary Provisions of Oxford in 1258. The only representative element was provided not by knights elected by the counties but by 12 *prodeshomes* chosen by the magnates, the purpose being to spare the latter the cost of coming to the three annual parliaments for which the Provisions called.[59] Nonetheless, the frequency of knightly summonses to parliaments or kindred assemblies was quickening. There had been one in the 1220s; none in the 1230s and 1240s; two in the 1250s. In the 1260s, there were between three and six.[60]

The rival parliaments of 1261

In September 1261, Simon de Montfort, Earl of Leicester, Richard de Clare, Earl of Gloucester, the Bishop of Worcester, and other opposition nobles summoned three knights from each county to St Albans "to treat with them about the common affairs of the kingdom". The king *e contra* ordered the three knights to come instead to see him at Windsor.[61] The summonses of 1261 were the first occasions since 1213 that men had been summoned from the shires with the general brief of discussing the affairs of the kingdom, though we do not know how far the knights were in any sense representatives or indeed how many actually turned up at Windsor or St Albans.

Simon de Montfort's parliaments of 1264-1265

In May 1264, Simon de Montfort defeated King Henry III at the battle of Lewes and assumed control of the government. In effect, therefore, it was Simon, in June 1264, who summoned four knights from each county "chosen by the assent of the county court" to come on behalf of the county (*pro toto comitatu*) to a Parliament at London "to discuss the affairs of the King and kingdom".[62] This Parliament was a landmark. It was the first occasion in which all the characteristics of the later parliamentary summons appears: the knights are representatives of their counties; they are coming to a Parliament; and their brief is general not specific. Later, in December, Simon went even further. He summoned the knights again, this time two from each county, and now, in addition, he summoned burgesses: each town was to send two. The ensuing Parliament which lasted from January to March 1265 was thus the first attended by representatives from the counties and boroughs: the House of Commons in embryo.[63]

The establishment of the Commons 1265-1327

The precedent set by the Parliament of 1265 was repeated with increasing frequency, although for many years it remained the exception rather than the rule. Knights alone were probably summoned to at least two parliaments between 1268 and 1270, and knights and burgesses together to at least one.[64] Both were summoned to the first Parliament of Edward I in 1275.[65] All told, in Edward's reign between 1272 and 1307, knights and burgesses were summoned to 13 of the 50 to 60 parliaments and knights alone to another four.[66] The pace quickened markedly after 1294. Knights alone, or knights and burgesses together, were summoned to five of the 10 parliaments held between 1294 and 1298. Of the nine parliaments held between 1300 and 1307, knights and burgesses were present at seven.[67] Their attendance was becoming the rule: the *Modus Tenendi Parliamentum* took it for granted, along with that of the lower clergy. Indeed, the *Modus* asserted that in all things "which ought to be granted, refused or done by Parliament" the knights from the shires carried more weight than the greatest earl.[68] The last Parliament without representatives was that of 1325.

The form of the summons of representatives

The form in which the representatives were summoned in the 13th century derived from administrative structures and practices of long standing. The county and its court dated back to Anglo-Saxon times. It had been the practice since at least the reign of Henry II (1154-89) for the county court to send groups of four knights to the King's court with the record of its proceedings.[69] Such knights were elected in the county court, just as were the later MPs. Indeed, by the early 13th century knights were elected in the county court to perform a whole series of local tasks. In 1215, Magna Carta stipulated such election for the four knights in each county who were to sit with the King's judges to hear petty assizes and for the 12 knights in each county who were to investigate the malpractices of local officials.[70] Equally established was the idea that knights so chosen represented the county court. Thus the knights bearing the record of the county court to the King were to come "on behalf of all the county court" (*ex parte tocius comitatus*) or "for the county court" (*pro comitatu*).[71] It was but a small extension for knights to come on behalf of the county as a whole, as they did in 1227 when they were summoned to explain grievances over Magna Carta "for all the county" (*pro toto comitatu*). Thereafter, various attempts were made to express the idea that the knights were indeed representative of everyone in the county. In 1254, they came specifically "in place of all and each of their counties" (*vice omnium et singulorum comitatuum*), but ultimately the government preferred to stress the community rather than the individual. In the final form of the writ of summons in 1295, the knights were to have power "for themselves and the communities of their counties" (*pro se et communitate comitatus*).[72]

The immediate reasons for the summoning of representatives.

The Edwardian writs of summons rarely stated specifically why representatives were being called to Parliament: from 1295 they were simply "to do what is ordained by common counsel". Under Henry III, by contrast, the writs and the circumstances in which they were issued are more informative. Together they suggest three broad and interrelated reasons for the summons of representatives. First, the need for political support, support which could be obtained by explaining to representatives the government's case and actions; second, the desire for information about the grievances and conditions in the localities, information which representatives could bring; and third, the need for taxation which the representatives alone could grant. Fundamentally, these reasons continued to operate under Edward I and under Edward II (1307-27), ultimately transforming the summons of representatives from an occasional event into a general rule.

a] Political support

When the King and the rebellious magnates summoned knights to rival assemblies in 1261, when de Montfort summoned knights in 1264, and knights and burgesses in 1265, the aim in all cases was the same, namely to gain political support. The same was equally true, in all probability, of John's summoning of knights and men in 1212 and 1213. All these summonses took place at moments of political uncertainty, even of crisis.[73] The aim of the regime was to explain and justify its proceedings. As Henry III put it in 1261, the knights were to come "in order that they might see and understand that we propose to attempt nothing save what we know will conform to the honour and common utility of our kingdom".[74] Having thus seen and understood, the knights were doubtless expected to return to their counties as the regime's apostles and recruiters. Even in more tranquil times, kings coveted popularity and support. They wished to broadcast triumphs just as much as they needed to refute slander. If, as seems likely, knights and burgesses attended Henry III's Parliament of October 1269, it was to witness the greatest triumph of his reign: the translation of Edward the Confessor's body to its shrine in the new church at Westminster.[75] Likewise in 1283, it was to witness the completion of Edward I's greatest triumph, the conquest of Wales, with the trial and execution of the Welsh Prince David, that knights and burgesses were summoned to Edward I's Parliament at Shrewsbury.[76] Indeed, the representatives from London took David's head back with them for display on the Tower of London.[77]

b] *Information from the localities*

Parliamentary representatives could thus take back information from the Court to the counties and boroughs. They could also bring information from the counties and boroughs to the Court. Indeed, in 1227 and 1258, as we have seen, knights were specifically summoned to councils or parliaments in order to ventilate local grievances. Later representatives were not specifically charged in this way. Few, moreover, seem to have presented individual petitions, and it was not till the 14th century that petitions from the Commons as a whole formed the basis for legislation. Nonetheless, the informal information which representatives could bring must have been extraordinarily valuable to the government. They could report on the political situation in their counties and on the competence and honesty of the King's local officials. They could be a vital link between the centre and the localities.

c] *The granting of taxation*

In 1254, as we have seen, two knights from each county were summoned to Parliament specifically to say what aid everyone in the county was prepared to grant the King. Likewise, in October 1269, knights and burgesses came not merely to witness the translation of Edward the Confessor, but to give consent to taxation.[78] There can be no doubt that the need to get consent to taxation was a major factor in establishing the place of the Commons in Parliament. The cardinal fact was this: from the 1260s no general tax was levied in England without the consent of representatives. The result was that representatives *were always* summoned to Parliament if taxation was in question. If the King wanted regular taxation, then representatives would have to be summoned regularly. More than anything else, this linkage established parliamentary representation during the reign of Edward I. Between 1275 and 1290, parliaments made four grants of general taxation to Edward I. Knights, or knights and burgesses, attended all of these parliaments; and, with one exception, these were the only parliaments which they did attend, the exception being the Shrewsbury meeting of 1283 where the business was the condemnation of David.[79] From 1294, as Edward's need for taxation multiplied with the wars in France and Scotland, so did the frequency with which representatives were summoned. Between 1294 and 1297, they came to four out of the eight parliaments, precisely those at which taxation was granted.[80]

In these watershed years, the very formula in the writ which summoned representatives to Parliament was developed so as to leave no doubt about their authority to grant taxation.[81] In the final version, in 1295, two knights were to be sent from each county "with full and sufficient power for themselves and for the community of the county to do what is ordained by common council ... so that for lack of that power the business will not remain unfinished in any way". Full power was likewise demanded of the burgesses. The purpose of requiring full power in this way was to ensure that the consent of the representatives to taxation was completely binding on the local communities.

Thus the only occasion, between November 1282 and October 1297, on which it was not demanded was likewise the only occasion on which there was no taxation, the business being instead, as we have mentioned, the condemnation of David.[82] Consent to taxation was not the only reason for the summons of representatives, as we have seen. Indeed, with the form of the writ now standardized, they appeared at parliaments after 1297 equipped with full power although no taxation was granted.[83] But the need for consent had played a central role, first in ensuring occasional attendance between 1275 and 1290 and then, between 1294 and 1297, in placing representatives in Parliament on a regular footing.

This conclusion is confirmed by two final considerations. First, the failure to summon representatives from the Welsh Marches to Parliament seems closely linked to the fact that no taxation was levied there.[84] Second, the summoning of representatives of the lower clergy to parliaments and other assemblies was related above all to the desire to secure their consent to taxation.[85] Indeed, the first known summons of such representatives to Parliament in 1254 was specifically stated to have that purpose.[86]

The underlying reasons for the summons of representatives

Knights and burgesses, therefore, were summoned to Parliament for reasons of politics, administration, and finance. They provided a channel of communication between the centre and the localities; they granted taxation. But if these were the immediate reasons for their summons by the King, why did those reasons apply in the second half of the 13th century but not in the first? The problem can be posed most starkly in terms of taxation. In 1207, 1225, 1232, and 1237 assemblies without any formal representative element granted taxes to the King. Then things began to change: in1254, as we have seen, knights were summoned to say what aid the counties would grant;[87] in 1268-9 they were present at several parliaments where taxation was discussed; in May 1270 they attended the Parliament which finally granted it.[88] Thereafter, the knights attended every subsequent parliament at which taxation was granted. What had altered? To answer that question, we need to look at theories of consent, changes in society, and developments in politics.

First, theory. In 1215, Magna Carta had laid down that general taxation could only be levied by "the common counsel" of the realm. It had then, as we have seen, defined how "common counsel" was to be obtained. The greater barons were to receive individual writs of summons. The other tenants-in-chief were to be summoned generally through the sheriffs. An assembly of tenants-in-chief, dominated by the greater barons, therefore, could apparently answer for the realm in the granting of taxation. The theory behind this has been suggested by J C Holt: "The magnates could give consent on behalf of the whole community, and they could do so because they spoke for the tenants-in-chief, whose consent embodied that of their tenants and therefore that of the whole realm"[89] A hundred years later, this confidence that the magnates could speak for the realm had entirely gone. The *Modus Tenendi Parliamentum* asserted that "each [of the magnates] is at Parliament for his own individual person, and for no one else."[90]

Even in the early 13th century, there had been doubts about the theory that baronial consent could bind everyone to pay taxation, particularly taxation levied on everyone's movable property. Rather, it was believed that the only taxes the baronage could answer for were taxes, in the first instance, paid only by themselves, taxes, that is, which took the form of scutages levied on the number of knights' fees they held in chief. To put it another way, a feudal assembly could only impose a feudal tax. If, on the other hand, the tax was one paid by everybody, then everyone in theory needed to consent to it, or at least everyone who was free.

These doubts about the authority of baronial consent were not universal. Occasionally, especially when writing to an individual baron, the King could imply that the great magnates alone had bound everyone to pay taxation on movables.[91] But usually, especially when announcing such taxes to the nation at large, the King shied away from any such suggestion.[92] Indeed, on occasion, he positively indicated that a tax paid by everyone had received everyone's consent. Thus in 1225, Magna Carta itself stated that the fifteenth on movables had been granted by archbishops, bishops, earls, barons, knights, free tenants, and everyone in the kingdom[93] The fortieth of 1232 was likewise conceded, so the writ said, by lay and ecclesiastical magnates, knights, free tenants, "and villeins", the addition of "villeins" indicating that the tax had received the consent even of the unfree.[94] In 1237, the writ for the levy of the thirtieth did not go so far, accepting that lords could answer for their villeins; but that only made the more pointed the absence of any claim that barons alone had answered for everyone else. Rather the writ stated that the lay and ecclesiastical magnates, clergy, knights, and freemen had agreed the tax for themselves and their villeins. The writ of 1237, indeed, suggests that the clerk had quite deliberately widened the circle of consent beyond the baronial. The sheriffs were informed that the archbishops, bishops, abbots, priors, earls, and barons "of all our kingdom" had assembled at Westminster. But in the next sentence, when it comes to the tax, this purely baronial assembly suddenly expands. The tax has been conceded by "archbishops, bishops, abbots, priors, *and clerks having lands which do not belong to their churches,* earls, barons, *knights and free men for themselves and their villeins*".[95]

It is only the writs dealing with taxation in the form of a scutage that make no claims of wide consent. The scutage of 1235, for example, was granted by "archbishops, bishops, abbots, priors, earls, barons, and all others of our kingdom *who hold from us in chief*",[96] that of 1245 was "by the common counsel of the magnates of England",[97] that of 1253 by "archbishops, bishops, earls, barons, abbots, priors, and other magnates of our kingdom".[98] It is easy to see the basis for this distinction. A scutage was a tax paid by the tenants-in-chief and levied on the number of fees they held by knight service. They then recouped the tax form their undertenants, who were bound to pay because they were simply fulfilling a basic obligation of their tenure.[99] The whole way in which the scutages were actually collected reflected and supported this theory. In 1235, the lay tenants-in-chief, through their bailiffs, collected the tax from their own tenants and then handed it to the knights appointed as receivers in each shire. Ecclesiastical tenants-in-chief were to pay the tax not to the knights at all but directly to the King.[100] This then was a tax which the barons collected themselves from their own tenants. No wonder they felt able to consent to it. Taxation on movables was very different. It was paid not simply by barons and their tenants but, as John put it in 1207 "by every layman of the whole of England".[101] It was usually collected not by baronial officials within each barony but by royal officials working within the shire. Only for the tax of 1232 was an exception made to this rule: then, after the tax had been assessed on each individual by the men of each village, the particulars were to be handed over to the steward of the baron in whose fee the village was, who could then collect it.[102] For all the other taxes of the early 13th century, collection was entirely in the hands of the sheriff and knights appointed by the King, who collected the tax from each village irrespective of the barony to which it belonged.[103] Thus John stated in 1207, the tax was to be paid "by every layman of the whole of England *whatever fee he may be*".[104]

In the early 13th century, therefore, there was a growing feeling that an assembly of tenants-in-chief could consent to a scutage paid and collected by themselves, but not to a tax on movables paid by everyone else and collected by the King. The fundamental principle underlying the distinction was that no one, or at least no one who was free, need pay taxes to which they had not consented, unless they were bound to it, as in the case of scutage, by the conditions of their tenure. This principle of individual consent to taxation was strenuously asserted by several great magnates in the reign of Henry III.[105] But it is equally clear that it was felt to apply lower down the social scale, even, so the writs of 1232 imply, to the villeins. It was a principle which derived from Roman and from Canon Law. The Roman Law tag, "what touches all shall be approved by all" (*quod omnes tangit ab omnibus approbetur*), was familiar in England long before Edward I cited it famously in his writ of summons to the Parliament of 1295.[106] The same principle was sanctioned in the law of the Church. A canon of the Fourth Lateran Council in 1215 stipulated that Church taxation required the consent of the bishop and his clergy as well as the permission of the Pope.[107] The principle that the lower clergy, who held the bulk of the Church's spiritual property, should indeed consent to such taxation was widely accepted in13th century England. In 1226 Henry III suggested that the bishops should convoke the deans and chapters, men of religion, and all the clergy of their diocese "whom this affair touches" (*quos dictum tangit negotium*) in order to induce them to grant a tax.[108] In 1240, according to Matthew Paris, the bishops delayed an attempt, this time by the Pope, to tax the lower clergy with the declaration that "this affair touches all; all therefore ought to be convoked; without them it is neither fitting nor expedient to reply".[109] In 1256, Lincolnshire clergy complained that, without any consultation, they had been taxed by the King; "something all the more grievous since when it is a question of anyone being taxed, his express consent is necessary".[110] Ecclesiastical and secular ideas were closely intermingled in the 13th century. The widely expressed principle that the lower clergy needed to consent to taxation may well have encouraged the belief that the same was true of knights and freemen.[111] Indeed, the principle was applied simultaneously on ecclesiastical and secular fronts in the writ which levied the thirtieth of 1237. The clerk, as we have seen, did not merely affirm that knights and freemen had given their consent; he also said the same of "clerks having lands which do not belong to their churches".[112]

In 1237, of course, as in 1225 and 1232, the claim that knights and freemen had consented to taxation bore limited relation to reality. Knights and freemen may well have attended the assemblies, but there is no evidence that there was any formal representation of the counties or the boroughs. Whatever the theory expressed in the writs, in practice the great magnates alone were granting taxation on behalf of the whole realm. What happened in the second half of the century was simply that practice came into line with theory. It was impossible, of course, for all knights and freemen personally to consent to the taxes they paid. The election of knights with full power to bind the whole community of the shire, which meant precisely everyone in the shire, solved the problem.

In asking why theory and practice came to coincide, we should not underestimate the influence of the theory itself. We should also acknowledge the force of ecclesiastical example. In 1254, as we have seen, the government ordered each sheriff to explain the King's needs to "the knights and others of their county" after which two knightly representatives were to come before the Council after Easter to say what aid "everyone" in the county would grant. Each bishop was likewise to explain the King's needs to the assembled clergy of his diocese after which "discreet men" were to come before the Council on the same day as the knights to say what aid the lower clergy would grant.[113] Here, ecclesiastical and secular representation at Parliament moved in parallel; but the letter in which the regency government explained these events to the King suggests that it was from the Church that the principle and the practice derived. It was the bishops, so the King was informed, who protested that "they were able to do nothing about giving an aid from their clergy, without the assent of the clergy". However, they promised to discuss the matter with them and try to induce them to make a grant. On the secular side, there was no statement of principle and no mention of discussion.[114] It is hard not to think that the procedure in 1254 – the sheriffs explaining the King's needs locally (clearly in the county courts), and the knights coming to the Council to say what aid everyone in the counties would grant was modelled, at least in part, on the ecclesiastical procedure where the bishops explained the King's needs to their assembled clergy, and representatives ("the discreet men") came to Parliament to report the results.

Neither the power of principle nor the force of ecclesiastical example, however, is sufficient to explain the transition from theory into practice, and fundamentally the explanation lies in the realm of practice rather than of theory. The essential problem with all taxation is its collection. Down to 1237, the perception was that the counties could be carried and the tax collected by assent given professedly by everybody, but in practice by an assembly dominated by great magnates and without any formal representation from the shires and boroughs. The perception was essentially correct for the taxes on the whole seem to have been efficiently collected.[115] Indeed, the counties may have been less worried about the theory of universal consent than the government. In Yorkshire in 1220, the complaint in the county court was the King's failure to consult the magnates, not the knights.[116] In the second half of the century, by contrast, the confidence that magnate assent alone could carry taxation evaporated. Reality and rhetoric had to come into line. Unless the counties had agreed the tax, the perception grew that it would not be possible to collect it. This was the crux which the regents recognized in 1254. As they told the King "from the other laymen [in the counties] we do not believe that we can obtain any aid for your use".[117] The necessity of consent, in some form, was here taken for granted. Indeed, it was already essential, as the regents went on to explain, to make political concessions to obtain it.[118] The situation was much the same between 1268 and 1270, the next occasion on which taxation was sought. Again the need to consult the knights was taken for granted, and this time concessions were made to secure it.[119] That the political perceptions of 1254 and 1268 were correct, that taxes could no longer be levied without the consent of the commons, was finally proved by the events of 1297. In July of that year Edward I attempted to levy an eighth on movable property. It had been agreed by a parliament, but one to which the magnates, it seems, had been improperly summoned, and no representatives had been summoned at all.[120] Edward, however, attempted to cover this up just as his father had done earlier in the century. The writ ordering the collection of the tax claimed that it had been granted "by earls, barons, knights, and laymen of all our kingdom".[121] This time the bluff was called. The Earls of Hereford and Norfolk marched into the Exchequer and declared that the writ lied; the tax had not been granted by the magnates or by "the community of the realm".[122] A little later, the opposition manifesto, the *De Tallagio Non Concedendo*, demanded that no tax be imposed without the consent of lay and ecclesiastical magnates, and the knights, burgesses, and other freemen of the kingdom.[123] In 1220, the complaint was the failure to consult the magnates. In 1297, the failure to consult the knights and burgesses seemed equally important. In 1215, Magna Carta had envisaged consent to taxation being given by an almost purely baronial assembly. In 1297, when Edward I accepted that taxes needed "the common assent of all the realm", he envisaged an assembly including knights and burgesses.[124] It was they, as the *Modus Tenendi Parliamentum* later stated, who, together with the proctors of the lower clergy, represented the community of the realm.[125]

Underlying these shifting perceptions were long term changes in the nature of baronial power. In the 12th century, when the structure of baronies was more intact, great barons might well have felt confident about collecting a tax on movables for the King and by extension of agreeing to it on behalf on everyone else. But in the 13th century, this structure was in decay. The arrangements of 1232 were a lone attempt to put the clock back; to restore a world which had gone, or at least was fast going. Tenants holding from several baronies; tenants living far from the chief residence of their lord; the division of baronies between co-heiresses; their passage to new families through the process of forfeiture, marriage, and escheat; all these factors over time, and at different speeds, tended to weaken the structure of baronies. This did not necessarily create a crisis for lords. If feudal ties weakened, they could be replaced by bastard feudal ties. But the barons recognized that they no longer had the administrative structures to collect taxes on movables. Indeed, they often lacked the power even to collect scutages, having to rely on the sheriffs to distrain their tenants.[126] The fact was that taxation, especially taxation on movables, was far more efficiently collected through the county administration of the King.[127]

The nature of that county administration was also changing in a significant way. The running of local government was passing into the hands of the knights and gentry. In the thirteenth century they came to dominate the most important local offices, those of sheriff, coroner, escheator, justice of assize, and, above all, collector of taxation. This was the King's system of local government which he had commissioned the knights to run. No baron could answer for it, at least not in any formal way, however much he might retain and control some of its agents. The truth was that the taxes themselves could not be collected without the cooperation of the knights. Why not make sure of the cooperation by summoning them to Parliament to consent to the taxes? Significantly, there was indeed a close connection between the knights who came as representatives to Parliament and the knights who actually collected the taxes. In 1292, in 21 of the 37 counties, tax collectors were also representatives.[128]

In the first half of the century the castle of baronial consent still stood, although undermined. It was the politics of the mid-century which fired the last props holding up the tunnels, and brought it tumbling down. In the course of the 13th century, the counties of England were radicalized politically. Already in John's reign, the counties had a political programme: they wished local government to be run by local men; an aspiration to which several clauses in Magna Carta bore witness. In the minority of Henry III and during his personal rule, the counties struggled to implement clauses in the Great Charter in the local courts and to secure the deforestation promised by the companion Charter of the Forest. After 1234, the abolition of the Justiciarship rendered central government more remote while the financial needs of the Crown made the sheriffs and the justices in eyre more oppressive. In 1254, when the regents advised the King that no tax could be obtained from the counties, it was precisely because of the widespread local discontent: above all, so it was claimed, Magna Carta was not kept by the sheriffs and other royal bailiffs. If the King was to secure a tax, he was advised publicly to proclaim the charters through the counties and order the sheriffs to keep them.[129] The King took this advice, but too late to influence the results of the ensuing Parliament, and no tax was forthcoming.[130] Such grievances, moreover, were not merely against the officials of the King, for those of the great magnates were equally unpopular. Indeed, the demand that the magnates should observe Magna Carta towards their own tenants and neighbours was one of the King's most constant refrains.

By 1254, therefore, it was already clear that neither the King nor the barons could take the counties for granted. Yet the pattern was not quite set. As we have seen, there was no suggestion that the three annual parliaments envisaged in 1258 should have representatives from the counties; and, despite the precedent of 1254, it was still possible to think that a purely magnate assembly might grant a tax to the King: at any rate, the Oxford Parliament of 1258, at which no representatives were present, appointed a body of 24 magnates "to negotiate about an aid for the King".[131] It was the revolutionary events of the next decade which tipped the balance firmly in favour of the counties. In 1258 itself, the whole structure of local government was overhauled to meet the grievances of the knights and those below them in local society. In 1259, the protest at the Westminster Parliament of "the community of the bachelory of England", a body broadly representing the knightly class, forced through legislation very much against baronial interests. In 1261, there was widespread resistance in the counties to the visitations of the King's justices and to the new sheriffs appointed by Henry in his attempt to recover power. Both sides vied for the support of the knights, summoning them to rival assemblies at Windsor and St Albans. And then de Montfort, drawing logical conclusions from these events, summoned the knights to his famous parliaments of 1264 and 1265. The middle years of the century, therefore, had brought the counties into the political limelight. Thereafter, the King never obtained taxation without their consent.

During the course of the 13th century, therefore, national assemblies of the realm had changed fundamentally in form and function and been given a new name: Parliament. The King's Council had emerged to form the heart of the institution. Lay and ecclesiastical magnates were summoned not as barons, but as their importance warranted. Increasingly, representatives of the counties, boroughs, and lower clergy were joining the assembly. One new function was the dispensing of justice through the hearing of petitions. Another was the granting of taxation. It was the granting of taxation, or rather the constant refusal to grant it, which put Parliament on the political map between 1237 and 1258. The name Parliament became established in precisely that period. This was no accident. The institution had achieved an altogether new political prominence. A new word seemed appropriate to describe it.

This structure of Parliament by the early 14th century was, of course, far from settled. In the next half century, a fixed list of parliamentary peers evolved to end the fluctuating numbers summoned around 1300. It was not till after 1325 that the summoning of representatives from the counties and towns became the absolute rule. Representatives of the lower clergy continued to attend Parliament throughout the 14th century, but they also formed a quite separate clerical assembly: Convocation. Since it was in Convocation that the clergy granted taxation to the Crown, this became the focus of their activities. They were present at Parliament, but had little role. In this sense, the parliaments of the later 14th century were less representative than those a hundred years earlier, which had witnessed an important but unsuccessful "attempt by the Crown to bring the clergy and the laity of the realm into one assembly".[132]

The functions of Parliament also developed. The hearing of private petitions as an important part of business dried up in the course of the 14th century, while the Commons' petitions presented by the representatives of the shires and boroughs became a great source of legislation.[133] As the King's demand for taxation, faced with the costs of the Hundred Years' War, became more and more insistent, the Commons conceived a whole series of demands in return for granting it. We have stressed that as early as 1254 the knights may well have demanded concessions before granting taxation. But a hundred years later this was taking place with an altogether new regularity: the House of Commons had arrived.

Where then does all this leave Stubbs's Parliament of 1295, that "model assembly ... serving as a pattern for all future assemblies of the nation", that assembly which "established" or "finally fixed" the right of shire and town representation, and after which "it may be fairly questioned whether any assembly afterwards held is entitled to the name and authority of parliament which does not in the minutest particulars of summons, constitution, and formal dispatch of business, answer to the model then established"?[134]

It is easy, in the light of what we have said above, to dismiss these claims. In the first place, Stubbs had concentrated almost exclusively on Parliament's development as an assembly of estates with the key feature being the emergence of the representatives from the shires and boroughs. He had thus sidelined the role of the King's Council in parliamentary development and the central part it had played in the dispensation of justice through the hearing of petitions. When Maitland told his readers that they would not be departing very far from the path marked out by works which were already classical, if they concluded that a session of the King's Council was the core and essence of every parliamentum, he was distancing himself from Stubbs while diplomatically pretending not to do so. For the whole thrust of Stubbs's discussion had been to see the King and Council as something growing up alongside Parliament rather than as part of it.[135]

Even on his own terms, Stubbs' claims for the 1295 Parliament were overstated, as he himself came close to recognizing. It can hardly be said to have established or fixed the right of town and country representation when many subsequent assemblies down to 1325, which contemporaries called parliaments, met without any such representation at all. Stubbs was perfectly aware of this and got round the difficulty by admitting that though the Parliament of 1295 established the rule and pattern, the rule "was not at once recognized". Thus "for many years", he acknowledged, assemblies of councillors and magnates without any representatives "share with the constitutional assembly of estates the name of Parliament".[136] That this admission virtually destroyed his whole hypothesis Stubbs did not appreciate, or at least hoped his readers would not appreciate. For how can the Parliament of 1295 be a model if it was a model unrecognized by contemporaries? Stubbs talked of anomalies, exceptional practices, irregularities, and confusion amid the "tender growth of the new system"[137], but of course the irregularities and confusion were entirely of his own making; the product of setting up a standard which at the time simply did not exist.

Why did Stubbs seize on the 1295 Parliament? There were various reasons, but one particularly stands out; namely the principle enunciated in the writ of summons to the bishops: "that which touches all shall be approved by all". It was this which made Stubbs sit up. The 1295 Parliament was, he wrote, a "precedent for all time to come, worthy of the principle which the King had enunciated in the writ of summons. This was to be a model assembly, bearing in its constitution evidence of the principle by which the summons was dictated, and serving as a pattern for all future assemblies of the nation."[138] Perhaps there was also another, more artistic reason for Stubbs's elevation of the Parliament of 1295. His account of the origins of Parliament is not easy going. Reading Maitland is like galloping a fine horse across open country; reading Stubbs is like following the plough through heavy soil. Stubbs desperately needed some landmark on which his readers could sit and view the surrounding fields. He found it in the Model Parliament. Having found it he was too good a historian not to recognize its difficulties; but he was not good enough to abandon the hypothesis altogether. So he compromised, establishing the Model Parliament and then immediately surrounding it with qualifications and explanations which, to the careful reader, destroy much of its value. Fortunately for Stubbs, the great Victorian and Edwardian public were not careful readers. They bought the book for show not for use; hence the many uncut copies, in their fading maroon covers, which gather dust in second hand book shops today.

We should not, however, abandon Stubbs and his model altogether. In concentrating on Parliament as an assembly of estates he was looking at only one aspect of its development in the 13th century. Yet, for the future, he was looking at by far its most important aspect. There was also something important going on around 1295. In the first half Edward I's reign, representatives had attended Parliament on an occasional basis. After 1294, their attendance becomes much more regular. Between 1294 and 1298, knights alone, or knights and burgesses together, attended five of the 10 parliaments. Between 1300 and 1307, as we have seen, they attended seven out of nine. If Stubbs' Model Parliament plants in the public mind the idea that Parliament was a construct of the 13th century and that the years around 1295 were decisive in its development, then it has not been without its value.

Footnotes to this Chapter may be found on page 187–196.

2: Simon Payling

The Later Middle Ages

AFTER dissolving the uncooperative "Addled" Parliament of 1614, James I remarked to the Spanish Ambassador that, "the House of Commons is a body without a head ... I am surprised that my ancestors should ever have permitted such an institution to come into existence".[1] This neatly expresses the paradox inherent in the history of the representative element in Parliament. On the one hand, local representatives were called to Parliament by a Crown anxious to extend its financial resources beyond its ossifying feudal revenues and to extend the scope of its government by establishing a dialogue between Crown and subject; on the other, these same representatives ultimately came to control the executive and subjugate the Crown. This paradox is to some extent resolved in conceiving Parliament, and particularly the Commons, as a body that served the interests of governor and governed: the forum in which the "growing authority of national kingship" was reconciled with "the rights of subjects".[2] Nonetheless, although Parliament served to resolve conflict between Crown and subject to the mutual benefit of both, parliamentary history can still be convincingly encapsulated in Chrimes's dictum: born as "the expression of the irresistible will of the King" Parliament came to express "the irresistible will of the people".[3]

The late medieval period appears to mark an important stage in this gradual transformation. It saw the House of Commons secure and defend rights – to assent to royal levies of taxation and to present the grievances of the community in the expectation of remedy – that were employed as weapons in a later constitutional struggle; and, after taking on the composition that was long to characterize it, acquire a strong sense of institutional identity manifest in the creation of the office of Speaker and the definition of due electoral process.[4] There are, however, as other contributors to this volume have emphasized, proper reservations about an interpretation which seeks to portray parliamentary history as a series of steps towards an inevitable sovereignty. To describe the late medieval period as one in which the Commons extended their influence, by implication at the expense of monarchial power, may be to project the constitutional preoccupations of the 17th century into an age in which they had no place, and to marginalize those aspects of Parliament, which, important to contemporaries, played little part in its subsequent history. The late medieval House of Commons certainly did not see itself as engaged in a struggle with the Crown for sovereignty, or even for a share in the formulation and execution of policy. When viewed in the context of such exalted ambitions, its aims on those occasions when it was drawn into dispute with the King were very limited. There is nothing in the contemporary record to justify the elevated place in the late medieval polity attributed to the Commons by 19th-century historians, most notably Bishop Stubbs in his influential *Constitutional History*. Indeed, some modern historians, in violent reaction to the work of Stubbs and other "Whig" historians, have painted a very unflattering picture of the lower house and denied it any meaningful role in late medieval government. Herein lies the main debate. While it is relatively easy to describe the institutional development of the House of Commons during this period, it is far more difficult to come to an accurate understanding of its political role. In part this is due to the inadequacy of the evidence, for we have almost no record of the debates in either the Commons or the Lords, nor any parliamentary diaries to give an idea of the motivation of individual MPs; in part, it is due to the undoubted fact that in this evolutionary period in its history (and beyond) its political role fluctuated with the political climate.

If, however, the House of Commons' political role is a matter for debate, the outline of its institutional development is clear. For convenience this can be described under three heads; taxation, legislation, and, for want of a better word, identity.

As the previous chapter in this volume has demonstrated, the representative element became a defining feature in the institution of Parliament early in the 14th century because of the King's need for general taxation that could only be levied with common consent. It is worth emphasizing that the novel principle here was not that taxation required consent – Magna Carta had affirmed the principle that extraordinary taxation could only be levied by "common counsel of the realm" – but that the representatives of the communities gathered in Parliament, rather than, as envisaged in Magna Carta, the greater barons and tenants-in-chief, were the body from which consent should properly be sought. This change reflected and reinforced the acceptance of the theory enunciated in the *Modus Tenendi Parliamentum,* a unique parliamentary manual of the early 1320s, that, since the magnates attend Parliament each " for themselves in their own person and for no other" it is the elected representatives who "represent the whole community of England" and hence "two knights who come to Parliament for the shire have a greater voice in the granting and denying [of taxation] than the greatest earl in England".[5] What quickly gave this "voice" such an immense practical importance was the military ambitions of Edward III which could not be funded without a considerable augmentation of the Crown's financial resources. Yet, although the Commons' right of assent to direct taxation had been established before the outbreak of the Hundred Years' War, during the early campaigns the Crown continued to levy highly lucrative indirect taxation, principally through a duty on wool, England's main export, without parliamentary consent.[6] Since, from the point of view of the Crown, this tax was paid by the merchants engaged in the wool trade, the King considered that the consent of the merchants was a sufficient justification for its levy. The Commons, as it made clear in several petitions presented in the parliaments of the 1340s, had a very different view: members recognized that the burden of the tax, although borne in part by the foreign consumer, also fell on the wool growers, to whom the merchants passed on the tax in the form of lower prices, and hence, since it was the community who paid a significant part of the tax, it was their consent that the Crown required. It was this view that prevailed for, from 1351, in response to yet another Commons' petition on the subject, the Crown routinely sought parliamentary consent to levy the wool subsidy. This could be said to be one of the main achievements of the Commons in the late medieval period – and in terms of the theoretical basis of taxation it was – but what did it mean in practice? The subsequent history of the wool subsidy and other customs duties demonstrates that they became a permanent levy with the Commons constantly renewing its assent, sometimes for a short period but at others, as in 1398 and 1415, for the life of the King. Although in theory such a renewal could be refused, the Commons does not appear to have systematically used its right of assent as a bargaining counter, nor even to have seen it as means by which it could oblige the King to summon regular parliaments. Indeed, on his accession in 1461, Edward IV did not wait for parliamentary sanction before collecting customs duties on the grounds that they were "due to the King of his inheritance", and the Commons' grant to him in 1465 of the customs for life can be seen as merely the reassertion of an empty privilege.[7] The explanation for this quiescence probably lies in the Commons' recognition of a practical truth: that, without the receipts of indirect taxation, the Crown could no longer meet its ordinary changes, and that this permanent necessity created a permanent obligation on their part to grant it. As Harriss has put it, this perpetual grant was the price the Commons paid to maintain, as a meaningful element of debate between Crown and subject, its right to grant direct taxation only as the occasion demanded.[8]

The Crown's dependence on indirect taxation is indicative of the long-term crisis in royal finance that was to endow the Commons' right of assent to taxation with greater political significance. In part, this crisis was a result of repeated outbreaks of war between England and France – not until the second half of the 15th century did the Crown's need for war taxation become less acute – but more important were the increasingly apparent structural defects of the system of public finance. These first became manifest in the rapidly declining yield of the levy on moveable property that was the basis of direct taxation: in 1290, such a levy imposed at the rate of a fifteenth had raised the remarkable sum of £116,000 and yet so quickly did the yield fall that, in 1334, the Crown was prepared to accept the fixing of the yield of a fifteenth (the rate was a tenth in the towns) at a comparatively meagre £38,000.[9] While this fixed rate may have been a sensible response to tax evasion, it rendered the fifteenth and tenth an inflexible form of taxation, incapable, since each county and town was assessed at the rate they had contributed to the levy of 1332, of reflecting changes in the geographical distribution of wealth. It also, conveniently for the parliamentary classes, obviated the need for regular inquiries into the social distribution of wealth and ensured that the greatest burden of taxation would fall comparatively heavily on those least able to pay. This inflexibility would have been of relatively little importance, either financially and politically, had the yield of indirect taxation not been afflicted with a similar decline. It is a striking fact that, in the 1360s, customs revenue, derived predominantly from the export duty on wool, yielded nearly £70,000 a year and accounted for nearly 70% of the Crown's revenue from all sources. The subsequent decline in the level of wool exports thus had serious implications. By the early years of the 15th century, annual customs revenue had fallen to less than £50,000 and, by 1450, to less than £30,000.[10] Such a steep decline increased the Crown's dependence on direct taxation, and hence placed a higher premium on negotiations between King and Commons.

Nevertheless, even though the demands of war and declining yields made the Crown heavily reliant on parliamentary taxation, it would be a mistake to see this dependence in the context of free bargaining between Crown and Commons over grants of taxation.[11] The Commons enjoyed a power of assent that was very short of that of free refusal. For just as the representative nature of the Commons gave it this right of assent, the Crown had the right to demand a share of its subjects' goods in times of common necessity. In the words of Sir John Fortescue, writing in the middle of the 15th century, but reflecting a long-established doctrine, the King's "reaume is bounde by right to susteyen hym in euery thyng necessarie to his estate".[12] Thus if the Crown could demonstrate a need then the community had an obligation to make a favourable response. In this sense, assent was an obligation rather than a privilege, and could not be denied without, as Harriss has written, "a repudiation of political authority on which the state rested".[13] But if the community had an obligation to extend aid to the King on a plea of necessity, it also had a part to play in defining necessity, a necessity first called into existence by the demands of war and thereafter defined in the same military terms. This balance of right and obligation is reflected in the formal opening exchange in Parliament – in which the King's representative made a speech outlining the necessity which justified a request for taxation – and, more significantly, in the language of debate between King and Commons at times of crisis. Even though the Commons did not have the right of free refusal, much that was inherent in its assent drew it into a political dialogue with the Crown, the content of which threatened, on occasion, to limit the King's freedom of action. The Commons' obligation to answer the plea of necessity in the affirmative obliged it to develop, if not a theoretical basis for its refusal, at least a *quid pro quo* for its acceptance. To take the most notable 14th century debate between Crown and Commons about taxation, that which took place in the Good Parliament of 1376, here the Commons justified its refusal to make a grant of taxation on the grounds that such a grant would have been unnecessary had not certain named courtiers misappropriated royal revenue to their own profit.[14]

The Commons was called upon to weigh conflicting interests: on one hand, the doctrine of necessity obliged members to look favourably on the Crown's demands for taxation; on the other, the expectations of their constituents, and in extreme cases the threat of local disorder in the face of exceptionally onerous taxation, demanded that tax grants be kept to a minimum. Naturally, the need to weigh these conflicting interests led the Commons into questioning royal expenditure. It is unfortunate that more evidence does not survive of the relations between the elected representatives and those who returned them, and a picture of the electorate's expectations of the Commons has to be built up from a variety of scattered and unsatisfactory references.[15] From such references we can infer that it was a common practice for MPs to report back to their constituents on what had occurred in Parliament, but only one such report, that made by the Colchester MPs of 1485, has so far been traced.[16] One recent commentator has remarked that these reports, so far as they related to taxation, were designed to justify the grant of taxation "before the bar of local opinion" and that they "marked the effect of taxation in setting MPs at odds with their constituents".[17] Further evidence of the tension inherent in this relationship is provided by the Parliament of October 1339, in which the Commons, nervous of the massive war expenditure to which the Crown was committed in the first years of the Hundred Years' War, asked for time to consult their constituents before increasing their grant.[18] While this is a unique example of resort to a practice which stood in contradiction to the *plena potestas* with which election endowed MPs and came at a time when the burden of direct taxation was especially burdensome, the threat of opposition in the shires, in other words, that the tax granted would either be uncollectable or produce serious local disturbances, "gave the Commons their most effective bargaining counter with the Crown".[19]

It is in this context that one must consider the doctrine of redress before supply, for although its development must partly be seen in terms of the growing self-confidence of the Commons, it also owed something to their need to justify grants of taxation to their constituents. This was the more necessary because direct taxation fell comparatively heavily on those least able to pay. The virtual tax immunity of the rich is a common refrain of early 14th century ballads. "Poem on the Evil Times of Edward II" complains that a man with £40 worth of goods was assessed at the same rate as a poor man with a brood of children, while the "Song against the King's Taxes" explicitly blamed the lords and gentry in Parliament for this state of affairs: "It does not hurt the great thus to make the King a grant; the lowly have to give all ... it is wrong to ordain that those who make a grant pay nothing".[20] The government was also infected with this view, for in 1336 commissions to the tax collectors threatened direct assessment by the Crown on all those "richer folk" who burdened the poorer subjects by evading the tax.[21] Thus it is not surprising that the Commons should have developed a strategy that increased its influence beyond simply accepting the King's plea of necessity and justified members' actions to those they represented. In the Parliament of March 1340, they presented a petition, the acceptance of which they made a condition of the grant of taxation the King so badly needed. MPs' most radical demand was for the appointment of a baronial council to supervise the expenditure of taxation, which in their view had previously been grievously misspent, and to answer in Parliament. Their hope was that the more efficient application of taxation would result in the lessening of future burdens. The most important point here is not that Edward III accepted the petition – the financial demands of war gave him little option – but that this was the first occasion on which the Commons had employed its right to assent to taxation to win concessions.[22]

Nonetheless, although the connection between the redress of grievances and supply was forged early in the history of the Commons, clearly the lower house did not thereby acquire the political muscle to bend the Crown to its will. First of all, its aims were limited, to control the burden of taxation. Second, Edward III's concession arose out of circumstances so extraordinary that they did not thereafter recur. Third, throughout the medieval period, the redress of grievances remained a matter of royal grace, while the Commons had an obligation to grant taxation as necessity demanded.[23] Indeed, when in 1401, MPs asked that they be given the answer to their petitions before making a grant of taxation, the King firmly denied their request on the grounds that such a procedure "had not been seen or used in any of the times of his predecessors".[24] This leads to a more general point. The relationship between Crown and Commons over the centrally important matter of taxation cannot be properly understood by concentrating on those occasions, such as, most notably, 1340 or 1376, when a clash occurred. Nor is it entirely helpful to characterize the Commons' attitude as being determined by "considerations of the kind that actuate modern rate-payers' associations".[25] As Edwards has pointed out, the Commons' right of consenting to taxation was gained by giving consent not by withholding it, and it could be argued that MPs owed their place in government to the House's effectiveness in facilitating the levy of taxation.[26] The recurrent grant of indirect taxation is one example of Members' willingness to cooperate with the Crown's reasonable demands as is the high level of direct taxation granted to support Henry V's successful campaigns in France. Moreover, it has even been suggested that, as the period progressed, the Commons was prepared to countenance an erosion of the link between taxation and war: in part, because the Crown came increasingly to face continuous items of military expenditure, most notably the maintenance of the Calais garrison, in times of peace, and this blurred the division between wartime and peacetime expenditure; but also, due to a widening of the definition of necessity.[27] Certainly, from early on, it had been established that taxation could be justified, for example, to maintain a defensive readiness in time of truce or to suppress a rebellion, both of which could be claimed as for the common good, and it soon became customary to make a grant of direct taxation in the first Parliament of a new king's reign.[28] The fact that twice as many fifteenths and tenths were granted between 1377 and 1422 as had been the case between 1336 and 1377 can also be cited in support of the view that the plea of necessity came to extend beyond war, but such a view is difficult to sustain in face of the declining number of grants after 1422. From 1450, this is readily explained by the Crown's disengagement from foreign war – less money was granted because less money was needed – but the meagre grants of direct taxation from 1422 to that date, as the government vainly struggled first to extend and then simply to maintain

Henry V's French conquests, contradict the notion of an extension of the plea of necessity. Further, although the connection between war and necessity may have occasionally been set aside in practice, it was held in theory long into the Tudor period.[29]

In short, the general attitude of the Commons to the granting of direct taxation was far from constant over the period as a whole. At times of successful warfare and strong kingship, they reacted with a generosity that extended monarchical power and funded warfare on a scale that would have been impossible without their cooperation. This truth was recognized by Commynes who remarked on the strength which parliamentary taxation brought to the English Crown, since, although taxation was restricted to war, for expeditions against the enemies of the realm Parliament granted money "very willingly and liberally".[30] Even when the Crown was weak and government lacked direction, the Commons' obligation to aid the monarch in times of necessity ensured that grants continued to be made although they became a matter of prolonged bargaining.

In one respect, however, the attitude of the Commons to taxation appears to have been constant. It is possible to see their bargaining over grants as an attempt to protect the goods of the King's subjects from the rapacity of the Crown, and there is certainly evidence that, particularly in the early years of parliamentary taxation, they viewed themselves as accountable to their constituents for the grants they made. They should not, however, be seen as the selfless protectors of the goods of the King's subjects. For one thing, it has been argued that the social changes occasioned by the Black Death – a shortage of labour with a consequent rise in wages and fall in the authority of landlords – transformed the Commons from "protectors of the shire poor against royal demands" into "exponents of forms of taxation which would tap the new found prosperity of the lower classes".[31] For another, there can be no doubt that the Commons encouraged the perpetuation of a system of direct taxation that deflected the bulk of its burden on the King's lesser subjects. As early as 1380, they themselves had described the traditional fifteenths and tenth as "very grievous" to lesser men,[32] but they consistently proved uncooperative in the search for a form of taxation that more accurately reflected the distribution of wealth. The obvious solution was a tax on landed income, either in place of, or as well as, the levy on moveable property, and, although several such taxes were granted during the course of the 15th century, the Commons consistently insisted, first, that such taxes should not be established as a precedent, and, second, that the records they produced should not come into the hands of the government.[33] Moreover, the response of landed society as a whole to such taxes was to return unrealistic assessments. For example, the combined tax on income and moveable property granted to Henry VII on stringent conditions in 1489, although far more renumerative than the income taxes collected under the Lancastrian kings, raised only about a third of its anticipated yield of £75,000.[34] When combined with the

decline in customs revenue, the resistance of the Commons to the replacement
or supplement of the long-established fifteenth and tenth with a form of direct
taxation that more accurately reflected the social distribution of wealth meant
that the English system of public finance, although still admired by Commynes,
was no longer the efficient instrument it had been in the mid-14th century.
As Harriss has remarked: "Its very effectiveness in financing war ... deterred
the medieval monarchy from contentious attempts to extend direct taxation
to peacetime or to make new assessments of taxable wealth," or to develop
new forms of indirect taxation.[35] In the longer term, this had profound
consequences for relations between the Crown and the Commons. It encouraged
the Crown to develop nonparliamentary sources of income, the so-called "fiscal
feudalism" of the Tudors, and threatened to diminish the importance of the
Commons' right of assent to taxation. These changes had political effects
which have no bearing on the period under review here, but they do show
that the medieval system of taxation, which had served the English Crown
so well during the wars of aggression fought by Edward III and Henry V,
was beginning to show signs of severe strain at the end of our period.[36] This
strain was in part a product of the resistance of the Commons to its effective
reform, and has led one scholar to the extreme conclusion that Edward IV
and Henry VII were "emasculated by the financial outlook of their subjects".[37]

While the granting of taxation was, for the Crown, the most significant purpose
of Parliament, from the point of view of the Commons and those they
represented, its chief importance lay in the opportunity it provided for the
presentation of petitions and the redress of grievances.[38] One of the central
functions of early parliaments was as a court in which the King could provide
justice to individual petitions from the highest to the lowest, and early
parliamentary records are largely a register of such petitions. Indeed, so
popular a forum for the presentation of private petitions did it quickly become
that, as early as 1280, petitions threatened to overwhelm other parliamentary
business and steps were taken to reduce the proportion of them that required
an answer from the King and Council.[39] And yet if Parliment had remained
a forum only for the presentation of the petitions of individuals seeking
individual remedies or favours, it would not have attained the central place
in the legislative process that was of such significance in its later history.[40]
Before our period, the making of new law had been established as a consensual
process, but only in the vaguest terms. It was yet to be established that
valid assent could only be given in Parliament, and, even had it been, the
frequent exclusion of the Commons from Parliament would have given them
no assured place in the legislative process. By the end of our period, however,
their assent was indispensable to the making of new law. This transformation
is probably the single most important development in the history of the
medieval Commons, and its first stage was a fundamental change in the
pattern of petitioning. In the early 14th century, Parliament became something
more than the forum for the presentation of the grievances of individuals or
even of communities, for the Commons began to present petitions, in the form
of a series of articles (known as common petitions), seeking remedies to

more general administrative, economic, legal, and other problems. Unlike an individual petition, which sought a royal favour or a remedy for a particular injustice, the common petitions sought general remedies that could only be provided by legislation. Although far more limited in scope than those baronial schedules of grievances which were of such importance in the 13th century, they stand in the same tradition. Their emergence reflects the "growing political cohesiveness" of the local communities from which MPs were drawn and, even more importantly, the transfer of the "voice" of the community of the realm from the Baronage to the Commons.[41] This change had been foreshadowed in the baronial articles themselves which reflected not only high politics and baronial concerns, but also the aspirations of the emergent gentry class. As David Carpenter has pointed out, already by the reign of King John, the counties had a political programme, manifest in their determination that local government should be run by local men, a subject that was later to become a frequent topic of common petitions.[42] In this respect, the main importance of these petitions is that they brought the voice of the localities to the centre of government, not indirectly through the barons, but directly through the Commons, and hence reflect the expansion of the political nation that was the driving force of the main parliamentary developments of our period.[43]

Moreover, this voice was more than simply heard, for with the emergence of the common petition came a fundamental change in the legislative process. In the reign of Edward I, legislation was expertly drafted by royal councillors and judges; in the second quarter of the 14th century, the basis of legislation became the King's answers to the common petitions. By some this has been seen as a seriously regressive step: Sayles argues that "the petitions of the Commons were a haphazard collection of unrelated requests", giving rise to legislation that was "often ill conceived, repetitive, [and] trivial" and not concerned with the sort of fundamental changes addressed by Edward I's statutes.[44] This is probably an exaggerated contrast. As Harriss has pointed out, the Edwardian statutes "were not a conscious programme of social engineering or tenurial reform so much as the answer to problems revealed in difficult cases in council and the voluminous complaints before the justices in eyre".[45] Moreover, the Commons-inspired statutes can be viewed in a more positive light than such a contrast allows. One of the functions of the Commons was to serve as a channel of communication from the localities to the centre, and, while some of their complaints were unwelcome to the Crown, not all of them were. Principally concerned with matters of local interest, which often required only uncontroversial administrative remedies, the content of common petitions demonstrated the representatives' familiarity with local conditions and provided the Crown with the sort of information that was essential to the framing of effective legislation. In this context, it is worth drawing a parallel with the making of law in the present day: in the words of Helen Cam, "Even if you admit that the responsibility for all legislation today rests with the government, you still have to find the government's source of inspiration."[46]

While there is no denying the importance of this shift in the legislative initiative, it should not be imagined that the power of the King, in passing statutes in response to the complaints of his subjects, was significantly diminished. Not only was he free to reject, without explanation, any legislation proposed by the Commons, but he also had scope to modify the intent of the petitions as his law officers drew them up into statutes. Indeed, in 1413, so wholesale were the modifications between petition and statute, that the Commons were moved to ask in the Parliament of the following year for an assurance that such modifications would only be made with their assent. Henry V replied with the limited concession that "nothing be enacted to the petition of his Commons that is contrary to their asking".[47] Moreover, a recent study of the reign of Edward III has concluded that the theory that no statute could limit the power of the Crown meant in practice that only those pieces of legislation positively advantageous to the King were ever actively enforced.[48] Most importantly of all, the executive could, at will, regrasp the initiative, as Richard II emphatically did in the last years of his reign. Only during the second quarter of the 15th century, when royal authority was eclipsed by minority and then by Henry VI's unfitness to govern, can it be said that nearly every addition to the statute book owed its place to the initiative of the Commons. Later in the century, a reassertion of royal power, under the Yorkists and Henry VII, saw important legislation passed at the King's behest.[49] Early in the next, Henry VIII was to show what could be achieved when the legislative authority of Parliament was harnessed to the royal will.[50]

This brings us to another apparent paradox. While what might be termed the "political" history of legislation shows the initiative of the Commons waning in the second half of the 15th century, the "procedural" history presents a very different picture with the Commons apparently gaining an ever-greater share in the legislative process.[51] Two developments are of importance here: from late in the 14th century, private petitioners increasingly came to address their petitions not to the King but to the Commons in the hope that the lower house would lend them its support;[52] and, more importantly, early in the 15th century, the King began to send private petitions, to which he had assented, to the Commons for their approval.[53] This second development explains the otherwise puzzling and unhistorical assertion of the Commons, in the 1414 petition mentioned above, that it "has ever been their liberty and freedom that no statute or law be made unless they have given their assent thereto", and that they "who are and always have been members of your Parliament, are both assentors and petitioners". It has been claimed that the establishment of this two-way traffic in petitions – or bills as they came to be known – "is the first of the really big developments to occur in the English Parliament subsequent to its transformation into a parliament that was representative",[54] and it certainly heralded what looks like an important constitutional change. From 1452, legislation, previously described as having been made "at the request of the Commons", came to be described as having been made "by assent of the Commons", and by 1489 the judges had ruled that legislation without the assent of the Commons was invalid.[55]

Clearly, these procedural changes were much more than cosmetic. They demonstrate, as Brown has pointed out, "how much the working atmosphere in Parliament and government" had changed since 1300.[56] With the benefit of hindsight, the transformation of the Commons from mere petitioners to assentors was of vital importance. Contemporaries probably had a slightly different perspective. Just as they became assentors, the Crown, by the simple expedient of introducing its own official bills among the common petitions, was reassuming the legislative initiative. This is difficult to reconcile with the view that there was an inherent conflict of interest between Crown and Commons, a struggle for legislative control that the Commons appear to have won and lost at the same moment.[57] What we are in fact observing is the waxing and waning of government activity; when the government lacked direction and purpose, the Commons held the initiative in the legislative process in the absence of an official legislative programme; when it was strong, the King was able, without resistance or rancour, to resume the initiative. In short, over the period as a whole, the Commons was drawn increasingly into the legislative process, but this did not come about at the expense of the King's power. Efficient management ensured that his official bills had a smooth passage through both Houses of Parliament, and he retained the power to veto any bill that was not official in origin. What had changed since the reign of Edward I was the degree of consultation involved in an increasingly sophisticated legislative process, not the fundamental balance of initiative between Crown and subject.[58] A recent survey of early Tudor government represents Parliament as the forum in which the Crown secured "the backing [of the political nation] for royal initiatives",[59] and so it would have been in Lancastrian England but for the exigencies of dynastic insecurity, war, minority and madness.

The evolving powers of the House of Commons were reflected, during the first part of our period, in the development of a firm institutional definition, and, in the second, in the members' sense that they formed a body to which special privileges attached. A rapid normalization of membership in the early 14th century was the basis of future developments. The demands of royal finance not only made the representatives of the communities a vital component of Parliament – the last assembly to which they were not summoned was that of 1325 – but also forged the representatives of shire and borough together. Under Edward I, their consent to taxation had sometimes been sought in separate assemblies, but it was obviously more convenient for the Crown to seek consent in a joint assembly.[60] Indeed, it was the Crown's preferred option to gain assent, in the same assembly, from the clergy to the taxes on clerical income that paralleled the levy on lay moveables. This, however, was resisted by the Church, reluctant to concede the principle that the secular authority had the right to compel their attendance at what was a lay court. By 1340, the King had accepted a compromise, with the clergy giving their consent in a manner that reflected the division of the Church into two provinces: in the provincial assemblies, called convocations, of York and Canterbury.[61] Thus, by the mid-14th century, the House of Commons had taken on the composition that was to characterize it for centuries to come. Thereafter, it quickly developed a sense of institutional identity. Particularly important in this respect was the period between 1376 and 1430 which saw the rise of the office of Speaker and the passage of legislation designed to protect freedom of election.

The history of the Speakership poses problems of interpretation.[62] On the one hand, the establishment of the office can be seen as a manifestation of the growing self-confidence of the Commons, determined to improve their rudimentary organization and to enhance their ability to negotiate with the Crown about taxation and redress. On the other, it could be argued that, even if the office did not originate in the government's perception that it needed to direct their affairs, the Speakership soon became one of the channels through which the King sought to bend them to his will. Such a dichotomy is, however, too stark. The bare facts would appear to support the second interpretation: from the first recorded speaker, Sir Peter de la Mare, in the Good Parliament of 1376, to the end of our period, the holder of the office was either a partisan of a baronial faction opposed to the Crown or, far more commonly, a high-ranking servant of the King with a place in the Royal Household or, particularly in the second half of the 15th century, on the Royal Council. In the first category can be numbered de la Mare himself as steward of the Earl of March and Sir William Oldhall, speaker in the Parliament of 1450-1 and chamberlain of Richard, Duke of York; in the second, most of the others who held the office. Indeed, from the accession of Edward IV, the Speaker can be said to have been a servant of the Crown in another sense, for he began to receive a handsome royal fee for his service in the office, and, under the Tudors, he came almost invariably to be a lawyer in royal employment. Nevertheless, to view the Speaker solely as an agent of the Crown or occasionally of baronial faction, is to misunderstand the dynamics of his appointment and his role in the Commons' proceedings. His office originated in an obvious institutional need, to provide a spokesman to communicate the results of the Commons' deliberations to the King and Lords. Hence it is not surprising that the Commons should have come to accept what amounted to a royal nominee, for someone known to the King (and probably familiar with the workings of central government) was likely to be an effective channel of communication. It certainly should not be imagined that the election of a royal servant as Speaker ensured a compliant Commons. The truculence of the 1406 Parliament, in which Sir John Tiptoft, a knight of the King's Chamber, held the office, is sufficient illustration of this point.[63] Several medieval speakers must have found themselves faced with the unwelcome task of communicating to the King news of the hostile disposition of the Commons. Instructive in this context is the case of William Stourton, who, elected Speaker in 1413, was removed from office on the Commons' complaint that he had acted *ultra vires* in accepting a royal request that their grievances be put in writing.[64] While it cannot be denied that an able Speaker in favourable circumstances was able to manage the Commons' deliberations in the King's interest – the best example is the royal councillor, Sir John Bussy, in the

Parliament of 1397-8 – there is, in general, no reason to believe that the Speaker "was able to speak other than as the Commons allowed him".[65] When the history of the office is seen against the background of other evidence suggestive of institutional identity, the emergence of the Speakership is "a sign of a quickening sense of corporateness among the Commons", and its development a contribution "to their growing constitutional and political importance", an importance which the Crown then sought to exploit by routinely securing the office for one of its servants.[66]

Further evidence of the Commons' growing sense of self-confidence and corporate identity is provided by the passage of a considerable body of electoral legislation, all of it at their petition. There is some evidence that, in the early 14th century, the main concern in the minds of the electorate was to return men who would serve for less than the standard parliamentary wage of 4 shillings a day for the county representatives and of half that sum for those of the boroughs. For example, in the early 1320s, the electors of Lancashire were angered by the sheriff's unilateral return of two knights of the shire not principally because they had been denied their right of election, but because those returned had taken wages of £20, "whereas the community of the county could have had by their own election two sufficient men to go to the Parliament for 10 marks or 10 pounds".[67] By mid-century, however, this attitude, at least in the shires, had changed and freedom of election was coming to be valued in its own right.[68] In the turbulent Good Parliament of 1376, the Commons petitioned that statutory penalties be instituted against sheriffs who failed to hold due parliamentary elections in the county court. This petition is to be seen in the context of the first appearance of complaints that Parliament had been packed. The earliest of these occurs in the chronicle of Thomas Walsingham, a monk of St Albans, who accuses John of Gaunt, Duke of Lancaster, who, as by far the richest lay landholder, had considerable influence in the localities, of packing the Parliament of 1377, which undid the work of the Good Parliament.[69] Thereafter, such accusations became, for the next 30 years, the common coin of political dispute: in the Merciless Parliament of 1388 it was alleged that the King's followers had caused sheriffs to be nominated who would arbitrarily nominate the shire knights; in 1399, one of the deposition articles against Richard II was that had interfered in elections through the sheriffs. The general view of historians is to doubt the truth of such allegations, largely because of the difficulties inherent in the exercise of wholesale interference. On Henry IV's accession, however, when the great estates of the duchy of Lancaster became part of the royal patrimony, the Crown acquired a much greater potential to influence local elections.[70] This was certainly the view of the Percy rebels of 1403, who claimed that they had been unable to obtain justice because of the King's interference in elections, and their complaint is echoed two years later when Archbishop Scrope demanded that elections be held freely. This is the immediate background of the centrally important Commons' petition of 1406. This complained of the corrupt election of some shire representatives through the partiality of sheriffs, and proposed a detailed and well-considered remedy designed to restrict the returning officer's freedom of action. It requested that, henceforward, the election return should no longer be made in its customary form of a simple endorsement on the writ of summons of the names of those elected, but rather as an indenture drawn up between the sheriff and the electors, who were to append their seals. The enactment of this petition as a statute made it a good deal more difficult for the sheriff to make a false return. While this important reform is to be seen in the immediate context of the complaints against electoral interference outlined above, it is better understood in a far wider context. Not only does it reflect the ever-increasing importance of the Commons, but it also implies increasing competition for seats. This in turn drew a greater number of local landowners into the electoral process.

What little is known of early elections suggests that they were dominated by the magnates, represented in the county court by their attorneys, and that so weak was the competition for seats that those returned were the nominees of the county court rather than candidates. In such circumstances, contests could not arise and hence there was no reason to define either the franchise or the method by which contested elections were to be resolved. By the second quarter of the 15th century, the whole pattern of the electoral process had been transformed. The Commons had become such a focus of communal aspirations that elections were a matter of much more general concern. If the petition presented by the Commons in the Parliament of 1429-30 is to be taken literally, the election process was now being threatened not by the corruption of sheriffs, but by the excessive number of people who attended the county court at election time, many of whom were poor and without property and yet claimed an equal voice in the election with the leading shire gentry. Clearly, in the view of the Commons, democracy could go too far, but it would be wrong to view this petition, and the statute which it produced, as designed to restrict the electorate to that comparatively small group of wealthy gentry from whom the parliamentary knights of the shire were predominantly drawn. Its purpose was rather to define the mechanism by which contested elections could be resolved. Thus it was that the resulting statute defined the franchise as all those who held freehold property to the value of at least 40 shillings and were resident in the county in which they cast their vote, and laid down that, in case of a contest, those with the support of the greater number of electors should be returned. Indeed, far from seeking to minimize the number of electors, the franchise was set surprisingly low, perhaps because the Commons feared the consequences of undermining their representative nature by depriving the lesser freeholders of the vote when they too bore the burden of parliamentary taxation and contributed to parliamentary wages. Although it would be foolish to overstate the democracy of elections after the statute – not only were elections frequently uncontested but it is unlikely that the enfranchised composed any more than, at most, 5% of the adult male population – the most important aspect of the statute of 1429-30 is its inclusivity rather than its exclusivity.[71] By the early 15th century, an interest in parliamentary affairs extended very far beyond those who could aspire to a place in the Commons.

Without doubt, the definition of proper electoral process at the petition of the Commons was the most important affirmation of their new found sense of institutional identity, but it was not the only one.[72] In the Parliament of January 1404, after a vicious assault on a servant of one of the sitting members, the Commons petitioned for the institution of a range of strong punishments to deter future assaults on MPs and asked that the murder of a MP be considered treason. While the statute enacted by the Crown was less extreme, it did acknowledge the special position of those elected to Parliament by providing them with a protection against assault that went further than the common law. More important was another privilege that the Commons assiduously sought through the 15th century, namely that of freedom from arrest for debt and other civil pleas during the course of a parliamentary session. They first claimed this privilege, so obviously to the advantage of individual MPs, on the grounds that it would benefit the King as much as they, for the arrest of members retarded the completion of parliamentary business, and, although this privilege did not achieve statutory definition, it appears generally to have been allowed, save in cases of particular political significance. All this demonstrates how far the Commons had come since the early 14th century: then not yet an integral part of parliament with representatives of shire and boroughs yet to be forged into a single entity and sometimes coming to Westminster reluctantly; by the end of our period the lower house had acquired a corporate identity with well defined rights, privileges, and procedures, and had become the focus of the political aspirations of a class far wider than those who took their seats there.

While there is little disagreement among historians about the development of the Commons in this crucial formative period of their history, the same could not be said about the question of their political role. Some have forcefully argued that the institutional development of the Commons was not, in this period, translated into a significant independent role in politics. The argument here, very clearly put in the extensive and forthright writings of Richardson and Sayles, is in two parts: first, that the right of assent to the levying of taxation and the ability to initiate legislation were not sufficient in themselves to give the Commons any more than a peripheral part in what was the real context of late medieval politics, the relations between King and Baronage; and second, that, on those occasions when they appear to be the focus of opposition to the executive, such as, for example, in the Good Parliament of 1376, they were not acting on their own initiative, but were merely the tools of their social superiors among the Baronage.[73] This second point brings into focus the relationship between the two Houses of Parliament. For Richardson: "The superiority of the Lords is too obvious to permit us to attribute to the Commons more than a subordinate, if respectable, part in the proceedings of Parliament".[74] This view is based in part on the "bastard feudal" ties that were part of the framework of late medieval landed society: many knights of the shire, the socially dominant members of the Commons, were in receipt of fees from or had a place in the households of individual lords. How then can they be seen as independent critics of royal misgovernment? The contrasting behaviour of the Commons in the parliaments of 1376, which saw an immoderate attack on the royal court, and January 1377, in which the work of the previous assembly was largely undone, appears to offer clear evidence of the Lords leading the lower house through their retainers. The Speaker of 1376, as already noted, was Sir Peter de la Mare, a servant of Edmund Mortimer, Earl of March, a powerful opponent of the royal court; in 1377, the same office fell to Sir Thomas Hungerford, a servant of the King's son, John of Gaunt.[75] The other main plank of the Richardson argument depends on the procedural device known as "intercommuning", by which delegations from the two Houses conferred together, and through which, in his view, the Lords dictated policy to the Commons during the course of a Parliament. While the work of Edwards has shown that "intercommuning" certainly did not fulfil this role – for not only was it the Commons who took the initiative in requesting these conferences, but it was they who nominated the lords who were to attend[76] – recent research has provided some support for the Richardson view. The latest volumes of the *History of Parliament*, covering the period 1386 to 1421, have shown that the political complexion of the Commons in parliaments called at moments of political crisis, such as the so-called Merciless Parliament of 1388, when Richard II's enemies, the Lords Appellant, attainted and executed some of his most intimate followers, and that of 1397-8, when the King took his vengeance, reflected the sympathies of the party in the ascendant. Several of the Appellants' supporters and retainers were returned in 1388; nine years later, such men were notable by their absence. Moreover, three times as many members of the Royal Household sat in the latter Parliament than had been the case in 1388.[77] This radical change in the composition of the lower house did not escape the notice of contemporaries, prompting one of the Appellants, Richard FitzAlan, Earl of Arundel, to assert that "the faithful Commons of the realm are not here" and leading to the charge of electoral manipulation among those charges levelled at Richard II at his deposition in 1399.

Nevertheless, although one can cite examples of the assertion of baronial influence in, and even leadership of, the lower house, there can be little doubt that Richardson has greatly exaggerated the political subservience of the Commons. The relationship between the two Houses needs to be placed in the context of the great political changes of the 14th and 15th centuries. Few would argue with the proposition that, as Elton has it, "the baronial opposition to Edward II took over the Parliament",[78] but, equally, few would accept that the peerage were capable of exerting the same sort of influence into the 15th century. Richardson has assumed a degree of dependence in the relations between peers and the wealthier county gentry, from whom the parliamentary knights of the shire were predominantly drawn, that most modern scholars, following the lead of McFarlane, would not accept.[79] Nor should we be too ready to believe that the majority of the parliamentary knights of the shire had baronial ties "close enough to cast doubt upon their political independence". A recent survey suggests that such knights formed a minority, albeit a significant one, of the shire representatives. Among the burgesses, more numerous but individually and collectively of less weight than the shire representatives, there were only very few with close links with magnates.[80] More directly, Richardson fails to consider those issues on which the interests of Lords and Commons came into conflict. In the fields of local government and the administration of justice, the Commons, through their petitions, consistently expressed a view that was very much at odds with that of the upper house. One specific example is in the field of electoral legislation, designed to diminish the influence of Crown and magnates on parliamentary elections. Another is their sustained campaign in the reigns of Richard II and Henry IV to diminish the unbridled distribution of livery badges by the peers, a practice which in their view endangered local order. Indeed, their determination on this issue led them into an open confrontation with the Lords Appellant in the Parliament of September 1388, one of several indications that, although the Commons had actively cooperated with the Appellants in the attack on the royal court in the Merciless Parliament of the previous February, they were not without an agenda of their own.[81] Indeed, we should not assume that their independence was manifest only in matters of local interest. The lower house could, albeit occasionally, take the initiative in matters of national politics. A good example is their demands for the resumption of royal grants in the early 1450s, which they saw as a vital preliminary to the restoration of the King's finances and about which the Lords, as a body with a greater fund of patronage to lose, were less enthusiastic.[82] More striking is the conclusion reached by a recent study of the Parliament of 1386, namely that the Commons was acting independently of the Lords in initiating the novel process of impeachment against the Chancellor, Michael de la Pole, Earl of Suffolk. This is indicated by the fact that, although the Lords adjudicated favourably upon some of the articles of impeachment, there were other articles upon which they did not.[83] There may be a parallel to be drawn here with the fall of the Earl's grandson, William de la Pole, Duke of Suffolk, in 1450. Even though there is good contemporary evidence that Suffolk's powerful enemy, Ralph, Lord Cromwell, played a part in initiating the parliamentary attack on him, inferential evidence implies that the Commons was far more committed to the process than the Lords, where Suffolk had friends deeply implicated in his unpopular policies. The hardline attitude of the Commons probably owed more to the popular hatred of Suffolk and the court party, reflected in many surviving contemporary ballads, than it did to Cromwell's prompting.[84] Moreover, even though it is clear that the baronial opposition to Richard II and Henry VI was able to orchestrate the hostility of the Commons against the monarch, this is not to say that it was they who called that hostility into being. The unpopularity of the government in 1376, for example, arose out of problems that were central to the concerns of the Commons, such as the misappropriation of public funds which placed an additional burden on the purses of taxpayers. Here it is worth remembering that they had constituents to answer to; the Lords did not.

But if the picture of a House of Commons dependent on the Lords for their political direction is inaccurate, what of relations between Crown and

Commons? Here Richardson and Sayles take the view, most clearly developed in the work of the latter, that to attribute any real political weight to the Commons in their bargaining with the Crown over taxation and the redress of grievances is to view Parliament from the perspective of a later age. As Sayles has pointed out, the Commons was "dependent on the will and caprice of the King. They came when he ordered it; they went away when so desired; so it was at the end of the Middle Ages when Henry VII found he could do without parliaments, and so it will remain until the Revolutionary Settlement of 1688."[85] He further points out that MPs were largely excluded from discussion of high politics, that, to use Stubbs's phrase, they did not have the "right of general deliberation on all national matters". In general terms, it might be said that important executive decisions were registered in the Commons rather than debated there. Moreover, when the King did seek advice on matters of policy from the leading county gentry, it might be outside Parliament. For example, in 1401 lords, prelates, and more than 200 knights and esquires were summoned to a great council to discuss the military threat to the kingdom.[86] More contentiously, Sayles claims that even the Crown's dependence on parliamentary taxation, on which in turn depended the capacity of the Commons to bargain with the Crown, diminished in the later 15th century as the Crown found sources of income more lucrative than the parliamentary grants of fifteenths and tenths, now limited in yield by outdated assessments. He concludes by dismissing the parliaments of the first part of Henry IV's reign, in which the Commons appears to have exercised considerable influence and demonstrated a precocious awareness of that prominent place in the constitution it was eventually to assume, as "no more than a curiosity of parliamentary history without any later significance".[87] While he undermines his own argument with the overstatement characteristic of his more polemical writings, there is much to support his view of the Commons. As we have seen, although they had won the right to consent to direct and indirect taxation in the 14th century, they did not have the right of free refusal, only the right to make a judgment on the King's plea of necessity. Even in the Good Parliament, their refusal to make a grant of direct taxation was balanced with the renewal of the wool subsidy and an affirmation of their readiness to aid the King in the event of necessity, and the Long Parliament of 1406 ended with their conceding, albeit reluctantly, a fifteenth and tenth and the renewal of the wool subsidy.[88] Moreover, as we have seen, ability to initiate and later to assent to new law placed a theoretical rather than a practical restraint on the Crown's freedom of legislative action. There can also be no doubt that the Crown developed effective methods of directing the deliberations of the lower house. One way was to call Parliament to assemble away from Westminster. A good example is the Parliament of 1447 summoned to Bury St Edmunds – where the influence of Henry VI's chief minister, William de la Pole, was strong – when the court party particularly needed a compliant assembly to secure the downfall of Humphrey, Duke of Gloucester; a further one is the Parliament held at Coventry in 1459. Another way was to encourage royal servants to find parliamentary seats for themselves. In the 14th century, relatively few MPs were royal officials or members of the Royal Household, but, in many parliaments of the 15th century, such men came to form a significant minority in the Commons. In 1447, for example, no fewer than 53 of the 272 MPs had places in the Royal Household.[89] This is not, of course, to say that the presence of such men ensured a compliant assembly – the strong opposition to the Crown in the Parliament of 1406 clearly shows that it did not[90] – but their presence provided the Crown with the opportunity to manage and direct its deliberations. This was particularly true during the reigns of Edward IV and Henry VII. For them, it was not simply the number of their own men who sat in the Commons, but the ability of the most senior of these men to manage the House. The increasing prominence of men of non-baronial rank, leading gentry servants of the Crown on the Royal Council, was of importance here. Such men had played a part in the Commons in earlier periods when the Council was not dominated by temporal and spiritual peers – most notably when Sir John Bussy acted as Speaker in the royalist Parliament of 1397-8 – but under Edward IV and more particularly Henry VII what had been an occasional expedient became a matter of policy. Indeed, so effective had the Crown's management techniques become at the end of our period that an historian of Edward IV's reign has attributed the apparent docility of the Commons not to any overt policy of cooperation, but to the Crown's skilful stewardship, and the same point could be made even more forcefully for the reign of Henry VII.[91]

Nevertheless, Sayles's view of relations of Crown and Commons must not be pushed so far as to deny the latter any freedom of action. The evolution of improved techniques of management by the Crown in the second half of the 15th century shows that even strong kings could not take the cooperation of the Commons for granted. Indeed, the fact that kings were then resorting to more refined methods in controlling the Commons than either Edward III or Henry V appear to have considered necessary is a sure indication of the growing political independence and assertiveness of local representatives. Although it is fair to conclude that a medieval king "got the kind of parliament he deserved", it is equally true that the Commons needed to be led rather than driven.[92] Nor can their opposition to Henry IV be dismissed as simply "a curiosity of parliamentary history". It may be that these parliaments were atypical in that Henry IV was readier to tolerate criticism than either his predecessors or successors, but this does not alter the fact that the Commons was simply acting in its well established role as the critic of perceived misgovernment. However much one may concur with Sayles's conclusion that the Crown had the reserves of power necessary to control the Commons, the fact remains that Parliament could be a place of confrontation between King and subjects. When the executive was weak, the Commons took upon itself the responsibility for correcting what members saw as royal misgovernment, as they did not only in 1406, but also in 1340, 1376, 1386, and 1450. Moreover, in discussing the question of their independence from Crown and Lords, MPs must not be isolated from their constituents. Their determination to secure statutory protection for the right of freedom of election and the comparatively broadly defined franchise of the famous statute of

1429-30 not only imply "a view of politics as a critical appraisal of government by all those whom it touched", but probably arose in part from pressure from a sector of society below that of the parliamentary knights of the shire.[93] Some of the most recent work on the 15th century has stressed the political literacy of this sub-gentry class; how, as Harriss has put it, "the reverberations of political debate extend beyond political society to the yeomen and artisans".[94] While this sector of society was largely disenfranchised, in that relatively few county elections were contested and many of its number fell below the 40 shilling franchise, this is not to say they were of no significance in the minds of their social superiors who sat in Parliament. Not surprisingly, given the nature of the sources, little evidence survives of the expectations constituents had of their elected representatives, but what does survive is of great interest. It suggests that if the Commons did not act independently of the King and Lords, MPs were perceived as failing their constituents. The clearest evidence is provided by the oft-quoted poem of *circa* 1400, *Mum and the Sothsegger*: "If we are false to those who provide for us, unworthy are we to earn our wages".[95] Although slender, also worth quoting is the evidence of a nascent political conscience on the part of the Commons. In his will of 1472, Nicholas Stathum instructed that a bribe of 10 shillings he had taken in the last Parliament should be restored to the donor not only because he had done "nothing therefor", but "for somoche as I was one of the parleament and shuld be indifferent in euery mater in the parleament".[96] Such sensibilities and independence of mind, allied to the fact that MPs brought with them to Parliament the expectations of an electorate that, as the period progressed, became increasingly diverse and sophisticated, must have restricted the scope for the exercise of influence from above.

It would, however, be wrong to end this essay by emphasising these moments of confrontation and by implying that it was only the active management of strong kings that kept this opposition in check. Arguments, such as those of Sayles, tailored to show that the medieval Commons was never sufficiently independent of the Crown to act as Stubbs's constitutional restraint on royal power, are apt to give the impression that Crown and Commons were in a constant state of potential conflict. This impression is reinforced by the understandable tendency of historians to emphasize the moments of crisis in their relations. Such an emphasis, however, can easily give rise to what Elton has dismissively described as "strange notions of kings calling parliaments which were designed to hamper their actions by opposing them".[97] It is thus important to give due weight to the uncontentious assemblies that were far more typical of medieval parliaments, and to see them as something more than the product of successful royal management of a naturally factious Commons. Parliament was, after all, designed to facilitate government; it was there "to do things that the King wanted done".[98] As Gillingham has remarked, "the powers of the Commons ... were ultimately based on their general willingness to cooperate with kings", and it was through consensus rather than conflict that they gained their power over taxation and legislation which were the basis of their future development.[99] For Elton, writing from the perspective of Tudor parliaments, "the vitality of the English Parliament is not to be measured by its willingness to oppose or its success in defeating the ambitions of kings, but by the degree to which it gathered all the interests – all the political nation – together to allow the conflict of interests to be resolved into positive action".[100]

With so many different perspectives on the medieval Commons reflecting their variant behaviour, from their apparent militancy in 1376 and 1406, to their readiness to act as the instruments of royal autocracy in 1397-8 and 1459, no conclusion about their place in the medieval polity is likely to meet with general acceptance. What, however, is not in dispute is that the period under review here was one of crucial significance in their institutional development. Before the beginning of our period, they had yet to establish their place in Parliament when the voice of the "community of the realm" was given expression by the Baronage; by the end of it, they had secured well defined rights in the fields of taxation and legislation and had been drawn into the circle of government. As Rawcliffe has justly concluded, the political influence of the Commons "being so dependent upon changing political circumstances, was never constant, but their impact upon judicial and financial affairs increased steadily throughout the 14th and 15th centuries".[101] But the story of the medieval Commons is not just that of an institution, it is that of a social class. The Commons has recently been described as "the mouthpiece ... of an emergent gentry", and it was in this period that the gentry became the separate and self-conscious class on which the Crown depended for the effective administration of the shires.[102] Just as the 14th century saw their political views expressed for the first time at the centre of government through their membership of the Commons, it also saw them establish a virtual monopoly of local administrative office. Particularly important here is the Crown's commitment of the main responsibility for the maintenance of local order to magistrates, the justices of the peace, drawn largely from the gentry. This owed much to the demands of the Commons and shows, better than any other single development, that the extension of royal government depended on the cooperation of the middling landholders of the counties. As Harriss has remarked, the "Crown's authority cannot be measured simply in terms of its ability to command and enforce, for it ruled through its capacity to invoke and mobilize the participation of the political elite".[103] The most important development of this period was the broadening of this elite beyond that small group of greater landholders whose claim to a share in executive authority was the context of much 13th century politics. This itself was a reflection of the expansion of government and the state. The power of the Commons is thus to be seen not only in terms of their rights in the fields of taxation and legislation, but also in the increasing participation of the gentry in government through their responsibility for local administration. Moreover, in the later part of our period, the gentry extended their parliamentary role by taking over the representation of the lesser boroughs.[104] This was the beginning of a long process, the chief significance of which lies outside the late medieval period, but already in the second quarter of the 15th century, the Commons contained many members who were not resident in the boroughs they represented. Greater competition between gentry for a parliamentary seat together with the government's determination to secure the return of its servants acted upon the willingness of the smaller boroughs to avoid the costs of representation to produce a Commons dominated not only socially but also numerically by the gentry. When added to the fact that a significant proportion of the gentry representatives of the boroughs were servants of the Crown, this is strongly suggestive of the central role the gentry and the Commons had come to play in national affairs by the end of our period.

Footnotes to this Chapter may be found on pages 196–201.

3: Jennifer Loach

The House of Commons, 1528-1603

THE FATE of the House of Commons under the Tudors has always attracted the attention of historians, who have traditionally seen the 16th century as the time when the lower house secured its place in the constitution. In this century, a great exponent of this view was the American historian, Wallace Notestein, who in his Raleigh Lecture for 1924, entitled *The Winning of the Initiative by the House of Commons,* argued that in the late 16th and early 17th century, the lower house became more important than the House of Lords. The Commons also, he suggested, grew immensely critical of the Crown, thus bringing about "one of the essential changes in the growth of the English constitution."[1] At much the same time, A F Pollard, in *The Evolution of Parliament,*[2] described "the strides" made by the Commons under the Tudors, and concluded that "but for that preparation under the Tudors there could have been no successful struggles under the Stuarts".

These assertions were subsequently given greater substance in the works of Sir John Neale. Neale, a pupil of Pollard, came to dominate the English historical scene in the 1950s and early 1960s, and his assertion that the 16th century, and especially the reign of Elizabeth, of which he made a particular study, had witnessed considerable, and highly significant, constitutional development, gained general credence. "At the opening of the 16th century," he wrote, "Parliament was essentially a legislative and taxing body, its meetings intermittent. Even at the end of the century, the same description might be formally applied to it; but, in the meanwhile, it had become a political force with which the Crown and government had to reckon. The change was brought about by developments in the power, position, and prestige of the House of Commons."[3]

Neale believed that the transformation in the Commons began under Henry VIII, and went further in the reign of Mary, when the development of what he saw as a principled, organized opposition to the restoration of Roman Catholicism marked a stage in the Commons' "apprenticeship to future greatness".[4] Under Elizabeth, the "militantly Protestant" House of Commons emerged triumphant: much less subservient to the Crown, and much less respectful of the House of Lords.

Notestein and Neale, and their very considerable number of pupils on both sides of the Atlantic, went on to suggest that in the 16th century, the House of Commons became more representative and more responsible.[5] While elections and the relationship between Members and their constituencies clearly were very different even at the end of the 16th century from those that subsequently evolved, the lower house, they argued, was becoming responsive to the anxieties and aspirations of those who had returned them.

As the Members of the Commons became more politically sophisticated, they also became more anxious to promote their own interests and those of the people they represented, even if by so doing they came into conflict with the Crown. The Lords, meanwhile, "stood in the wings and made their rare appearances as a body – rather like the chorus in *Iolanthe*."[6]

However, while united in their estimate of the significance of the 16th century for the development of the House of Commons, these historians did not always agree about the reasons for the change. Was it, as Pollard and Neale had suggested, an almost inevitable consequence of the break with Rome and the establishment of the Church of England, a process carried out by statute? Did the subsequent flooding in of puritan-minded gentlemen necessarily increase the weight and authority of the lower house, and bring about the development of a principled opposition? Or was the fact that the lower house was increasingly dominated by landed gentlemen, far more socially and politically confident than the timid burgesses of Middle Ages, more decisive? Or perhaps the explanation was to be found in the superior educational accomplishments of late 16th century Members: by 1601, almost half of the House was university-educated, and more than a half had been admitted to an inn of court.

Before these questions could be finally decided, a generation of young historians came along, who wished, as young historians so often do, to turn them on their head. Perhaps, they argued, there was no need to explain why these changes had occurred, since it was obvious to them that the House of Commons at the end of the 16th century – and, indeed, well into the 17th century – was an insignificant part of the political and constitutional scene. Far from having "won the initiative", as Notestein had suggested, the Commons, they argued, remained subservient to the Crown and its ministers, anxious at all costs to avoid confrontation.

In justification of their position, the "revisionists", as they came to be called, pointed to the comparative ease with which Tudor – and, indeed, early Stuart – monarchs obtained grants of taxation. This is surprising, since the burden of taxation was sometimes, as in the 1540s and the 1590s, very heavy. Moreover, Tudor monarchs were asking for parliamentary taxation with greater and greater frequency: in the 16 parliaments between the battle of Bosworth in 1485 and the accession of Edward VI in 1547, there were four in which no grant of taxation was made, and three others in which no grant was made during the first session.[7] But things were very different under Elizabeth. Elizabeth was the first of the Tudors to ask for taxation in the first parliamentary session of a reign, and only one of her parliaments, that of 1572, was to pass without any grant of taxation being made.[8] Finally, although Tudor monarchs increasingly ignored the medieval convention that taxation was only asked for in time of war, their requests were never turned down, and rarely, after the debacle with Wolsey in 1523, even reduced. Most Members seem to have concurred with the view expressed by Francis Bacon in 1597 that "the treasure that cometh from you to her Majesty is but a vapour which riseth from the earth and gathereth into a cloud and stayeth not there long, but upon the same earth it falleth again."[9]

The revisionists partly explained such easy concurrence by pointing to the government's adroit handling of the Commons during this period. The Speaker, for example, remained a royal nominee, paid by the Crown. Since he had the right to choose not only who spoke in debates, but also the order in which bills were discussed, and the moment at which a vote was taken, he possessed considerable power, and that power was usually used for the benefit of the Crown. Moreover, the fact that from the reign of Henry VIII royal councillors and ministers were elected to the Commons if they did not have seats in the Lords strengthened the links between the Speaker and the Crown, for councillors were placed in the House next to the Speaker's chair, and "whispered" advice to him. Thus, the sessions in which there were fewer councillors than normal in the Commons – 1555, for instance, or the first session of James I's reign – were also sessions in which the Crown found it particularly difficult to get its will done.

Nonetheless, the revisionists saw the real explanation for the docility of the lower house in the Members' inherent desire to avoid confrontation with the Crown. After all, for much of the first half of the 16th century, Englishmen still worried about, and desperately sought to avoid, those internal struggles that we call the Wars of the Roses, and for much of the second half they prided themselves on avoiding the dissensions that tore apart their European neighbours. Peace and tranquillity were therefore all important, and the Tudors, who had saved England from internal warfare, had to be supported almost irrespective of the cost.

Clear evidence of this desire to avoid confrontation emerged in the course of the monopolies debates of 1597 and 1601, that is, in the last two parliaments of Elizabeth's reign. By 1597, monopolies had become a serious grievance, about which the Commons expressed much eloquent dissatisfaction. Elizabeth, whose prerogative right it was to grant monopolies, was able to defuse the situation only by a promise of reform. But she was too financially dependent on monopolies as a means of rewarding her courtiers and servants – see, for example, the monopoly right to import sweet wines which she granted to her favourite, the Earl of Essex – to undertake thorough-going reform, and the Commons of 1601 complained yet more bitterly. There were now even demands that reform should be accomplished by means of statute, which would have involved constitutional innovation, since the assumption always had been that the prerogative could not be "invaded" by statute. Again Elizabeth thanked her loyal Commons for drawing to her attention abuses about which she was ignorant, and again she promised reform. Again, and despite its experience of how little that promise meant, the House allowed itself to be fobbed off, and shied away from constitutional change.[10] It was not until 1624 that an Act of Monopolies was passed, an act that has been described as "the first statutory invasion of the prerogative".

The arguments of the revisionists have, in the main, prevailed. Most historians would now accept that the House of Commons in the 16th century believed in consensus and agreement, and was not especially interested in winning the initiative from anyone. Despite occasional spats between Crown and Commons, such as the conflict of 1555 over a bill that would have allowed Mary to confiscate the property of those who left the kingdom for religious reasons, or the very bitter disputes in the early years of Elizabeth's reign about the Queen's refusal to give a firm promise that she would marry and settle the succession, the prevailing mood was amicable: in general, the Commons seems to have seen its relationship with the Crown and the Crown's ministers very much as a meeting of shareholders sees itself in relation to the chairman and board of a company – devoted to the same purposes (in this case, peace and prosperity), but occasionally disagreeing about how best to achieve them.

But if the House of Commons did not "grow to adulthood" or "win the initiative" from the Crown or the Lords in the course of the 16th century, it did experience two immensely important changes, both of which are indisputable, and, in a sense, permanent. One is a change in the Commons' meeting place, the other a change in the size of its membership.

One of the most remarkable features of the House of Commons in the 16th century was its growth in size. The lower house, which consisted of the knights of the shire and the burgesses from the enfranchised boroughs, contained only 296 members in 1504. By the beginning of Elizabeth's reign that number had risen to 400, and by her death it was 462.

During earlier centuries, the membership of the House of Commons had fluctuated considerably: 302 men had been summoned to the Parliament of 1295, for example, but by the early 15th century, numbers had fallen back to about 250. The attitude of monarchs, whose prerogative it was to enfranchise boroughs, to the creation of new seats had also fluctuated.[11] For example, although early in his reign Edward IV had created five new parliamentary boroughs, none seems to have been added after the early 1470s. Henry VII probably added only one extra seat – at Much Wenlock, which had previously been a single-member constituency. Only with Henry VIII did a consistent policy of enlargement begin. Thus Henry considerably reduced the size of the House of Lords by the abolition of the abbots and priors who had sat there, and added 45 new seats to the Commons, 31 of them through the enfranchisement of Wales and Cheshire. Edward added 34, Mary 25, and Elizabeth 62. James I was to continue this process, creating new seats such as those for the Universities of Oxford and Cambridge, and "restoring" numerous others.[12] Why?

Although 16th century England witnessed considerable population growth – indeed, the number of inhabitants came near to doubling – the increased size of the lower house was in no way a response to this growth. There was at this time no belief that regions that were increasing in size had any particular claim to representation. Some of the boroughs enfranchised on the whim of earlier monarchs were by the 16th century more or less nonexistent, like Gatton, in Surrey, with an electorate of one, or Old Sarum, a deserted village, and few of the boroughs newly enfranchised in the 16th century were economically or socially advancing. At the time of Liverpool's enfranchisement late in Henry VIII's reign, for example, the town was described as decayed and isolated. Some of the boroughs newly enfranchised in Elizabeth's reign were also, like Grampound, decayed, and some, such as the Isle of Wight constituencies and Andover, were truly "rotten".

What was represented in the House of Commons until, and beyond, the 19th century reform acts, was not people but property. Thus, those who were eligible to vote had to fulfil some property qualification: in the counties they had to have an income from freehold land of at least 40 shillings a year, and in the towns they had to be ratepayers, or possess a "hearth". Enfranchisement could always be justified in terms of land, even if it could not be justified by population size or prosperity, giving the monarch a totally free hand. Under Elizabeth, this was to result in a substantial increase in the number of enfranchised boroughs in Devon and Cornwall, counties with small and even shrinking populations; moreover, these enfranchisements included a number of stannary towns, despite the decay of their only industry, tin mining. Meanwhile, prosperous and expanding areas of the midlands and the north remained under-represented – Durham, for example, despite some discussion in 1563, was to remain without representation until 1673.

The Crown was not, then, looking at economic and social factors when deciding upon new enfranchisements. Enfranchisements were the result of royal whim and royal policy alone. Thus, one reason for the growth in the size of the House of Commons in the first half of the 16th century was a government drive towards further unification of the realm. Berwick, for instance, restored to the English in 1482, was enfranchised early in Henry VIII's reign. Tournai, which surrendered to the English in 1513, sent representatives to the parliamentary session of 1514, and probably also in 1515, before being returned to the French in 1519[13] Calais also returned Members between 1536 and the French recovery of the town in 1558. Not surprisingly, therefore, the Earl of Hertford, the future Protector Somerset, assumed in 1541, perhaps as an analogy with Calais, that Jersey, of which he was at that time captain, had the right to return two members of the Parliament summoned for 1542[14]

After the English county system was extended to Wales and Monmouthshire in 1536, the Welsh counties were given the right to return one knight each (unlike the English counties and Monmouthshire, which each elected two), and the enfranchised boroughs in those areas were authorized to return a single burgess each. After a petition in the Parliament of 1542, Cheshire and Chester were also each permitted to return two members.[15] Here, then, as with the overseas possessions, was a coherent policy of extending representation to the regions as they were more firmly secured under the thumb of Westminster.

Behind other new enfranchisements perhaps lay a feeling that areas losing some other form of representation should be compensated with the right to return Members to Parliament. Thus, the loss of an abbot or prior with a seat in the House of Lords may have been of importance in the decision to enfranchise Abingdon, Peterborough, and St Albans and, in particular, Westminster, which first returned members in 1545. Similarly, the decision to grant representation to Chester seems to have been a consequence of the abolition of the inhabitants' right to prevent the imposition of laws and taxes agreed in Parliament by withholding their consent at the county court.[16] The complaints of the Pilgrimage of Grace in 1536 and 1537, and, in particular, the rebels' demand that a parliament should be held at York, elicited from Henry VIII a suggestion that some new boroughs might be enfranchised such as Pontefract (where the rebels' articles were drawn up), Richmond, and Beverley – although the king prudently made his offer conditional on an agreement by the inhabitants of those boroughs that they would find the money for their representatives' wages and expenses; nothing came of this proposal at the time, but Beverley and Richmond were to be enfranchised in Elizabeth's reign, and Pontefract in James'.[17]

This extension of representation was surely a consequence of the royal desire to extend the scope of taxation. Thus, from the passing of what is sometimes called "the second act of union" in 1542, Wales dropped from the list of areas exempted from the payment of subsidies and fifteenths and tenths. Some minor concessions were, it is true, made during the reigns of Edward VI and Mary, but from 1576 onwards, "in the most palpable manner imaginable, through their pockets, the inhabitants of Wales joined the realm of England".[18] The cry of "no taxation without representation" carries with it a corollary, it should be remembered, that representation may well involve taxation.

What considerations, besides a desire to unify their realm, led Tudor rulers to increase the number of enfranchised boroughs? One obvious possibility is that the Crown was "packing" the House, that is, filling it up with royal nominees. However, this suggestion does not stand up to close scrutiny: after all, several of the newly-created constituencies were permitted to return only one representative. The Welsh constituencies were, as we have seen, all single-member, probably "to prevent the Commons from being swamped by the arrival of a group of Members whose potential influence was disproportionate to the political, social, and economic importance of the region which they represented",[19] and Mary later gave Banbury, Higham Ferrers, and Abingdon the right to return one member only, although Aylesbury, enfranchised at the same time, was, for no obvious reason, empowered to return two members. The creation of single-member constituencies would have been unbelievably foolish if what the Tudors were primarily concerned about was packing.

But although the Tudors never went in for systematic packing, they undoubtedly did have a need – and a growing need – for seats into which they could put useful men: councillors, civil servants, and courtiers. Monarchs always used the seats over which they had influence for such men. Thus, the duchy of Lancaster borough of Preston, for example, produced seats for noted Crown servants such as Sir Ralph Sadler, John Hales, and, in Elizabeth's reign, for William Fleetwood's son and for Thomas Cromwell. Another duchy town, Lancaster itself, provided a seat for Fleetwood in 1559 and 1563.[20]

The more seats the Crown had for such men, the better. Not surprisingly, therefore, the seats newly created in the 16th century were often in areas of Crown influence, where the monarch effectively had the nomination of the member. Many of the freshly enfranchised boroughs were in areas under the sway of the Council of the North, like Thirsk, or that of the duchy of Cornwall, like Camelford, or were stannary towns. Sometimes the enfranchised boroughs were on manors in royal possession, such as Banbury. Above all, the new enfranchisements were duchy of Lancaster boroughs such as Thetford, Liverpool, Wigan, Ripon, Higham Ferrers, Stockbridge, and Sudbury.

These boroughs were controlled by the chancellor of the duchy, and could therefore easily be persuaded to find seats for useful and experienced Crown servants. Thus, the duchy of Lancaster borough of Knaresborough, first enfranchised in 1553, provided a seat for the civil servant and diplomat, Sir Thomas Chaloner, as well as a number of duchy officials; the secretary of state for the Netherlands, William Davison, was returned for the borough in 1586. Fowey, a stannary town that first returned in 1571, chose an exchequer official and Thomas Cromwell in 1571, sending in blank returns the next year. Grampound, a duchy of Cornwall borough, first returning members under Edward VI, frequently sent in blank returns, as did another duchy borough, East Looe, which began returning in 1571.

The Crown's own interests, then, in some part explain the 16th century increase in the size of the House of Commons. But if the Crown needed to provide seats for its own servants, it was also constantly being asked by other influential persons – noblemen, courtiers, and royal ministers – for seats for their followers. Any local potentate worth his salt would, at this period, have some parliamentary patronage, and the mighty – holding influential offices such as that of lord lieutenant in a county, or high steward in a borough – had a great deal. Thus the Howard Dukes of Norfolk owned the Sussex boroughs of Bramber, Horsham, and New Shoreham, where they nominated almost all the borough representatives. They could also usually nominate at King's Lynn and Great Yarmouth.[21] The three Elizabethan Earls of Pembroke totally controlled the boroughs of Wilton and Old Sarum, and were usually able to put a secretary or a treasurer in at Shaftesbury.[22] Even a small country gentleman might have one or two seats at his disposal, as Sir Thomas Copley had at Gatton.

If such men needed more seats into which to put their clients, they asked the monarch for further enfranchisements, and the monarch usually agreed. Of course, monarchs did sometimes refuse these requests, as Elizabeth did in 1579, when we find Thomas Wilson telling the Earl of Rutland about a charter for the town of Newark, to which the Queen had agreed in all parts, "save the nomination of two burgesses ... [Since] it is thought that there are over many already",[23] but rejection seems to have been rare. As Sir John Neale put it: "The monarch was obviously a mere agent, yielding to pressure for more seats ... If it was his prerogative to dispense privileges, it was also his function; and with Court life exquisitely organized for powerful begging, the most alert and well-willed of monarchs had often to yield...".[24] It has been suggested that as many as half of the new Elizabethan boroughs received their franchises in this way, through the offices of peers.[25] While some historians of the Commons, and Neale in particular, have been perhaps too eager to see evidence for such initiatives,[26] clear instances of magnate pressure for enfranchisement do exist, and others may be assumed with fair certainty. Thus, it was surely the Duke of Norfolk who persuaded Mary to enfranchise Castle Rising in 1558, and the Earl of Rutland who secured the enfranchisement of East Retford in 1571. There is firm evidence that Elizabeth's cousin, Sir George Carey, was responsible for the enfranchisement in 1584 of three boroughs on the Isle of Wight, of which he was then captain. (He then put his clients into these seats, demanding that the boroughs send him blank returns for the purpose.)[27]

What did magnates gain by placing their clients into parliamentary constituencies? They did not, it would seem, in general use their patronage "to promote a personal interest group or faction", but rather "to secure the selection of men whom [they] thought ought to be present in the lower house".[28] They seem to have seen their ability to nominate to a parliamentary seat largely in terms of honour and prestige, expecting in return merely expressions of "service" and loyalty. Only very occasionally, and in the most extreme of circumstances, did magnates think of using their influence in a factional manner. Cardinal Wolsey, it was thought by contemporaries, might have done so in the Reformation Parliament, had he lived, and Thomas Seymour, Lord Seymour of Sudeley, certainly planned to do so in Edward's reign. There are hints of such a situation in the 1590s with the bitter rivalry between the Earl of Essex and Robert Cecil.[29] But, in general, magnates seem to have regarded the placing of their clients in the Commons as an end in itself – it was something that enhanced their reputation, but not something from which they expected to derive personal advantage.

However, even if we can explain the increased number of seats by the exigencies of royal and aristocratic patrons, we are still left with a problem; why did clients ask their patrons to find them seats in the Commons? In earlier times, it had often been difficult to persuade men to sit in the Commons, and especially difficult to persuade them to fill the less prestigious borough seats. However, in the 16th century, boroughs that were, by statute, required to return resident townsmen came to be represented by gentlemen, and nonresident gentlemen at that. While some towns, such as Cambridge and Bristol, persisted during the 16th century in returning true townsmen, and many boroughs did so occasionally, the general trend was towards representation by gentlemen and by outsiders. In most of Elizabeth's parliaments, one third of borough members were in fact country gentlemen, and another quarter to a third government officials or lawyers. Only a small proportion of Elizabeth's House of Commons were true townsmen: 24% of the burgesses of 1559, 19% of those of 1571, and 14% of those of 1601.[30]

Why did 16th century gentlemen so much want a seat in the Commons that they were prepared to accept even a borough seat, so much less prestigious than that of the knight of the shire, or to ask their patrons to secure a new enfranchisement for them? One explanation lies in the increasing range and scope of legislation in the 16th century, when statute came not only to shape the Church, but also to deal with many social and economic problems, such as poverty and prices. By the reign of Elizabeth, it was statute that determined the meaning of, for example, "murder, bankruptcy, perjury, charity, usury, poor relief, and rape".[31]

However, the reasons of these 16th century gentlemen were not entirely political. Although gentlemen wanted seats,they were curiously unenthusiastic about attendance once they had been elected. In theory, no member should have absented himself without securing a licence from the Speaker, a licence usually given for reasons such as family illness or death, or Crown service. However, whenever a "call", that is, a count, of the House was taken, the number of absentees without licence was found to be large. No figures were then recorded, however: the figures that are extant are known only when a counted vote, or division, took place. In the early years of Elizabeth's reign only 276 of the 400-plus members who had been returned were ever present at a division: in the controversial Parliament of 1601, less than half the House was ever present at a division, and in one vote the number fell to 80.[32] Division figures are likely to give an inflated impression of the attendance, since it is probable that more members than usual came when some controversial issue was being discussed, so that the figures that we have may reflect an uncharacteristically large attendance. The norm was probably much lower.

So why were gentlemen so anxious to find a seat, if they then occupied it only rarely? A seat in the Commons carried with it certain privileges, and these may have been of great interest to some. Members of Parliament enjoyed the privilege of freedom from arrest, for instance, and some members clearly sought election to order to secure this privilege. In 1571, the Queen's circular letter to sheriffs before the elections warned that "many in late parliaments,

Her Majesty thinketh, have been named [that is, elected] for private respects and favour upon their own suits [or] to enjoy some immunity upon arrests upon actions during the time of parliaments". Despite this warning, the poet George Gascoigne, who was said to have "lurked at villages" until he was elected as Member for Midhurst, afterwards openly showed his face "in despite of all his creditors". In 1593, the Lord Keeper again advised members to be certain that "the protection of your House be not worn by any man for a cloak to defraud others of their debts and duties": he may have been prompted by the attempted arrest for debts of £5,500 of one of the Members for Newcastle under Lyme.[33]

However, it would be unduly cynical to suggest that the 16th century House of Commons was simply a sanctuary for debtors and criminals. What was probably more important was the growth of London as a centre of conspicuous consumption, and the development of the London season, which brought more and more nobles and gentlemen to the capital for the winter months. If one was in London anyway, then it made sense to belong to the Commons, to have, as it were, a club in which to meet one's friends. Doting fathers seem, indeed, to have regarded the Commons as a means of giving their sons a little polish. Thus, one father wrote in 1597 that "as my son is as it were entering into the world and to those years that may fit his country's service ... I am minded to advise him to stand to be knight of the shire for Surrey against the next Parliament".[34] County families, therefore, tried to share out the advantages of a spell in Parliament among them. As the second Earl of Pembroke wrote in 1572: "I would have all gentlemen to have their due reserved unto them, which is, from time to time, as parliaments fall out, to be chosen; now some, and then some, as they are fit; to the end they may be [experienced] in the affairs and state of their country."[35] Thus, we should set the 16th century expansion of the Commons primarily in a social, rather than a political, legal or constitutional framework: the Commons grew because the charms of London and the Court became at this point so attractive.

Other significant changes in the nature of the Commons in the 16th century occurred as the result of a change in its meeting place. In earlier times, the Commons had met in either the chapter house or the refectory of Westminster Abbey. These were places of beauty, but, as we shall see, not necessarily suitable for such gatherings. In the reign of Edward VI, after the dissolution of the chantries, the House of Commons acquired St Stephen's chapel for its meeting place. The layout of that building profoundly altered Commons' procedure. The refectory at Westminster Abbey was a long, narrow room, with a fixed high table at one end. Whether the other tables normally used by the monastic community stayed in place around the walls during parliamentary sessions is unclear, but the fact that in 1489 the monks prudently removed the mats that normally covered the stone cloister walks and placed them in their dormitory for safe keeping, no doubt on the assumption that "the boots of heavy-footed knights and burgesses" would destroy them, perhaps implies that little of value was left around during a parliamentary session.[36]

It therefore seems probable that most members had to stand during debates. However, the chapel, when fully converted for the Commons' use, allowed many members – but not, as we shall see, all – to sit.

St Stephen's chapel, to the south and east of Westminster Hall, the site of the Lords' meetings, had been built by Edward III, on the site of King Stephen's earlier foundation.[37] Most of the chantry's considerable lands and endowments were on 22 July 1550 granted to a prominent courtier, Sir Ralph Vane, with the exception of the upper part of the vault of the chapel which was retained "pro domo parliamenti et pro parliamentis nostris ibidem tenendis".[38] Quite when the Commons took possession of their new home is unclear, although a warrant for payment of "workes aboute the Parliament House" of 2 December 1549 may imply that it was being used for the session that began in early November that year.[39] By the time John Hooker wrote his account of Parliament in the early 1570s, the Commons' meeting house was "more of length than of breadth", made "like a Theater, having foure rowes of seates one aboove an other round about the same".[40] At "the higher end in the middle of ye lower rowe" was the Speaker's chair, with a table in front of it for the under-clerk of the Parliament, usually known as the Clerk of the Commons. Round about the Speaker, as we have learnt, sat the privy councillors, and the representatives from London and York sat on his right, but no one else had a seat by prescriptive right.

The layout of the chapel was crucial to the development of procedure in the Commons. Firstly, debates became lengthier and lengthier. No longer worried about their aching feet, Members took to more and more elaborate forms of discourse. Session after session, Speakers urged the Commons "to spend little time on motions, and to avoid long speeches", but to no avail. As Members were also becoming better educated, so their desire to show off their classical learning in speeches full of elaborate metaphors and references to obscure texts triumphed over the government's wish to speed business through. Secondly, the chapel contained an ante-chamber next to the meeting-room, in which the clerks and various suitors to the Commons normally sat. The existence of this room was to bring about a great change in the way in which the House voted. At the beginning of the 16th century voting in the House, like voting at elections, was by acclamation: members shouted either "yea" or "no", and the Speaker decided which response was the louder. Only if he could not decide, or his decision was challenged, would there be a counted vote. The counted vote seems to have been taken originally within the chamber itself, but with the acquisition of the ante-chamber a procedure developed whereby the party in favour of a bill went into the ante-chamber, being counted as it returned.[41] Hence, the development of the division.

However, St Stephen's chapel was not big enough to accommodate the rising numbers in the Commons: had all members turned up, many would have needed to stand. This shortage of seats seems to have made some Members reluctant to move in a division for fear of losing their places. In 1601, one

Member noted: "I have observed it that ever this Parliament, the noes upon division of the House have carried it. The reason whereof, as I conceive it, is because divers are loth to go forth for losing of their places. And many that cry 'aye, aye, aye' will sit still with the Noes."[42] His statement was backed up by the Comptroller of the Household, who agreed that he had heard "fault found before this time" with Members who were reluctant to leave their places. Thus, the growth in the membership of the House of Commons, and the consequent pressure of space, seems to have led to the loss of some controversial measures.

Finally, it may well be because the Commons now had a permanent place for its meetings, with accommodation for clerks and other staff, that contributed to the increased formality of procedure in the lower house, and to the improvement in record keeping epitomized by the Journal, which was maintained continuously from 1547. While the House of Commons may not have "won the initiative" from the Lords in the 16th century, it certainly came to emulate the upper chamber in its methods of handling business. Commons procedure, therefore, became more formal, with the number of readings given to a bill stabilizing at three, and the establishment of committees to scrutinize draft legislation became commonplace.

Nonetheless, despite such changes, the House of Commons in the 16th century never became as efficient as the House of Lords. In the first half of Elizabeth's reign, for example, four-fifths of the bills originating in the Commons failed, and one-third of those in the Lords. In the latter part of her reign, 70% of bills initiated in the Commons failed, and only one half of those beginning in the Lords.[43] Of course, the Lords had less business to do than the Commons, and they had, in the judges, better legal assistance, but they were also better behaved. The lower house in the 16th century, like the lower house revealed today by the television cameras, was extremely rowdy. Members coughed, whistled, and spat, they would not yield to each other if two stood up at the same time, and they – and their servants – were very ready to punch each other in the face. Members were not good at listening to each other, and they were ready to show their disapproval of long or boring speeches. In 1572, for example, Arthur Hall was treated to such "shuffling of feet and hawking" that he could not be heard. At Mr Hele's speech on the subsidy in 1601, the House "hemmed and laughed and talked". The Speaker produced a stern rebuke, declaring that "it is the ancient use of every man to be silent when anyone speaketh", but when Hele went on to cite a large number of historical precedents more "hemming" broke out.[44] Later in the same Parliament, an aged doctor of civil law made what was obviously a very long and boring speech, and the House "hawk'd and spat'. As one government minister remarked sternly, "this is [behaviour] more fit for a grammar school than for a court of Parliament".[45]

Here, then, we have a House which in its procedure and its physical setting closely resembles that so familiar to us today. Nonetheless, the House of

Commons of the 16th century was, in fact, vastly different from its successors: the main concerns of its members were local and personal rather than political, and neither electors nor Members saw it as a major forum for political or social or religious change.

Footnotes to this Chapter may be found on page 201–3.

4: Kevin Sharpe

James I, Civil War, and Restoration 1603-1660

WHEN WE look at an object what we see is conditioned by a number of factors: the distance at which we stand (or crouch), the angle from which we view, the nature of our eyesight in the biological sense; what we might call our "cultural vision" (what we have been trained to see). And we might add to such a list a wide variety of possible technical aids, from the simple telescope, to 3D, X-ray, and the infra-red lens. In the cultural and technological senses, what we see is a product of history and change, and in turn what we see reshapes history. To take a 17th century case, the first audiences at Inigo Jones' new perspective stage in Jacobean Whitehall, untrained in its mathematical principles, were confused about what was going on. Before long, however, the perspective stage was the normal arena of theatrical production. Moreover, by placing the King and courtly spectators according to the lines of perspective, the new way of seeing reinforced the position of the monarch and the lines of authority among the audience as well as actors, so connecting a privileged vision to a vision of privilege and status.[1] Similarly, the invention of X-ray, infra-red, and ultra violet have affected our sense of reality as well as vision, providing the possibility and stimulating the language of looking *through* as well as *at*. Computer graphics take us still further into the possibilities of constructions and simulations in three dimensions of what is "observed" only on two planes, apparently enabling the observer to view an object from a number of positions simultaneously.

All of this is obvious enough to a contemporary photographer or an historian of the image. But it has been curiously lacking in much recent work of the historians of 17th century parliaments who nevertheless have written, revealingly, of placing parliaments in "perspective" rather than in *a* perspective.[2] The significant omission of the indefinite article, I would like to suggest, has led to the generation of more heat than light and ultimately left the subject still in the dark.[3]

In the last 20 years, the most heated debates among English historians of any period have been about 17th century parliaments: their "nature", their power and importance, their role in the origins of the English Civil War, their place in the larger story of English history, and, beyond, their contribution to the history of freedom in the West. In part, those discussions have been prompted, as new historical interpretations and debates often are, by the discovery or availability of new evidence: the papers of individual MPs and elections in local archives, the use of manuscript versions of the Commons and Lords Journals rather than the hotch-potch compilations of 18th century editors; most of all the listing and printing of numerous private diaries for almost all the early Stuart sessions, published by the Yale Center for Parliamentary History. Rather than settling disagreements, as some might expect, the profusion of new evidence has sharpened scholarly disputes. This is not only because all the evidence can be viewed from a number of angles, but also because the search for evidence, certainly the type of evidence given greatest weight, has also been determined by historians' angle of vision.[4] Enamoured of the "big story" of English liberties, J H Hexter and T K Rabb have little patience with the sources dominated by daily minutiae or localist preoccupations; viewing Parliament as an organ of business rather than debate, Sir Geoffrey Elton is more concerned with the clerk's notes than the diarists' self-promoting rhetoric; suspicious of printed matter on principle and of *post hoc* perspectives in general, Conrad Russell spurns the contemporary broadsheets and the later narratives which polemically constructed and distributed the perceptions, fears, and hopes of a number of early Stuart actors and their heirs.[5] Observing (as any historian must) from a particular standpoint and preferring some types of evidence over others, each scholar has studied 17th century parliaments from and in *a* perspective. It may be time to see whether, rather than simply selecting one photograph and renouncing the rest, we cannot examine the shots taken by different lenses from different angles: to see whether some composite picture might be constructed which draws upon them all. Though any such arrangement, collage, or computer model must itself be a personal design, it at least compels an incorporation of "perspectives" and dispels the illusion of any authoritative *one* perspective.

Let us start with the photograph taken with the wide-angle lens, more usually referred to as the Whig interpretation of the 17th century. This is a picture of the past taken with the viewfinder framing the 17th century and the Victorian House of Commons. Its most famous photographer was Thomas Babington Macaulay, an historian, MP, and Secretary for War in Lord Melbourne's government.[6] It offers a panorama of English history intended to explain the origins of the Victorian constitution to which, in the words of Samuel Rawson Gardiner, "every step was constantly tending".[7] The author of the massive and learned 10-volume history of England from the accession of James I to the outbreak of the Civil War, Gardiner's name should be a sufficient reminder that, *pace* some revisionists, the Whig view of the past need not eschew detail. Indeed, within the parameters of his subject, Gardiner worked chronologically, so that his account was written as he proceeded from strictly contemporary rather than later documentation – rather as revisionists have attempted to do. But for all his fine, often unsurpassed, miniatures, Gardiner's vision of history, like Macaulay's, was focused on a large picture that was determined by the stance of his own age and intended to explain to him its constitutional triumphs.[8] The wide-angle lens was deployed not only by the Whigs. From the 19th century, Marxist historians offered an alternative panorama of the past, with the viewfinder not primarily focused on the constitution, but ranging over the landscape from feudal institutions to the triumph of the proletariat. In the case of English history, where too many objects failed to fit, the photograph required some elaborate touch ups in the studio, which successions of Marxists have continued to refine.[9] While the Victorian constitution is undoubtedly identifiable, whatever significance we may give to it, the triumph of the proletariat has had to be "painted in" on the negative of English history and the studio has never succeeded in masking the artifice of its production or selling it as a natural image of the past. Finally, more familiar with the wide open spaces, several American historians have fitted a wider angle lens still. To Professor Wallace Notestein, the big picture of English history opened onto a larger picture still. If the English past showed how human beings had learned to govern themselves, the panorama of history embraced the spread of that lesson to America whose Manifest historical Destiny it had been and was to preserve and disseminate that lesson in self-government.[10] It has taken only refinements of Notestein's technology to enable Professor J H Hexter to get into his frame this history of freedom and its establishment and advancement throughout the Anglophone world.[11]

In some of these photographs, as critics have complained, the wide-angle has reduced the 17th century House of Commons to an indistinct blur. But in each case, though indistinct in detail, early Stuart parliaments are central to the large composition, and derive importance from it. To the Whigs, the Stuart Commons was the arena in which English subjects fought to preserve their liberties and properties against absolutist monarchs, and the Civil War and 1688 Revolution the occasions of their decisive victories in that struggle. For the Marxist historian of England, the English revolution represents the overthrow of a feudal monarchy and aristocracy by a rising bourgeois class of trade and capital, and the emergence of radical Levellers and Diggers, the brief dawn of a truly proletarian revolution that was (inconveniently for the Marxist model) aborted. The early 17th century, too, witnessed for Notestein, Hexter, and others the emigration from old to new England which exported the institutions and values of parliamentary government and liberties to the wider world. In each case, younger generations have criticized the technique, composition, and vision of these historical pictures. Against the Whig picture it is argued that early Stuart MPs were not seeking parliamentary government, nor did they secure it: no Parliament was in session in 1688 when a Whig coup brought William III to the Throne. The Marxist picture is rejected on the grounds that the Civil War was not a bourgeois revolution, but an aristocratic rebellion whose outcome saw no permanent social revolution. After 1660, the English state remained an *ancien régime* run by an aristocratic oligarchy of land and birth.[12] As for the Americans' manifest destiny and the history of freedom, the English revisionists have been quick to deride pictures which seem obviously drawn by contemporary ideological perspectives, and focus little on the meaning of "liberties" and indeed "parliaments" to those who spoke of them in the 17th century House of Commons. At the core of all the criticisms are charges of anachronism, teleology or, to return to our metaphor, distortion in the Whig/Marxist wide-angle pictures which reveal so little of the details of 17th century parliaments that we are unable to see what they were, or how they worked.[13] While this is undoubtedly true, such criticisms may amount to disliking a mural done in broad strokes because it is not a miniature of filigree delicacy. The panoramic photo of the Grand Canyon may lose the detail of rock-formation shown by the close-up, but it remains *a* picture which represents what we see when we look up and around. If some historians in the 19th and early 20th centuries could see the 17th century in a clear sweep of the camera that panned to their own time, there is importance and validity enough in that. If by the late 17th century we find men, some of whose experiences and memories went back decades, already sketching that picture, already seeing themselves in that perspective, we must keep it on our table, as a perspective we cannot lose sight of.[14]

For the moment, however, we turn to its opposite: the close-up photograph. It was Sir Geoffrey Elton who first asked historians to focus on 17th century parliaments rather than sweep across or over them, and John Kenyon who began to show how differently they would appear viewed through a lens that spanned only their own century – or half century before 1642.[15] During the 1970s, a new generation of scholars set out with their cameras and a kit bag, from which the wide-angle was banned, to take a number of new shots of the early Stuart parliamentary scene. All were engaged in close-up work. One focused on one MP, another on an election, yet another on the passage of a bill, or some weeks of a parliamentary session. With more ambition and experience, Conrad Russell set out to re-photograph each of the parliaments of the 1620s and, in consequence, to reorientate our vision of them all.[16] With reels of film devoted to the details of what had been a point on a larger panorama, the historical picture of parliaments was radically transformed – often beyond recognition. Indeed, the detailed close-up at times revealed the opposite of the hazier wide angle. Where the Whigs saw the Commons forging their way to power at the expense of the Crown, Russell found MPs uninterested in taking the reins of government and reluctant to oppose the monarch, or to use their control of subsidies to get their way. Where the Whigs panned their camcorder to present a continuous narrative of parliaments growing from childhood to confident maturity, Russell presented intermittent snapshots of a faltering adolescent body which had little continuity of institutional life, which jumped from issue to issue and which declined in significance during the decades before the Civil War. Far from the Commons being the centrepiece of the picture and the champions of constitutional rights, Russell showed an assembly which failed to discharge its functions and one whose members' frustrations reflected political problems beyond their resolution and even in some cases their comprehension.[17]

Some of those dissatisfied with Professor Russell's pictures were just too set in their angle of vision to see things another way. But there were legitimate worries about the new pictures, worries that have grown as the excitement of their first publication has passed. In the first place, even on Russell's videotape, for all the quality of the picture, the sound is missing. There was noise and passion in early Stuart parliaments and much heated discussion of them which finds only intermittent voice here, leaving in places an eery quiet where an animated soundtrack should be.[18] For all its use of the newly published parliamentary diaries, Russell's book is more confident in analyzing political moves and manoeuvres than in examining the rhetoric of parliamentary speeches. Secondly, Russell is inclined to view the Commons from the perspective of the "county community" and a historiography, now criticized, that depicted MPs as preoccupied with local questions and interests, rather than as men participating in the government of the nation or the public sphere of discourse about it.[19] Most seriously, the narrow focus on the 1620s restricted the historical vision and exacerbated the problems of historical explanation. If the Commons was so insignificant and declining in importance why was it called in the 1620s so frequently?[20] How did the issues and mood of the House in the 1620s compare with Elizabethan assemblies? How, if parliaments were a series of events, did some MPs attain a sense of institutional identity and pride? How did the experience of parliaments and memory of past parliaments shape individuals' political consciousness – to the point that MPs, like Pym in 1641, were to appeal to it with such telling effect?[21] Professor Russell, rightly critical of the fuzzy lines of the big Whig picture, was nevertheless wrong to claim that he had placed 17th century parliaments in perspective. He had, very ably, shot them from a different perspective, which highlighted important features and details lost in the big sweep, but which also fragmented and cut off aspects – some would say the core – of its subject. We must endeavour to put the pieces together again.

The microscope enables us to probe beneath the surface of objects to see how they function and what parts they consist of. In the first case, the old Whig view was concerned more with the function of the House of Commons in the long historical story, than how contemporaries viewed it in early 17th century England. If any consideration was given to the latter, it was assumed that early Stuart MPs saw themselves as fighting an historic struggle for parliamentary government, whose preservation and advancement was their primary function. This, of course, too easily ignored the fact that it was the King who summoned parliaments, presumably for some other reason than their advancement at his own expense. The view of the Crown was that parliaments were called to vote taxes in extraordinary circumstances, to pass legislation, to offer advice and – too seldom mentioned – air grievances and criticism. As they looked closely at the workings of parliaments, the revisionist historians discovered paradoxically that the Crown's view of their functions was shared by most MPs, but that they were functions the Commons were failing to perform.

In the case of taxation, the theory governing royal and parliamentary attitudes – that the King should live of his own revenues in peacetime – had long been unrealistic. Perhaps by the 13th century, the royal demesne was insufficient to bear the costs of government. Though the century of war with France brought almost permanent taxation, it hid the reality that even in peacetime the Crown did not have the resources to sustain its obligations to defend and protect its subjects. A real opportunity to restore the Monarchy to fiscal strength and independence was presented to Henry VIII when he inherited the Yorkist, Lancastrian, and Tudor estates and added to them the lands of the dissolved monasteries. However, as a true Renaissance prince, Henry preferred the glories of war against France to pacifism and fiscal rectitude. By the end of his reign, most of his substantial resources had been dissipated, and the beginnings of the greatest inflation ever known quickly eroded the rest.[22] This was also the century when changes in weapons and tactics, sometimes called the military revolution, escalated defence costs even faster than the runaway inflation that rocked a realm used to stable prices.[23] Even withdrawal from continental warfare would not alone solve the problems: after the break from Rome, England was always the likely target of a Catholic crusade, and the realm needed to be kept in a state of preparedness for defence and war.[24]

The gap between the needs of the Crown and its resources grew to a chasm. This is the gap that, Whig historians argued, Elizabethan and early Stuart MPs took advantage of, to force the Crown to concede more power in return for votes of subsidies. Conrad Russell argued, from close examination, that if anything the Commons was weakened by these developments. Though he showed that from Elizabeth's reign onwards that the Commons voted increasingly frequent and large grants of taxation, even in peacetime, the value of such levies declined, as assessments for the subsidy failed to keep pace with inflation.[25] In 1628, after Parliament had granted five subsidies, the Privy Council was frantically endeavouring to get a yield per subsidy that matched that of 1572: they failed; subsidies declined in value from £130,000 to £50,000.[26] The only light at the end of the tunnel of fiscal gloom was the rising value of customs duties with expanding trade, and the value of extraordinary measures such as the grants of monopolies. In so far as the Commons questioned royal fiscal expedients as grievances, they threatened to cost as much as they contributed. As a source of revenue therefore, Russell argued, the Commons had all but lost its function. This is a provocative conclusion, hard to square with the frequency with which parliaments were called, especially in the 1620s. Though the Crown necessarily resorted to fiscal expedients, as much to reward its servants as to gain revenue, what is still remarkable about early Stuart England is the Crown's limited exploration of extraparliamentary revenue. In early Stuart England, there was no large scale sale of hereditary offices like the *paulette* in France.[27] The Monarchy and the Commons were both caught up in a set of traditional customs which were strained at the edges but not broken, leaving the Crown unable to govern and the Commons, rather like modern critics of the health service, irritated at deficiencies and grumbling at the costs. Had it wished to loom large in government, the Commons perhaps could have done so through the voting of an annual revenue even in peacetime, but it showed little enthusiasm, in 1610 for example, to do so. It took the fact of Civil War and parliamentary government to change the fiscal system. Before 1642, the Commons may have failed to meet the Crown's fiscal needs in practice, but it did not veer much from customs and traditions in which King and Parliament were both trapped.

The second important function of a parliament was legislation. Strangely, the Whig wide-angle paid little attention to parliamentary bills and acts, concentrating on moments of constitutional dispute – the Apology or Protestation – which impeded the progress of legislation. Yet legislation was arguably what gave English parliaments their power and importance. By the 16th century, statute law was held to be supreme and royal proclamations were used only to enforce or gloss rather than to change the law. For all his claims to Caesaro-papism, Henry VIII enacted his Reformation through statute and the Elizabethan religious settlement was made in Parliament. Scholars have long observed that from the reign of James I the number of official acts declined, and Conrad Russell has developed the point to argue that, after the failure of his project for full union with Scotland, James had no legislative programme and Parliament's rôle as a legislator declined. The statistics show a decline in the number of acts from Elizabeth's reign.[28] But it is worth remembering that in terms of royal legislation, the 16th century, with the need for religious settlement and new treason laws, was exceptional rather than typical.[29] During the early 17th century, the number of royal proclamations remained stable, and reached their lowest during the 1630s when no Parliament assembled.[30] The absence of official bills then did not signal a monarchy looking to enact its will outside Parliament, but a return to stability after the heady changes consequent on the Reformation.

What is more interesting is the paucity of public bills initiated by the Commons in this period – even on matters about which they expressed concern.[31] In part, this was due to incompetence and bureaucracy. For all Notestein's talk of procedural developments, the Commons often appears disorganized, unfocused, and badly led.[32] Many bills of no obvious contention disappeared into committees from which they never emerged, perhaps because more educated MPs (rather like academics on committees) talked much but resolved little. Jennifer Loach, however, has interestingly suggested that the Elizabethan House of Commons was reluctant to legislate against the burden of monopolies because they trusted the Crown to reform the abuse.[33] If this were the case, the succession of James, who announced his enthusiasm to listen and reform, may have added extra goodwill to the traditional honeymoon for a new monarch and led to fewer bills and more petitions to the King. The range and number of petitions to the King is striking, and his response no less so.[34] It may be James' willingness to suspend patents by proclamation, for example, that took the heat out of the issue; for it was not until 1624 that a statute against monopolies was passed, and then with the active encouragement of the Prince of Wales. Though James' openness to reform and petition did not fulfil the hopes for reform of abuses, it did mean that those hopes, like the hopes of the religious reformers, were never dashed.[35] The obstacle to reform and to legislation, as the debates about purveyance or the Great Contract reveal, was a conservative resistance to fundamental change – among MPs as much as, if not more than, by the Crown. After 1618, the focus shifted from domestic to foreign affairs with the eviction of James I's daughter and son-in-law from their lands in the Palatinate and the outbreak of the Thirty Years' War. Politics and pressure (from outside as well as within the Commons) took over from legislation, the session of 1621 producing no legislation but the subsidy act. While the succession of the more rigid Charles I ultimately changed the atmosphere of openness to petition and reform, the new King began with a fund of goodwill, not least owing to memories of his championship of reforms in 1621 and 1624.[36] War and high politics dominated the parliaments of 1625-28, but for all their frustrations at burdens, policies, and ministers, the Commons still preferred to reform through petition to the King rather than legislation – even in 1628 when the procedure by bill was dropped for a Petition of Right. After 1610 and before 1640, therefore, the Crown had a minimal legislative programme and the Commons preferred petition to statute. Curiously, even when the Long Parliament met after 11 years of nonparliamentary government, it took more than six months before a series of reforming bills became law. Though the removal of what were perceived as excrescences on and abuses of customary government was sought by the backbenches, the manoeuvres for a resolution of the main political crisis were going on elsewhere. Legislation in early 17th century England failed because (with the exception of the union) neither the Monarchy nor the Commons considered pursuing the radical reforms of the system that necessitated statute. It was not an index of the redundancy of parliaments, but of the stranglehold of conservatism on all government.

The third function of parliaments, and especially of the Commons, no less in the eyes of the Crown than of the MPs themselves, was advice. The whole theory of personal monarchy as it developed in England was based on the centrality of counsel – from ministers, magnates, and Privy Councillors and from the representatives of the political nation in the shires. Before the development of party institutionalized the connections, good counsellors were the vital link between the Crown and the political nation, the essential component of that trust on which the workings of the system depended. MPs came to Westminster with a unique knowledge of the problems and views of the counties and boroughs they represented and, even when the advice they gave the King was unwelcome or unpalatable, it was important and valued.[37] Or nearly always. James' openness to petition and counsel appears to have been dented by the Commons' response to his scheme for a union of Great Britain, a response which he believed (not unreasonably) to be dictated by nationalism, avarice, and fear of rivalry for trade and places rather than considerations of the public weal. During the 1620s, the Commons' advice on foreign affairs he viewed – again not unreasonably – as ill-informed, if not ignorant, few MPs having any idea of the intricacies of European diplomacy or the costs of war. In Charles I's eyes, fighting a war as soon as he ascended the Throne, the Commons' counsel was not only misguided, but inconsistent with its earlier exhortations and members were downright irresponsible in denouncing the measures that the war they had urged necessitated. The Crown's growing disenchantment not with the theory of counsel but with the Commons' unhelpful advice was matched by MPs' growing dissatisfaction that their counsel was either not heard or unheeded. In some respects, the Duke of Buckingham, who, a recent biographer suggests, was greatly misunderstood and undervalued, became the scapegoat for a breakdown over Parliament's rôle as an adviser: a breakdown as important as the fiscal problems of the regime.[38] For kings traditionally called parliaments for advice, even when they did not seek supply; the crisis of counsel, as MPs themselves discerned, threatened the survival of parliaments.[39] By 1629, it was because Charles I had resolved that their counsel was more a hindrance than aid to his government that he embarked upon a period of rule without them. For all his action was understandable, however, it underlined the importance of Parliament's counsel. Superficially, the 11 years of nonparliamentary government appear to support arguments for their declining function and significance. Government continued and worked reasonably well. But the government lost a vital opportunity to communicate and explain its programmes and a sounding board to test the mood of the nation. As Charles I found in the late 1630s and Oliver Cromwell in the 1650s, the absence of regular parliaments detached the central government from the political nation, placing strains on the patronage chains of command.

For all then that, as Professor Russell argued, Parliament appeared to be losing its usefulness – as a supplier, as a legislator, as a source of counsel – it never lost importance. The kings, and indeed the Protector, continued to view parliaments as the only organ for granting supply (all else were expedients), the only way to change the law, and a vital source of counsel. Still more they recognized its importance as a symbol of the traditional courses. Neither Charles I's nor Cromwell's speeches about the importance of parliaments should be dismissed as insincere rhetoric. They believed in parliaments and were as confused at the Commons' failure to act in harmony with them as MPs were devoted to monarchy and unable to understand why it failed to heed them. Interestingly, for all Conrad Russell's observations, the decline (and perceived decline) in Parliament's functions did not lead to any reduction of the importance contemporaries (Councillors and commoners) attached to them. If anything, as we shall suggest, the reverse was the case.

While we are observing through the microscope, we need to examine the structure and form of parliaments. Superficially, we do not need to look very closely to see that they consisted of King, Lords, and Commons – though, having recognized that, much of the historiography has in practice ignored the first two. What we do need to appreciate and study is that the relationship of the constituents – of the Lords to the Commons, of the King to each House, of the full House to its committees – changes over time, as does the membership, the procedure, and the practice. Such changes in parliaments were a consequence of broader social and political shifts, and in turn tended to shape those broader developments. The Whigs, knowing already what they wanted to see, pronounced confidently after the briefest of looks, on what important changes the 17th century saw in the structure and constitution of parliaments. A new dynasty of kings, Scottish, ignorant of English law and traditions, bent on absolute rule, faced a new class of MPs, men newly educated in the universities and Inns of Court, whose humanist and legal studies equipped them to be champions of the resistance and fight for freedom and democracy. The Marxists, too, quickly discern a shift that fits into their wide-angle picture. During the 16th and 17th centuries, they detect the decline of a feudal aristocracy and the rise of a gentry and bourgeois class, often of men who had risen through trade, who came from the counties and especially the boroughs determined to dismantle the vestiges of feudal authority and to remake the constitution in their own interests. While they have returned to the laboratory and made minor modifications to the theory, whole generations of students have followed their Marxist professors, from Christopher Hill through Lawrence Stone to Derek Hirst, and most recently (albeit old experiments only just published) Robert Brenner.[40] Recent research, however, has convincingly demonstrated that in their enthusiasm for their own model, these scholars were blind to some very important data. In the brilliant *Parliamentary Selection,* Professor Mark Kishlansky showed that, far from being revolutionized by social change, the processes of selecting members for Parliament was characterized by norms of deference and consensus, and dictated by traditions of aristocratic patronage and honour. As a consequence, MPs sent to Westminster until at least the eve of Civil War came from the same social class, and often the same families, as their forebears.[41]

As for the House of Lords (curiously ignored by the Whigs), as other scholars have shown, the peers refused to act as the declining class that the Marxists believed they saw. As a class, the peerage still expected and were accorded deference; and as a House, the Lords was prominent in the parliaments of the 17th century. In 1621, for example, the impeachments of the patentee, Sir Giles Mompesson, and the King's Lord Chancellor, Francis Bacon, depended upon the House of Lords, the revival of whose judicial powers enhanced their political importance for the rest of the decade. In 1628, in seeking redress of their grievances by a petition of right, the Commons were – necessarily – anxious at all points to have the support of the Lords. Without it they could do little. The support the Lords gave the lower house in 1628 directs us, far from the Marxist focus, to a problem still in need of exploration: why, by the late 1620s, had the Lords ceased to be the reliable supporters of the Crown?[42] Detailed studies have shown how leading magnates such as the Earls of Arundel and Bristol became disaffected by the rise of a favourite in the 1620s, and conspired with their clients in the Commons to bring the Duke of Buckingham down.[43] Close analysis of the politics of the winter of 1640-41 have shown the centrality of the magnates in the machinations to resolve political crisis by changes in the King's Council.[44] A young scholar, researching the activities especially of the Earl of Essex and Lord Saye and Sele, has argued suggestively that, far from a revolution of a new rising bourgeoisie, the English Civil War originated in the revolt of a baronage steeped in the history and values of their Lancastrian predecessors.[45] Though it is not here our central object of focus, it is clear that, in order better to understand the House of Commons, we need to know a great deal more about a House of Lords whose membership rose from 55 in 1603 to 126 in 1628. How far did the great expansion and, in some cases, change in the membership, affect the politics of the House of Lords?[46] Did divisions within the Lords undermine its value to the King? Were the difficulties James I and Charles I faced with the Lords occasioned by more than the rise of a *parvenu* favourite? How did "opposition" peers come to control the House in 1641 so as to secure the execution of the King's chief minister? Such questions dictate the need for a full study of the politics of the Lords from the failure of the Jacobean Union to the Civil War – and beyond. Evidently, Oliver Cromwell came to regard the absence of an upper chamber in the 1650s as an impediment to constitutional settlement, and to consider the conferring of titles an essential element in social and political stability.[47] After 1660, the House of Lords and the peerage were central to the politics of the restored kingdom, and the improved relations between Crown and peerage provide a key to the political stability of the years after 1688.[48] Given what we have begun to learn about the links between the houses at particular moments in the 1620s, a better understanding of the Lords promises to place the Commons in a very different perspective.

That, however, should not detract from the extensive research that still needs to be done on the House of Commons and its members. While Kishlansky is right to counter the claim that MPs came from a new class, it cannot be denied that the speeches reveal members better educated – in the classics, the law, and Scripture. Whether this better equipped the House to articulate its grievances against royal policies or bogged its proceedings in self-promoting speeches of hours' duration is a moot point.[49] The speeches themselves, their purpose, their rhetoric, the responses they received, inside and outside the House, have been curiously neglected. In some recent scholarship, too little consideration is given to the relationship of the speakers and rhetoricians to the "silent" backbenchers whom the orators were presumably trying to persuade.[50] Were the silent those more concerned with the business of the House, where the orators sought to capture attention outside it? Were MPs ambitious for office and place pursuing quite different courses from those whose social and political ambitions were centred on representing their county? How were local and national perspectives weighted by men of strong local attachments, but education in and experience of national affairs? While scholars have debated some of these questions in general, we still have few case studies of MPs, either as individuals or representatives of a county; and those we do have are of members such as Eliot, Wentworth, or Pym who (in different ways) were quite untypical.[51] The microscopic analysis of 17th century parliaments has scarcely begun.

Such microscopic study, however, must not preclude study of the surrounding tissue. Ironically, the Whig wide-angle and the Russell close-up on parliaments have failed fully to study them in relation to the other organs of government, as participants in the government, still more in the broader political culture and public sphere. Traditionally, the relationship of the House of Commons to the Privy Council and the Court was described as one of contest or opposition. But as soon as we acknowledge that 17th century politics was characterized more by personal relations than institutional parameters, we see how inappropriate it is to study parliaments discreetly. Nearly all Privy Councillors were Members of Parliament, and many MPs too were a part of the Court – either narrowly defined (as the Royal Household and entourage) or more broadly conceived (as all who held office of the Crown, including keepers of royal manors, forts and castles, or escheators of Crown lands like Pym). Moreover, during the 17th century, several MPs, most famously Wentworth, Noy, and Digges, became Councillors and courtiers – and it was perfectly natural rather than exceptional for them to do so.[52] If MPs sometimes took the route to office, it was no less true that Councillors and courtiers at times championed parliamentary grievances; and in turn used their allies in the Commons to win a dispute within the King's Council, even to put pressure on the monarch himself or, since the case is very well demonstrated for Elizabeth, herself.[53] Historians have demonstrated this for particular episodes and in the specific context of faction.[54] But the interrelations of Parliament, Council, and Court went beyond the narrow politics of faction and we await a study of the Commons in the context of these broader, complex, and fluid arrangements – in the context of patronage.[55]

Similarly, the relationship of various MPs to their localities needs to be reconfigured in the light of recent scholarship. During the 1960s and 1970s, the historians of the county communities presented a picture of the typical county MP sent to Westminster with provincial political perspectives and ends, keener to press for the repair of Dungeness lighthouse or the bridge over the river Nene, than to be involved in national issues. As Clive Holmes, Anne Hughes, and others have argued, this is only a half truth.[56] Most MPs were lifted beyond their county horizons by university, often a period at one of the Inns of Court and by business, kinship, and marriage. Moreover, when sitting at Westminster, they shared the experiences of other members and became part of an active London culture which was the metropolis of news as well as (often political) entertainment. How did individual MPs negotiate their duties of serving their locality, serving the Crown, and advancing the public weal? Such questions of choice and conscience always were, and still are, part of being an MP. But if, as has been persuasively argued, the tensions between centre and locality were increasing, it was natural that they were reflected in Parliament. If the Commons was only the barometer indicating stormy political weather, we cannot hope to explain the storm only by staring at the barometer. We need to examine the broader political structures, political culture, and, as important, contemporaries' perceptions of them.

Once, historians of ideas confidently described early modern political culture as characterized by order, harmony, and obedience, not least because contemporary writers rehearsed such terms almost as a litany of state.[57] What we now appreciate is that the repitition of such axioms announced insecurities about their cohesion and fears about their subversion. As on the continent, the English Reformation threw up awkward questions about personal faith and conscience in relation to duty and obedience to the magistate: questions that went to the heart of the nature of power, authority, and obedience. Subjects began to read the Bible, the classics, the law in very different ways and came to different conclusions about the priorities of government. Such real tensions and fissures were often masked by a language of consensus and by rituals of community which served to shelve and exacerbate the problems: problems not only of religion, but of the role and authority of the state (at a time of military escalation and endemic warfare) in relation to the rights and properties of subjects.[58] Themselves a microcosm of a larger cultural incapacity to acknowledge differences, the rituals and rhetoric of parliaments emphasized unanimity and concordance. To MPs whose (or whose constituents') experience was rather one of discord and division, this led to confusion and frustration, and a need to place the blame somewhere "outside". Like the European witch craze, English hysteria about popery undoubtedly signals a larger psychological phenomenon: a need to explain ills that could apparently be ascribed to no natural causes. But if these were problems for parliaments, they were not problems caused by them. They were the problems of a culture which could not easily voice opposition and acknowledge conflict, the first steps in the resolution of problems.[59] Each MP's experience of the Council, the Court, and his county, his own readings of the supposedly shared texts and codes of the political culture, are the essential contexts for an understanding of parliaments.

Nearly all historical analyists of Stuart parliaments have taken it as given that they were an unusual specimen, exhibiting abnormalities that revealed ills in the body politic. If, however, we are to conclude that, and explain how, 17th century parliaments were abnormally contentious, we need a comparative sample of others of supposedly greater normality and harmony. Yet historians of medieval parliaments have been less inclined to see the 17th century as special or very different from the mix of harmonious and stormy scenes that characterized the 12th to 15th centuries, or from the crises of Richard II's, Edward II's or Henry VI's reigns which led to the deposition and murder of anointed kings.[60] To come closer to the early Stuart decades, recent researches on Elizabeth's reign have not only shown that beneath the rhetoric of love and harmony were sharp clashes over the Queen's marriage, the succession, religious and foreign policy, but also that, as in the 1620s, Privy Councillors were often behind the pressure voiced noisily in the Commons.[61] After the Civil War, the hero of the Parliamentarian cause, Oliver Cromwell, found it no easier to work with parliaments than his royal predecessors, and was dogged by the same issues (unparliamentary taxes, religious disputes) that had plagued them.[62] Noise, division, and conflict, in other words, were the practical norms of parliaments, for all the rhetoric of harmony; and it is not absolutely obvious that the early Stuart parliaments were any worse than most. Indeed, even during the 1620s, there were occasions of cooperation and accord (as in 1624) rather than a smooth graph of escalating contention. Such observations pose a conundrum. If tension and contention were normal to the history of parliaments,why did 17th century conflicts lead to violent civil war where others – if not all – were resolved by more peaceful means? Here it is worth remembering that throughout the 1620s and even in 1641, the measures pursued to restore harmony were steeped in precedent and tradition. What was different about the so-called Bedford plan, to place trusted magnates in the King's Council, was the context rather than content of the proposals: the presence of a Scottish army and demobilized English troops. What this constituted, far more serious than a "British problem", was a condition of violence in which, as often, political solutions were nigh impossible to negotiate. Thereafter, thanks to the Irish rebellion of 1641, there was never a window of demilitarized opportunity for peaceful settlement. After 1660, significantly, for all that the issues returned to parliamentary politics, as sharp and divisive as ever, their resolution always stopped short of battle. The memory of civil war and, related, the determination to exclude any standing armies in England, again provided a context for the resolution of normal political conflict by the normal processes of negotiation and compromise. Later, the party system institutionalized those processes and also reduced the likelihood of clashes between Crown and Parliament by requiring royal ministers to have a base of trust in the Commons. Even the perceived hysteria about popery did not again erupt into internecine violence. If sharp conflicts between Crown and Parliament were not themselves a sufficient cause for civil war, the history of early 17th century parliaments may have been written to explain what they did not cause.

Our laboratory analysis may also benefit from continental as well as chronological comparisons. Certainly, such a comparison is implicit in the traditional Whig history. English parliaments, the assumption goes (like the English race, then spreading its beneficence to the colonies), were more robust than and morally superior to those of other nations.[63] Where the English Commons "won the initiative" (against the odds?), the French Estates General meekly accepted its own demise in 1614 and succumbed to the growth of Bourbon absolutism; and the Paris Parlement proved pusillanimous and compliant. In Spain, English ambassadors were struck by the willingness and generosity of the Cortes in granting taxation.[64] Where the English Commons held to the principle of no extraparliamentary levies, the French and Spanish crowns taxed without consultation. Such observed differences were not just in the imagination of staunch Victorian patriots. Seventeenth-century Englishmen and MPs drew attention to the eclipse of representative institutions overseas and some feared their own would follow.[65] While the differences between English and continental assemblies were undoubtedly important, I wish to suggest that their importance has been misunderstood. Rather than weakening the Monarchy, the English parliaments were a source of strength to the Crown, and one which continental monarchs lacked. At first it appears odd that the Venetian Ambassador to England should in 1607 describe James I as having "reached such a pitch of formidable power that he can do what he likes".[66] But if this was to go too far, it was pardonable exaggeration. During the 16th century, uniquely, the English Monarchy had been able to carry through a break from Rome, a Protestant reformation, a return to Rome, and the resumption of reform without religious civil war. Henry VIII's (sincere) rhetoric that he never stood so high as when in Parliament was proved by events.[67] In England, the negotiations between the Crown and political nation, the cynosure of *all* early modern governments, were worked out in parliaments rather than through aristocratic risings and revolts. The most important, and least pondered, difference between English and continental parliaments further enhanced social stability and the power of the Crown. In England, taxes were paid as well as voted by the nobility and gentry who, in France, were largely exempt from payment. The burdens were not simply transferred to the poorest, and early modern England was largely free of the peasant uprisings which were endemic on the continent. There was surprisingly little class warfare in England; even the Civil War saw no agrarian revolution, and its relative social cohesion strengthened the English state.[68] Secondly, the fact that the propertied in England were the taxpaying class presented a phenomenal potential for raising revenue, not at the disposal of foreign monarchs. While, as we have seen, for much of the period medieval attitudes to finance trapped the King and Members of Parliament, taxation bought Oliver Cromwell military and naval victories over powerful neighbours.[69] In the 1690s, with King and Commons in partnership, William III, supported by the new National Debt, crushed a Louis XIV who struggled to raise money for long campaigns from private creditors.[70] As Henry VIII had believed and predicted, the King in Parliament could be the mightiest monarch of all and, as the country MPs might have said during the 1690s, with a parliament managed by patronage and place, the most absolute at home. There were no intrinsic peculiarities in the English Parliament that secured its strength at the expense of the Crown.

As we lay out our photographs of parliaments, some old and faded, some new, wide-angle, close up, microscopic, some of the Commons alone, some with other subjects in the frame, we are struck by the fact that they appear to be images of quite different objects, but in reality are visions of the same one. That recognition prevents us simply discarding any photograph and suggests that we should endeavour to make some composite of them all.

Was the 17th century after all a period of unique constitutional conflict between Crown and Parliament, and was it a quest for power by the Commons that led to civil war? As soon as we return to these basic questions, we are immediately struck by a number of paradoxes. Although on the one hand, many MPs expressed anxiety about the survival of Parliament, we have seen that Parliament did less and less; moreover, there were few demands that it should meet more frequently, and absenteeism remained from Elizabeth's reign onwards a problem.[71] Even in 1641, when momentous matters were being discussed, the Commons ceased to be quorate. Secondly, if the Commons wished to participate more in government during the early Stuart decades, it is remarkable how slowly and reluctantly they took up the reins of power in the 1640s, and how willing they were to surrender them to a Protector, a new royal dynasty in the house of Cromwell, and in 1660 to the Stuart heir – with no extra guarantees of their position or restraints on the Crown. Evidently, what the Commons wanted, as they often said, was traditional government by a king in parliament, ruling in the interests of the gentry. This is what a succession of monarchs also claimed to desire, so we need to understand why it did not happen. Professors David Willson and Hugh Trevor-Roper once suggested that the explanation lay in a failure of royal management: that where Elizabeth and Burleigh managed the Commons, James I did not ensure adequate numbers of Privy Councillors in the House; and Cromwell failed to rig the elections to secure a compliant following.[72] Stability returned only with the brilliant skills of a Danby, or a Walpole, who forged a sense of common interest between King and Commons.[73] While there may be some truth in this, it is one more complicated than personalities. The English state was stronger in Walpole's time, the patronage at the Crown's disposal greater; but just as importantly the King and political nation had been shaken out of an unworkable set of values and arrangements by the experience of civil war and later developments.

The early modern period, in England as on the continent, had seen new problems and tensions which placed peculiar strains on a still essentially medieval polity. The alleged "absolutism" of the Stuarts was not a cause, but sign of these strains. James I and Charles I were not more "absolutist" than Henry VIII, Elizabeth, or the first two Georges.[74] But they reigned during a time when the expanding business of government and the dangers to national security occasioned by religious division, necessitated some extension of the executive. To carry out their traditional duties of protecting the realm, the monarchs had to pursue some untraditional courses. MPs and others who feared that the old customs and balances were being upset were right. But their proposed solution, from outside the circles of government, was adherence to the very traditions that could not serve the new circumstances. King, Lords, Councillors, and Commons were all trapped by (sincere) devotion to custom – a dilemma nicely illustrated by ministers like Sir John Coke who as MP abhorred the novelty of the measures he took as Secretary of State in wartime.[75] The experience of government during the 1640s broke the stranglehold of custom. It was a parliamentary government that instituted peacetime taxation, excise, and monthly assessments, set up a salaried Protector and established not only a powerful naval defence, but a military basis for successful war and colonial expansion. Participation in government led the Commons to a greater understanding of the problems of rule and to a renewed basis of partnership between the ruler and the political nation. That partnership also depended on the gradual diminution of the heat of religious conflict. The break from Rome and spread of Protestantism bequeathed fundamental problems which a Hookerian rhetoric of harmony and an official policy of *via media* served more to conceal than cure. Recently, some historians have argued that the English Civil War was the "war of religion" that resulted from divisions and fears that eroded trust between the Crown and significant parts of the political nation.[76] Again, a shared rhetoric of concern for the Church of England masked long-standing differences about what the Church was and should be, different visions for which a few were willing to fight. For all the talk of the success of Elizabethan moderation, it was perhaps only after the experience of radical extremes during the 1640s and 1650s (Catholic uprising and revolutionary sectarianism) that the political nation was bonded by a common support for one Church and Faith, whatever men's private beliefs and preferences.[77] A civil settlement of the religious problem was one of the important consequences of civil war – albeit it took until 1689 before the passing of a Toleration Act neutralized the threat of denominational division to political concord.

By the late 17th century, then, such changes in state and Church helped to resolve the issues that had strained the relations between the Crown and the political nation. They were not issues created or caused by parliaments, but problems that parliaments (that is King, Lords, and Commons) had to tackle, but were ill-equipped to solve. Custom, the mantra of early modern political discourse, was the obstacle to settlement, to the reestablishment of the mixed polity in new circumstances, and so the destroyer of the Commons as well as the Crown. The Civil War led not to the triumph of Commons over the Crown, but to a polity in which both increased in effectiveness and strength.

At the centre of the problems before 1642 lay the disjuncture, on all parts, between reality (the reality of change) and perception (the perception that things should be as they were). In that disjuncture too lies some of the explanation for the great difference between historians of Stuart parliaments. Professor Russell points revealingly to the political realities of declining subsidies, administrative weaknesses, and the diminishing functions of parliaments. But, as Cust and Hughes argue, he pays inadequate attention to the devotion to parliaments and customary ways loudly articulated in speeches and pamphlets attacking the Crown. If this appears contradictory, our own experience reminds us that our sense of the importance of institutions is often most vocalized when they appear not to be working – to the frustration of all concerned. The expressions of passionate commitment to parliaments were not confined to members of the Commons. They should be read not as the creed of a party seeking more power, but as a shared hope and anxiety of men living in a period of instability and change which they could not conceptualize or verbalize in the paradigms of custom that dominated their values.[78] Ironically, it was revolution that enabled the reestablishment of the traditional polity they desired – a renewed traditional partnership only made possible by an altered political culture.

Footnotes to this Chapter may be found on pages 203–8.

5: W A Speck

The Glorious Revolution and the Hanoverian Succession, 1660-1734

THE HOUSE of Commons in the late Stuart and early Hanoverian period has not had a good press. On the contrary, it was accused at the time of being incorrigibly corrupt, a charge which has been repeated ever since. The Cavalier Parliament of Charles II, which lasted from 1661 to 1679, first attracted charges of systematic corruption to explain its longevity. Thus, in 1677, there appeared *A Seasonable Argument to persuade all the grand juries of England to petition for a new Parliament or a list of the principal labourers in the great design of popery and arbitrary power.*[1] This listed more than 200 MPs who were alleged to be placemen or pensioners, that is members who had accepted offices or money from the Crown with the expectation that they would support the government in the division lobbies. It described Samuel Pepys thus: "Once a tailor, then serving man to the Lord Sandwich, now Secretary to the Admiralty, got by passes and other illegal ways £40,000." Sir Thomas Williams appears as "once a poor quack chemist, now the King's chemist, has got at least £40,000 by making provocatives for lechery." Baptist May's entry claims that he received £1000 a year as privy purse, but "got besides in boons for secret service £40,000. This is he that said £500 per annum was enough for a country gentleman to drink ale, eat beef and to stink with." In the 1690s *The Danger of Mercenary Parliaments* accused the Court of seeking to buy the House of Commons.[2] It claimed that the government

> had made two hundred members absolutely dependent upon them. And what points might not such a number carry in the House, who were always ready and constantly attending with more diligence to destroy our constitution than the rest were to preserve it? who represented not their country but themselves, and always kept together in a close and undivided phalanx, impenetrable either by shame or honour, voting always the same way, and saying always the same things, as if they were no longer voluntary agents, but so many engines merely turned about by a mechanic motion, like an organ where the great humming basses as well as the little squeaking trebles are filled but with one blast of wind from the same sound board?

The pamphlet was reissued in 1722, when the danger was perceived to have grown. Charges that the Court was corrupting the Commons reached their peak under Sir Robert Walpole. In 1734 one of his leading Tory opponents addressed the House.[3] He invited the members to

> suppose a gentleman at the head of the administration whose only safety depends upon corrupting the members of this house ... most of their seats purchased and their votes bought at the expense of the public treasure. In such a parliament let us suppose attempts made to enquire into his conduct, or to relieve the nation from the distress he has brought

upon it ... suppose ... these reasonable requests rejected by a corrupt majority of his creatures, whom he retains in daily pay, or engages in his particular interest, by granting them those posts and places which ought never to be given to any but for the good of the public; upon this scandalous victory, let us suppose this chief minister pluming himself in defiances, because he finds he has got a parliament like a packed jury, ready to acquit him of all adventures.

Why was there this constant complaint about corruption, reaching a crescendo in the 1730s? One possibility is that the times were corrupt. Certainly, there were flagrant examples of MPs feathering their nests. In 1695, the Speaker, Sir John Trevor, was discovered to have accepted £1100 from the Common Council of London to promote a bill. He was voted to be guilty of a high crime and misdemeanour and expelled the House. Under the first two Georges, William Yonge came to epitomize, in Lord Hervey's words, "everything pitiful, corrupt and contemptible."[4] Hervey also claimed that Yonge "had a great command of what is called parliamentary language and a talent of talking eloquently without a meaning and expatiating agreeably upon nothing." At the time of the South Sea Bubble, Yonge was one of the members bribed by the Company with a "present" of its stock, "in his case £3000 at the current price of 350." In 1727, John Ward, who had embezzled £70,000 from the Duke of Buckingham, was expelled from the House for forgery and after absconding for eight months was finally brought to trial, fined £500, and sentenced to one hour in the pillory. Perhaps the most sensational case of corruption leading to an expulsion from the Commons was that of Sir Robert Sutton in 1732. Sutton was one of the managers of the Charitable Corporation, an institution created to lend small sums to poor persons at legal rates of interest to prevent them from falling into the hands of usurious pawnbrokers. Thus, where the corporation charged 10 per cent, pawnbrokers charged 30, 40 and even 50.[5] In 1728, he persuaded the government to increase the capital of the corporation from £100,000 to £300,000, and again two years later to £600,000. On each occasion, the value of the corporation's shares rose and Sutton, through what would nowadays count as insider dealing, profited handsomely. In 1732, an inquiry into the ways in which the managers had benefited from the manipulation of the corporation's shares led to charges of defalcation in which Sutton, who protested his innocence, was nevertheless implicated. The opposition moved in for the kill, and Walpole, suspecting that the defence of a supporter would also implicate his ministry in corruption, left Sutton to twist in the wind.

These cases added to the general impression that the House of Commons was soused up to its ears in corruption. But the notion that the Court could actually control the Commons by bribing a majority of its members was an opposition fantasy. Although Walpole was alleged to have said that every man in it had his price, this was an apocryphal story. The bulk of the MPs, even those in the pay of the Court, cannot be shown to have voted against their principles for material considerations. Take the case of William Hay, MP for Seaford from 1734 to 1755. The Cinque Ports were notorious safe seats for government members, and Hay got his as a gift from his cousin, the Duke of Newcastle, one of the most powerful men in Walpole's ministry. Hay voted with the Court in every division, for which he was rewarded in 1738 with the place of commissioner of the victualling and when he had to resign it to stay in the House received a secret pension *in lieu*. Here was a perfect example of a placeman and a pensioner if ever there was one. Yet from the private diary he kept of his attendance in Parliament, it is clear that he acted on principle. He believed in liberty, and objected to a bill in 1736 because it would create one law for the rich and another for the poor "and tended to create an invidious distinction in a free people like that of patricians and plebeians among the Romans".[6]

Concern about corruption in these years arose not because the Commons was peculiarly corrupt under the later Stuarts and early Hanoverians, but because contemporaries were particularly concerned about it. As Professor Pocock has been at pains to demonstrate, the prevailing ideology of civic humanism was obsessed with the notion in general.[7] In terms of the House of Commons in particular, it was the principal arena in which the struggle for sovereignty, which marked so much of Stuart history, was finally resolved.

At the Restoration of Charles II in 1660, there were still three main contenders in the conflict for sovereign power in the constitution: the King; the King in Parliament; and the people. By the general election of 1734, the rivals of royal and popular sovereignty had been eliminated, and the victory of the King in Parliament was assured.

That the King alone was still a serious contender for sovereignty as late as the 1680s was demonstrated by the virtual disappearance of Parliament during that decade. The House of Commons could only act in partnership with the Crown if it was allowed to assemble. Historians of the early Stuart period have rightly challenged the interpretation which sees the Crown in conflict with Parliament at that time by pointing out that for most of it there were no parliamentary sessions. Parliament in their view was an event not an institution. It is true that the Long and Cavalier Parliaments became something of an institution. But that the Houses had not yet established themselves as a permanent part of the constitutional machinery became clear when Charles II dissolved Parliament in 1681 and did not call it again. James II summoned one shortly after his accession in 1685, but prorogued it at the end of that year and it never met again before being dissolved in 1687. Another parliament was not elected until after the Revolution. So Parliament was unable to check the later Stuarts' attempts to make themselves absolute because it simply did not exist for most of the 1680s.

A more powerful threat to parliamentary limitations on the Royal Prerogative during that decade was the Crown's drive to reduce the Commons to an instrument of the royal will. This was seriously attempted in the 1680s after a majority of members had demonstrated opposition to the Crown

longtain voyage: quil souffira de porter seulement vng
las de soye a vng ymage de sainct george pendãt a icelluy.
Aussi se ledit colier dor auoit besoing de reparacion il pora
estre mis en la main de souurier iusques a ce quil soit
repure. Lequel colier aussi ne pourra estre enrichy de
pierres ou daultres choses, reserue les ymage qui pourra
estre garny au plaisir du cheualier. Et aussi ne pourra
estre ledit colier vendu engaigie dõne ne aliene pour
necessite ou cause quelconque que ce soit

Alexander rex Scotor̄   lewellin princeps wallie

CARDINAL WOOLSEY

E

G

H

after three general elections held between 1679 and 1681. There followed a sustained campaign to rig the electoral system to procure a packed parliament. Had it succeeded, then the theoretical sovereignty of the King in Parliament would have become a façade behind which the sovereign power of the Crown would have been established in reality.

The vulnerability of the Commons to royal regulation under the later Stuarts lay partly in its electoral basis. Although the lower house purported to be the representative of the people, it was notoriously elected by a minority of the population. "The third estate, which is the House of Commons," observed a Tory MP in 1689, "are not the fourth part of the Kingdom."[8] Modern estimates assess the electorate at about a quarter of adult males.[9] Although this is a somewhat larger proportion than is sometimes credited with the franchise, it was very unevenly distributed among the various types of constituency. Of the 300,000 or so voters, at least 200,000 were 40 shilling freeholders who had the right to vote for knights of the shire in the counties of England and Wales. But these comprised only 52 of the 269 English and Welsh constituencies. The remaining 217, apart from the Universities of Oxford and Cambridge, were boroughs. The latest, and as it turned out the last, addition to the constituencies by royal fiat was made by Charles II when he granted a charter enfranchising Newark in 1674. The Royal Prerogative of creating seats in the Commons could have been as powerful a means of political control over the lower house as that of creating peers was over the upper. However, it was never employed again.

Nevertheless, the Crown had at its disposal other techniques for procuring pliant MPs. Most of the parliamentary boroughs owed their right to return representatives to charters granted by the Crown. If they had abused any of the privileges conveyed by their charters, the Crown could revoke them and issue new ones. After the general elections between 1679 and 1681 had produced anti-Court majorities, Charles II embarked on a policy of revoking charters to eradicate his opponents. The process of *quo warranto* was used as a pretext to discover that boroughs had been acting *ultra vires*. Thus London was found to have passed bylaws regulating markets which were not warranted by its charter. As a result, the charter was forfeited to the Crown. The real aim had been to destroy the hold of the Whigs on the City. In the new charter, the right to elect a common council was revoked and the City was run by royal nominees.[10] Similar steps were taken against more than 50 other boroughs. This interference with the electoral machinery helped to ensure an overwhelming majority for the Court in the elections held in 1685, after the accession of James II.[11]

Rigging the charters, however, could not in itself guarantee a built-in majority for the Court. This became obvious in the second session of James II's Parliament when the House of Commons objected to the King's pro-Catholic policies. One problem was that, without detailed local knowledge of his likely supporters in the constituencies, James II did not have enough information at the centre to nominate willing collaborators in the boroughs. He therefore set up a commission for regulating the parliamentary boroughs in 1687. This employed paid regulators who went down to the localities to purge, purge, and purge again until they got electorates who would return candidates hand-picked by the Crown. In the process, 97 boroughs were regulated, some several times in the effort to procure pliant voters.[12]

How far this process would have reduced the Commons to a cypher can only be surmized, for a general election was never held on the basis of the regulation. Historians, therefore, disagree about its efficacy. Some, including the editor of the official History of Parliament for the years 1660 to 1689, conclude that a successful outcome for the King was "at least a possibility".[13] Others remain sceptical.[14]

The speculations of historians, however, are less significant than those of contemporaries. Although some of those expressed scepticism too, many if not most seem to have been genuinely worried that the King would get his way. In that eventuality, James would have established absolute monarchy not despite Parliament but with it. It would not have been like the Estates General, which the absolute rulers of France failed to summon, but like the provincial estates, such as Languedoc, which they had reduced to a rubber stamp. As one pamphleteer put it, James would have a House of Commons "shuffled, cut, and packed" by the regulators.[15]

The campaign to pack Parliament, therefore, became one of the major causes of the Revolution of 1688. According to J R Jones it was "easily the most important ... more resented and feared than even the attack on the Church".[16] The Bill of Rights condemned it with the assertion that elections to Parliament "ought to be free". This is usually dismissed as a vague generalization, a mere pious platitude, but it went very much deeper than that. As with so many aspects of the Glorious Revolution, the spirit of 1688 was more important than the letter. Thus there was nothing on the Statute Book to stop William III from appointing judges at his pleasure, but all his judicial appointments were on good behaviour. The King knew that it would have violated Revolution principles to try to pack the judicial bench. So would any attempt to pack Parliament by the methods employed under James II. The clause in the Bill of Rights declaring that elections ought to be free served notice on the Crown that attempts to regulate the returns of MPs by direct executive action were unacceptable. The power of the King over Parliament was thereby curtailed.

Of course, the influence of the Crown over the House of Commons was not restrained by the Revolution. On the contrary, it grew steadily between the accession of William and Mary and that of George II in 1727. The judicious dispensation of patronage to reward MPs was developed to a high degree in those years. Under Anne, 120 members had places under the Crown, ranging from Cabinet posts to the purest sinecures. These placemen, as they were known, were regarded as Court fodder in the division lobbies. Under Walpole, their numbers rose to about 150, and their loyalty to the ministry became even more notorious.

Again the Crown used its influence in the constituencies to return Court supporters to Parliament. Several boroughs were amenable to government pressure. The Admiralty, for instance, had substantial influence over such ports and dockyard towns as Portsmouth, Southampton, and Weymouth. It even had an impact on electoral fortunes in Kent, influencing voting behaviour in parishes close to naval bases along the Thames and the Medway.[17] Such measures as the promotion of placemen and the use of electoral interest in the so-called Treasury boroughs, while it created a strong Court party in the Commons, cannot be compared with the deliberate attempt by James II to pack Parliament. It merely served to strengthen the influence of the Crown in Parliament, not its power over it.

Placemen were seen as a means of corrupting the Commons, of subordinating the legislature to the executive, and of superseding the sovereignty of the people with that of Parliament. These criticisms added up to a Country ideology against the Court. To adherents of this attitude MPs were answerable not to the Court but to their constituents. They could not serve God and Mammon. Macaulay, as usual, summed up the Country mentality perfectly when he observed[18]

> The House swarmed with placemen of all kinds, Lords of the Treasury, Lords of the Admiralty, commissioners of Customs, commissioners of Excise, commissioners of Prizes, tellers, auditors, receivers, paymasters, officers of the Mint, officers of the household, colonels of regiments, captains of men of war, governors of forts. We send up to Westminster, it was said, one of our neighbours, an independent gentleman, in the full confidence that his feelings and interests are in perfect accordance with ours. We look to him to relieve us from every burden except those burdens without which the public service cannot be carried on, and which therefore, galling as they are, we patiently and resolutely bear. But, before he has been a session in Parliament, we learn that he is a Clerk of the Green Cloth or a Yeoman of the Removing Wardrobe, with a comfortable salary. Nay we sometimes learn that he has obtained one of those places in the Exchequer of which the emoluments rise and fall with the taxes which we pay. It would be strange indeed if our interests were safe in the keeping of a man whose gains consist in a percentage of our losses.

The incompatibility of interests between revenue officers and electors was held to be so great that customs and excise officials were not allowed to sit in the House of Commons by Acts passed in 1700. The following year, the campaign against placemen reached its zenith when a clause was inserted in the Act of Settlement making the acceptance of any office under the Crown incompatible with a seat in the Commons. Had this clause come into effect, it would have eliminated all placemen from the lower house, not just sinecures like the farmers of the green wax but ministerial posts such as Chancellor of the Exchequer and Secretary of State. In consequence, the Cabinet system could not have evolved. Instead, the House of Commons would have become like the American House of Representatives, bereft of ministerial members. Indeed, in many ways, the American Constitution enshrined 18th century Country ideology, which was ultimately based on the notion of popular sovereignty, encapsulated in its opening words, "we the people".

The tradition of popular sovereignty based on natural rights which the Levellers had maintained in the Interregnum was by no means dead under the later Stuarts. It informed republican or "commonwealth" thought from Algernon Sydney to John Trenchard and Thomas Gordon. Although pure republicanism was marginalized during the Revolution of 1688, the notion of the sovereignty of the people continued to be opposed to the concept of the sovereignty of the King in Parliament. As Blair Worden observes, John Toland argued that if Parliament, through its corruption, betrayed the trust which the electorate had "delegated" to it, then the people "may defend themselves against their legislators".[19]

Fortunately for the advocates of parliamentary sovereignty, the blanket proscription of placemen in the Act of Settlement did not become operative until the death of Queen Anne, and during her reign they took the opportunity to amend the provision. The Regency Act of 1706 repealed the place clause and substituted it with a complex measure, the gist of which was that offices regarded as essential to Cabinet government were spared the general prohibition. The notion that the ministry should be accountable to the electorate as well as to the Crown, however, was upheld with the provision that any MP appointed to an office deemed to be incompatible with membership of the Commons should nevertheless vacate his seat and seek fresh endorsement from his constituents at a byelection. Byelections upon taking office indeed were required until the provision was repealed in 1926.

During the debates about the replacement of the place clause in the Act of Settlement with a less restrictive arrangement, a significant divergence in attitude emerged between backbench Tories and Whigs. Tories wished to preserve the blanket proscription of placemen. Some were doubtless motivated by genuine Country sentiments, being suspicious of the executive's infiltration of the legislature by rewarding MPs with places. Others, however, were more inclined to reduce the influence of the future Hanoverian dynasty over the Commons in order to strengthen the position of the Jacobites, the adherents of the exiled Stuart claimant of the Throne, James II's son, the so-called Pretender. The Whigs were divided. Some supported the Court's attempt to remove all impediments to promoting MPs to posts under the Crown. These were anxious to retain a strong executive for the incoming Hanoverians, not least to stand up to Jacobite pretensions. Others, while no less hostile to the Pretender's claims, were sufficiently suspicious of the executive to wish to reduce the Crown's ability to reward MPs with places. While agreeing to repeal the measure preventing the King from employing members altogether, in its place they proposed to identify offices essential to a smooth working relationship between the Crown and the Commons, and therefore to which MPs could be promoted in the interests of efficient government. In the event this positive way of dealing with the problem did not prevail, and instead the Regency Act adopted the negative course of identifying those offices which were deemed to be incompatible with membership of the Commons.[20]

These rather complex proceedings revealed that different Country attitudes could be adopted by backbenchers depending on their relationship to the two major parties in the House, the Tories and the Whigs. By the 18th century, these were informed to a large extent by the dynastic problem created by the Revolution of 1688. They can be traced back before that, however, to the different views which the parties adopted to the question of sovereignty. At their birth in the reign of Charles II, the Tories regarded the King as sovereign. They accepted his divine, indefeasible hereditary right to rule, and denounced any right to resist it. The Whigs upheld the right of Parliament to alter the succession and even the right of the people to resist a tyrant. After the Revolution, divergent attitudes in Tory and Whig ranks became more and more apparent. These were most clearly revealed in the trial of Dr Sacheverell for high crimes and misdemeamours in 1710. The Sacheverell trial was one of the high points for the Commons of the whole period.[21] Sacheverell was impeached, a process brought by the Commons as prosecutors against an individual before the tribunal of the Lords. The articles of impeachment accused the Anglican minister of preaching that the Glorious Revolution had not changed the Church's traditional doctrines of passive obedience and nonresistance since there had been no resistance in 1688. The Whig majority in the lower house regarded this as an attack upon the Revolution settlement. Although there could be little doubt that the doctor asserted the unlawfulness of resistance to the Crown on any pretext whatever, his defenders, in a superb exercise in damage limitation, argued that the supreme power which could not lawfully be resisted was not the King alone but the King in Parliament. Since Parliament had not been in session in 1688, there could be no question of resistance to it. While the Whigs insisted that there had been legitimate resistance to the Crown on that occasion, they were reluctant to justify the right to resist thereafter, since the Revolution settlement had established a regime which upheld the rights of Englishmen, and, therefore, resistance to it could not be justified. It seemed that there was a growing consensus that sovereignty now lay in the King in Parliament. Under the Hanoverians, only a minority of Whigs continued to stress the sovereignty of the people, while paradoxically more and more Tories, even Jacobites, were prepared to appeal to it.

The theoretical paradox can be resolved by the practical results of appeals to the sovereign people. The fact of the matter was that the Whigs lost their electoral appeal during the 1690s, while the support for the Tories in the popular constituencies grew.[22] Whig confidence in the electorate was still sufficiently strong for them to advocate the Triennial Act in 1694. This made the maximum interval between general elections three years. In fact, 10 elections occurred between 1695 and 1715, one every two years on average. Of the 10, one produced a hung parliament, four produced clear Whig victories, and five resulted in an overall Tory majority, that of 1713 being the greatest lead of one party over another in the 18th century.

Not surprisingly, the Whigs lost their appetite for frequent elections, and when they won the 1715 election, more by management than by luck, they determined to extend the intervals between contests. In 1716, they put the Septennial Act on the Statute Book, lengthening the maximum gap between elections to seven years. By and large this was maintained, so that in the following 20 years, only three general elections took place.

Moreover, these elections were scarcely appeals to the people. On the contrary, the last one, held in 1734, was in popular terms a defeat for the government. In terms of votes cast, there can be no doubt that the majority of the electorate rejected Sir Robert Walpole and his fiscal policies. Yet the great man's ministry could command the confidence of the Commons when the House met. As Paul Langford observes, "in open constituencies, counties, and large boroughs alike, the government was trounced. The Tory party returned 149 MPs to Westminster: this was the only election between 1713 and 1760 in which it improved its parliamentary position."[23] Walpole survived because of Court and Whig influence in the more numerous constituencies where only a handful of electors had the right to vote. By 1734, these were completely under the sway of patronage. Most of them were not even contested. Their existence enabled ministries effectively to get round the requirement that MPs appointed to office should seek reelection. Most appointments in Walpole's day went to men whose returns were so certain that hardly any had to campaign against a rival to be returned to the Commons.

The last vestige of popular sovereignty had thereby been evaded. Supporters of the Walpole ministry's lack of popular support were frankly disdainful of the electorate at large. "Supposing it true that the Majority of the people are against the Ministry, what does that prove?" challenged the *London Journal* in 1734. "The people are sometimes right and sometimes wrong."[24] The general election of that year proved a turning point in political history. Election contests slumped thereafter, far fewer constituencies going to the polls at the next contest in 1741. Opposition politicians conceded that appeals to the electorate to defeat the government were pointless. The sovereignty of the King in Parliament had finally triumphed over the sovereignty of the people.

Footnotes to this Chapter may be found on pages 209–10.

6: Jeremy Black

The Rotten Borough Commons, 1734-1832

CORRUPTION is commonly seen as central to the political system of Hanoverian Britain. Traditionally, it has been particularly associated with the elections and electorate of the period. The very phrase "pocket borough", meaning an urban seat that was controlled or heavily influenced by a patron, is symptomatic of this analysis. How true was it? How much freedom did electors enjoy? How representative was the Commons of its electorate?

Let us first take the traditional view. This would present the corrupt nature of pocket boroughs as integral to the ministerial stability that characterized so much of this period. In this view, the government had little to fear from the electorate, for even if the ministry was generally unsuccessful in the larger "open" constituencies – the counties and the large cities, such as Bristol and London – they could rely on the large number of pocket boroughs. There were many boroughs with small electorates, such as Malmesbury with 13 votes, Gatton with 22, and Whitchurch with 85. In many of the small constituencies, there was rarely a contested election. The Jacobite Earl of Orrery complained in 1721, "there are so many little venal boroughs that 'tis to be apprehended a majority will hardly be carried by the inclinations of the people only." William Pitt the Elder, the so-called Great Commoner, came into Parliament when he was elected unopposed for Old Sarum in 1735. This quintessential rotten borough returned two MPs, though it was entirely depopulated. Pitt's grandfather, Thomas "Diamond" Pitt, who had made a fortune trading to India, had purchased the property that carried the right of election in 1691, and at the general election of 1734 William's elder brother was returned unopposed by the five voters. As he had also been returned unopposed for Okehampton, where he owned much property, Thomas brought his brother in for Old Sarum. William sat for that seat until 1747, then for pocket boroughs of the Duke of Newcastle. In December 1756, he was elected for Okehampton and for the pocket borough of his Grenville in-laws at Buckingham and in 1757 he transferred to Bath, which he had been invited to represent by the corporation, which enjoyed a monopoly of the franchise. Only one of his elections, Seaford in 1747, was contested, and Newcastle was able to swing that election.

Irrespective of any urban property, local aristocrats and gentry could be of considerable consequence in controlling or influencing borough representation; for example, the Dukes of Buckingham in Winchester, the Dukes of Grafton and the Earls of Bristol at Bury St Edmunds. Many boroughs, such as Exeter, that, in the 17th century had chosen townsmen as MPs, chose country gentlemen in the following century. The country elite dominated Parliament. The peers had a considerable influence in the Commons. "Corruption" acted as a harness between the Lords and the Commons, with MPs often reflecting the views of their patrons in the Lords; and thus, prevented conflict between the two chambers. The growth of the peerage, particularly from the reign of George III, reflected a trend of promoting MPs to peerages. The cost of county elections and a desire to avoid contests helped to lessen the number of county contests: after 1754, there was no Oxfordshire contest until 1826. There was a similar process in some boroughs.

The central point in the traditional interpretation of the Hanoverian Commons was, therefore, that it was unrepresentative not only of the population at large, but even of the electorate. As a corollary, it could not be expected to take much of an interest in society other than in order to sustain its position and oppose reform. Indeed, Sir Lewis Namier, the great mid-20th century historian of the Commons, emphasized the social and nonpolitical factors that encouraged people to go into the Commons, as well he might given the numbers who never or rarely spoke in the House. Thus, the Commons stood as a central aspect of an unreformed political system treated by later writers rather as the contemporary Church of England was: apparently ripe for the evangelization of zeal and commitment.

Such a view is increasingly suspect, for an important reevaluation of the Hanoverian political system is in train. Attention has been cast on electoral independence and the role of issues in politics at the local and national level. Indeed, corrupt practices can be seen in part as a means by which politics continued in a world in which ideology and conviction played a great role. The absence of an electoral contest did not necessarily mean the absence of political activity.

At the local level, the independence of the electorate can emerge clearly, as can the role of issues. The two were sometimes combined in a preference for local men as MPs against the choice of borough magnates. Thus in 1722 and 1748, Derby successfully resisted the usually dominant interests of the Duke of Devonshire and the Earl of Chesterfield. It is clear that electors expected their MPs to promote local interests. Elected for the populous and politically aware seat of Bristol in 1774, Edmund Burke wrote to his constituents that an MP should be guided by "the general good ... he owes you, not his industry only, but his judgment; and he betrays you, not serves you, if he sacrifices it to your opinion". Burke's neglect, however, of "local prejudices", in the shape of Bristol's negative views on proposals of freer trade for Ireland, helped him to come bottom of the poll at the next election.

Thus, MPs were expected to forward local legislation at Westminster, one of the most important links between localities and national institutions; and this was a period when local legislation was proportionately far more important than today. Private and local acts took up much parliamentary time and reflected the often very specific importance of legislation. The number of private bills passed by the Commons rose from 68 in 1760 to 210 in 1800. Parliament, therefore, played a crucial role in serving the interests of the localities as understood by and mediated by the local elites. It was representative, yet undemocratic, arguably intrinsically English and just what made it work. In his *The Role of Transportation in the Industrial Revolution: A Comparison of England and France,* Rick Szostak argues that the political institutions and culture of England were more conducive to the local initiatives and control required for the creation of new transport links – canals and turnpikes – whereas in France control lay more in the hands of a small bureaucracy that was less responsive to local needs. The situation in England was eased by the possibility of establishing trusts by private acts of Parliament, while in France the insistence on central government control precluded necessary private investment and led to a concentration on a small number of prestige projects. This view of Parliament, as a very sensitive legislative tool, contrasts, however, with much of the political narrative of the period. Parliament was also useful at the national level. First, Parliament played a crucial role in legitimizing the constitution, especially after the settlement of the Hanoverian succession by the Act of Settlement of 1701. At a time of dynastic conflict, it was important that a forum for legitimization existed. At one level, this could and can be presented as a form of corruption. In purely dynastic terms, the Jacobites had the best claim and the Glorious Revolution was a usurpation or, as Lord Glenamara, formerly Ted Short, Labour Secretary of State for Education, put it in the House of Lords in 1986, a squalid *coup d'état.* Parliament was, therefore, invaluable to William III and the Hanoverians as it provided a means of legitimizing this *coup.* The Glorious Revolution and the Hanoverian Succession were confirmed by Parliament. Furthermore, Parliament had an important comprehensiveness: between 1689 and 1750, a significant proportion of the Commons, albeit a clear minority, was sympathetic to Jacobitism, but, even so, retained a commitment to the parliamentary system.

Secondly, the Commons was important because of the role of Parliament in enabling the government to harness national resources for conflict. The 18th century was an age of conflict, far more so, indeed, than the century from Waterloo to the guns of 1914: in the latter period, Britain only once fought one European power (Russia) and the Crimean War involved no threat to British security or independence. Possibly, therefore, the Whig historians of the period paid insufficient attention to the importance of military strength and success. This was scarcely true of the Nine Years' War (1688-97), the War of the Spanish Succession (1702-13), the War of the Austrian Succession (1743-8), the Seven Years' War (1756-63), the War of American Independence (1776-83), and the French Revolutionary and Napoleonic Wars (1793-1815). These were not wars on the margins of empire, nor were they the essentially contained conflicts of the 1620s, 1650s, 1660s and 1670s with Spain, France, and the Dutch. In the 18th century wars, the independence of Britain was at stake. The French contemplated invasions of Britain in 1692, 1708, 1744, 1745-6, 1759, 1779, 1798, and 1805. They sought to exploit opposition in Ireland and Scotland. In 1778-83, they played a crucial role in dividing the English-speaking world, a crisis of empire that was more serious than any until the loss of Britain's Asian empire in the 1940s. Britain was demographically weaker than France and for most of the 18th century not noticeably stronger economically.

Parliament has been seen as enabling Britain to overcome these difficulties by raising taxation and guaranteeing low-interest national debt. Warfare was extremely expensive, in large part because of the cost of the largest navy in the world, as well as the burden of subsidizing allies on the continent. In the War of American Independence, for example, expenditure rocketed: £114.6 million was spent in 1776-82 and the national debt rose from £127 million (1775) to £232 million (1783). In the Seven Years' War, the government spent about £83 million.

The parliamentary-secured funded National Debt, based on the Bank of England, enabled British ministries to borrow large sums at low rates of interest. Whereas, in the early 1690s, the government was paying up to 14% for long-term loans,the rate of interest fell to 6-7% in the war years of 1702-14. Due to the debt burden of war, the peacetime rate of interest was also very important. This was only 4% in the late 1720s, and, after a wartime rise 3 – 5% in 1750. The French government was in a weaker financial position. Rates of interest were generally higher, government finances were intertwined with those of the private financiers, there was no consolidated revenue fund, the Treasury's authority and knowledge were limited, and the public had limited confidence in a system that was all too private.

In Britain, Parliament provided an opportunity for commercial groups to exert influence and to seek to define public support for commerce, greater than that offered by the French Council of Commerce of the 1700s or the Bureau of Commerce of the 1780s. Commercial pressure groups played an important role in the House of Commons. These could be either narrow, for example the Liverpool MPs who sought to defend the Slave Trade, or formidably broad, such as the extensive pressure in the Commons for war with Spain in 1739. More indirect, but also considerable, was the pressure exerted by those engaged in one way or another in the trade with India and the Far East, partly, but only partly, institutionalized in the East India Company. Commercial pressure did not lead to social tension: an appreciable number of the businessmen in the Commons came from elite families; there was little class barrier here between upper and middle class. Indeed, "rotten boroughs" provided an important route for the political expression of the aspirations of such groups. An important aspect of the success of the Commons was its admission of the new emergent mercantile and industrial interests of the century; both in membership of the Commons, and in the House's consideration of commercial interests.

The conclusion might therefore seem clear. Parliament was the crucial nexus of political, social, and economic relationships. Thanks to Parliament, it was possible to obtain public support for the government's fiscal needs, through borrowing and through taxation. An income tax was introduced in 1798 when wartime needs called for far more than traditional expedients.

This is the current Whiggish, teleological account of Britain's rise to greatness. Parliamentary authority was the crucial source of national strength and imperial expansion. It is, however, an analysis that is questionable for a number of reasons. First, it was by no means the case that Parliament accepted what the government felt to be necessary. Walpole's proposals to extend new excise regulations to wine and tobacco in 1733 provoked a furious political row, and the ministry had to abandon the scheme. The absence of a reliable party unity, on which government could rest, left ministers feeling vulnerable to attack. Despite devoting so much of their time to electoral patronage and parliamentary management, ministers such as Walpole and Newcasle knew that it was difficult to maintain the impression of governmental control of the Commons. In 1744-6, Carteret was weakened by his inability to secure the management of the Commons. In October 1756, the approach of the parliamentary session destroyed the Newcastle ministry and in the subsequent political crisis the creation of a workable leadership in the Commons was the key issue.

Even if Parliament did support government proposals, that did not necessarily imply that popular consent was gained. The Cider Excise of 1763, a tax upon cider and perry made in Britain, encountered considerable opposition and was repealed in 1766. After the Seven Years' War, the government sought to ease the burden of its debts and to reaffirm parliamentary authority in American affairs by imposing a number of duties, including those on stamped paper (Stamp Act, 1765) and on glass, paper, lead, and tea imported into the American colonies (Townshend Act, 1767). These played a major role in exacerbating Anglo-American relations. Indeed, the danger of a parliamentary system, whether democratic, quasi-democratic, or neither, was clearly reflected in this episode, because those who cannot prevail in the assembly or feel unrepresented in it will not necessarily accept its injunctions.

Even if consent could be obtained, it is far from clear that Britain's success should be ascribed primarily to parliamentary public finance. The great French historian, Fernand Braudel, suggested that the volume of borrowing might have had very different results had Britain been defeated in her quest to become a world power.[1]

The comparative perspective can be helpful here. The Hanoverian age was not a great one for representative institutions. The role of the British Parliament appeared especially important to continental visitors, for only in Sweden, Poland, and the United Provinces (Netherlands) were there comparable institutions, and none was so successful: the Swedish Age of Liberty came to an end in 1772, while the Dutch Estates General and the Polish Diet were proverbial for delay and disagreement. Their systems of government were also discredited, the Dutch by the political breakdown and civil conflict of 1786-7, the Polish by the failures leading to the three partitions of the country. The British system, in contrast, could be presented as excellent, an excellence that reflected the balanced nature of the constitution and that was demonstrated by the successes of Britain: in avoiding autocracy at home and in gaining imperial triumphs abroad.

Thus Parliament enabled Britain to compete successfully with the growing military strength of the other European powers – a different constitutional cum governmental route to military power – and at the same time was crucial to the global power of the British state: there was no collapse of naval finances during the Seven Years' War comparable to that which affected France.

Yet this analysis is all too simplistic, and bears little reference to the hopes and fears of contemporaries. The modern tendency to concentrate on "structural" factors, the inherent strength and character of the two states of England and France, are of considerable importance, but they lend a misleading appearance of inevitability to the outcome of the conflict. To treat the wars as a single unit entails offering a somewhat schematic interpretation that diminishes the role of circumstances and individuals. In order to understand the military and political nature of the conflicts it is necessary to rediscover the play of contingency, to recover narrative.

It is easy to point to crises, such as the congruence of Jacobite advance and French invasion preparations during the '45, the disastrous early stages of the Seven Years' War, the Bourbon invasion attempt of 1779, or the repeated failures at the hands of Revolutionary and Napoleonic France. It is then possible to ask how far Parliament helped in the response. On occasion this is not a pertinent question. The Hanoverian Parliament sat for less than half the year and, in particular, was in recess during the summer, the campaigning season. Thus, Parliament was not in session during the 1779 invasion panic, or when the Revolutionary French overran the Austrian Netherlands (Belgium) in November 1792, or when George II and Carteret mishandled the victory at Dettingen in 1743.

For much of the course of the War of American Independence, Parliament provided firm support for the government, helped by Lord North's victories in the elections of 1774 and 1780. There were serious domestic problems, particularly in Ireland, the Association Movement and the Gordon Riots, but Parliament was firm. Yet after Yorktown, this support collapsed. There was increasing pressure for a change of ministry or at least policy. One MP wrote on 30 November 1781:

> There was a strong opposition to the Address in both houses on the ground of their pledging themselves by it to American war ... It seems to be pretty generally allowed that the prosecution of it internally is no longer possible.

The country gentlemen who usually supported the government in the House of Commons were no longer willing to continue supporting the cost of an unsuccessful war. On 7 February 1782, the ministry's majority fell to 22 on a motion of censure. On 22 February, an Address against continuing the American war was only narrowly blocked and on 27 February the government was defeated on the issue. The motion encapsulated the opposition view on policy towards America:

> ... that the further prosecution of offensive warfare on the continent of North America, for the purpose of reducing the revolted colonies to obedience by force, will be the means of weakening the efforts of this country against her European enemies, tends under the present circumstances dangerously to increase the mutual enmity, so fatal to the interests both of Great Britain and America, and, by preventing a happy reconciliation with that country, to frustrate the earnest desire graciously expressed by His Majesty to restore the blessings of public tranquillity.

Lord North announced the government's resignation to the Commons on 20 March 1782. Britain, of course, was at war at this point. Her forces still held New York, Charleston, and Savannah. The naval war with France was starting to turn in her favour. Thus, the role of Parliament can be presented in two lights. It can be seen as forcing a change of policy on an unwilling government, especially on George III, or as dangerously and publicly undercutting a ministry seeking to adapt to adverse circumstances. The latter claim can also be made about Shelburne's subsequent failure to win parliamentary support for the peace terms.

Similar comments can be made about the 1740s and 1750s. In 1745 when Charles Edward Stuart invaded Britain, Pitt the Elder saw the parliamentary session as an opportunity to put pressure on George II, in order to force his way into office. On 23 October 1745, he moved a motion designed to embarrass the ministry, an Address to George to recall all British troops still remaining in the Austrian Netherlands. All the infantry had, in fact, already been recalled to confront the likely Jacobite invasion of England, and cavalry were difficult to transport, but Pitt's motion offered an opportunity to press the ministers on a sensitive subject and to demonstrate the problems he could create. Henry Pelham defeated the motion by a majority of only eight, an extremely low figure by the standards of an age when the absence of marked party discipline lent an air of instability to ministries that could not command substantial majorities.

Pitt's tactics led to a government attempt to win him over, but his demands were impossible if Britain's alliances were to be maintained. The Earl of Chesterfield complained that Pitt's speeches needlessly exposed views "both to the Dutch, and to the French". On 19 December 1745, Pitt attacked the use of foreign troops, at the very time when the Hessians, whose use Pitt castigated, were widely seen as necessary for planned operations against the Jacobites. Pitt again attacked Britain's foreign and military policy in 1756, for example, unsuccessfully opposing an Address to George II to send for Hanoverian troops to prevent a threatened French invasion of England. Pitt's policy helped to lead to the resignation of the Duke of Newcastle's ministry that year.

Again, the role of Common's opposition can be seen in two lights. Pitt can be seen as a cynical opportunist, needlessly threatening political and governmental stability at a time of national crisis. Alternatively, it can be argued that the existing government could not cope, that war accented a central feature of the political system, namely that successful parliamentary management required competent leadership and acceptable policies, as well as patronage, and that, especially in periods of real and apparent crisis, such policies had to take note of the wider political world.

Parliament's political role thus has to be considered in the context of contemporary controversy about policies and personnel. It is difficult to be conclusive about its importance, because the very nature of a political crisis was that it involved a number of factors. The extent to which government policy, and the response to it which indeed could play a role in shaping policy, were affected by the existence of Parliament and the consequent need for government to consider how best to win parliamentary support or reply to parliamentary criticism, were unclear to contemporaries. Much clearly depended on the particular issue and occasion. As Parliament was the public forum in which the ministry formally presented and defended its policy and was criticized in a fashion that obliged it to reply, it was Parliament where the public debate about policy can be seen as most intense and effective. There was an obligation to respond that was lacking in the world of print, and an immediate linkage between the taking of decisions and the debates, the debates themselves being occasioned by the discussion of these very decisions. Thus, Parliament had a role that it otherwise lacked in a direct constitutional sense. To note the problems created for government by Parliament is to emphasize that its existence created serious difficulties, as well as the advantages that are generally stressed in schematic accounts. It is unclear how much weight should be placed on these problems. Much clearly depends on an obviously subjective response to the issues of stability, continuity, and order. What can be emphasized is that at a time when the modern role of Parliament is being questioned, and may be fundamentally revised as a consequence of devolution within Britain, and both federalism and constitutional-legal changes within Europe, it is possible to look back and note that even in an earlier glorious era doubts had been raised. Yet, it is also worth stressing that the alternatives were bleak. Enlightened Despotism was not only autocratic; it could also be inept and unsuccessful, as the Emperor Joseph II showed in the 1780s. France was scarcely much of an advertisement for a more "constitutional", yet still powerful monarchy. Impatience with representative assemblies led to William IV of Orange's seizure of power in Holland and Zealand in 1747 and to Gustavus II doing the same in Sweden in 1772. Both led to serious problems and were unsuccessful in the long term.

The Westminster Parliament was one of the sole successful representative assemblies of the period. By 1800, Poland had been partitioned and the United Provinces, Swiss Confederation, and Venice conquered by the French. Republican experiments in France had proved short-lived. Only in the United States did distance from powerful enemies permit the development of a decentralized representative system. In Britain, the Westminster Parliament extended to incorporate those of Edinburgh and Dublin. As already indicated, this should not be seen in a triumphalist fashion, but it can be viewed as an increasingly distinctive feature of Britain in this period. The relationship between centre and locality, state and population, sovereign and subject, was more, apparently and obviously, formally and informally, consensual than in most of the rest of Europe: tension was integral to this relationship, but it brought important advantages and was fundamental to British political culture.[2]

Footnotes to this Chapter may be found on page 210.

7: Valerie Cromwell

The Victorian Commons, 1832-1884

IN 1832, the House of Commons appeared in many ways substantially the same as it had been in 1780 and earlier. Although the procedure and practices of the 18th century Commons had developed in significant ways to enable Parliament to cope with pressures at home and abroad, the ways of conducting parliamentary business had changed little. At home, these pressures resulted from a deluge of private legislation, associated first with land enclosure and later with the building of canals: from abroad the needs of conducting war on land and sea on an unprecedented scale forced some emergency procedures related to legislation and the voting of supply. In contrast, by the late 19th century, the role of Parliament in British society and the way the Commons functioned had been profoundly transformed. Against a background of accelerating industrialization and urbanization, the important effects of easier communications and an ever cheaper press offered new opportunities for wide scale political activity to an increasingly politically sensitive nation. The key to Parliament's survival in anything like its earlier form lay in the ways it would adapt to these new developments. Public opinion seemed to demonstrate its power over Parliament in a most dramatic way during the Reform Bill crisis of 1830-32. It is now generally accepted, however, that at no point in the period 1815-1918 did Britain experience democracy. More importantly, perhaps, Britain did not and has not experienced any type of violent political revolution such as have almost all continental states in either the 19th or 20th centuries. Some explanation of these apparently antipathetic phenomena must be found in the functioning and responsiveness of Parliament to active external political forces.

There can be no doubt that the passing of electoral reform legislation in 1832 appeared as an important example of this responsiveness and was also of great symbolic importance to contemporaries. Great were the hopes of the reformers and great the fears of the opponents of reform for the future. For many years, reformers had railed against the unrepresentative nature and the apparent general unresponsiveness of the Commons. Their hopes centred on the potentially beneficial effects of a wider franchise and the increased representation and, in some cases, new representation of the growing industrial towns. In addition, great inequality existed between the large number of "pocket boroughs", with negligible electorates, and the increasing electorates of county seats. Outside Westminster, the activities of the Political Reform Associations, building on 50 years of argument for the redistribution of parliamentary seats and for the rationalization of the qualifications for the vote, presented an almost unstoppable case for electoral reform. In Parliament, the Whigs had certainly become convinced of the need for change: the strength of the rioting, especially in Bristol and Nottingham in 1830-32, furnished excellent witness of what might happen if reform were to be blocked.

The rioting also fuelled the fears of those who trembled for the position of the old political balance, in which political power was linked to the ownership of land or wealth, if the right to vote were widened. Any move towards a wider franchise was always attacked as opening the door to the sway of demagogues and the domination of MPs by the electorate: the image of Wilkes' case cast a long shadow.

So what was so significant about 1832? The very passing of the 1832 Bill was clear evidence of the responsiveness of the unreformed Commons to outside opinion. The Bill's first reading was carried in an excited House with 607 members present. Recent scholarship has indicated the vitality of 18th century political life. John Phillips has analyzed borough elections in the unreformed Parliament and found a very high level of local electoral involvement.[1] Paul Langford has pointed to the liveliness of 18th century parliamentary activity and demonstrated the links between the property owned by MPs and that parliamentary activity. MPs regularly acted as agents for parts of the country unrepresented in Parliament in such a way as to satisfy their legislative needs.[2] Apart from noting the passing of such legislation in the late 18th and early 19th centuries, Peter Fraser has drawn attention to the importance of public petitioning to Parliament for the raising of matters of moment in the Commons, thereby enabling the unreformed House to respond constructively to stresses in society.[3] It should also be pointed out that the 1830 election was the first election that a government had lost since the early 18th century. It is, therefore, clear that the electorate's role and extraparliamentary political activity were in no sense negligible before 1832.

There are many problems associated with the interpretation of the motives of members of the government in steering the Bill through both Houses in the face of strong opposition, particularly in the Lords and also in assessing the Act's effects. There can be no doubt that the significance of the 1832 Reform Act was largely symbolic. For the reformers it opened the door if only a little to wider representation: the unexpected threat that the new King (William IV) would agree to create enough new peers to ensure the passage of the Bill through the Lords was an indication of their apparent success. The passing of the Act, even though limited in its effects, was of enormous importance because it encouraged the belief that further reforming legislation might be passed in future. For many in the Commons greatly disturbed by the level of public rioting, the Act represented a necessary concession to ensure public order. The rioting also provided justification for the reformers. However, some saw it as bluff. John Arthur Roebuck, the radical reforming MP, recalled later in 1848,

> ... to attain our end, much was said that no one really believed; much was done that no one would like to own ... often, when there was no danger, the cry of alarm was raised to keep the House of Lords and the aristocracy generally in what was termed a state of wholesome terror. When the Bill proceeded with ease ... a grave calm was preserved in

> our demeanour and writings ... when its provisions were threatened ...
> black clouds rose obedient to our call, as regularly as on the stage at
> the scene-shifter's command; our language grew violent, we stormed,
> we threatened and prophesied, and, like some other prophets, we were
> determined to accomplish our own predictions. Processions, meetings,
> harangues, revolutionary resolutions, banners, mobs, assemblages both
> by night and day, all like a furious hurricane, swept over the face of the
> political waters.[4]

Against this noisy background, the passing of the Act must be seen. The
parliamentary debates over the details of the proposed legislation, however,
seemed to take place in a very different world. Moderate Whig support for
radical demands lay in the presentation of extremely modest proposals. Whig
leaders regarded these as necessary concessions to strong popular demand,
which would, however, ensure that they remained in power. The opponents
of reform argued quite correctly that any change in the electoral system would
open the floodgates to further radical measures just as the radical reformers
hoped. The Whig reformers replied that the proposed changes would improve
and perfect the constitution thereby rendering further electoral change
unnecessary. They dissociated themselves from earlier radical cries for
manhood suffrage. Grey was careful to emphasize the cautiousness of the
government's proposals in the Lords in October 1831,

> I deny, therefore, that these changes will have the effect of injuring the
> landed interest, strengthened as it will be by the addition made to the
> county representation ... when the abuses of such a system have been
> generally exposed, is it possible to maintain it?
>
> In removing the odium of such a system, and introducing another, in
> which the legitimate influence of rank, and property, and intelligence
> will have their due weight, this Bill affords the most effectual security
> to those interests which it is alleged to destroy.[5]

The changes effected were in the event minimal. The worst pocket boroughs
and the worst anomalies in the franchise were eliminated. The Act
disfranchised 56 boroughs with fewer than 2,000 inhabitants, which had
previously returned 111 MPs. One member was removed from 30 boroughs
with a population of between 2,000 and 4,000 and the representation of a
few others was altered. Ninety-seven new seats were distributed to English
constituencies, one to Wales, five to Scotland, and three to Ireland. These
were allocated mainly to large towns, but also went some way to improve
county representation. A standardized qualification (£10 Householder) for
male voting in boroughs was introduced in place of the multiplicity of local
qualifications which had become established over time. In the counties, the
ancient 40 shilling freehold franchise was supplemented with a few new
franchises. An irony is that the framers of the Act had very little idea of what
the numerical effects of the changes might be. Lack of reliable census
information, or evidence on the variations of local property values made this

uncertainty inevitable. The total electorate in England and Wales which resulted was approximately 653,000 males.

Tory fears of the Act's effects on the House proved to be ungrounded. The influx of new members, who had never sat in the House before 1833, was 37% of the total membership, but to put that figure into perspective, the comparable turnover in 1826 had been 26%. The explanation of the relatively low turnover figure in the circumstances of 1832 lies in the personnel changes which had already occurred after the elections of 1830 and 1831. It was not surprising that the electorate in late 1832 reelected those members who had supported electoral reform, when they had apparently elected them in 1831 for that purpose. When the new House met in 1833, its composition proved little different in social and political complexion from that of its predecessors. Long before 1832, the purchase of small boroughs had provided an easy route into the Commons for men of means, whether their wealth derived from land or industry. The change that came in 1833 was that the modest redistribution of seats resulted in such men as William Ewart Gladstone, a Liverpool merchant, who had sat for Bletchingley or Thomas Houldsworth, a Manchester cotton spinner, who had sat for Newton (Lancs), before 1832, came to represent the areas of their business interests or the counties in which they lived rather than rotten boroughs. The country gentry were also affected since the number of county seats went up from 94 to 159 in England and Wales. Having represented Bramber in 1831, William Dugdale of Blyth Hall, Warwickshire, became member for the northern division of Warwickshire in 1832: James Wortley of Wortley Hall, Yorkshire, who had sat for Bossiney in 1831, was elected for Halifax in 1832. Thus the effects of the Act in terms of members might be described as a rationalization rather than a transformation of the interests represented there. It is always difficult to determine a definition of individual sources of income. In the 1830s, as before and after, many merchants and traders were also substantial landowners. Although the sons of merchants might not be involved in the family business, they often depended on it for financial support. William Ewart Gladstone and his brother, Thomas, were the sons of the wealthy Liverpool merchant, John Gladstone. Despite these problems of definition, an analysis of the financial resources of members of the Commons reveals a surprising continuity in the proportion of those with mercantile, as compared with those with landed, interests before and after 1832. If anything, not only was the percentage of merchants, manufacturers, and bankers in the 1833 House, including those with only marginal claims to be listed as such, relatively low (13%), but oddly that figure is slightly lower than that in the last unreformed Parliament.[6] Similarly, the House was not to be swamped with radicals and demagogues as the Tories had feared. In fact, the Tories remained a very large minority which included abut 150 staunch opponents of the Act. Thus, for all these reasons, the 1833 House portrayed by Sir George Hayter looked very much the same as the unreformed House.

The electoral system which remained left many of the arguments for reform unsatisified. What was wrong with the system from the point of view of the reformers, apart from the question of extending the right to vote, was the survival of different borough and county and representation and, what was worse, of the gross imbalance between county borough representation in the distribution of constituencies. This imbalance was only to be effectively addressed in the Redistribution of Seats Act of 1885 when the majority of the old parliamentary counties and boroughs were broken up into single-member constituencies. Two interrelated factors ensured that the nature of electoral politics remained much the same. The first was the survival of electoral corruption associated with the essentially local character of English political life in the first half of the 19th century. The reformed system made very little difference to the style of local election campaigns. The second was the continuation of open voting. After 1832, there were still many constituencies with small numbers of voters. Seven English boroughs, Tavistock, Totnes, Reigate, Chippenham, Harwich, Horsham, and Lyme Regis, polled fewer than 200 votes at the 1832 election. There are many instances of the persistence of aristocratic influence in borough and county elections; the Cavendishes in Derbyshire, the Russells in Bedfordshire, and the Longs in Wiltshire were probably the most obvious examples. It is relevant to note that 13 of the 60 Tory members elected in 1832 were returned for the same seats they had held in 1831: eleven of those unseated in 1832 returned to the Commons later. Twenty-six members for the disfranchised boroughs returned in the 1832 election represented other constituencies, nearly half of them county seats in areas where they owned land: a further 22 found similar seats in later elections. Philip Miles, a Bristol merchant, MP for Corfe Castle before 1832, was returned for Bristol in 1835. One interesting side-effect of the disfranchisement of boroughs was that, of the 22 merchants and bankers who had sat for them, only six got back to the Commons in 1832 and another six in later parliaments. Thus, paradoxically, the disfranchisement of 56 small boroughs removed a route into the Commons just as smooth for merchants, bankers, and industrialists as for landowners. The continuation of electoral bribery and corruption was inevitable as long as borough constituencies with small electorates and open voting remained. "Treating" and even violence continued. William Gladstone's first seat in 1833 was for a pocket borough.

What was therefore new? Most important was an acceptance that change was possible. The weaknesses of the electoral system had been admitted and the transformation so dreaded by the Tories had been begun. The group of radicals who entered the Commons in 1833 soon pressed for a number of important legal and social reforms, which were achieved in the 1830s – anti-slavery legislation, the reform of local municipal government, factory reform, and the new poor law as well as much legislation to regulate commercial matters. The passing of such extensive legislation significantly increased pressure on the limited parliamentary timetable. Most important, the Act itself introduced a requirement for electors to be registered. Procedures for registration had to be devised: the elected overseers of the poor in each parish found themselves responsible for compiling the registers and a system of revision courts presided over by a Revising Barrister was set up to see fair play. This requirement for registration provided an important encouragement for the development of more sophisticated methods of local political organization. It also offered the opportunity to devise new forms of electoral corruption and sharp practice. The purchase of property for political supporters and large-scale objections to the names of political opponents on the register soon became accepted practice.[7] The effects of these changes were, however, only to become clearly visible after 1867.

From 1832, it is important to note that until 1868, the 1841 election remained the only clear example of the electorate's choosing a government by reducing the representation of the party in power at the time of the Dissolution of Parliament. Thus the 1832 Act had little significant effect on the role of the electorate in determining the composition of the Commons. More important was that the Commons remained unrepresentative in terms of electoral contests until well into the 20th century. In the period 1832 to 1867, there were approximately 400 constituencies, the vast majority of them electing two seats each. In the first election after the passing of the 1832 Act, when great interest would have been expected among the electorate, there was no contest in 48 boroughs. Thus, apart from the new boroughs, the proportion of contested to uncontested boroughs was about three to one. Strangley, six of the new boroughs were uncontested, Birmingham, Cheltenham, Gateshead, Kendal, Wakefield, and Merthyr Tydvil. In the counties, an even greater proportion of seats were uncontested: of 80 county constituencies, 32 were uncontested. Given the relative rarity of electoral contests in the counties in the 18th century, this situation is not perhaps entirely surprising, but, against a background of the unsettled political state in the country, it is an indicator of the persistent strength of influence. It also reflects the high cost of contested elections in counties with large electorates. The total number of seats uncontested in 1832 was 124, that is more than a quarter. The number of uncontested constituencies rose to a peak of 240 in 1859, well over half the total. In the period after the 1867 Reform Act until 1884, there were 420 constituencies, some electing three MPs, the bulk two, and a few one. At the 1874 election, with the further extension of the franchise and the introduction of the secret ballot, 122 seats were surprisingly uncontested. From that election, the number uncontested fluctuated erratically. In the 1880 election, the most expensive election ever before the passing of the 1883 Corrupt Practices' Act, 67 seats were uncontested.[8]

In many ways, the 1867 Reform Bill represented a second stage of what had been begun in 1832. It extended the franchise from 1,300,000 to 2,500,000 votes, opening the vote to many skilled male artisans. The relatively modest nature of this increase may be indicated by noting that the total population of the time has been calculated at approximately 26 million. The act extended the borough franchise to householders with a one-year residential qualification and to lodgers who had occupied lodgings worth £10 a year, also for a year. In the counties, it created an occupation franchise for those occupying lands worth £12 a year and a property franchise for those with lands worth £5 a year. Although there had been for some time external pressure for further electoral reform, but not rioting as in 1830-2, the atmosphere of the Commons' debates was totally different this time. The final form of the Act resulted from extraordinary manoeuvrings in the House as a result of the defeat in 1866 of a Liberal reform bill by an unexpected combination of Tories and dissident Liberals.[9] The bill that was eventually passed was at the initiative of a Tory government. Hasty draftsmanship, sudden changes of mind, and constant revision by amendment meant that the Act passed bore little resemblance to the text initially introduced by ministers. This was Derby's "great experiment and 'taking a leap in the dark' ", and represented a great political gamble for the Tories. They were banking on future electoral support from the skilled artisans. Even more than in 1832, the drafters of the 1867 clauses had very little idea of the possible effects of the complex changes likely to result. This time they should have had a better idea of the shape and distribution of the population. By then, three reasonably well constructed and administered national censuses had been carried out. Redistribution of seats was again undertaken, but the distinction between the counties and the boroughs remained. Unlike 1832, when a significant number of redistributed borough seats went to the counties, in 1867 it was the borough electorates which benefited. A few experiments were tried including the allocation of a third seat to a few substantial towns: in these the voters still had two votes. This oddity created a splendid chance for electoral manipulation. In Birmingham, the Liberals operated a "vote as you're told" strategy and won all three seats. The enlarged electorate encouraged the Westminster parties to extend party organization into the constituencies. These fledgling organizations proved as adept in exploiting old electoral practices as landowners, manufacturers, and the election committees had been in the period after 1832.[10] The slackness of control of the preparation of the voting registers was matched by the continuing failure to control the process of voting. There was still much intimidation of electors especially in 1868 when the number of voters increased and also extensive treating and bribery: corruption seemed to increase. So much is known of electoral politics in the period up to 1872 because of the survival of printed electoral poll books for the bulk of contested parliamentary constituencies. Although varying a good deal, a large number of these poll books give not only the political sympathy of the voter, but also his address and his source of income. Only in the last 20 years with the help of computers have historians been able to analyze in a systematic way these splendid sources for large scale analysis of local electoral politics. The introduction of the secret ballot in 1872 inevitably ended poll book publication.

Within the House, much appeared to remain the same on the surface. Many of the old forms survived in the shape of ceremonial and the formalized styles of address, many of which are still current. The number of members in the chamber on an average working day remained much the same until well into the 20th century when it slightly declined. In this period, members were rarely dragooned by the whips into the division lobbies except on matters of great political significance. Table A indicates the low rate of participation by MPs in Commons' divisions in this period and the effects of gradually increasing pressure by the whips over the period 1861 to 1926. Here, again, the availability of computers has provided the means for interpreting the

Table A
Voting participation by MPs in selected sessions

Total in brackets gives number of MPs eligible to vote in the session, but who did not vote.

Session	Total no. of divisions in the session	Highest no. of votes by an MP in the session	No. of MPs voting in any division in the session	MPs voting over 50% of total no. of divisions	Percentage of MPs voting who vote in 50% or less than 50% of the total no. of divisions
1861	187	182	654 (662)	71	89.14
1871	270	269	648 (655)	127	80.40
1876	242	241	652 (660)	125	80.82
1881	411	408	647 (649)	153	76.35
1886	143	139	676 (677)	166	75.44
1891	416	415	675 (685)	136	79.85
1896	419	418	670 (675)	205	69.40
1901	482	481	671 (673)	246	63.34
1906	501 (2)*	500	680 (683)	421	38.09
1911	451	443	688 (692)	335	51.31
1916	67	65	609 (678)	121	80.13
1921	370	356	641 (650)	180	71.92
1926	563	560	615 (620)	363	40.98

*One unnumbered division included.

(Table derived from research funded by the Economic and Social Research Council, Research Grant E 00 23 0051)

pattern of voting behaviour of members from the printed Commons' Division Lists, published from 1832. All these continuities of behaviour should be seen against a complete transformation of the physical parliamentary environment and a profound change in the relationships between the Commons and the world outside, and between the executive government and the independent members of the Commons, the world of the new.

The most profound change was precipitated by the destruction of the bulk of the buildings then in use by both Houses in the terrible fire of the night of 16 October 1834. The majority of the buildings had been in use since the early 16th century and before. The fire had been caused by the burning through that day of tally sticks from the Exchequer Office, wooden tally accounting having been abandoned in 1826. London's worst fire since 1666 drew enormous crowds. Everything was destroyed apart from Westminster Hall, the walls of the Painted Chamber and St Stephen's Chapel, the Crypt Chapel and the Cloisters, now the members' cloakroom. Since 1801, the Lords had been sitting in the old Court of Requests, which is now the site of the statue of Richard Coeur de Lion. In the emergency, they offered their building to the Commons. Surveyors had judged its walls sound enough to be converted for use as a temporary House of Commons. Thus some of the earliest and best speeches of Gladstone and Disraeli were heard in the Lords' Chamber. The Lords themselves would move temporarily into the remains of the Painted Chamber. At this early stage after the fire, some members considered that enough remained of the Palace of Westminster for the old buildings to be refurbished appropriately. This view was rapidly suppressed. For a long time, criticism had been growing in the Commons about their accommodation. In the 30 years before the catastrophic fire, this concern about working conditions had led to a little rebuilding work to remedy the worst disrepair and also the cutting of recesses in the medieval arcading of the crowded and hot St Stephen's: nothing, however, had been done about the totally inadequate provision for the conduct of burgeoning Commons' business, in particular the increasing number of committees. The fire, therefore, offered "English architecture its finest opportunity since the Great Fire of London".[11] The Commons' committee set up in 1835 under the chairmanship of the first Lord Sudeley to consider the future building decided to institute a competition for a design in the Gothic or Elizabethan style and to appoint a Royal Commission to decide on the winner. The competition resulted in the choice of Sir Charles Barry who was assisted in the drawings needed for the estimates by A W Pugin. In 1844, Pugin returned to work with Barry on designs for the decoration of the new building. When Barry died in May 1860, the new Palace of Westminster seemed almost complete. His second son, Edward Barry, completed the work.

There is little evidence of any debate about the layout of the two new Houses. For the Commons, it appears that the committee and Barry deliberately adopted the shape of the old one, though it is known that Barry had wanted a spacious square shape to accommodate all the members with ease. The total membership was now 658 after the Union with Ireland. Delays caused by haggling over the proposed costs of the building and revisions in the design resulted in the laying of the foundation stone of the new palace only in 1840, nearly five years after the announcement of the chosen architect. The designs were constantly altered in the next 10 years as the result of pressures from future users and in response to artistic opinion, technical advice, and financial considerations. At one point, the construction of the towers was nearly cancelled. To achieve completion required phenomenal determination and energy on the part of Barry. He catalogued his problems,

> I have also been called upon to remodel the internal fittings of the Two Houses and to vary from time to time the arrangement and appropriations of the Offices, the Division lobbies &c of each House owing to the changes made in the mode of conducting the business of Parliament and the vagueness and insufficiency of the information afforded for the preparation of the original design which information upon being reconsidered by committees appointed from time to time during the progress of the works has been found in many instances to be altogether at variance with the requirements ... The entire plan and construction of the building has had to be modified and recast over and over again...[12]

By 1870, the building was complete. Wren's classic mouldings had been replaced by Gothic arches: Pugin's carving had replaced the work of Grinling Gibbons. There have been many alterations to the building since completion mainly as a result of Second World War bombing. More recently, however, both Houses have been concerned to restore the Palace as closely as possible to its original form. Simultaneously, other accommodation has been acquired and a second new building is under construction to accommodate the needs of Parliament in the 21st century. For guidance in the restoration of the Palace, Barry's competition drawings are unfortunately lost. Consequently, the architectural drawings by George Penrose Kennedy are of great value: Kennedy worked in Barry's office together with at least 18 other assistants. These drawings are now in the House of Lords' Record Office as are Thomas Greene's papers. Greene was a conscientious Conservative MP for Lancashire. He became Chairman of Ways and Means in 1841 (till 1847) and was one of the three commissioners for the completion of the New Palace of Westminster (1848-1851). The commission was intended to speed the new building's completion and to control the finances for it more carefully. It was inevitable that it would soon find itself in a difficult relationship with Barry. There can be no doubt that, as Michael Port has explained, "it was Barry's 'cool determination to act without leave' that built the New Palace at Westminster."[13]

In 1850, the Commons was able to move into its new chamber and then the complaints from members began. The new chamber was only a little wider and shorter than the old St Stephen's Chapel. Thus, the inadequacy of seating provision was soon clear. The main discomforts, however, concerned ventilation and lighting. The design and effectiveness of both of these services were to be profoundly handicapped by the personal differences which developed between Barry and his scientific consultant, David Boswell Reid. This friction was the result of the division of authority between architect and technical adviser, and had reached such a level in 1846 that committees of both Houses investigated the situation. This led to Barry becoming responsible for ventilating the Lords and Reid the Commons. The real technical innovation in the construction of the new Palace was the proposed intricate ventilation system. Reid faced the same procedural handicaps in the design of this system as Barry and Pugin were experiencing with the architectural and interior designs: he was finally dismissed in 1852. After the system had been running for only a short time, successive efforts to improve it seemed to make things worse. The Thames "stank unbearably in hot weather". Artificial ventilation recycled the foetid air. In May 1865, "between the hours of four and six in the afternoon, many members were in a state of semi-asphyxia."[14] These poor conditions inevitably affected the attendance of members, especially in warm weather and also limited the length of sessions. The problem was never really solved. Certain improvements were eventually made by Dr John Percy and the system survived into the 20th century. The ventilation problems were made worse by the new lighting system, which at that date required some form of combustion. By 1852, the gas lighting system incorporating huge gasoliers, which had been included by Barry in 1847, designed on Faraday's principle, had already been replaced on the grounds that it gave off too much heat. The new system then recommended by David Reid and installed was itself replaced a year later by one designed by Goldsworthy Gurney. Although grumbles continued, many years were to pass before electric lighting was to be introduced.

Together with the complete transformation of the working environment of the Commons came a much more open relationship of the Commons with the world outside. Until the beginning of the 19th century, the proceedings of the Commons were very private. Before the end of the 18th century, the printing of the Commons' Journals had begun, thereby making the proceedings of the House more publicly available. The press reported members' speeches only if members supplied copies. Sometimes important parliamentary figures published volumes of their speeches. In 1803, it was on the initiative of the radical William Cobbett, when he commenced the publication of *Parliamentary Debates*, that any reasonably full published reporting of what was said in the Commons began. In 1812, this pioneering publication passed into the hands of Thomas Hansard, who had always printed it. In this period, *Hansard* was in no sense an accurate or full record of Commons' debates. Members could supply their own speeches and also amend the proposed printed versions. It was not till the 20th century that Hansard became an official and verbatim publication. Even so, press coverage of debates in Parliament became much fuller and more authoritative in the 19th century. Some leading politicians, in the case of Palmerston, a prime minister, wrote extensively, sometimes anonymously, in the press. An enlarged electorate and increased literacy among the population ensured a growing readership and encouragement of a more popular press. Journalists found themselves more welcome in the lobbies of the Commons. Soon the first lobby correspondent was to appear, Henry Lucy, eventually to be popular Toby MP in *Punch* and knighted. The public became much more aware of the personalities of their political leaders.

Large print runs of engravings of portraits were sold out. At country fairs, cheap Staffordshire pottery portrait models were keenly purchased and prized by supporters. Gladstone took advantage of the railway network to address massive public meetings from the 1860s and was to pioneer "stumping the country" in Britain: his Midlothian campaign in the late 1870s was an exhausting whistle-stop tour. The political world had become noticeably wider.

Parliament was also helping the public to become better informed. The growth of parliamentary inquiries by select committee together with the appointment of many royal commissions led to an extraordinary increase in the publication of parliamentary papers on a multiplicity of issues. External pressure led to the setting up of many of these inquiries and the reports in their turn fed campaigns for legislative initiatives particularly on social problems. Factory and prison conditions, industrial pollution, the poor law, schools and universities are just a few of the issues which fill the 19th century parliamentary papers, the Blue Books, so named from the colour of their stiff covers.

In this new political world, new style political parties emerged with constituency based organizations. The first half of the 19th century witnessed the appearance of a series of ever more sophisticated extraparliamentary, single issue pressure groups culminating in the Anti-Corn Law League in the 1840s. The organizational expertise developed in such organizations was to be seized by Westminster party managers. The Liberal party was to benefit from the adoption of the methods used by the Liberation Society's network of paid agents. Popular Liberal and Conservative associations were set up in most towns and the Primrose League was founded to appeal to middle-class Conservatives. Political parties had long existed in both Houses of Parliament. It was the 1867 extension of the franchise which encouraged Liberal and Conservative party activists to develop networks of central and local organizations. In this period, the chief function of these fledgling organizations was to remain predominantly that of providing a machine to win elections by the employment of numerous solicitors and election agents to manage the registers and to supervise election tactics. The channelling of opinion from the grass roots to the parliamentary leadership or *vice versa* played a very small role in party activities until well into the 20th century. In the Commons, the tightening of party organization was beginning to erode the independence of the private member, whose position was already becoming weakened by the steady growth of legislative activity by the executive government in the face of massive industrial and social change, the emergence of the collectivist state.

The two important functions of Parliament, the granting of taxes and the passing of legislation, were profoundly altered in the 19th century by this emergence of the collectivist state. During the second half of the 18th century, the Commons had gradually assumed control of all government spending on civil and military business. Although it had thus assumed responsibility for paying for them, there was no system of account and audit to check an extravagant or incompetent government. As the "economical reform" movement with its attack on sinecures gained momentum, the network of Crown patronage which had oiled the wheels of the 18th century political system began to collapse. Thus, by the 1820s, attacks on ministerial "influence" had given way to cries for "retrenchment" in government finances. The next 40 years saw numerous Commons' debates on the detail of government spending. It was not, however, till the 1860s, with Gladstone as Chancellor of the Exchequer, that the Commons was provided with a machinery for full, if retrospective, control of government spending. It is ironic that, with the appointment of the Comptroller and Auditor General, and the setting up of the Public Accounts Committee to implement that control, the House of Commons ceased to discuss financial matters in detail. Debates in the Committee of Supply began to focus on general government policy rather than on the supply votes under discussion. By the 1870s, the Commons had lost its preoccupation with "cheap government". The only vestige of the old principle of redress of grievance before supply lay in the use by members of the motion that the House go into Committee of Supply to raise matters of concern.

It was in the relationship between the executive government and the Commons that another enormous change was experienced in this period. The shift came in the balance of parliamentary time. In the early 19th century, the bulk of the parliamentary working week was devoted to business raised by private Members of Parliament. The steady pressure of government business associated with substantial legislative programmes eventually proved beyond the capacity of the accepted parliamentary timetable. Gradually, as the century progressed, the opportunities for private members to raise matters of concern were tightly limited. The first important restriction was imposed in the 1830s: it removed the right to debate the subject of petitions on their presentation. An innovation, the parliamentary question, slowly came to replace some of the older procedures. Although governments encroached more and more on the time for private members' business, they still found themselves unable to complete their legislative programmes. It has been shown in work on failed bills in Gladstone's first administration (1868-74) how, quite apart from difficulties within the governing party, it was to be cumulative legislative congestion which demoralized the administration.[15] So intense was private members' activity, of all parties or of none, in prolonging debate that it verged on the style of deliberate obstruction which was so skilfully deployed later by Charles Stewart Parnell and his Irish party in the 1880s. The parliamentary session was short. It rarely began before early February and usually ended in late July or early August. Irish members did not like an autumn sitting, which would mean more travelling. Members wished to avoid the unpleasantness of the Thames in hot weather. The parliamentary day usually began at 3.45 pm except on Wednesdays and other days when morning sittings were arranged. Then the House usually met at 12 noon and sat till 6 pm. Certainly, the House could sit for long hours on a normal working day other than a Friday. Business could restart at 10.30 pm after the motion to adjourn at 10pm. The voting of supply required substantial time in each session. The accepted convention was that the House would sit till members were too tired to continue. The problems experienced by governments led to the emergence of delegated legislation and the consequent further weakening of the power of the private members of Parliament.

The passing of the Corrupt Practices Act in 1883, which finally ended the kind of electoral corruption which had characterized parliamentary elections for many previous decades and had even survived the introduction of the secret ballot in 1872, fundamentally altered the nature of British electoral politics. The activities of the party organizations and the cost of the 1880 election indicated to most members of the Commons that significantly greater control of electoral spending was necessary. A reformed electoral system soon followed on the heels of the 1883 Act which had fixed a limit on the election expenses any candidate might incur. Radicals in his party persuaded Gladstone of the need to give counties the same franchise as the boroughs in order to reduce landlord influence. In 1877, in a population of eleven and a half million people in the English counties, H J Hanham has calculated that the electorate there was only 785,343 and, including the boroughs, the ratio overall one elector to eight people.[16] The Conservative opposition struck a deal with Gladstone that substantial extension of the franchise by granting the household qualification to the counties must be accompanied by a large scale redistribution of seats. A pair of substantial reform acts followed, very much more far-reaching than their 1832 and 1867 predecessors. The Representation of the People Act of 1884 gave any householder or lodger who had occupied his house or lodgings for a year before the registration date could now vote. The Redistribution of Seats Act of 1885 broke up the old county and borough two – and three – member constituencies into new single-member constituencies. The basis of the 20th century electoral system had been created.

These three significant changes combined to push the political parties towards much tighter party organizations in the constituencies and also into a more controlling relationship with their parliamentary candidates. The control of electoral spending meant that parties had to recruit armies of volunteers to assist with elections and only they could provide the back-up necessary for candidates in the new electoral world. For many women, as yet unable to vote, this new voluntary work for local party organizations offered their first chance to involve themselves in political work. Everything seemed to be working towards the reduction in the role of the private MP. The success of Parnell's Irish Nationalist party in its strategy of obstruction throughout Gladstone's second ministry had led to the reluctant introduction of a number of tough procedural restrictions, the guillotine and the closure. The pace of growth of delegated legislation was accelerating. The government had assumed almost complete control of the parliamentary timetable. The pathway was now open for the domination of the Commons by the government. That domination would be dependent on its Commons' majority. Continuing strong party discipline would be necessary to ensure this.

Footnotes to this Chapter may be found on pages 210–11.

8: Michael Fry

Universal Suffrage: The Modern House

THE PERIOD between the Reform Acts of 1884 and 1918 produced a remarkable shift in debate about constitutional reform of the United Kingdom. Right through the 19th century, the debate had focused first and foremost on the electoral franchise, on how far to extend the right to vote. By the end, democracy had not quite triumphed, but popular government was clearly here to stay. Its pressures prompted questions about broader defects in the way the country was run, and a search for better ways of running it. The debate came together with another imposed by Britain's external circumstances, the need to maintain, amid growing difficulties, her position as an imperial power. The whole bore directly on the competence of Parliament to exercise the absolute sovereignty which it claimed.

The Reform Act of 1884 still fell some way short of introducing universal male suffrage. It doubled the total electorate, to more than 5.6 million, but this meant that one man in three still had no vote. The Act also preserved certain inequalities, in the business and university constituencies. As a general rule, nevertheless, every ratepayer, together with many lodgers and agricultural tenants, could now register to choose their representatives in the House of Commons. From there it was a relatively short step to granting the franchise to all adult men and to most women in 1918, in acknowledgment of the people's exertions during the First World War.

By itself, the Act of 1884 generated a certain impetus towards broader reform. It was most thoroughgoing in introducing uniform suffrages, in place of the varied and unequal suffrages, according to the place where the vote was cast, that had survived the Acts of 1832 and 1867. Through imposition of uniformity, this latest Act had more dramatic results in some parts of the United Kingdom than in others. In England, it increased the electorate by 67%. In Scotland, it increased the electorate by 80%. In Ireland, it more than tripled the electorate. If we add together the total numbers in the Celtic countries who now enjoyed the franchise, we get, with more than 700,000 from Ireland, almost 600,000 from Scotland, and 300,000 in Wales, very nearly 30% of voters who were not English. That figure stayed much the same till 1918. In no other period have the Celtic counties carried such numerical weight in the political system of the United Kingdom.[1]

For two or three centuries past, those countries had seen England increase its dominance of the system.[2] Now they had some chance to redress the balance. All experienced an upsurge of popular nationalism. In Scotland, it was moderate and cautious, because Scots were satisfied with most aspects of their membership of the Union of 1707, and especially with the access it gave them to the Empire. Still, the governmental structure of the Union was the aspect with which they were least satisfied. They complained about Westminster's neglect of Scottish affairs and about obstacles there to even the most urgent Scottish legislation. Now the protests reached a new pitch, and political leaders on all sides agreed that in prudence something ought to be done. The result, in 1885, was the restoration of the Scottish Secretaryship which had been abolished in 1746 out of misguided political spite after the last Jacobite rebellion, and the creation of the Scottish Office, thus giving the country the foundations of its modern system of government.[3]

There was no such focus of discontent in Wales, because she had lacked all national institutions since her union with England in 1536. But before long, in the course of the 1890s, the Young Wales movement arose out of a genuine religious and linguistic populism. David Lloyd George became a leading figure in it, and so launched his political career by playing a nationalist card. Not for that reason alone, the movement could on the whole be absorbed by the Liberal party, which dominated Wales, so that nationalism did not emerge as an independent political force. Still, the sentiment did as much as anything to preserve Welsh cultural identity into the 20th century.[4]

The most far-reaching consequences came in Ireland. That can be appreciated just by looking at the electoral pattern. The Irish Home Rule League, afterwards known as the Irish Nationalist party, had been formed in 1873. In the two subsequent general elections, on the franchise of 1867, it won about 60 of the 105 Irish constituencies in the House of Commons. A turnover of only eight seats would, therefore, have deprived the party of its majority, and on that reckoning there might still have been some faint hope of turning back the nationalist tide. After the Act of 1884, there was no such hope. In the general election of 1885, the Irish Nationalists won 86 seats out of 103, and despite severe internal dissensions never fell much below that level at later polls. Their majority became overwhelming and impregnable. Meanwhile, they pursued at Westminster a policy of obstruction and disruption which strained politicians' nerves and created terrible practical problems with a parliamentary timetable that was already felt to be grossly overloaded.[5]

To this complex of difficulties, William Gladstone came up inside a year with what he hoped would be a definitive solution, to grant Home Rule to Ireland. But he proposed to do so in a form regarded by many as excessively radical, with exclusion of Irish MPs from Westminster. Unable to carry Parliament or the country with him, Gladstone paid a heavy price. In 1886, he split his own Liberal party, created out of his opponents a Unionist party and brought on, with one brief interval, 20 years of Tory government. He caused besides a general polarization in British politics, all without getting one inch nearer his goal.

Why was there this extreme reaction? Many just could not stomach any loosening of the bonds between Ireland and Great Britain. Ireland had posed a danger to Great Britain while still outside the union of 1801. That union had indeed been immediately prompted by the Irish rebellion and French invasion of 1798, at a time of mortal peril to British independence. The same danger was to exercise Winston Churchill during the Second World War, when the Irish Free State remained neutral. In 1886, the United Kingdom, once the only imperial power of any consequence and still mistress of the seas, was being challenged by a newly united Germany and by other countries. It seemed unthinkable to recreate the remotest possibility of a threat through Ireland. Ireland, after all, remained restive. She had old grievances stretching back centuries, the destruction of Gaelic culture, the penal laws, the failure to grant Catholic emancipation at the time of the union, the potato famine. Her intractably wretched social condition gave rise to endless new grievances, rackrenting landlords, the loss of the talented and industrious through emigration, the coercion continually needed to keep the place in some sort of order. Perhaps the extreme reaction to Gladstone's proposal also reflected an uneasy awareness that many of the grievances were justified.[6]

If remedy was necessary, but Gladstone's remedy was unacceptable, then the problem had to be looked at in a different context. One available context was the Empire. If Ireland could be found some place anchored in an imperial framework, then it might be possible to loosen the bonds of a union which she increasingly rejected, without losing her altogether in an unpredictable and perhaps ultimately dangerous way. The idea seemed propitious because the Empire had visibly reached a crucial formative stage, with developments in certain respects positive and in others negative from Britain's point of view. She had been sending her surplus population out to live in Canada, Australia, New Zealand, and the Cape of Good Hope, and these colonies of settlement were loyal. Equally, India, the jewel in the Crown, was firmly held. She had to all intents and purposes been ruled as a military dictatorship since the Mutiny of 1857, and little change was in prospect. For the rest of the world, British strategy had so far consisted in establishing what is now known as the informal Empire. That is to say, distant parts were held in primarily economic dependence, on the whole, if with exceptions, eschewing formal political sovereignty for Britain. At the same time, she tried to keep other powers out of them. But in this sytem, in Africa especially, though elsewhere too, a great transformation was under way, not always to her advantage. A complex of events culminted in a severe diplomatic defeat for Britain at the conference held in Berlin in 1884 to settle colonial differences among the European powers. It ended in sanctioning the scramble for Africa, so that here the British global strategy collapsed, as it did later in the Far East, Oceania, and eventually the Middle East. There was the added discomfiture that Britain had just failed in the first Boer War to impose her sovereignty on the Afrikaner republics in South Africa. It was clearly a time for reassessing priorities and trying to decide what new territories were to be acquired, under what form of authority and, indeed, for what ultimate purpose.[7]

The colonies of settlement appeared to offer some sort of guide. Britain was the only power in possession of such colonies. If, spanning the world, they could all the same be brought together under a novel arrangement, they might furnish means for her to maintain her position as a global power. Unfortunately, since no one before had dreamed that maintenance of global power might become a problem, the tendency of policy had for nearly half a century been in the opposite direction. Since the 1840s, the colonies of settlement had been granted responsible government. In other words, Westminster no longer claimed in practice any right to control their internal affairs. It appointed governors, but those governors, acting in effect as constitutional monarchs, formed governments out of majorities in elected legislatures answerable to their own local populations.

The Canadians had taken this a step further in the confederation of 1867, bringing together provinces most of which had had separate governments, not least because some lay 3,000 miles apart. One thing this did was to demonstrate the value of combination against an external threat. In part it was a response to the ambition of the United States, on the agenda since 1776, to unite the whole North American continent, which meant the annexation of Canada. Indeed, many Canadians had supported the idea, not only radicals who admired American democracy, but also businessmen who saw markets of the future as continental rather than oceanic. Only by heavy-handed manoeuvres had British Columbia and the Maritime Provinces been brought into the confederation, while a rebellion had to be suppressed in Manitoba to achieve the same end. Still, by hook or by crook, disparate and recalcitrant colonies had been persuaded to embark on an experiment in unity which was yet not an experiment in uniformity, because it tolerated anomalies and made special provision for this and that. But it seemed to be working. A new country formed which, with due allowance for the French, was recognizably British, owing allegiance to the Crown.[8]

Could it be an example which, on a grander scale, the Empire might follow? With this in mind, in 1884, the Imperial Federation League held its inaugural meeting in London. It had been formed as a nonpartisan or rather cross-party pressure group. Apart from independent figures, most of its sponsors were Tories, but it attracted significant support from Liberals too. Representatives of the colonies were also invited. The biggest catch was Sir John Macdonald, Prime Minister of Canada and architect of confederation. He brought along his friend and colleague, his former minister of finance and now Canada's first High Commissioner to the United Kingdom, and fellow-Scotsman, Alexander Galt. He was an enthusiast for the imperial project. He thought there could be some kind of imperial assembly, to include representatives from legislatures in the colonies of settlement, then from England, Scotland, and Ireland. Amid the various domestic and imperial crises which ensued, the idea had a growing resonance in Britain. It brought varying responses among the main currents of her politics. But each had some bearing on the role of the Parliament at Westminster and on the question whether it should become, in a deeper sense than it already was, an imperial Parliament.[9]

Gladstone was Prime Minister at the time and, in this and his later governments, British radicalism almost achieved the breakthrough which might have altered the course of the country's history. He, who from high Tory beginnings moved steadily leftwards, never became a radical himself in the full sense of the word, but he won the loyalty and devotion of most who laid claim to that name. He had always deplored the foreign adventurism of his great rival, Benajamin Disraeli. When he came back to office in 1880, he was determined to reverse it. He failed. Imperial commitments rather multiplied, threatening to overwhelm a Liberal government prepared for them neither materially nor mentally. The whole business became a nightmare, culminating in the martyrdom of General Gordon at Khartoum. In foreign policy, this sequence of disasters spelt the death of radicalism, though few were aware of it at the time. In any event, Gladstone himself was not interested in grandiose schemes for the Empire. While wanting to solve the Irish problem, he sought a simple, bold, clear-cut solution, and he sought it for Ireland alone. He would not listen to advice that he needed to blur the edges, to generalize the solution in some wider scheme. So he was defeated on the Second Reading of his Irish Home Rule Bill, went to the country in the first general election under the new franchise, and lost.[10]

As Gladstone's critics inside his own party departed to form the new Liberal Unionism, the rump left round him became more radical and proletarian, though it would ultimately fail in competition for the working-class vote with the still newer Labour party. That was because its radicalism remained old-fashioned and Victorian, extolling the individual and his moral qualities, distrusting the state. The radicals were strong in the great industrial regions of the country, in the North of England, in Scotland, and in Wales. In the last cases, because radicalism was genuinely a people's movement, it responded to popular nationalism. Therefore, despite Gladstone's own reluctance, it espoused Home Rule for these countries too. But it did so not as part of an imperial scheme, rather in order to limit Westminster's power over Ireland, Scotland, and Wales and give them the right to decide domestic policies for themselves. By the time Gladstone retired in 1894, radicalism had joined to this programme of internal constitutional reform a strong anti-imperialist stance. It saw the Empire as an oppressor of helpless foreign peoples, as a cause of war, of heavy taxes, and of interventions by the state bound to sap British resources and moral fibre. The Empire was in other words a burden, and radicals could only look forward to the day when Britain would be rid of it, though few could say when or how this might happen. The way in which the train of thought thus tails off justifies a description of it as old-fashioned. It held Victorian values to be absolutes and was not interested in rethinking them for new conditions, neither in relation to the British state, nor to the Empire. Its actual historical role was to stop the old Liberal party adapting to those new conditions: hence the fate of the old Liberal party. Still, radicalism remained powerful enough to dominate that party for the time being. Finding at length a new leader in Henry Campbell-Bannerman, it won Liberalism its last great victory in the general election of 1906.[11]

Yet not all those who stayed loyal to Gladstone in 1886 were radicals of this old-fashioned sort. There remained in his party a considerable modernizing faction, stronger in the upper ranks than in the lower. It represents a second current of thinking which, starting from traditional Liberal principles, did seek to adapt them to the new conditions, above all to the Empire. Its leader was Lord Rosebery, who attracted to his side several rising political stars, Herbert Asquith, Robert Haldane, Sir Edward Grey, and others. Rosebery was a protégé of Gladstone's and, if not wildly enthusiastic about his leader's course from 1886, stuck by him, to be rewarded with the Foreign Office on the Liberals' return to office in 1892, and with succession to the premiership in 1894. He gave it up, in evident disillusion, only a year later.[12]

But he then had the freedom he wanted to chart a future course for Liberalism, Britain, and the Empire. It was, to use his term, a search for National Efficiency. In most aspects of it he was vague on detail. But obviously it had to do with the loss of Britain's position as industrial leader of the world, the competitive successes of Germany and the United States especially, their long-term implications for British global power, and ultimately for the security of the United Kingdom. We have to look more at Rosebery's disciples than at the man of vision himself for what was in mind, but it had to do with better education and training, industrial reconstruction, more positive social policies, the standard recipes of modernizers even today. Where the generalities did attain some degree of precision was in the constitutional sphere.[13]

Ireland remained the great constitutional question, and here these men thought they did indeed have the answer to Gladstone's problem without Gladstone's solution. It was Home Rule all round. That is to say, each of the nations of the United Kingdom should be given its own parliament to decide matters of purely domestic concern to them. Westminster would no longer have to deliberate on bills for the draining of Irish bogs, or the creation of crofting tenure in Scotland, or the disestablishment of the Anglican Church in Wales. Instead, freed of legislative triviality, Westminster would be equipped to pursue higher social and economic goals for the whole United Kingdom, which on that level would remain united. This sounded fine in itself, but encountered the obvious problem of England. Logically, England ought to share in Home Rule all round, but being much larger than the other nations would unbalance the structure. It appeared besides superfluous to have a parliament for the United Kingdom and an English parliament sitting in London. Yet the basic principle seemed to have a good deal of mileage in it, and it was Winston Churchill who, as Home Secretary in a Liberal Cabinet again able to consider these matters after 1910, proposed dividing England into regions, each with its own subordinate parliament. This forms part of the Labour party's programme today. At the time, it seemed to answer, or at any rate an answer, to the problem of giving Ireland more rein without letting her run away.[14]

It then appeared to open up a still more exciting prospect. Rosebery and his friends were also imperalists. They wanted to consolidate the Empire and to expand its scope as an instrument of modernization on a global scale. If they could have succeeded in devising a workable scheme of Home Rule all round, with a Parliament for the United Kingdom dealing with the big issues on top, then that might indeed have led to the creation of an imperial parliament, including representatives of the colonies, to perform the same service for the whole Empire. This vision thus encompassed a solution for Britain's hardest internal problem and for her most taxing external problem, of finding means to maintain her global power. The practical difficulties were, of course, formidable. In any case, the whole project was blown off course by events, above all by the second Boer War, fought by the Conservative government which came back to office in the general election of 1895. The British won, but not very gloriously. Their performance was at times so blundering as to call into question not only military organization, but also the whole nature of a society trying to exercise imperial responsibility under an aristocratic ruling class of apparently very limited capacities. The Liberals, from the opposition benches, had every chance to press these points home. Unfortunately, they were divided over the war. Rosebery and his friends supported it, while pointing out how it proved National Efficiency to be all the more essential. The radicals opposed it, saying that the failures served Britain right for her ruthless and unworthy aggression. With the party split, Rosebery and Campbell-Bannerman fought a duel for its leadership and its soul. Campbell-Bannerman was victorious, and more or less put paid to Liberal imperialism.[15]

Still, issues raised by the Empire cut across party lines, just as issues raised by Europe do in our own day. Before long, the Conservatives were to be split over them too. A minority party after the Reform Act of 1832, they might have been destined for oblivion in an age of democracy. But Disraeli saved them, not least through imperialist appeals to the working class. Then Gladstone's miscalculation in 1886, and the formation of a Unionist party which eventually joined the Tories, brought a decisive accretion of strength from sections of the middle class which had been the mainstay of Liberalism. The Conservative party thus became a broad church, capable of combining many strands of thinking. The Unionists especially preferred for some time ahead to preserve an identity. Part of this, especially in Scotland, and above all in Glasgow, consisted in commitment to Home Rule all round, combined with the same imperialism as Rosebery and his friends on the opposite side espoused.[16]

That was not true, however, of the Unionists' leader, Joseph Chamberlain. As "Radical Joe" he had been the pioneer of municipal reform in Birmingham and, till 1886, the champion of every progressive cause. One gets the impression that the vehemence with which he could say something was to him always more important than what he actually said. Having split from Gladstone, he became the great jingo, a term coined with reference to him and his followers. He rejected all internal constitutional reform. But he did have big imperial ideas. As Colonial Secretary at the time of the Boer War, he passionately supported it. Since the Empire emerged somewhat tarnished from it he, with his taste for drama, decided in 1903 to launch the new grand design of Imperial Preference. His aim was to forge the disparate countries of the Empire into one single trading bloc, which would bid fair to become the mightiest in the world and restore Britain's lost position as economic leader. But that meant abandoning free trade, the official doctrine of the British state, almost fanatically adhered to ever since the repeal of the Corn Laws and of the Navigation Acts in the 1840s. Another obstacle had arisen from the granting of responsible government to the colonies of settlement. The advent of free trade had indeed been one of the main reasons for granting it, since the old mercantile control of colonial economies was now superflous. Some colonies soon claimed full fiscal freedom and imposed duties on imports from the mother country. Duties imposed in Australia and New Zealand were at first disallowed by the Colonial Office, but it gave way when the much more politically formidable Canadians wanted to follow the same course. The lessons of the American Revolution had been well learned. One might almost say that with this the United Kingdom had declared its independence from the Empire. Still at the time the world's leading industrial power, it had asserted a right to get cheap food for a burgeoning population from wherever it liked, without favour to colonial producers. But by the turn of the 20th century, with the world moving back towards protectionism, that looked like a mistake. It was in response that Chamberlain sought to draw the imperial economies together again.

Since free trade had, meanwhile, served Britain well, it would have been an about-turn in policy as dramatic as Margaret Thatcher's in 1979, and met a similar wall of opposition. Curiously but significantly, Chamberlain launched his campaign not from Westminster, nor yet from Birmingham, but from Glasgow, a strongly imperialist city, but one also where Adam Smith had taught, and where belief in his teachings remained deeply rooted. If Chamberlain could conquer such territory, the rest might fall into his hands. His Prime Minister, A J Balfour, feared him as a rival, but did not seek to block him. He said, however, that if this was the cause that Chamberlain truly had at heart, a cause which formed as yet no part of the government's policy, then he ought to resign to pursue it. Should he convert the country, the government would follow. At the same time, Balfour found a pretext to sack from his Cabinet those free traders who were going to oppose imperial preference come what may, so leaving his own options open. In fact, Chamberlain failed, and Balfour remained at the helm till he lost the general election of 1906.[17]

So we arrive at a fourth school of imperial thinking, if indeed it can be dignified as such, because it really consisted in the British tradition of pragmatic Conservatism distrusting all fixed bodies of doctrine. In the context of the time, it also represented a truer assessment of what the colonies themselves wanted, something that did not often seem to bother Chamberlain. If he had looked back, for example, to what Sir John Macdonald had said at the inaugural meeting of the Imperial Federation League, he would have found caution counselled. Macdonald ruled out parliamentary federation as impracticable and a uniform tariff in the Empire as contrary to the colonies' interests, though there was scope for other forms of cooperation on trade, and for a common system of defence: he had at any rate no doubt that the daughters would always come to the aid of the mother country.[18]

But what was Balfour's own answer to the great problems of Britain's and the Empire's future which Chamberlain and the Liberals opposite had been trying to solve? Balfour has a low reputation as a prime minister. In many respects, however, he was a far-sighted man whose influence has been deeper than is generally thought. In the circumstances of 1903, he believed that fanatical adherence to free trade had become counter-productive to a country in danger of being overtaken by younger and more vigorous industrial powers. At the same time, he distrusted big ideas, the kind of sweeping reconstruction of an economic system that Chamberlain had in mind. He not only saw the difficulty of pushing it through against established habits and interests, but also doubted if any new system would be on balance better, whether indeed there is any magic wand that can be waved to solve the world's problems. He had little time at all for imperial federation.

As it happened, the concept of federation did mark up some successes in the first decade of this century. Australia was federated in 1901. After the Boer War, in 1902, the much more formidable task was accomplished of federating the four provinces of South Africa, two of which had been British and two of which were newly conquered. The energy and industry of Lord Milner's kindergarten, idealistic young imperialists recruited for the purpose, swept aside all difficulties. Most then returned to Britain in the conviction that commitment alone could work wonders. They found a domestic political situation no less difficult. Once the Liberal government had got rid of the House of Lords' obstruction with the Parliament Act of 1911, it turned straight back to Irish Home Rule. It also encountered the same problems as in 1886, only worse. That was why members of the kindergarten, notably Philip Kerr, later Marquess of Lothian, revived the idea of Home Rule all round and tried harder than anybody else to work out a practical scheme for it. Tories rather than Liberals, they still felt it necessary to strike out in some new direction to save the country from an increasingly dangerous constitutional crisis. Because they were imperialists, they saw this also as the counter to centrifugal forces in the British Empire. They achieved nothing: the leaders on their own side were not interested, and the Liberals were determined to solve at least the problem of Ireland, with Home Rule first for her, only then perhaps for others. Everything was nevertheless abandoned on the outbreak of the First World War. Shortly after the peace, the United Kingdom in fact broke up, and Ireland became effectively independent.[19]

The Parliament Act had been intended merely as a means of solving problems perceived to be much deeper. In the event, it turned out to be an end in itself, a solution to such problems as needed to be solved. It got rid of a block to efficiency in the political system by establishing the Commons as superior to, not coordinate with, the Lords. A government supported by a majority in the lower House was now sure of getting its legislation through, subject only to some delaying and revising powers in the upper House, which have not proved especially effective. It has not, therefore, been necessary to do much more about the other House. Contemporary schemes for transforming the Lords into a federal or imperial chamber, as the prelude to making the Commons acknowledge some wider sovereignty that the Crown in Parliament, simply vanished from the agenda, or were pushed off by the graver business of war.

The war had a profound effect on the Empire. All its members stood together, showed unquestioning loyalty, and did their duty when the King simply declared war against Germany on their behalf. Some at home hoped the spirit of which they gave proof might produce a fresh impulse towards unity after the terrible sacrifices they endured together. But the reverse happened. Many in the dominions, while making no protest in 1914, had still felt disturbed at being dragged into such an awful conflict without reference to themselves. They did not want it to happen again. Imperial conferences had taken place regularly before the war, but none was held afterwards till 1926. There was good reason for that: the colonial prime ministers sought a showdown to define the exact degree of their independence from the mother country. When a new conference at last met, it asked Balfour to draft a document in suitable terms. As a realist, he knew that Britain would in future have no real hold over her self-governing colonies, but he wanted to salvage something. It was he who formulated the concept of a free association of sovereign states, united by no more than self-interest and sentiment: what we have come to call the Commonwealth. So the Empire finally found its definitive political form. That still left open the question of its economic form. In 1931, amid the onset of the great depression, a system of imperial preference was in fact to be set up. But, since it failed in the end, it can safely be left outside the scope of this chapter.[20]

The purpose here has not been just to breathe life into some long-dead controversies. It is easy to see with hindsight why the general course of events went the way it did, and why most of the ideas discussed above never got anywhere. That is not the same as saying they were bad ones; the inertia of institutions and of people means that many good ideas remain stillborn. The men involved can still speak to us. They lived, after all, in a Britain not too remote from ours, with some of the same problems, of an advanced industrial society trying to cope with competition from others. They had to consider what political apparatus was best for doing so and they wondered whether some broader framework than the United Kingdom was the right one. In the days of the Empire that led straight on, just as it does now in Europe, to questions of the sovereignty of Parliament, its nature and extent.

Here, then, is the basic question these men faced: was it necessary to embark on systematic reform of the British state, to interrupt its organic growth, or perhaps its habit of mend-and-make-do, to set the whole thing on some more rational basis, calculated to meet its problems? To that question, Gladstone, Campbell-Bannerman, and the radicals said there should be internal reform but not external reform; Chamberlain and the jingos said there should be external reform, but not internal reform; Rosebery and his imperialists said there should be both; Balfour and the conservatives said there should be neither. There were perhaps too many contradictions in the two partial solutions. The non-solution won, but there may be no harm in speculating what might have happened had the total solution won instead. If, for example, Irish Home Rule had been pushed through in 1886, in the days before Irish Nationalism and Ulster Unionism hardened, and as the prelude to some broader arrangement, it might have been possible for the United Kingdom of Gladstone's day to stay united, though federalized. That could have spared us the tragedies of Ireland in the 20th century, for which it would have been worth paying a lot. Suppose, then, a more ambitious imperial scheme had followed. That may appear a fantastic notion. But remember that it was meant to address one of the difficulties that still confronts us today, of defending our economic position against powerful rivals, of finding the right political means to do so, of "punching above our weight", as Douglas Hurd has put it. We seek to answer the difficulty through union with Greece and Portugal, among others, and eventually, it seems, with Slovakia and Latvia. That is a notion which our grandfathers would have found fantastic. In any event, it does not face up to one question which at least some of them did try to face up to, whether the difficulty can be answered at all without internal reform, reform of the British state. It may be significant that so many of the politicians discussed here were Scotsmen. Scots, as junior partners in the Union, have to be hard-headed about it, and have always thought more seriously about its nature than the English. In view of the lost opportunities of the past, of the roads not taken, it might be as well to listen to what Scots are saying about the Union today.

Footnotes to this Chapter may be found on page 211.

9: L W Gormley

Layman's guide to the European Union and the British Parliament

WITH THE accession of the United Kingdom to the European Communities on 1 January 1973, a new era dawned in the constitutional history of the House of Commons. No longer was Parliament the supreme forum for legislation. No longer was the House of Commons the fount of legislative activity. The House of Commons certainly did not become a parish council, but an additional and superior source of law took effect in the United Kingdom. The ability of the House of Commons to affect that source of law is at best indirect, although there has never been any doubt that the United Kingdom would be able to withdraw from the European Union should Parliament so wish.[1] In the absence of withdrawal, even subsequent national legislation will be interpreted in such a way as to give effect to rights conferred by Community law.[2] Section 3(1) of the European Communities Act 1972 requires the British courts to have regard to the principles laid down by any relevant decision of the European Court, or any court attached to it. As one of these principles is the supremacy of Community law,[3] it follows that the United Kingdom courts must recognize that supremacy.[4] If Parliament were to enact legislation inconsistent with Community law, it is now highly unlikely that the United Kingdom courts would enforce such legislation in the absence of a clear repeal of Sections 2(4) and (3)(1) of the European Communities Act. This is all the more true since the European Court has made it clear that national courts are bound to give interim relief – in effect setting aside (or disapplying) provisions of an act of Parliament – where failure to give interim relief would impair the full effectiveness of Community law.[5] The limitation of sovereignty which Parliament accepted when it enacted the European Communities Act 1972 was, however, a wholly voluntary act with at the very least a clear undertaking to conform to Community law for such time as the United Kingdom is a member state of the European Union. Enactment of, and giving effect to, legislation incompatible with Community law would constitute infringements of that law which could be the subject of infringement proceedings under Articles 169 or 170 of the Treaty of Rome. Any withdrawal from the Community would in practice be effected by treaty between the United Kingdom and the remaining member states.

Membership of the European Community (now of the European Union) was achieved by a perfectly orthodox constitutional procedure: the Treaty of Accession was signed by ministers on behalf of the Crown, in accordance with the Royal Prerogative. Their action is not open to review by the courts.[6] However, Parliament has been jealous in trying to keep its options open in relation to agreements at European level which expand the powers of the European Parliament: hence Section 6(1) of the European Parliamentary Elections Act 1978 (as amended) requires that no treaty which provides for an increase in the European Parliament's powers is to be ratified by the United Kingdom unless it has been approved by an act of Parliament. European Community law is brought into the United Kingdom's domestic system by the European Communities Act 1972 (as amended). The 1972 act effectively operates rather like the space shuttle's fuel tank: it is the shuttle itself which effects the mission; the fuel tank serves its purpose and is then discarded – at least in this case as far as the operation of Community law itself is concerned.

The House of Commons and European legislation

Any assessment of the House of Commons and the European dimension must have regard to scrutiny of Community legislation[7] and in particular to the operation of the House of Commons Select Committee on European Legislation. Much United Kingdom law actually originates in Brussels. Community regulations are directly applicable in the member states[8] and thus bypass national parliaments. The only possibility for national parliaments to influence them is to ensure that their governments take account of views expressed in the national parliaments at meetings of councils of ministers. In the case of directives, there are two opportunities for national parliamentary input: first, in the same way as with proposed regulations, at the negotiating stage; secondly, in relation to the form and methods of implementation of directives. Directives have to be implemented in the national legal systems[9] and, while they are binding, they leave the choice of form and methods open to the member states, subject to the obligation to implement by legally certain means rather than by mere administrative circulars which can be changed at the whim of the administration. The chosen form and methods may be primary legislation, which will go through the normal procedures for the enactment of acts of Parliament, or it may be delegated legislation. If the government choses delegated legislation, it may chose to present the draft for approval by resolution of each House, or it may adopt an Order in Council on the regulations concerned, but the instrument is subject to annulment on resolution of either House.[10] It may be, though, that the government choses a different legal basis for the secondary legislation from that provided for in the European Communities Act 1972; in such cases, the procedure applicable is that provided for by the primary legislation chosen as the legal basis. If the government wishes to designate a particular treaty as one of the Community Treaties[11] a draft of the Order in Council must be approved by resolution of each House of Parliament. Accordingly, while the government is free, in the exercise of the Royal Prerogative, to negotiate amendments of the Community Treaties, irrespective of the wishes of the House of Commons, there are two important constraints: first, as mentioned above, ratification of any treaty increasing the European Parliament's powers requires approval by an act of Parliament; secondly, rights and obligations flowing from such amendment will have no internal effects in the absence of an Order in Council, the draft of which has been approved by resolution of each House. The possibility for the government to negotiate treaty revisions ignoring the wishes of the House of Commons is thus subject to legal and practical constraints.

With European legislation, as in all other fields, information is power. The scrutiny arrangements which apply in the United Kingdom Parliament represent by far the most systematic scrutiny of EU legislation in any member state.[12] Two key practices are important: the early deposit of texts, and the undertaking to defer any decision at Community level until Parliament has been able to express its opinion on the proposal concerned. As will become apparent, the latter practice is far from a watertight guarantee of parliamentary influence as both of these practices depend upon the cooperation of the government.

All proposals for EU Council regulations, directives, and decisions, all draft reports, resolutions or programmes submitted for adoption by the Council, all proposals submitted to the European Council (where these are available in advance), and Commission Green and White Papers (to mention only the principal documents) are deposited within two days of their receipt in London by the government. This means that they often reach Parliament before they are published in the *Official Journal of the European Communities*. While most Commission (as opposed to Council) legislation is not deposited, it will be available in the *Official Journal*. The potential for national parliaments to influence treaties concluded with third countries or international organizations is, however, limited. Such documents are not deposited in draft until the negotiations have been concluded by the Commission and the draft is submitted to the Council for approval. If the agreement is a mixed agreement, *ie* one to which the Community and its member states are parties as well as third countries, the possibility of a debate on the treaty or approval by resolution if the treaty concerned is to be designated a Community treaty, does offer the opportunity for some scrutiny of the arrangements entered into. When a document is deposited, the government provides an explanatory memorandum, detailing the procedure involved in the proposal, its legal basis, and expected timetable, the responsible United Kingdom minister for the field involved and the impact of the proposal on United Kingdom law. The explanatory memorandum may well set out the probable form of implementing legislation and always includes a discussion of the policy implications of the proposal. This may well include an indication of the government's views. The memorandum is signed by the responsible minister.

Since accession in 1973, governments have always undertaken to await the opinion of Parliament before agreeing to a proposal at Community level. This has been formalized by a resolution of the House of Commons[13] which requires a minister not to consent to the adoption of a proposal (or to the adoption of a common position on a proposal where this is provided for in Community law) which is still before the Select Committee on European Legislation, or is awaiting consideration by the House. Ignoring this resolution would cause a minister to be in contempt, although routine confidential, trivial, or urgent matters can be agreed.[14] If the matter is urgent and cannot await the results of scrutiny, the minister must explain the reasons to the House or the appropriate committee as soon as possible. The minister is not obliged to follow the views expressed in any debate in the House, unless they are contained in a formal resolution adopted after the debate, although this occurs very rarely. Even if the minister's hands are tied by a formal resolution, in meetings of the Council the members of the Council (the ministers) are obliged to act in the Community interest, albeit inevitably "viewed through the spectacles of national interests. According to the subject-matter and political climate in the Communities these will be more or less dark."[15] When unanimity was more frequently required than nowadays, the tying of ministerial hands could at least in theory frustrate Community decision-making. It is important to remember, however, that the member states are just as responsible for the safeguarding of the essential interests of the Community as is the Commission.[16] Moreover, the fact that a member state has voted in favour of a proposal will not prevent it seeking to have the legislation concerned annulled by the European Court of Justice.[17] Now that qualified majority voting has been greatly extended, the effectiveness of any attempt by the House of Commons to tie the minister's hands is less certain, as the minister may well follow the House's wishes, but be unable to prevent the adoption of the proposal or of a common position on a proposal.

The number of European documents deposited in Parliament is enormous and, while all are examined, very few are actually debated by the House. The sifting is undertaken by the Select Committee on European Legislation which consists of 16 members, the quorum of the committee being five. Standing Order No 127 sets out the committee's terms of reference, but while it may report its opinion on the legal and political importance of a document and on any matters of principle, policy or law which could be affected, may also make recommendations for further consideration of documents and consider issues arising, its reports do not express views on the merits of a proposal, as that is a matter for the House itself or for a European Standing Committee in accordance with Standing Order No 102. The reports therefore identify the issues involved and it is to the official report of the debate in the European Standing Committee that reference must be made if the views of the members of the committee on the proposal are to be discovered. In examining documents, the select committee is assisted by notes prepared by its officials, which enable matters of scant importance to be dealt with quickly so that attention may be given to more weighty ones. The select committee may enlist the assistance of expert advisers or take evidence; it may even meet in joint session with the House of Lords Select Committee on the European Communities, although it appears that this power is hardly ever used. The House of Commons select committee reports after each meeting which documents it has considered, setting out those it considers to be of little significance and those which it feels should be further considered by the House because of their legal or political significance. Since the beginning of the 1990-1991 Session, further consideration takes place in one of the two European Standing Committees, each consisting of 10 members, although if the House so decides a debate may be held in the full House. Matters discussed in the European Standing Committees are debated for a set period of two and a half hours in the presence of a minister who answers questions at the start of the sitting of the Committee; the sitting ends with the adoption of a resolution which is reported to the House. While the resolution is formally moved, no further debate takes place.

The activities of the Select Committee on European Legislation are really technical in nature, those of the European Standing Committees being more substantive. In this the House of Commons procedures are substantially less refined than those applicable in the House of Lords, where the Select Committee on the European Communities and its various subcommittees undertake many inquiries and deliver substantial contributions, sometimes involving suggestions for amendment of Commission proposals, which do find their way into the final Community legislation.[18] One advantage of parliamentary scrutiny is that it does enable national parliaments to keep a weather eye open for compliance with the terms of Article 3b EC which requires that in areas not within its exclusive competence, the Community must act in accordance with the principle of subsidiarity. This means that the Community may act "only if and in so far as the objectives of the proposed action cannot be sufficiently achieved by the member states and can, therefore, by reason of the scale or effects of the proposed action, be better achieved by the Community." Moreover, Article 3b EC requires that any action (not just in areas in which the Community does not have exclusive competence) must not go beyond what is necessary to achieve the objects of the EC Treaty. Parliamentary scrutiny will now have to involve the assessment of whether a proposal complies with these requirements. While subsidiarity itself has not yet been the subject of judicial consideration – and it is by no means clear that the Court of Justice will wish to get involved in the examination of complex political issues involving such a discretionary evaluation – no such inhibitions apply in the discussion of proposals by national parliaments. There are ample opportunities for the scrutiny committees of national parliaments to cooperate, should they so desire, in such a discussion. Indeed, the Conference of European Affairs Committees provides a forum within which chairmen and members of such committees may exchange views and coordinate their positions, meetings being hosted by the national parliament of the member state holding the presidency of the Council. However, if the House of Commons' scrutiny system is to be as effective as that of the House of Lords, radical revision will be necessary, although the pressures on parliamentary time in the House of Commons are, it is true, substantially greater than those in the House of Lords.

Scrutiny of European legislation by the House of Commons is extremely indirect. While the filter mechanism means that unimportant proposals do not clutter up the agenda, it may be wondered whether a debate of two and a half hours, including the time taken by questions to the minister, is always enough to permit a detailed evaluation of the issues which the select committee has identified. Moreover, it would be useful if the select committee were able to express its own view, if necessary by proposing the resolution to be debated by the House or by the standing committee. Such an approach would be more in line with the workings of the committees of the European Parliament which present resolutions for discussion and adoption by the whole House.

Future perspectives

As the European Parliament's role in the adoption of Community legislation increases, another source of democratic legitimacy takes its place in the sun. But as long as the interest in elections to the European Parliament continues to be so low in the United Kingdom, the constitutional perception remains that it is the House of Commons which matters. Yet the advent of direct elections to the European Parliament in 1979, the Single European Act in 1986, and the Treaty on European Union in 1992, the role of the European Parliament in the adoption of Community legislation has increased dramatically. That body is, though, still far from a fully-fledged parliament with legislative capacity. Although the European Parliament undoubtedly has formal democratic legitimacy, the poor turnout in direct elections inevitably means that its claim to be a European expression of the democratic will of the people is harder to sustain given that national parliaments attract substantially greater electoral participation. As long as the democratic deficit in the Community is not remedied, the future of the House of Commons as the main democratic representative of the will of those in the United Kingdom remains intact. Once the European Parliament – and not the Council – is perceived as having real power, in the sense that it alone can adopt legislation and set the budget of the European institutions, and that it, as well as the Commission, may propose legislation, the future of the House of Commons is that of an important regional assembly. Indeed, at that point, there may well be moves to question the present function of the United Kingdom Parliament as such, with parliaments being established for England, Wales, Scotland, and Northern Ireland (unless the latter decides to be independent or unite with Ireland). But that also depends on a fundamental shift in the nature of the European Union, from being a union of member states based on the European Communities, to being a union of the peoples of Europe. In such a union, the Council might function as an upper chamber of a new European Parliament, or representatives from national parliaments might be elected by their bodies to an upper chamber which would represent regional interests (with regions being understood to be what are now the member states). In either of these possibilities, assuming that the United Kingdom remains united, a role for the House of Commons exists, controlling the actions of ministers or, albeit indirectly, of the European Parliament. The House of Commons would certainly have its say before any such developments could occur, as, of course, would the parliaments of the other member states. In view of the close shave by which the Treaty on European Union was ratified by the member states in accordance with their constitutional requirements, it may well be a long time indeed before the political will on the part of the people matches that of the pro-integration sections of the European political and intellectual élite. Accordingly, on the occasion of this anniversary of the

Mother of Parliaments, it may safely be said that any newspaper reports of the demise of the House of Commons have been greatly exaggerated.

Footnotes to this Chapter may be found on pages 212–13.

10: Michael Stephen MP

Life of an MP

HOW DOES one become a Member of the United Kingdom House of Commons? The simple answer is to get elected, but it is very rare today for anyone to be elected in his own right. The party system here is now so well developed that it is almost essential to secure the endorsement of one of the political parties to stand as their official candidate, for a constituency which that party has reasonable prospects of winning.

The methods by which the parties choose their candidates vary, and I will confine myself to the Conservatives, of which I have direct experience. The first step is to join a constituency Conservative Association and work for the party at ward level, canvassing from door to door, distributing leaflets, collecting subscriptions, helping to man a committee room at election time, and doing all those practical tasks which have to be done if local and national elections are to be won. At the same time, it is useful to join one of the national groups such as the Young Conservatives, the Conservative Political Centre, or the Society of Conservative Lawyers, to take part in political debate, and to write or help to write political pamphlets. A degree in politics is not necessary, and may even be a disadvantage.

In due course, the new member will be invited to join the committee of the ward branch of the association, and if well regarded, will be elected secretary, treasurer, or chairman of the branch, and can go on to stand for election as an officer of the association itself, and/or as a Conservative candidate for the local council. In addition to service to the party, it is highly desirable to be able to show some achievement in a business or professional career unrelated to politics. There are some notable cases of MPs who have done nothing except politics, but "professional politicians" are not universally admired within the Conservative party. A broad understanding of the problems which constituents and businesses have to face in the real world is considered important. It is not essential to have served in local government, but anyone wishing to become an MP is well advised to do so. The experience is invaluable, and successful service in local government provides solid evidence of political ability and commitment to the party, which parliamentary selection committees will be looking for.

After some years satisfactory service to the party, application may then be made to join the approved list of parliamentary candidates. This does not guarantee selection as a candidate, and still less election to Parliament, but it shows that in the opinion of the National Union of Conservative and Unionist Associations the person concerned understands and subscribes to Conservative principles, and has the necessary experience and ability to stand as a Conservative parliamentary candidate. Applicants for the Candidates List are invited to attend for a weekend appraisal at an hotel or conference centre, where their suitability to stand as a Conservative candidate will be assessed by senior officers of the National Union, by Central Office officials, and by Members of Parliament. Candidates are divided into groups of about 15, and are required to make a speech, to take part in a debate and an informal current affairs discussion, to act as interviewer and interviewed on closed circuit television, and to submit a piece of written work. The candidate is not only assessed on his individual merits, but also on his interaction with other members of the group.

If successful, the next hurdle is to secure selection by a Conservative association in whose constituency there is a vacancy for a parliamentary candidate, and people on the Candidates' List are informed by Central Office when vacancies arise. Normally, a candidate will apply in the first instance to associations where the seat is currently held by another party, and I was selected by the Doncaster North Conservative Association as their candidate for the 1983 general election. Doncaster North is a seat with a solid Labour majority, considered to be a stronghold of the National Union of Mineworkers, and although we did not expect to win the seat it was important that people in the consituency who supported the aims and principles of the Conservative party should have a candidate for whom to vote. On my first day out canvassing in one of the mining villages, I was told on the doorstep that if I was from the Labour party I could push off. From that encouraging start we went on to win 13,915 votes. After the count, the victorious Labour candidate asked, "where can you find so many Conservatives in a place like this?"

Having fought a "loser", the next step is to secure selection as parliamentary candidate in a "winnable" seat. This is the most competitive stage of all, as a Conservative seat with a good majority will normally attract about 250 applicants. I was notified by Central Office in the summer of 1991 that Sir Richard Luce, who had held the Shoreham seat in West Sussex for 20 years, intended to retire at the next general election, and that the local Conservative association was inviting applications. Having sent a written cv to the association, I was fortunate enough to be invited for interview by a selection committee comprising 12 of the most senior officers of the association, who had decided to interview about 20 applicants. The second stage was for six of us to appear before the executive council of the association, comprising about 50 of the most active party workers in the constituency; and the final stage was for two of us to appear before the whole association in general meeting. Voting at each stage is by secret ballot, and while an official of Conservative Central Office is present to advise on procedure, he has no vote. The choice of a parliamentary candidate in the Conservative party is, therefore, a balance between the national party organization, which approves the Candidates' List, and the local party workers who choose the candidate for their constituency.

The new "prospective parliamentary candidate" must then get to know the members of the association, the constituency, and the electorate as well as he can before the general election is announced, and to argue the case for his party as well and as often as possible.

The first day in the life of any Member of Parliament begins at dawn on the day after the election when, tired but exhilarated by the election campaign, he wakes to his new responsibilities. But what are those responsibilities? What is he meant to do? Very soon, he learns that no one tells him anything – he must find out for himself. I was elected at the general election of 12 April 1992. No summons arrived the next day, nor the day after, so I thought I had better go to Westminster to find out what was happening. On entering the members' cloakroom I noticed a small loop of red tape attached to each of the coat-hangers. These are for members to hang their swords. I have yet to see one of my colleagues wearing a sword, but those loops of red tape have an important purpose. They are there to remind us that not so many years ago men settled their disputes by the sword, and might was right. Today we fight with arguments and with votes, and Parliament is – thankfully – a talking shop.

Sometimes our verbal battles are of great ferocity, and lest there be any temptation to reinforce the argument with blows, there are two lines drawn on the floor of the House of Commons chamber which we may not cross during a debate. These lines are two sword-lengths apart. Watching proceedings on television can give the impression that MPs are constantly at each other's throats, for it is in the nature of television that the exciting and the dramatic are given prominence, and careful constructive debates, perhaps on matters of great importance but with limited audience appeal, are ignored. Relations between members from different parties are actually quite good, and many genuine and long-lasting friendships have developed across party lines. There are many all-party groups on such things as sport and the arts, charity groups, and country groups, where members of all parties sharing an interest in a particular subject or foreign country meet regularly. A long-serving Labour MP said to me quite early in my parliamentary career, "you can have friends on both sides of the House, but watch out for those sitting behind you!"

Members of the public watching proceedings from the public ("Strangers'") gallery often remark that very few members are present in the chamber. This is because only about 10 members on each side can expect to be called in a debate, and other members will not normally sit through the debate unless it is on a subject of particular interest to their constituents. There are many other matters to which members must attend while the House is sitting.

The mood of the House can change rapidly from tedium to high drama; and the Labour MP Dennis Skinner ("the Beast of Bolsover") once remarked that the House is sometimes like a church, and sometimes like a zoo. The hours of work of the House are often criticized. Some say that proceedings in the chamber should commence at 9.30 am every day instead of at 2.30 pm on Mondays to Thursdays. This has its attractions, but there is already more than enough to do in the mornings. It would also be popular among members if sittings finished not later than 10 pm every day, but sometimes the pressure of business is such that the House must sit until the early hours of the morning. Often this happens because the Opposition are using their democratic right to delay legislation. Some people say that the Summer Recess should be shorter, but this is the only part of the year when MPs can spend much time in their constituencies, make parliamentary visits abroad, take family holidays, and attend their party's annual conference. Some limited changes have, however, been recently introduced on a trial basis.

A Member of Parliament has duties to his constituents (whether they voted for him or not); to the national interest; and to the political party which he supports, and whose members support him. Otherwise, the life of an MP is essentially what he or she wants it to be. Each member is an individual, with his own view of his responsibilites, and each organizes his time in the way which suits him best, and which will in his view lead to the achievement of his particular objectives. The smoking room of the House of Commons is a place where some of the most interesting and significant political discussion takes place. It is also the place where Sir Winston Churchill used to spend much of his time in his last years in Parliament. On one occasion, one new MP said to another "That's Winston over there – they say he's in his dotage now." "Yes," said Churchill, "and they also say he's deaf." The members' tea room is also a favourite place for intrigue, and it is there that many of the political plots are hatched.

Today the pressures on an MP are much greater than even a few years ago, and the days are gone when a member need visit his constituency only three or four times a year. Constituents expect much more of MPs and governments than they ever have, or ever will have, the capacity to deliver; they expect their MP to be an expert on every national and international issue, and still to have time to solve the constituent's individual problems. They expect him to work full time, by which many of them mean 24 hours a day, 365 days a year. They sometimes forget that they have sent him to Westminster, and wonder why he is not in the constituency more often. If he does manage to spend time in the constituency he ought, they say, to be attending to their affairs at Westminster. If he makes witty speeches they say he is frivolous – if he makes serious speeches they say he is boring. If MPs spend hours discussing issues, the people say we ought to get on and *do* something – but if Parliament takes action without giving every conceivable point of view a hearing we are called dictators.

An MP must divide his time between his constituency and the House – and may if he is lucky find a few minutes for his family. In London, only a small part of our time is spent in the chamber of the House on legislation, on general debates, and on parliamentary questions. We must also attend committees of the House, party groups, all-party groups, meetings with interest groups on a wide range of subjects; meetings with constituents and others who visit the House and much else. We must deal with an avalanche of constituents' letters every day; we must provide the press and radio and television with information, and respond to their requests for interviews; we must read widely, and read in-depth on our specialist subjects; and we must try to think ahead.

In the chamber of the House of Commons, the government and opposition parties sit opposite each other. These were the seating arrangements when the House first met in the choir stalls of St Stephen's chapel in the royal Palace of Westminster, but they have been retained to the present day for good reasons. When a minister stands at the Despatch Box to speak or to answer questions, the opposition members are only a few yards away. They get a good view of him, and can establish personal eye-contact. In a semi-circular chamber where ministers sit at the front the only view normally available to ordinary members is the back of their head.

Perhaps the most daunting prospect for any new MP is his first (or maiden) speech in the chamber. I made mine about a month after being elected, but some members take much longer. Edward Gibbon could not face the prospect at all, and decided instead to go away and write *Decline and Fall of the Roman Empire*. Some maiden speeches are memorable, but most are not. The newspapers said of Thomas (brother of W E) Gladstone's maiden speech that he "made a few remarks inaudible from the gallery". It is customary for maiden speeches to be uncontroversial, and to include some remarks about the new member's own constituency. The House will normally listen politely and will not make interruptions, unless the new member breaches convention by being controversial.

Question Time is one of the best known features of the parliamentary day, and the Prime Minister himself answers questions on Tuesdays and Thursdays from 3.15 to 3.30 pm. The occasion is broadcast on national television, and most backbenchers try to be present. Constituents often ask why we always ask him a general question such as "will he list his engagements for today?" or "will he visit my constituency?" The reason is that if we asked a specific question it would be referred by the Clerks of the House to the minister whose department deals with that area of policy. We are not of course interested in the PM's answer to the formal question, but once it has been answered we can then put a "supplementary" question on any subject we please.

This is seen by opposition members as an opportunity to score political points, and since the PM has no notice of the supplementary question he must be very well briefed on a wide range of topics. Members of the governing party will usually tell his Parliamentary Private Secretary what they are going to ask. Some members on both sides try to turn their question into a speech, but they are usually stopped by the Speaker before they get very far. If we wish to ask an oral question of a minister, it is advisable to submit it in writing beforehand at the Table Office, and it will be entered in a ballot. However, those who are unlucky in the ballot may still get a chance to ask the question because between calling the balloted questions the Speaker will usually call two or three other members. Anyone watching question time in the House of Commons will see that about 20 members on each side rise in their places at the end of each question and each answer. These are the members who wish to ask a question, and they are seeking to "catch the Speaker's eye."

The main business of the House is of course legislation. Each Session of Parliament runs from early November to late July the following year, with a two-week recess at Christmas, Easter, and Whitsun, and in an average Session the government will introduce about 10 bills. A bill must pass through all stages in both Houses before the end of the Session, otherwise it will in normal circumstances lapse and will have to begin again. Controversial bills are normally introduced in the Commons and less controversial bills in the Lords. Those bills which are nearly completed when the House rises for the Summer Recess will normally be finished in a "spillover" period of about 10 days in late October/early November immediately before the House is prorogued and the new Session begins, with the State Opening of Parliament.

Most ministers are Members of the House of Commons, who have the same constituency duties as their non-ministerial colleagues, and a minister in charge of a bill in Parliament has a particularly heavy workload. For backbenchers (ie other members of the governing party, and opposition members who are not front-bench spokesmen for their party) their involvement in the bill will depend upon whether they have a particular interest in the subject. If they have no specialist interest, they will normally maintain a general awareness of the bill, and focus their minds only upon controversial points which may arise, or points of particular concern to their constituents.

Those who do have a specialist interest will often seek to serve on the committee of about 15 members from each side of the House, which will consider the bill in detail in one of the committee rooms upstairs. Exceptionally, a bill of major constitutional importance (such as the bill to implement the Maastricht Treaty), or bills on which there is general agreement, will be considered by a "committee of the whole House". This is an odd name, for a committee comprising all the members of the House is hardly a committee; but MPs soon get accustomed to odd terminology.

I have a particular interest in criminal justice, and made it known that I wished to serve on the committee considering the Police and Magistrates' Courts Bill (enacted 1994). The Committee Stage of this bill took five weeks, during which the committee sat every Tuesday and Thursday, and considered the bill line by line. Most of the speeches were made by the ministers in charge of the bill and opposition members who wished to change or delay it.

The bill then went back to the chamber of the House for its Report Stage and Third Reading (both stages normally taken in the same sitting). This is the opportunity for members who have not served on the committee to table amendments or to speak on particular amendments of concern to them. When passed by the Commons on Third Reading, the bill was then sent to the House of Lords, where it passed through a similar, but not identical procedure, and then received Royal Assent. This is usually given in the House of Lords on behalf of Her Majesty by senior peers sitting as Commissioners, and not by the Queen in person.

At the end of each stage of a bill in each House, there is a vote, and there is also a vote during Committee and Report stages on each clause or amendment on which there is any disagreement. It is of obvious importance to any government that its legislation is passed by Parliament, and the members of the governing party will therefore be given clear written notice each week of when votes are expected to occur. Likewise, opposition members will be given notice of votes considered important by their leadership. This notice is called "the Whip". If the notice is underlined three times (a "three-line whip") we are expected to attend and vote with our party. If the notice is underlined twice, we must still attend and vote with the party unless we have agreed with a member of the main party opposite that neither of us will vote, and have registered that "pair" with our party whips' office. If the notice is underlined only once, attendance is optional.

When we vote on a matter proceeding in the chamber of the House of Commons, we have to be physically present in one of the two "lobbies" or wide corridors which run parallel to the chamber. One is called the "aye" lobby, and the other the "no" lobby, and our vote is recorded by the clerks and counted by tellers on each side as we leave the lobby. The only exception is for a seriously ill member who can be "nodded through" by agreement between the party whips, provided he is within the precincts of the House, even if in an ambulance. The advantage of voting in person, rather than by using a vote-recording machine, is that ministers, including the Prime Minister, have to be in the lobby too, and it is a very useful opportunity for colleagues to have a personal talk with them, and with other backbenchers whom we might not otherwise see for weeks. By comparison, there must be very few opportunities for a US Congressman to talk face to face with the President or his Cabinet officers.

The procedures of the House also enable an individual member to raise in the chamber a matter of particular concern to him, and this may even be the individual case of just one of his constituents. This can be done in an "adjournment debate" which lasts for 30 minutes (or longer if it starts before 10pm) at the adjournment of the House for the day. The member seeking the debate must write to the Speaker giving the subject, and his name will be placed in a ballot for Monday to Thursday. On one day each week, adjournment debates are at the personal discretion of the Speaker. A minister always replies to an adjournment debate, and it is normal for the member whose debate it is to allow the minister at least 15 minutes. It is the convention that other members do not take part in the debate except by prior agreement. Recently, adjournment debates have also been held on Wednesday mornings.

Most bills are introduced by the government, since they have been elected to govern the country, and they need most of the available parliamentary time, but private members do have limited opportunities to introduce legislation. There are two main ways in which this can be done. The first is to win by ballot a place on one of the 12 Fridays in each Session set aside for Private Members' Bills; the second is to use the "ten-minute rule" by which private members get 10-minutes in which to persuade the House to give them leave to introduce a bill. If a member wins a place high up in the ballot, he is guaranteed some parliamentary time for a debate, but his bill will not pass into law if the government or the opposition, or any other significant body of opinion is against it. In the case of Ten Minute Rule bills, it takes only one MP to shout "object" when the bill is called for Second Reading for it to go back to the end of the queue, and to be effectively dead. For a private member to succeed he must, therefore, prepare a bill which will receive wide support in all parties, and must try to identify and neutralize such opposition as there may be.

I have not so far been lucky in the ballot, but I did manage to persuade the House to give me leave to introduce a bill under the Ten Minute Rule. This was a bill to give the prosecution a right of appeal where magistrates courts release on bail accused persons whom the prosecution believe should be kept in custody until trial, for the protection of the public. I had wanted to make this change in the law long before I became an MP, because I knew of so many cases where persons on bail had committed serious offences. One particularly tragic case was that of Anna McGurk, who was raped and murdered by a man who had already been arrested for rape and released on bail. I received a lot of support from Anna's parents, who helped me to secure the backing of 100 MPs of all parties. When I felt that I had enough support, I discussed the bill with the Home Secretary personally, and he gave it his approval. This did not, however, make it a government bill, and it was still possible for a single member to wreck it. I therefore talked to everyone I thought might object and then summoned up the courage to table it for Second Reading. On Friday 19 February 1993, the Clerk of the House called the name of my bill so that the House might decide whether it should receive a Second Reading. I held my breath for the few seconds allowed to objectors, but no objection came. The bill was formally read a second time and sent to a committee.

The Committee Stage of my bill was the same as for government legislation, save that as the member in charge of the bill I had the right to choose the members of the committee, except the minister and the opposition spokesman. Naturally I chose colleagues from my own and other parties who supported the bill. The committee stage was useful because in considering the bill in detail, colleagues drew to my attention potential difficulties which I had not foreseen, and I was able to agree to most of the amendments which they tabled. The bill in its improved form passed its Report Stage and Third Reading without dissent, and was sent to the House of Lords.

On second reading in the Lords, it was clear that a small number of peers thought the bill infringed civil liberties because it provided that the accused person be kept in custody from the moment the prosecutor gave notice of appeal. This provision was necessary because it would have been contrary to the whole purpose of the bill for the accused to be able, pending the appeal, to abscond or commit further offences. I therefore, arranged, with the help of the Home Office Minister of State, to meet the doubtful peers and was able to allay their fears by accepting a very short timescale within which the appeal against the grant of bail must be heard, and certain other amendments. The bill then passed its remaining stages in the House of Lords without further difficulty, and I am told that this was the first time a bill had ever had an "informal committee stage" in the House of Lords. The bill received Royal Assent on 20 July 1993 and is now the Bail (Amendment) Act 1993.

My experience on this bill has made me even more convinced of the value of the House of Lords as a chamber for serious debate and for careful revision of draft legislation. Its active membership consists for the most part of men and women who have reached the top of their chosen profession – in business, the Church, the law, medicine, politics, and the armed forces. The House is an immense reservoir of knowledge, experience, and judgment, and we would be very foolish to destroy it. The fact that peers are not elected is, I think, a virtue, because they do not have to conform to the political pressures of the day, and because they are not elected it is accepted that the will of the House of Commons must prevail. If both were elected, there would be a constant power struggle, especially if different parties were in control of each House. I have noticed that the more the House of Lords makes life difficult for the government, the less enthusiasm my Labour colleagues in the Commons have to abolish it.

I had 71,252 constituents eligible to vote at the 1992 general election, and although I am the representative in Parliament of all those people, and also of those who were too young to vote, it is clearly impossible to give effect to the wishes of everyone. In the first place, no MP can know the views of all his constituents on all the issues, and even if he did he would find that on almost every issue the views and interests of some constituents conflicted with those of others. A Member of Parliament cannot, therefore, be a mere delegate; he must get to know the views and interests of his constituents as best he can, and must give effect to them as far as possible, but he is not a local councillor, and he must use his experience and judgment for the benefit of the nation as a whole. While I do not know what all my constituents think, I do know that by voting for me, twice as many voters preferred the principles and programme of the Conservative party to those of any other party. There is controversy about whether members ought to vote with their party or to vote according to their own views on each issue as it arises. On matters of conscience, such as capital punishment, abortion, or Sunday trading, there will normally be a free vote, and if there is a particularly strong constituency interest a member may sometimes obtain a dispensation, but apart from these I take the view that a member ought to vote with his party. The reason is that in the United Kingdom, parliamentary candidates are elected because they support the principles and programme of a political party, by people who voted and campaigned for them because they too support that party. This is not to say that an MP should not use all his skill and tenacity to argue within his party for the policies he wants; but if he fails to persuade a majority of his colleagues I believe that he should support the majority decision save in the most exceptional circumstances. Politics is a team effort, and if all MPs were free to act as they pleased it would be impossible for the government to implement its programme, or for the opposition to mount any effective opposition to that programme.

A relatively recent feature of British politics, imported from the United States, is the growth of professional lobbying on behalf of charities, environmental groups, trade unions, commercial organizations, and many single-interest pressure groups. Some MPs object to the existence of lobbyists, and try their best to deny them access to the Houses of Parliament, arguing that they are suborning members and subverting democracy. I take the view that lobbyists can help the democratic process by drawing members' attention to issues, preferably before they have been decided by the executive, and by providing facts and arguments. No member is so stupid as to think that such material is likely to be impartial, but it can be very useful as a statement of one side of the case. The member must then look for the other side to the library of the House of Commons, to his own research staff, or to a rival lobbyist. However, some lobbyists, and in particular those with a measure of public support, go much too far. So concerned are they that their point of view shall prevail in Parliament that they seek to apply heavy pressure and even to intimidate Members of Parliament. No MP can ever submit to such methods, and must always remember that however vehemently some members of the public, and indeed some of his own constituents, may support a particular cause, he must vote in such a way as in his judgment is best for the nation as a whole, even if by so doing he makes himself and his party unpopular at the time.

Very recently, members have had access to information via the Parliamentary Data and Video Netweork, to which personal computers can be connected. This gives on-line access to the *Official Report* of both Houses of Parliament (Hansard), to newspaper reports, and to other information sources. The system is still in the process of development, and some members can now see and hear proceedings in the chamber of both Houses on a television monitor in their office. In this respect, the UK Parliament is far behind some other legislatures. Some members have very recently been connected to the Internet.

In addition to national issues, a Member of Parliament today is expected to be well aware of local issues, and to have an opinion on matters which are really the responsibility of local councillors. Often, when a constituent is unhappy with the action of a local authority, he will expect his MP to solve the problem. In addition to our mailbag, MPs also hold "surgeries" in the constituency where constituents can have a personal talk about national, international, local, or personal issues. I have on behalf of constituents solved a wide range or problems, including failure of the state to pay the correct social security benefits, concerns over the location of a refuse transfer station, the construction of flood defences for constituents' homes, concerns about the action or inaction of the police, the maintenance of drains and sewers, the choice of route for a new road, concerns about medical treatment, and many many others. I even had a constituent who demanded that I do something about the flying saucers landing on the Downs behind her house. I also do everything I can to improve employment prospects in the constituency, and have arranged for two foreign trade delegations to make a visit.

I have been seconded to British Rail under the Industry and Parliament Trust scheme, which aims to make parliamentarians and industrialists more aware of each other. Secondment is for a few days at a time over a period of 18 months, and I was able to see for myself what happens on the railway from the point of view of the chairman of the board, and the carriage cleaners, and almost every grade in between, in many different parts of the country. I was also able to visit French, Swedish, and Dutch railways, and found the international comparisons immensely valuable. I have recently been invited to accept a secondment to the Royal Navy under a similar scheme. I believe it is vital that MPs keep closely in touch with the world outside Parliament, and should take very opportunity to keep themselves informed on what is happening and on what people are thinking.

At the end of each day's proceedings in the House of Commons, the police call out "who goes home?" This tradition has survived from the days when members returning late to their homes would be set upon by cut-purses and other villains, and would therefore be entitled to a police escort. Today members run much the same risks, but no escort is provided.

11: Edward Pearce

Parliament and the Press

"FAUSTUS, this night thy soul shall be required of thee". The soul of government certainly. The soul of Parliament is in such a state that one is far from sure that there are any takers for it in hell. Why should any such dangerous pacts be needed? A time was when Parliament held the press (which it did *not* call the media), in a grand, altitudinous contempt and the press responded with a spaniel-cringe of devotion. The reporting of Parliament was a privilege, but it was a privilege gratefully devoured by page upon page of reporting of proceedings *in extenso* in retina-detaching type. The feeling among Victorian journalists was that, made privy to sonorous pronouncement, they were under obligation to disseminate it. They were more fortunate in this than the casual hearers of Pericles; not quite the position of Mr Kelvin Mackenzie. That golden world of god-like politician and horsewhipped editor is deader than any parrot. If Parliament as a whole is deferential to government, we have seen in recent years a shift by which government defers to certain newspapers and those papers play an essential part in determining who, by becoming government, shall control Parliament. The process of reverse-deference has been accelerated lately. Less recently, in what the Russians might call the near-past, an election would be marked by the devotion of *Express, Mail, Times, Telegraph,* and some of the fallen: *Graphic* and *Sketch*, say, to announcing in plain or gaudy ways that the Conservatives were best.

In 1959, the slogan on the hoardings was "life's better with the Conservatives. Don't let Labour ruin it." The message of the newspapers was indistinguishable. But the relationship of the Conservative party to the press, which largely means of government to the press, behind which Parliament comes limping behind, was simple and subordinate. It could be given as an order of service in a cathedral. "Her Majesty's imperial press, men in pork pie hats carrying emblematic notebooks and wearing the traditional dirty macs of state, shall periodically cry 'Vivat'. All the congregation shall kneel or rise, whichever seems more appropriate, and with or without the Archbishop of Canterbury, the Conservative and Unionist party shall be elected." But you cannot always count on that sort of magic. In the 1960s, the old, respectable Tory press made a lot of Richard Dimbleby noises to settings of Parry in A Major without any effect at all. Labour was returned in the elections of 1964, 1966, February and October of 1974 with only 1970 going the correct way. The old *Times, Telegraph,* and *Daily Express* were not delivering, David English's super-professional Pravda-ization of the *Daily Mail* was still under construction. Clearly rougher trade was called for, and accordingly we get to Faust Part One.

Margaret Thatcher, leader of the opposition from 1975, went out of her way to win the support of Sir Larry Lamb, then the editor of the *Sun,* and something began to happen which has transformed the relationship of press, government, and Parliament in what commonly seems to be that order. In the process, we were told something about our society (if we are allowed to have one). The feeling was that out there across Britain were hundreds of thousands of *Sun* readers. They were working class; they liked a bit of smut (and most days, a couple of bits of overkill); they liked horrible murders in an old working class tradition which goes back via the Newgate Calendar to 16th century broadsides sold beneath the gallows. But there were an awful lot of these readers and did they really have to vote Labour? Well now the paper was the sales sensation of its day, "Your super soaraway *Sun*" reaching at its high point, something well over four million copies sold daily. It was a line to the working class, to what we have been told to call "the C2s". If they could be induced to like what Mrs Thatcher and her party stood for, clearly this would be very good political business. But then the arrangement made by Johannes Faust with Mephistopheles, head of corporate affairs at Astaroth Holdings PLC, was also an attractive deal. (Faust you recall, got further with Helen of Troy than the Conservatives ever did with Samantha Fox).

Sir Larry and the *Sun* delivered. The Prime Minister became "Battling Maggie"; she was "battling for Britain", her enemies were variously "Worzel Gummage" and "the Welsh Windbag". Something like nine million people were told every day when it mattered that the Tories were a good thing and Mrs Thatcher a wonderful thing. Across three elections, the *Sun* produced virulent, high volume, low veracity progaganda for the Conservative and Unionist party. And beyond the natural period of upper working class prosperity – a South of England, in-work, doing all right sort of prosperity at the best of times – the Tory message was carried sweetly to the upwardly mobile voter. Now as long as Sir Larry was around, the *Sun* was not entirely a bad thing. It was cheerful sexiness and disrespect rather than malignancy. Sir Larry was and is a nice man. He once thought of hiring me and took me to lunch to that end. What did I like to drink? I said, like a fool, that I was quite happy with cheap Italian wine. "Stuff that for starters," he said and ordered a Montrachet. A man like that, even if he did support Margaret Thatcher, had something to be said for him. But Sir Larry belonged to the early days. For a long time until recently, the *Sun* has been edited by Mr Kelvin MacKenzie.

Politically, he has most in common with the unlamented Horatio Bottomley whose paper, *John Bull*, preached during the First World War and the 1920s the glory of the British bulldog, the contemptibility of lesser races, and of course the especial evil of the Hun and the need on that account for young men to get themselves killed on the Somme. If patriotism is, in Dr Johnson's phrase, the last refuge of the scoundrel, then the next scoundrel who flees to it, will find Mr Mackenzie in the bar. As for journalism, well, Mr Mackenzie is to journalism what the Black and Tans were to the Brigade of Guards. We speak, do we not, of the very poor and hopeless, the dynastic unemployed, as the underclass? With the accession and growing influence of Kelvin Mackenzie, we in Britain acquired an "underpress". However, the implication for Parliament, as I will make clear, is that this is not a pathetic gathering of dog-plate rattlers, but a ravening underpress with some of the implications for government as the Paris Mob in the 1790s. Except that such papers only visit politics on an awayday ticket ... rather in the way of football hooligans. For much of the time, its papers are not newspapers at all. Nothing in government, in foreign news, in the economy is as important as the sexual deviations of an actress in a soap opera. The required central front page issue of a Murdoch/Mackenzie popular daily has been, over a couple of decades, that Fred had intercourse with Fifi ...

It is then a quite luscious irony that the *Sun* is the heir of the *Daily Herald*. The *Daily Herald,* I must remind those under 40, was a dull, decent, sober, inept newspaper attached to the Labour party, whose leaders were unable in 1961 to stop its sale by Odhams Press to IPG, owners of the *Daily Mirror*. Let me reminisce. I was present as an undergraduate at the Oxford Union debate in which Hugh Gaitskell was taking part, when the message came through that Christopher Chancellor, head of Odhams, had agreed the sale. The leader of the opposition hurried out and went into a long, anxious phone call from the president's office. He was worried that something rather dreadful might have happened. He was right to be worried. But not just immediately. Hugh Cudlipp, a highly successful *Mirror* journalist and executive, part of an old ascendancy we can barely remember, tried to revamp the old *Herald* into a broadsheet and gave it the exciting title the *Sun* which, give or take about 7½ per cent, was dull, decent, inept, and attached to the Labour party. After losing more money on it, the IPG 10 or so years on, sold the title for a song to the son of a respected Australian proprietor-journalist, Sir Keith Murdoch. (It was Sir Keith's widow, Lady Murdoch, who said in a musing kind of way, "I don't understand Rupert. His father was such a nice man!"). I tell this known but disregarded tale because it symbolizes something. The failure of the Labour *Herald* and the Labour *Sun*, both of them responsible and honest, neither of them attracted to smut and both of them esteeming their audience much too high, reflects on more things than the villainy of Rupert Murdoch. If you cannot sell to a working class audience a moderately demanding if flavourless publication, but you can sell a daily catalogue of little-screen starlets and starlings, getting high, following one another in and out of bed, and having fights in pubs, then the achievement of public education falls somewhere below where Mr Doug McAvoy and the NUT think it does. Think how much faith went into the idea that education would save all, would raise people, show them the well-lit civilization in which the idealistic middle class themselves lived. It was the dream of Hardy's Jude, Jude Fawley, who aspired to be the equal of the inheriting class by reason of the books he had read, the subjects he had mastered. It was Hardy's Christminster University, which of course is Oxford University, that turned him away with a little note explaining that such things were not for labouring men, not for the likes of him.

The triumph of the underpress is that at the moment when Christminster stretches out to Jude's tribe both arms of its elbow-patched, don's jacket and says, "please come with priority", that tribe embraces an ignorance wholly voluntary. Consider the calculating mind of Mr Rupert Murdoch. If mass public education had not failed, the *Sun* would be popularizing science, reporting on the Taiwanese economy, analyzing developments in Central Europe, and grumbling about the latest production of Don Giovanni. It would also be reporting debates in Parliament *in extenso*. If intelligent, disinterested reflection upon serious issues sold papers and made money, Mr Murdoch would send out for some. As it is, he inherits a sump of quarter-literacy, inert, incurious, dirty-minded lumpen slobbishness – and he caters for it to the height of his formidable powers ... and daily sells four million copies.

You know the old cliché that we get the press we deserve. If that is true, what sort of people must we be to deserve the press we have got? And how comprehensively have we failed to turn modest economic growth and genuine belief in a participatory democracy into anything at all. I do not pretend to know, do not even undertake to guess whether the failure of light is the product of underspending on education, a crank mentality among educationists coupled with the dim producer instincts of the NUT, a union with great negative strength, or the awful finite limits of human intelligence. I recall the words attributed to Ernest Bevin about the working class and "the terrible poverty of their expectations". I can only say that Britain as a whole has lived up to them. You will also be familiar with Aldous Huxley's account of newspapers in *Brave New World* where science and universal artificial insemination (and artificial incubation) have produced nicely balanced numbers: of upper and lower executive minds, steady clerks and skilled men, toiling workers and semi-morons, the categories, alphas, betas, gammas, deltas, and epsilons. Each has its newspaper, from the thoughtful *Alpha Argus* to the simple *Delta Despatch* and below them all, printed on yellow paper in words of one syllable with many pictures, especially for the semi-morons, is the *Epsilon Echo*. Well now Rupert ...

But the implications of this for Parliament and government are those of manipulative populism. Once a paper has made itself immensely popular with no reference whatever to Parliament or government, such political influence as it chooses to exert is potentially very great. Mr Murdoch in one sense is not political at all. He wants to break the common restraints of monopolies and mergers legislation and get networks he should not have and accomplish takeovers which tend against fair trade. To that end, he wants a government creaturely to him in the things he values. In return, he will be creaturely to it in its requirements. He may or may not deserve the credit for the government's success, but he will claim such credit in 80 point type – IT'S THE SUN WOT DONE IT – and be believed. The *Epsilon Echo* is thus enormously influential with government because it is deemed to have been enormously influential in the election of Parliament. But the *Sun* latterly *has* been getting political, not more than 5% of its printface, but made up for in emphasis and virulence. It has preached a systematic hatred of Europe coupled with a still more unpleasant and specific hatred of Germany. You can laugh if you like, at the headline, "Up Yours Delors", laugh rather more uneasily at "Hop off Frogs". But I have to say that "The Sun Bans the Hun" does not strike me as funny at all.

The little episode of the German troops who might have taken part in celebrations of the end of the Second World War, symbolizes quite neatly the whole state of play on Europe. Joined by the *Daily Mail* which talked of "German troops marching on Whitehall", the *Sun* set about stirring up every comforting hatred that might lie latent within the British soul. It spoke in terms which Norman Tebbit had used about the Treaty of Maastricht: "Jackboots in Whitehall". The thought that a 14-year-old boy fighting in the ruins of Berlin in April 1945 will now be 65 years old, will very likely have a grandson at the end of his teens, and that the guilt of Germans *under* 65 is nil, is not permitted. The idea that a distinction should be drawn between the Nazis and the Germany which boringly elects a dull, decent, right of centre party in marginal preference to a dull, decent, left of centre party, is pedantic fact and by definition irrelevant. The anti-Germanism was, of course, in perfect sync with the views of the *Sun's* heroine. It was Margaret Thatcher who said in the hearing and presence of Helmut Kohl at Cambridge in April 1990: "The British people will need 40 years to forgive the Germans." I think that for a head of government to speak in that way in that context was clinically crazy. But a baton was handed on, not to Mrs Thatcher's successor, but to her heirs in the press. The *Sun,* following Margaret Thatcher, wants us to hate Germany, and by extension, wants us to hold out to the peoples of Europe the sort of civilized understanding which might be offered to foreigners in a very rough pub at about quarter to eleven at night. The attitude is the one described in a *Punch* Cartoon:

> First Rough: Joe. That's a Foreigner.
> Second Rough: Right Fred. 'Eave 'alf a brick at 'im.

Well now, if you talk like that to a certain kind of backbench MP, you are likely to bring out the worst in him. The French are our enemies, the Portuguese are Third World – the view of one of the genteel nasties on the *Spectator* – the Belgians are comic. No Irish need apply. This is a proletarian version of the world of Nancy Mitford's Uncle Matthew: "Abroad is unspeakably beastly and all foreigners are friends".

I speak of the *Sun*, but of course the *Sun* is only the flagship of the Murdoch armada. What the *Sun* says, *Today* echoed, and the *Times,* a rather unwholesome resurrection, that deconsecrated chapel now run as a rather flashy funeral parlour, also proclaims. And they are joined in their hostile view of Europe by two non-Murdoch papers whose editors take like views, the *Daily Mail* and the *Sunday Telegraph*. The effect upon government confidence, government ability to make rational judgments, upon the courage of government, and its sense of community with friendly neighbouring countries with whom we have entered into an historical and binding treaty, is extensive and damaging. It works in part through Parliament. John Major's government was not perceived to be legitimate by a vigorous group (or coven) of rightwingers in regular communication from its pentacle with the late lady. Margaret Thatcher hated Europe irrationally, so did they. Major was dealing with Europe, I would say, with hard-negotiated sense and great success. But according to this press, nothing achieved in Europe, not the strongest, most advantageous compromise, must be endured. In all our dealings with Europe, the government must now accommodate a virility test. These negotiations, usually about pettifogs and arcania, ball bearings and carrot jam, must be fought to the death. It is essential that our chap shall swagger, strut, cause affront and meet the testicular norm demanded by a bar full of subeditors. He must quarrel where he might have reasoned quietly. He must never on any account reach a conclusion which might be good for Europe as a whole. Only wimps compromise. Only traitors make concessions. Only by stealth can you behave sensibly.

Now Europe, the European Union itself, is a strange animal. It is compelled by its own nature to *do* things. It must go forward in one of several optional directions in order to be sure of its existence. It is an organization embodying Cartesian gradualism: "I edge forward, therefore I exist." It has devised for itself ways of going forward in smoke-filled rooms in which the clocks have been stopped. Glassy-eyed men, who have not slept for 48 hours, emerge with bits of paper to wake sleeping journalists in hotel foyers with the news that Europe has achieved a 15-sided compromise, a common air-freight policy or whatever. It is bizarre, but it more or less works and while, of course, everybody there has fought his corner, in not one of the other 15 countries is it thought that points lost, concessions made, represent a victory for its enemies over one's country or personal disqualification in a prime minister for leadership. But the British, precisely through taking this press-created, overwrought attitude, suffered earlier in 1994 a real defeat and the Prime Minister a mighty humiliation. There was no other intelligent explanation of Mr Major's action in seeking to resist the routine arithmetical racking up of the veto quotient, the so called qualified majority voting, from 23 to 27. It simply takes notice that Austria, Sweden, and Finland have joined. The increase was, of course, a retention of the *status quo* under new numbers brought up by those acceding countries. It left things as they were, as 10 of the 12 wished to leave them.

Spain opposed and she did so for reasons of healthy low commerce. Spain benefits from most of the inequities (and iniquities) of the Common Agricultural Policy. The wine she cannot sell goes into the Wine Lake which lies adjacent to the Olive Oil Lake into which the olive oil she cannot sell either also flows. It is free money for farmers and whatever the charm of *that* to anyone blissfully setting aside between Oxford and the Welsh Border, there is no defence to be made for it. The inequity of the CAP, put together by the French and the

Bavarians during our first sulk (post 1957), is something about which the most committed pro-Europeans in Britain are agreed. It is, however, the most natural thing in the world that Señor Felipe Gonzalez, enough of whose voters are onto a good thing, will fight for an actual reduction of the veto number to help keep them on it. That is good old fashioned dirty politics, but one no blames Señor Gonzales, because this is an act of rational self-interest which the rest of Europe comprehends as certainly as they rationally vote it down.

What possible advantage had Britain to gain from staging a 15 round contest on an issue which gave her nothing if she won and which, for not one nano-second spent calculating the odds, was she ever going to win? The answer resides in a large commanding piece of the press followed avidly by, and in communication with, the dissentient faction in the government party. Although the chief engine of press menace is the underpress, the same politically motivated message is coming through more genteel channels. Listen to the *Times,* sister paper of the *Sun*:

> Mr Major must not lose his nerve. All the hardest deals in the EC are settled at the very last minute. In holding out for a compromise that allows minority countries an indefinite delay, he will not just be giving succour to a small wing of his party, he will be in tune with the vast majority of Conservatives and with most of the electorate. The centre of gravity has shifted within his party and the country. And the Prime Minister needs to take this into account. The few Tory MPs who oppose his position are looking ever more isolated. And only yesterday an NOP poll in the *Mail on Sunday* found that 61% of voters in Southern England thought that the European Union had too much power over British domestic policy ... Interestingly, this poll suggested that the Conservatives may not fare as badly in the European elections as had been feared ... To Labour attacks that he is merely patching up internal divisions, he can reply convincingly that unlike the Opposition, he is prepared to defend British interests abroad.

Thus did the Murdoch *Times* instruct the government and it did so in terms of "Essex before Europe". Paralyze the Community because there are votes in it. That entire leader, even to an intelligent opponent of the European Union, was nonsense, nonsense in its own terms, but also nonsense as the government did it, nonsense as the Murdoch *Times* applauded it. Schiller sweetly observed: "Against thickheadedness the gods themselves struggle in vain." But what influential thickheadedness! The only way that we might have extracted from what would have been a permanently embittered and alienated 12 and an outraged new three, any sort of reduction of the veto quotient, would have been by withholding with Spain our assent to the accession of Sweden, Finland, and Austria. This is the equivalent of getting a better table in a restaurant by threatening to set fire to the table cloths. This is more than thickheadedness. This is a leader in the *Times* of London, the Murdoch *Times,* the *Sun* with long words and no nudes. Not only does that leading article betray an award-winning ignorance of the state of play and the power balance in Europe. Not only does it exemplify the uncomprehending in pursuit of the unattainable, we were recommended to this absurd and forlorn objective because it would help the Tories to do better in the European elections (which in a pig's ear it would. They went onto those elections and held only 18 seats).

Putting aside miscalculations, did you ever see a more desolating piece of provincialism? "It will keep the Tory party sweet." End of argument. But you see the development of the press and governmental relationship set out. The press feels closer to the electorate than government because it is nearer to the party. But in both cases it is a prime instructor itself. Effectually, the press is telling government to get in line with itself. Fourth estate indeed – nothing so lowly.

Now I have long suspected that many Conservatives when they speak of "the people", or indeed "the world", have in mind a wine and cheese party in Angmering. But this is a piece of self-preoccupation which imports a suave cosmopolitan quality to that 19th century Irish editorial punchline: "The Tsar of the Russias should know that the eye of the Skibereen Eagle is upon him". It makes Señor Gonzalez's efforts for unsaleable Spanish commodity surpluses at least seem a *rational* selfishness. Unwanted wine may do a lot better over the next three years than the Conservative and Unionist party. What the *Times* is trying to say with the felicity of a verbally challenged weasel, is that the Tories might be able to play the patriotic card. It and the rest of the Murdoch press were therefore delighted, rapturous when Mr Major vetoed the appointment of Jean-Luc Dehaene. Some legitimacy can be claimed for the Prime Minister's act this time. The German and French governments did concert too privily over the name. They accept as much. But the name was a good one. M Dehaene is a talent big enough for the job and the depressing dream of the British government and the newspapers perched on its shoulder is that M Jacques Santer may not be. This commitment of the British to the promotion of the second rate in the hope that it will suit their domestic ends is depressing. But the British government gave a good impression throughout these proceedings of seeking extended permission to exist from Mr Murdoch and his allies. I rather suspect that the Scoundrels' Bar has an annexe, the Wimps' Snug.

Take the underlying *Times* point that the centre of gravity has shifted, that people are resentful of Europe in Southern England (I can think of some places where people are resentful of Southern England, but no matter). Such hostility, such resentment, such flight from the community simply could not have occurred without the relentless activity of seven newspapers, the Murdoch five, the *Daily Mail,* and the *Sunday Telegraph*. Of course, that hostility takes variable forms, some more reputable than others. The racism of the *Sun* – and I think that invoking malignant rage against Germany *is* racism – is paralleled by earnest playmaking about small regulations, in which the *Sunday Telegraph* specializes. Of course, there are any number of issues on which we might all wish to be constructive critics and reformers, but still positive Europeans. But the press opposition is systematic and reflexive. It has little to do with reform, everything to do with sustained nag and rabbit resentment.

We have reached the point in Britain where the government doing routine European business – which is what this footling veto-quotient was – becomes wry-necked with anxiety at the opinion which a body of newspapers can stir up against it. The John Major who actually negotiated a very skilful deal for Britain at Maastricht, an opt-out from a fair measure of overheads and exemption from about a quarter of EU domestic regulation, would not have dreamt at that constructive time, of touching the OMV nonsense which he fell into in the spring. Over Maastricht he fought a rational, patient case and came away with exceptionally good terms. But in Parliament, he was hardly met with acclamation. A section of his party treated us to a long hot summer of filibustering resistance to ratification. They went on auto-witter. Compared with Mr Bill Cash, Fidel Castro is terse. Compared with the Maastricht debate, the Crucifixion was a mercy killing.

It is a long-accepted convention that in Parliament government commands, government gets what it wants. The Lords may do as they please, but they do not know any better and besides they do not get jobs as number three at the environment dangled at them. The spring and summer of 1993 were spent rebutting the whole assumption. Is that not then a good thing? After all we want a healthy Parliament arguing with the executive. Respectfully, I do not think that people happy with the sort of consultative conciliation which brought us the Poll Tax, are the ideal spokesmen for healthy pluralism. There is nothing very Popperian about Sir George Gardiner.

What we saw over Maastricht and the more general undermining of Mr Major was the rage of Thatcherian authoritarians *in* Parliament allied with a press happy at every clicking of her fingers as long as its mergers went through Any pluralism there is of a distinctly Pickwickian sort. Home, bruised and burnt in the last whisper of Maastricht, it is not altogether surprising that Mr Major acted over qualified majority voting to appease the very people who had given him hell over the treaty. He did so after that long, inveterate campaign of anti-Europeanism coupled with the argument that the desperate Tory party might be seen as "defending Britain's interests abroad". On this occasion, he abandoned a normally very good political judgment and "gave over to party what was meant for mankind". He acted foolishly, but not characteristically. He acted under pressure and, I think, we know under what pressure. Mr Major who has no talent for vulgar abuse, was persuaded to call the late John Smith "a Euro-poodle". The patriotic card was played, the papers which had persecuted Mr Major as an underendowed feebleton, said warm things about the crass folly he was committing. In the real world, our friends – which is what the Europeans are – were first furious and then unbending. The Foreign Secretary was brought close to resignation, the patriotic card was withdrawn, and the same newspapers, which had egged Mr Major on, portrayed him instantly as an underendowed feebleton. The *Daily Mail's* cartoonist, Michael Cummings, had his drawing of Mr Major as a poodle put on the front page.

Mr Major had sought to serve the right in the right's terms. He had done so because behind the right stood the press. And when he pulled back from exclusion of the Scandinavians, pulled back from simple wrecking, the right and the press behind it tore out his guts and devoured them: "Faustus this night thy soul shall be required of thee." But the consequences of that Faustian pact and the growth of the power of the underpress does not stop there. The hole in which the Tory party stands is fathoms deep. Taxes, unemployment, past interest rates, and a dislike which grows ingrained cannot be removed except by one thing. Suppose that the *Times* is right, that anti-Europeanism really is a card to sweeten the Southern English voter. Any leader of that party has to please the same people, his activists and the rightwing newspapers. This is true of Mr Michael Heseltine who dropped hints of rightward conciliation. It is, of course, true of Mr Michael Portillo who is playing to this gallery with every breath he draws, though happily Mr Portillo's cleverness never goes on stage without being accompanied by his stupidity. He is not Jekyll and Hyde half so much as Morecambe and Wise. It is true of Mr Major. The Prime Minister behaves more often than not with great skill. His death is everywhere reported and anticipated, ham is ordered for the celebration of his funeral tea, but Mr Major turns up at it. He loses the European elections all right, but loses them moderately badly. He carried out a challenge to himself in July 1995, which he won and now Mr Major may be Prime Minister at the election of October 1996 or March 1997. He has paid a high price. He has fed the right, he has fed the Murdoch press. His position in respect of the media is like that of a turn at the old Glasgow Empire in the 1930s. This music hall was attended by shipyard workers of critical cast of mind who used to carry rivets in their pockets. It was said, as it might be of the Murdoch press, "if they liked you, they let you live".

To live at the next election he will need to bring the Murdoch press exactly where Mrs Thatcher had them – in line behind and blowing like a trade wind. He picks a big fight, he wrecks something, the Murdoch press sings *Te Deums.* He is obliged to balance more Indian clubs than his concert party performer father ever did. He must somehow embrace the vulgar nationalism of "the Sun bans the Hun" while signalling frantically to the weary occupant of the German Chancellery and to the Berlaymont that, though for the moment he must half-wreck Europe, nevertheless, he still wants us at the heart of it after the election. "Faustus this night thy soul shall be required of thee". Newspapers, which had essayed political power in 1930 and been beaten off by Baldwin, which had tried again (Lord Beaverbrook and the *Express* over Europe in the 1960s) and failed again, can now claim that the centre of gravity has indeed shifted – from government to the underpress. If that new balance describes us the way we are, the way we are is no way to be. But is that to be the final word? Do we accept that a group of newspapers should think they can instruct a government, that a cause they have picked must be followed, that ignominy works?

Mr Major handles the underpress by being adroit, by giving them something of what they want, but then sneakily going round their backs over essentials. He has the dilemma of Stanley Baldwin, but he stands on weaker ground. Government in Baldwin's day possessed mystique and a mantle of natural authority even if the generality of dithering stuffed shirts then in government did not deserve either. Newspapers at that time, despite their solid fare and tedious responsibility, were thought flashy and not quite respectable, apart that is, from the turgid, intolerable old pre-Murdoch *Times,* whore turned kept woman, turned duchess. For Beaverbrook and Rothermere to attack Baldwin was not done. It was visibly a fusillade mounted by bounders. When Baldwin roused his natural decency from the lilo of his temperament, deployed the lines written for him by his literary cousin, Rudyard Kipling, and spoke of "the prerogative of the harlot down the ages", older and wiser heads nodded in expression of the sort of approval they would have called "sage".

Government today stands at the end of a long and sustained period of derisive contempt worked upon it by its actual failings and by the Murdoch style. You cannot say, "cor, what a wally" to 10 million people reading with one finger as often as it has been said, without grinding government pretty fine. The relationship of the press and Parliament has been transformed. Mystique and the mantle of natural authority have gone the way of snuff boxes and powdered hair. In principle I do not regret that. The old lapel-clutching political class which, "Like Cato gave its little senate laws/And sat attentive to its own applause" was not to be admired. The opposite extreme is worse. Government ought to have a furious respect for the people and opinion, but what opinion? Press semimonopoly means that three men, Conrad Black, Rupert Murdoch, and more tentatively, Vere Harmsworth, *make* opinion. A Tammany boss in America once said, "I am the law". These three can say, "We are opinion ... We are the people". Remember, "It's the Sun wot won it".

"Speak for England", said Leopold Amery on a celebrated occasion. Well now, a renegade Australian with an American passport, a south Canadian who identifies with the United States as the Cause of Good and Right, and a slightly valetudinarian gentleman who lives in France speak for England. Like Rosencrantz and Guildernstern, they play upon our stops and what a poor thing they would make of us. Opinion when marshalled, heavily influences policy, and opinion is made by papers carrying politics pig-a-back upon the carnalities of soap starlets. Opinion is a parenthesis in a comic. The opinion of the people is obtained, proclaimed, and brandished by people who have planned their papers upon a sovereign and total contempt for the people. This is a country crying out for antitrust legislation, for stern merger regulation, for state resistance to monopoly. Government needs to breathe, the public needs to form opinion from a diversity of sources. The concentration of the press is the concentration of power. I cannot think that we are stronger as a polity when government, reflecting on the new press, has to keep remembering that advice given by deep sea divers on meeting a shark: "You're perfectly all right as long as it never smells either blood or urine". Unless until another government erects a law to confine press ownership (and TV franchises) the soul of Faustus will be required of him, not perhaps this night, but will instead go on being sold on hire purchase – death on the instalment plan, the privatization of politics. Power without responsiblity indeed, but power in the semimonopolitistic hands of worse people than harlots.

12: Adam Bruce

The Parliament of Scotland 1296–1707

IT IS NOT auspicious that, while the majority of essays in this book look back to the English "Good Parliament" of 1295, this essay begins one year later with the deposition of King John of Scots by King Edward I of England. King John's demise was followed by the English Parliament at Berwick which received on 28 August 1296 the Ragman's Roll containing the names of some 2,000 Scottish freeholders who had sworn fealty to Edward I. If Scotland had a contemporary "Good Parliament", it was that held in St Andrews in 1309 which settled the Crown of Scotland on King Robert I (the Bruce) and commenced the final phase of the Wars of Independence, culminating in the Treaty of Northampton in 1328.

More significantly, the time frame provided by this book has allowed for an intriguing examination of Scottish constitutional history, beginning as it does in 1296 with the deposition of one monarch, John I, and culminating in 1689 with the deposition of a second, James VII and II. Both of these events received the "sanction" of contemporary representative assemblies and both provided fertile ground for 18th and 19th century debate between Jacobite and Whig historians. The deposition of John Balliol provided ammunition for Whigs who saw it as precedent for the removal of James VII and II.[1] Jacobite historians countered by arguing that Balliol had been forced on Scotland by Edward I, and that the true royal line, represented by the Bruces and latterly by the Stewarts, was restored with the culmination of the Wars of Independence. More importantly, the Jacobites strenuously denied that the Scots monarchy was limited or elective.[2]

For the historian of the Scottish Parliament, works written in each of the three centuries after the Union of 1707 bring different obstacles that must be overcome. Eighteenth-century histories are redolent of the intellectural struggle between Whigs and Jacobites. Nineteenth-century Whig historians, ashamed at the apparently retarded nature of the Scots Parliament, and the lack of a glorious constitutional history in the English mould, wrote off Scotish parliamentary history as irrelevant.[3] Even 19th century histories of Scotland were less than generous in their treatment of Parliament.[4] In the 20th century, parliamentary histories have reflected contemporary politics. At the start of the century, at the height of imperial lustre, and when Bishop Stubbs' star was at its brightest, analysis of the Scots Parliament remained in an anglocentric context.[5] By the end of the century, renewed interest in Scottish history reflected calls for constitutional reform. However, this current renaissance in the history of Scotland has yet to produce a revisionist treatment of her parliaments.[6]

There remains one further obstacle for the historian who completes this historiographical maze. Writing a brief history of the Scots Parliament in a collection of detailed essays on particular eras in the history of the English Parliament may lead at best to a perception of lack of scholarship, and at the worst to accusations of partisanship. The English parliament was a unique institution, and much of its history and tradition, mythical or not, has been incorporated into the United Kingdom parliament. While its birth was in terms similar to many medieval representative assemblies, Scotland's included, its development was moulded by a series of dynastic struggles, civil wars, and foreign expeditions not experienced in Scotland. There is probably little to be served in a direct comparison of the two institutions. What is more useful is to examine their development in a European context. Here too the historian faces an obstacle: examining anything in Britain in the late 20th century is likely to give rise to an equally partisan debate between Europhile and Europhobe, as that which existed between Whig and Jacobite historians in the 18th century.

A reexaminaiton of the early development of the Scots Parliament can be continued to look at its growth in the later medieval and early modern period. At a time when the English third estate was beginning to exert its influence over the first and second estates, a comparable lack of advance in the Scottish third estate needs to be explained again by comparison, this time with other domestic institutions, in particular the Convention of Royal Burghs and the General Assembly of the Church of Scotland. There are also other factors beyond the scope of this essay that require to be examined, especially the nature of monarchy in late medieval Scotland and the relative lack of royal authority in the localities. The medieval and early modern constitutional make-up of Scotland was very different from that of England. The relative stability in Scottish constitutional affairs between 1399 and 1603 under one dynasty compares starkly with the five changes in dynasty in England in the same period. The most immediate consequence for Scotland of these bloody upheavals in England was that the usurping monarch usually launched an invasion of Scotland in the age-old routine of deflecting opposition at home by concentrating on adventures abroad.[7] In the main, the lack of Scottish royal adventures abroad and the consequent lack of requirement for taxation, coupled with the relative stability in the localities, ensured that few parliaments were called and, when they were, they were brief and lacking in contentious disputes and grievances.

The Parliament of Scotland developed unique characteristics principally in its composition. Throughout its existence, it was unicameral, despite an attempt by James I to introduce a "House of Commons" by requiring the third estate to elect a speaker. Until the construction of Parliament Hall in 1639, it was peripatetic, although from the 16th century onwards it sat principally in Edinburgh. Its composition changed over time, first, with the attempts at creating county representation and, secondly, with the exclusion of the clergy after the Reformation. In administration, it delegated almost all its legislative functions to a committee known as the Lords of the Articles and it lost its civil judicial authority to the Court of Session in 1532. Disputes about whether actions before the Session were appealable to Parliament continued into the 17th century. In the course of its existence, its authority was compromised by other national assemblies, particularly by the General Assembly. Its rules of procedure were limited in scope and yet complex in detail; concepts of "privilege" and "sovereignty" only emerged in the latter part of its life. Ultimately, by a series of ill-judged acts, it so aggravated the Crown of Great Britain that it was abolished in an incorporating union in which the possible contribution of its traditions was ignored while, in contrast, its wholly deficient franchise was maintained until 1832. The manner of its passing continues to spark debate and, unfortunately, the shock of its complete disappearance, Jonah-like, into the belly of what had been the English Parliament, has led to a number of erroneous propositions about its powers in life and the extent of its life after death. The two most serious of these errors are the notions, wholly unsubstantiated by historical fact, that in Scotland sovereignty lay with "the people" and not with Parliament and that in Scotland one Parliament could bind its successor.[8]

In his *History of Scotland,* first published in 1759, the Revd William Robertson, one of the Scottish Enlightenment's principal Whig historians, traced the origins of the Scottish Parliament to the King's own Baron Court whose members comprised his tenants-in-chief who attended out of feudal duty.[9] This analysis in its broadest terms fits within the framework of the development of representative assemblies in Europe through the course of the 12th and 13th centuries. These 13th century *concilia* differed little in composition, and all recorded their business in the universal language of Latin. Occasionally, assemblies convened without being called by their king. In time of dynastic upheaval or war, such as in Poitou in 1246, or in Scotland after the death of the Maid of Norway in 1290, councils were assembled to attempt to restore the *status quo ante.* In Scotland, as elsewhere in Europe, the form and content of these early assemblies followed the procedures of clerical synods, with feudal obligation tempered by principles of civil law. It was an accepted tenet of private law even in the 13th century that *quod omnes tangit ab omnibus approbetur,* that which touches everyone should be approved by everyone. It was this that the Holy Roman Emperor Frederick II referred to when he summoned the assembly in Verona in 1244 and likewise Edward I when calling the Parliament of 1295.[10] The early Scottish parliaments of the late 13th and early 14th centuries were attended at least by the bishops, earls, and barons. Representatives of the burghs appear to have attended on an *ad hoc* basis. These assemblies met to ratify important acts of state and to consent to the levying of taxation. In this they were no different from representative assemblies across the continent.

Representatives of the burghs and of the clergy appear in Scots records of parliaments in the late 13th and early 14th centuries, contemporaneously with their appearance in other European states. The "Auld Alliance" between

Scotland and France, ratified by the Treaty of Dunfermline of 1296, was accepted by the "prelates, earls, barons, and communities of the towns of Scotland," and the seals of six burghs were appended to the deed.[11] It is unclear, however, whether representatives of these burghs attended the Parliament held at Dunfermline at that time. The burghs were certainly represented in the Edinburgh Parliament of 1328 that ratified the final peace agreement between Scotland and England. The summons called "bishops, abbots, earls, barons, freeholders, and six sufficient persons of the various burgh communities specially empowered for the purpose."[12] The presence or absence of burghal representation is not too significant, as the four principal burghs (Edinburgh, Stirling, Roxburgh, and Berwick) had met in the Court of the Four Burghs since the 12th century. The existence of the Court, later the Convention of Royal Burghs, had a limiting effect on burghal representation in Parliament. In exchange for bearing the burden of taxation on the third estate, the royal burghs enjoyed a monopoly in foreign trade. This monopoly was jealously guarded by the Convention. It laid down regulations for the number of burgh commissioners who could attend Parliament; it met before each session of Parliament to agree the business to be proposed and the "line" to be taken in each session. The Convention also regulated the admission of burghs to Parliament. Not all burghs were "royal" or free. A number were burghs of barony or regality, and were represented in Parliament by their lay or clerical superior. Even after an "unfree" burgh had received its royal charter, elevating it to the status of a royal burgh, it needed to receive the consent of the Convention before it could send representatives to Parliament.

In the late 16th century, the Royal Burgh of Crail in the East Neuk of Fife persuaded the Convention to delay the recognition of its neighbouring burghs of Kilrenny and Anstruther Wester, even after they had received their royal charters.[13] The real significance of the Convention was that it set the rules for the administration of the burghs, and not Parliament. It regulated foreign trade, and the operation of the Scottish Staple at Veere in Holland, and it was the Convention that often funded embassies from the Scottish Court to foreign states to discuss trading matters. The influence of the Convention was such that representatives of the burghs played a limited role, not only in the Scottish Parliament, but latterly in the United Kingdom Parliament, until the Franchise Reform Acts of 1832 and 1918.

The second institution that impinged on the working of Parliament in its latter years was the General Assembly of the Church of Scotland. The Reformation in Scotland took place in two stages; the first the move from Rome and the second, more lengthy and more hotly disputed, the abolition of episcopacy and the establishment of the Presbyterian kirk.[14] Until the Reformation Parliament of 1560, each of the 13 sees of Scotland were represented in Parliament by its bishop. Despite the radical nature of the Reformation of 1560, bishops continued to sit in Parliament until 1639 when episcopacy was abolished, only to be restored in 1661. The bishops returned to Parliament in 1662, and were present in the Convention Parliament of

1689 which nominated William and Mary. None attended the "revolution" Parliament later that year and episcopacy was finally abolished by Act of Parliament on July 1689 when the established Church of Scotland was confirmed as Presbyterian. Representation of the clergy ended in 1689 as in 1638 the General Assembly had decreed that no minister of the church should "ride or vote" in Parliament.[15] This underlies the enduring contrast between the two established churches; that of England being part of, and therefore, represented in the state; for the Scottish church, the absence of representation in Parliament is a corollary of its absence from the secular state. The General Assembly was formed as a representative national assembly.[16] In its early years, its deliberations were as much doctrinal as political, resolving in 1594 that the King's subjects put themselves in arms to answer the threat from Spain and, in 1596, on a visit of James VI it occupied itself in discussing the manifest sins of the King.[17] In 1638, the General Assembly held in Glasgow overtly refused to recognize the authority of the Crown and ratified a number of measures that led to the Bishops' Wars and the termination of Charles I's personal rule in England.[18]

One particular facet of the early years of the Scottish Reformation was the creation of a *noblesse de robe* comprised of men rewarded by the King with the lands of religious houses to be held *in commendam*. Known as commendators, they sat in Parliament in the estate of the clergy as *de jure* lay heads of their respective houses. This position was maintained by the principle of Scots Law that the right to representation in parliament was a *jus in re* and not a *ius ad personam*; the right to attend Parliament ran with the land. In the late 16th century, Edward Bruce, one of James VI's Council, a Lord of Session, and latterly Ambassador to England and immediately after the Union, Master of the Rolls in that country, was made commendator of the abbey lands of Kinloss. Summoned to Parliament in that respect as "Dominus de Kinloss" he sat in the Estate of the Clergy whence he lodged a protest against the resolution in 1587 of the General Assembly that no layman be allowed to sit in that estate.[19]

The composition of the Estate of the Baronage has already been described in the sister volume to this book.[20] Its representation is worth some further examination. The Estate comprised greater and lesser barons, all of whom, at least until the 16th century, sat in Parliament by virtue of their landed tenure. On his return from captivity in England in 1424, it appears that James I attempted to remodel the Scots Parliament on English lines, by splitting it between Lords and Commons. By Act of 1428, the lesser barons were excused personal attendance, provided they elected commissioners to represent them, two from every shire, save the two smallest shires which sent one each.[21] The Act called for the shire commissioners to assemble and elect one of their number as speaker, "who shall propone all and sundry needs and causes pertaining to the Commons in the Parliament." The main obstacle to the creation of a bicameral assembly, if one was mooted by the King, was that, unlike in England, the representatives of the shires and the representatives of the burghs formed separate estates and were unwilling to combine. This bifurcation in the representation of the "commons" is one of the reasons for the very different development of local politics in Scotland in this period from that in England and the consequent disinterest of historians in whether the Scottish gentry rose or fell in the same manner as their English counterparts.[22] The Act of 1428 was not universally upheld. Some small barons continued to attend Parliament, irrespective of whether they had been chosen as shire representatives. The need to clarify the rules of attendance for the small barons became apparent in the Reformation Parliament of 1560 when a larger number of barons appeared and demanded admittance.[23] The County Franchise Act of 1587[24] effectively limited the franchise to all freeholders possessing land of the annual value of 40s "old extent" (land valued at 40s in the reign of Alexander III – 1249-86) which was held directly of the Crown by ward tenure (ie military tenure) or blench tenure (ie tenure based on a nominal annual payment). By the end of the 17th century, it was highly unusual for land to be conveyed on ward or blench tenure and most property was sold in feu-hold. However, the possession of land in "old extent" remained the franchise even after the Union despite two 17th century Franchise Reform Acts in 1661 and 1681. As the years progressed, so the electorate dwindled so that by 1832, when the population of Scotland was more than two million, the county electorate was barely 3,000. These happy few hardly represent the "popular sovereignty" that, according to some, underpinned the parliaments of Scotland.

Despite the restricted franchise, the county electoral system was well regulated and the seats eagerly contested. In 1669, Parliament set up a "committee anent controverted elections" to deal with contested election results. Unlike in England, the county representatives were paid an attendance fee of £5 a day and they also received travelling expenses.[25] Every sheriff was expected to keep a roll of the freeholders entitled to vote in his sheriffdom and appeals for inclusion or exclusion from this register were heard by the Court of Session. Mandatory electoral registers were not introduced in England until 1832.

In their critiques of the Scots parliaments, 18th and 19th century historians singled out one particular feature as the focus for their ire. The almost universal argument from historians of all shades of opinion was that the Scots Parliament failed to "develop" (along English lines) due to the existence of the Lords of the Articles. The Committee of the Articles can be traced back to the medieval parliaments, charged with preparing and drafting legislation to be presented to Parliament.[26] The committee consisted of eight representatives of each estate and the officers of the Crown. The method of election of the committee was first described in 1633.[27] First, the bishops selected eight barons, who in turn chose eight bishops. Together the representatives of the first and second estates chose eight burgesses. By the turn of the 17th century, the Committee was, in effect, an extension of the royal will. It had changed from a committee of the legislature to a committee of the executive. Its association with royal absolutism saw its abolition in the interregnun (1649-60) and then, after its restoration in 1661, it was finally abolished by the revolution Parliament of 1690.[28] The existence of the Articles and the lack of a fully fledged third estate effectively prevented the Scots Parliament from developing along the "ideal" route established by Whig historiography, but this failure to fit into the Whig historical narrative does not mean that Scotland lacks a distinct parliamentary heritage.

By the 17th century, the Scots Parliament was a mature and well-established assembly with detailed rules of procedure and lengthy regulations on protocol. In the age of absolutism, it stands out with the Parliament in England as one of the last representative assemblies in Europe to have existed in unbroken form since its inception in the Middle Ages. Unlike the English Parliament, which had vested its civil appellate powers in its upper house, the Scots Parliament divested itself of its appellate authority with the creation of the Court of Session in 1532. The Session had originally been a judicial committee of the estates with the task of meeting at "twa sessions yerly."[29] In 1458, Parliament devolved its judicial functions to the Session, declaring that cases that came before it were to be "utterly decided and determined by them without any remeed or appellation to the King or to Parliament."[30] The Act of 1532 created a permanent court to exist separately from Parliament. However, throughout the 17th century, Parliament and Session clashed over the boundaries of their respective jurisdictions. Parliament agreed that the principle that it was able to redress grievances arising from acts of members of the executive or the judiciary had not been devolved to the Session. The abilities of parties before the session to protest to Parliament for "remeid of Law" was much contested in the 17th century, so much so that the Claim of Right contained a clause asserting that it was the right and privilege of subjects to protest for remeid of Law to the King and Parliament against sentences pronounced by the Lords of Session.[31] The crucial distinction between a Protest and an Appeal was that, while an Appeal stopped execution of the decree of the Court, a Protest to Parliament did not. Given the relative infrequency of Parliament. Protests were rare beings. In counter to this perceived incursion into their jurisidiction, the Court of Session held that it could review and suspend Acts of Parliament. In the second edition of his *Institutions of the Law of Scotland* published in 1693, James, Viscount Stair, Lord President of the Session, wrote that "the Lords (of Session) may, and sometimes must, suspend Decrees of Parliament. . . but they cannot suspend *simpliciter* but only until the Parliament may determine."[32] The principle was that the Court could not overturn or set aside an Act, rather suspend it for further consideration by Parliament.[33]

The ability of the Court of Session to review Acts of Parliament has led to recent assertions that in Scots Law certain law can be held to be "fundamental" and ring-fenced from amendment or repeal by later parliaments and that the doctrine of parliamentary sovereignty, as known in England (and as defined by Dicey), has no precedent in Scotland. This argument developed from the desire of some Scots lawyers to argue that the Act of Union of 1707 was fundamental law and, in effect, a written constititution for Great Britain. Over the centuries since 1707, certain articles of the Act of Union have been repealed, which has reduced the fundamental law argument to one that certain articles were more fundamental than others. This argument has been set out in two recent judgments of the Court of Session.[34] Unfortunately, it appears from contemporary sources that the late 17th century Scots Parliament did not believe that one Parliament could bind its successors. Barely 80 years after Lord Justice Coke wrote that the Acts of Parliament of England were subject to the common law and could be set aside in the courts,[35] Lord President Stair wrote that, in Scotland: "Whatever a Parliament can do at one time, in making of laws or determining of causes, may be at their pleasure abrogate or derogate."[36] His son, the first Earl of Stair, expanded this argument in his speech in Parliament in the debate on the Union where he is reported as stating that: "The sum of the whole matter can be stated like this; that although our Parliament is founded on law and flourished by law, yet by law it may also be dissolved. Our authority over it is total. We in Scotland . . . acknowledge no laws or constitutions as binding for ever."[37]

In November 1705, the Earl of Roxburgh wrote of the proposed Union of parliaments that: "The motives will be, Trade with most, Hanover with some, ease and security with others, together with a general aversion to civil discords, intolerable poverty and the constant oppression of a bad ministry."[38] Roxburgh continued by arguing that whatever the inconveniences of Union, they were as none compared to the prospect of the accession to the throne of Scotland of Queen Anne's half-brother, the *soi-disant* Prince of Wales. Sir John Clerk of Penicuik assented, and wrote that the Union was "the best expedient to preserve the honour and liberties of Scotland".[39] The debate that took place in Scotland in the years immediately preceding the Union centred on the question of the Succession.[40] The deaths of the Duke of Gloucester, the future Queen Anne's heir, and James VII and II in 1700 brought into sharp focus the debates on Union that had started with the accession of James VI to the English Throne in 1603. For the second time in almost 10 years, there was a disputed succession to the thrones of both kingdoms. The case for the Electress Sophia of Hanover was not helped in Scotland by the manner in which the English Parliament passed the Act of Succession in 1701. The Scottish parliament was given no opportunity to voice its opinion, despite the terms of the Claim of Right in 1689. For the first time since Edward I had chosen John Balliol as King of Scots, the English Parliament had chosen the line of succession to the imperial crown of Scotland. In the Scottish elections of 1703, the court party was decisively defeated, and in August 1703 Parliament passed the Act of Security, giving it the authority to choose a successor for Queen Anne as King of Scots, thus raising the possibility of the ending of regal Union. More worryingly for Anne's ministers, it raised the spectre of a Roman Catholic king and a francophile nation to their north.

The year 1705 was not a good year to be an Englishman abroad in Scotland or *vice versa*. The Aliens Act of February 1705 had threatened to treat all

Scots resident in England as aliens, and proposed a trade embargo on Scotland. Anglo-Scottish relations froze. In retaliation, the captain and two members of the crew of the *Worcester,* an English merchant vessel seized off the port of Leith, were summarily tried and executed in Edinburgh, the victims of circumstance and bitter feeling. The Administration in England was determined to prevent the accession of the Pretender, and realized that the price they had to pay was full Union with Scotland. This essay does not give the scope for a detailed examination of the reasons for Union, or the manner in which it was achieved. Whatever the contemporary feelings in Scotland for or against Union, it was not until Anne's English ministers appreciated the great danger of not securing the succession in Scotland, that Union became inevitable. No matter that there was little real prospect of the Pretender becoming King of Scots, while he remained a Catholic, or that Scotland's economic interests were impelling her to Union, it was the crisis of 1703-5 that was the catalyst.

Like all great acts of state, the Union of Scotland and England was achieved as much by the immediate circumstances of 1705, as by the impetus that had been drawing the two countries closer together since 1603. By 1705, the consensus of opinion in Scotland favoured a federal Union. In 1706, the Convention of Royal Burghs called for "an honourable and safe Union" with England. In reality, faced with cessation of trade with that country, whose markets consumed more than half of Scotland's exports, and confronted with the possibility of English invasion, the Scots Parliament had little option but to consent to the terms offered by the Union commissioners. With the independence of the church and the law secured, and with parliamentary opposition to the Union divided and effectively leaderless, the legislation was passed. On 28 April 1707, the Parliament of Scotland was finally dissolved. At its demise, the Parliament of Scotland was a mature and developed organism. It was one of the few remaining representative assemblies in Europe at the start of the 18th century. In the two centuries since 1707 it has been largely ignored by historians, being neither a romantic failure nor a heroic success. The fact remains that together with the Parliament of England it can claim to have been the most successful and most durable representative assembly in Europe for more than 500 years. It deserves to be reexamined.[41]

Footnotes to this Chapter may be found on pages 213–15.

Notes

A full reference to each work appears on its first mention in each chapter; later references in the same chapter appear under the author(s)'s surname(s) and a short title. The following abbreviations have been used:

chaps(s)	chapter(s)	ed(s)	editor(s)
edn	edition	esp	especially
et al	and others (where there are more than three editors).		
et seq	and the pages following.		
Ibid	The same book or article as in the preceding note.		
n	note	no	number
NS	new series	OS	old series
p(p)	page(s)	pt	part
repr	reprinted	rev	revised
ser	series	vol(s)	volume(s)

The following titles of journals have also been abbreviated:

Arch Journ	*Archaeological Journal*
Bull Inst Hist Res	*Bulletin of the Institute of Historical Research*
Econ Hist Rev	*Economic History Review*
Eng Hist Rev	*English Historical Review*
Haskings Soc Journ	*Haskins Society Journal*
Hist Journ	*Historical Journal*
Trans Roy Hist Soc	*Transactions of the Royal Historical Society*

Introduction (Pages 1 - 25)

1 J S Moore, R Smith, eds, *The House of Lords: a thousand years of British tradition* (London, 1994).

2 *Ibid*, pp 19, 137–41, 143; P A Bromhead, *The House of Lords and Contemporary Politics, 1911–1957* (London, 1958), chaps VIII–XV; D Shell, *The House of Lords* (London, 1988, 2nd edn, 1992, chaps 5–8; D Shell, D Beamish, eds, *The House of Lords at Work* (Oxford, 1993), chaps 3–7, 10.

3 W Cobbett, *Cobbett's Parliamentary History* (London, 36 vols, 1806–20), vol XV, pp. 725–8, 735–40.

4 Moore and Smith, eds, *The House of Lords,* chap 1.

5 S Roskell, L Clark, C Rawcliffe, eds, *The House of Commons, 1385–1421* (Stroud, 4 vols, 1992), vol I, p 41.

6 C A V V Conybeare, *The Place of Iceland in the history of European Institutions* (Oxford, 1877), pp 37–46, 49–53, 65–7; P Foote, D M Wilson, *The Viking Achievement* (London, 1970), pp 56–61, 92, 377, 402; M H Kirby, *The Vikings* (Oxford, 1977), pp 78–80, 190; F D Logan, *The Vikings in History* (London, 1983), pp 68–70; M McCririck, *A History of Iceland; Eleven Centuries, 874–1974 A.D.* (Bangor, 1984), pp 5–8.

7 Below, p 210, n 8.

8 Below, p 209, n 9.

9 Surviving poll books are listed in J S W Gibson, *Pollbooks, circa 1692–1872: a directory to holdings in Great Britain* (Birmingham, 1989). For a good example of their utility, see J R Vincent, *Pollbooks. How Victorians Voted* (Cambridge, 1967).

10 C R Hudleston, 'Gloucestershire Voters in 1710' (*Trans Bristol and Gloucs Arch Soc,* vol LVIII (1936), pp 195–205).

11 E A Wrigley, R S Schofield, *The Population History of England, 1541–1871* (Cambridge, 1981, repr London, 1989), pp 208–9, provides a reconstruction of population-trends which is generally accepted from *circa* 1600 onwards; the earlier period is rather more controversial and certainly less well documented (see my forthcoming *'Troublous days of Affliction'. Disease, disaster and death in mid-Tudor England*). Previous estimates for the period before the start of parish registers are assembled and discussed in Wrigley and Schofield, *The Population History of England, 1541–1871,* pp 563–76; see also T H Hollingsworth, *Historical Demography* (London, 1969), Appendix 3. Figures after 1871 are derived from the *Reports of the Census of Great Britain.*

12 The expansion of the urban sector, and the reasons for this expansion, are analysed in C G A Clay, *Economic expansion and social change: England, 1500–1700* (Cambridge, 2 vols, 1984), vol I, pp 165–214.

13 Eg R Tittler, 'The Incorporation of Boroughs' (*History,* LXII (1977), pp 24–42) and 'The Emergence of Urban Policy, 1536–58', in R Tittler, J Loach, eds, *The Mid-Tudor Polity, c. 1540–1560* (London, 1980), pp 74–93.

14 S T Bindoff, ed, *The House of Commons, 1509–1558* (London, 3 vols, 1982), vol I, p 4; R Sedgwick, ed, *The House of Commons, 1715–1754* (London, 2 vols, 1970), vol I, p 1.

15 E H Phelps-Brown, S V Hopkins, 'Seven Centuries of building wages' (*Economica,* NS XXII (1955), pp 195–206); E H Phelps-Brown, S V Hopkins, 'Seven Centuries of the prices of consumables compared with builders' wage rates' (*Economica,* NS vol XXIII (1956), pp 296–314); both repr in E M Carus-Wilson, ed, *Essays in economic history* (London, 2 vols, 1954, 1962), vol II, pp 168–96, and in E H Phelps-Brown, S V Hopkins, *A Perspective of Prices and Wages* (London, 1981), pp 1–12, 13–59. The wheat prices quoted are derived from E Miller, ed, *Agrarian History of England and Wales, III, 1348–1500* (Cambridge, 1991), p 504, and G E Mingay, ed, *Agrarian History of England and Wales, VI, 1750–1850* (Cambridge, 1989), p 975.

16 D Hirst, *The Representative of the People? Voters and Voting in England under the Early Stuarts* (Cambridge, 1975), pp 29–43. Thus the south Gloucestershire poll book for 1710 noted that voters could be 'Cottagers', 'Leaseholders' and 'Copyholders' (Hudleston, 'Gloucestershire Voters in 1710', pp 195–6).

17 Hirst, *The Representative of the People?*, p 30.

18 J S Moore, 'Introduction', in Moore and Smith, eds, *The House of Lords,* pp 4, 11–14, and references cited at p 183, n 32.

19 A H Johnson, *The Disappearance of the Small Landowner* (Oxford, 1909, repr London, 1963).

20 J H Plumb, *The Growth of Political Stability on England, 1675–1725* (London, 1967), pp 45–6.

21 F W S Craig, *British Electoral Facts, 1832–1987* (Aldershot, 5th edn, 1989), pp 21–50; C Rallings, M Thrasher, *Britain Votes, 5: British Parliamentary Election Results, 1988–1992* (Aldershot, 1993), p 163.

22 W Stubbs, ed, *Select Charters* (Oxford, 9th edn, 1913), p 480. Only the ecclesistics were deemed worthy of a quotation from Roman Law; the knights and burgesses received simple writs of summons without any explanatory preambles.

23 V H Galbraith, *The Making of Domesday Book* (Oxford, 1961), p 60; V H Galbraith, *Domesday Book: its place in administrative history* (Oxford, 1974), p 34.

24 C P Lewis, 'The Domesday Jurors' (*Haskins Soc Journ,* vol 5 (1993), pp 17–44).

25 H C Darby, *Domesday England* (Cambridge, 1977), pp 62–3.

26 For the beginnings of inflation, see P D A Harvey, 'The English Inflation of 1180–1220' (*Past and Present,* vol 61 (1973), pp 3–30), and for its continuance see Miller, ed, *Agrarian History of England and Wales, III, 1348–1500,* pp 432–67, 502–16. For the development of personal serfdom and villeinage tenure, see P R Hyams, *Kings, Lords and Peasants in Medieval England. The Common Law of Villeinage in the Twelfth and Thirteenth Centuries* (Oxford, 1980), to which A J Frantzen, D Moffat, eds, *The work of work: servitude, slavery and labour in Medieval England* (Glasgow, 1994), adds nothing. For the decline of slavery after the Norman Conquest, see J S Moore, 'Anglo-Norman Slavery' (*Anglo-Norman Studies,* XI (1989), pp 191–220) and D A E Pelteret, *Slavery in Early Medieval England, from the reign of Alfred until the Twelfth Century* (Woodbridge, 1995), esp pp 232–40, 250–5.

27 E A Kosminsky, *Studies in the Agrarian History of England in the Thirteenth Century* (Oxford, 1956), p 228. Regrettably, there is no attempt to elucidate the ratio of free to unfree in this crucial period in H E Hallam, ed, *Agrarian History of England and Wales. II, 1042–1350* (Cambridge, 1988), chaps 6, 10.

28 Roskell, Clarke and Rawcliffe, eds, *The House of Commons, 1385–1421,* vol I, pp 61–2.

29 For population-trends, see J Z Titow, *English Rural Society, 1200–1350* (London, 1969), which adds new evidence to that very poorly assembled in J C Russell, *British Medieval Population* (Alburquerque (USA), 1948); B F Harvey, 'The Population Trend in England between 1300 and 1348' (*Trans Roy Hist Soc,* 5th ser, vol 16 (1966), pp 23–42); the discussion in Hallam, ed, *Agrarian History of England and Wales. II, 1042–1350,* chaps 5, 10, is very unsatisfactory. For the changed agrarian circumstances of the 14th and 15th centuries, see J Hatcher, *Plaque, Population and the English economy, 1348–1530* (London, 1977).

30 R H Hilton, *The decline of serfdom in Medieval England* (London, 2nd edn, 1983); Miller, ed, *Agrarian History of England and Wales, III, 1348–1500,* esp chaps 5–8.

31 J P Cooper, 'The Social Distribution of Land and Men in England, 1436–1700' (*Econ Hist Rev,* 2nd ser, vol 20 (1967), pp 419–40); J C K Cornwall, *Wealth and Society in Early Sixteenth-Century England* (London, 1988), pp 120–53, 253–76; Clay, *Economic expansion and social change: England, 1500–1700,* vol I, p 143.

32 For medieval warfare in general, consult C Oman, *A History of the Art of War in the Middle Ages* (London, 2nd edn, 2 vols, 1924); J F Verbruggen, *The Art of*

Warfare in Western Europe during the Middle Ages (Amsterdam (Netherlands), 1977); P Contamine, *War in the Middle Ages* (Oxford, 1984). Medieval warfare in England and Wales is studied in greater detail in F M Powicke, *The Thirteenth Century, 1216–1307* (Oxford, 2nd edn, 1962), pp 549–53; M McKisack, *The Fourteenth Century, 1307–1399* (Oxford, 1959), pp 238–41; J Beeler, *Warfare in England, 1066–1189* (Ithaca (USA), 1966); M Strickland, ed, *Anglo-Norman Warfare: studies in late Anglo-Saxon and Anglo-Norman military organization and warfare* (Woodbridge, 1992); S Morillo, *Warfare under the Anglo-Norman Kings, 1066–1135* (Woodbridge, 1994). The later developments are studied in J E Morris, *The Welsh Wars of King Edward I* (Oxford, 1901); R Nicholson, *Edward III and the Scots. The Formative Years of a military career, 1327–1335* (Oxford, 1965); E Perroy, *The Hundred Years War* (London, 1951); A H Burne, *The Crecy War. A Military History of the Hundred Years War from 1337 to the peace of Bretigny, 1360* (London, 1955); A H Burne, *The Agincourt War. A Military History of the latter part of the Hundred Years War from 1369 to 1453* (London, 1956); K A Fowler, *The Hundred Years' War* (London, 1971). For the development of castles after the Norman Conquest, see E S Armitage, *Early Norman Castles of the British Isles* (London, 1912); A Hamilton-Thompson, *Military Architecture in England during the Middle Ages* (London, 1912); S Painter, 'English Castles in the Early Middle Ages' (*Speculum,* vol 10 (1935), pp 321–32); R A Brown, 'Royal Castle-Building in England, 1154–1216' (*Eng Hist Rev,* vol LXX (1955), pp 353–98); R A Brown, 'A List of Castles, 1154–1216' (*Eng Hist Rev,* vol LXXIV (1959), pp 249–80); B K Davison, 'The origins of the castle in England' (*Arch Journ,* vol 124 (1967), pp 202–11); R A Brown, 'An Historian's approach to the origins of the Castle in England' (*Arch Journ,* vol 126 (1970), pp 131–48); D F Renn, *Norman Castles in Britain, 1066–1216* (London, 2nd edn, 1973); R A Brown, *English Castles* (London, 3rd edn, 1976); C Platt, *The Castle in Medieval England and Wales* (London, 1982); D J C King, *Castellarium Anglicanum* (New York (USA), 2 vols, 1983); R A Brown, 'The Castle of the Conquest', in A Williams, R W H Erskine, eds, *Domesday Book Studies* (London, 1987, reprinted in R A Brown, *Castles, Conquest and Charters* (London, 1987), pp 65–74; D J C King, *The Castle in England and Wales: an interpretative history* (London, 1988); J M Counihan, 'The Growth of Castle Studies in England and Normandy since 1850' (*Anglo-Norman Studies,* vol XI (1989), pp 77–85); N J G Pounds, *The Medieval Castle in England and Wales: a social and political history* (Cambridge, 1990); M W Thompson, *The Rise of the Castle* (Cambridge, 1991); R Higham, P Barker, *Timber Castles* (London, 1992). Useful but not comprehensive coverage of data on garrisons, and references to original sources, neither of which are always accurately reported, occur in P Warner, *Sieges of the Middle Ages* (London, 1968); Brown, *English Castles,* pp 173, 185–9, 191–4, 198–9; Pounds, *The Medieval Castle in England and Wales,* pp 90, 122–3; J Bradbury, *The Medieval Siege* (Woodbridge, 1992); J S Moore, 'Anglo-Norman Garrisons', forthcoming in C Harper-Bill, R Harvey, eds, *Knights and Knighthood,* VI. Some figures on the size of English armies are assembled and criticised in J H Ramsay, 'The strength of English armies in the Middle Ages' (*Eng Hist Rev,* vol XXIX (1914), pp 221–7), and in A E Prince, 'The Strength of English Armies in the Reign of Edward III' (*Eng Hist Rev,* vol XLVI (1931), pp 353–71), but the topic needs much more archival research to be done. The evolution of medieval armour is studied in C H Ashdown, *Armour and Weapons in the Middle Ages* (London, 1925); A Borg, *Arms and Armour in Britain* (London, 2nd edn, 1979); C Rothero, *Medieval Military Dress, 1066–1500* (Poole, 1983); H M Zijlstra-Zweens, *'Of his array telle*

I no lenger tale': aspects of costume, arms and armour in Western Europe, 1200–1400 (Amsterdam (Netherlands), 1988). For the development of the sword, see E Oakeshott, *Records of the Medieval Sword* (Woodbridge, 1991) and E Oakeshott, *The sword in the age of chivalry* (Woodbridge, 3rd edn, 1994). The growth in the size and stamina of horses is shown by R H C Davis, *The Medieval Warhorse: origin, development and redevelopment* (London, 1989), to which A Hyland, *The Medieval Warhorse from Byzantium to the Crusades* (Stroud, 1994) adds relatively little. The evolution of archery is examined in J Bradbury, *The Medieval Archer* (Woodbridge, 1985) and R Hardy, *Longbow: a social and military history* (Portsmouth, 2nd edn, 1986).

33 S K Mitchell, *Studies in Taxation under John and Henry III* (New Haven (USA), 1914), as modified by S K Mitchell, *Taxation in Medieval England* (New Haven (USA), 1951) (both these works are in need of correction and updating); for the 1203–4 tax on the ports, see D M Stenton, ed, 'The Great Roll of the Pipe for the Fifth Year of the Reign of King John' (*Pipe Roll Soc,* NS vol XVI (1938), pp xii–iii); D M Stenton, ed, 'The Great Roll of the Pipe for the Sixth Year of the Reign of King John' (*Pipe Roll Soc,* NS vol XVIII (1940), pp xliii–v).

34 Moore, 'Introduction', in Moore and Smith, eds, *The House of Lords,* p 4, Table 1.

35 For the growth of towns and their increasing economic importance, see now E Miller, J Hatcher, *Medieval England: II, Towns and Trade* (London, 1995).

36 W L Warren, *The Governance of Norman and Angevin England, 1086–1272* (London, 1987), pp 109–22, 126–8, 187–9, 198, 215–6.

37 *Ibid,* pp 65–6, 73–6, 79–83, 98–100, 125–9, 145, 155–7, 172–6, 185–90, 192–4.

38 For the developing 'equity' jurisdictions of the Chancery and Exchequer, see A H Marsh, *The History of the Court of Chancery and of the Rise and Development of the Doctrines of Equity* (Toronto (Canada), 1890); W P Baildon, ed, 'Select Cases in Chancery, A.D. 1364 to 1471' (*Selden Soc,* vol 10 (1896), pp xii–xlv); M E Avery, 'The history of the equitable jurisdiction of Chancery before 1460' (*Bull Inst Hist Res,* vol 42 (1969), pp 129–44; W J Jones, *The Elizabethan Court of Chancery* (Oxford, 1967); W H Bryson, *The Equity side of the Exchequer: its jurisdication, administration, procedures and records* (Cambridge, 1975); A Harding, *The Law Courts of Medieval England* (London, 1973), pp 100–3; A L Brown, *The Governance of Late Medieval England, 1272–1461* (London, 1989), pp 132–4. For the courts of Requests and Star Chamber, see I S Leadam, 'Select Cases in the Court of Requests, AD 1497–1569' (*Selden Soc,* vol 12 (1898), pp xv–xlv); I S Leadam, ed, 'Select Cases in . . . the court of Star Chamber, 1477–1509' (*Selden Soc,* vol 16 (1902), pp ix–lxxi); J A Guy, *The Cardinal's Court: the impact of Thomas Wolsey in Star Chamber* (Hassocks, 1977). For the continuing judicial role of the Council down to the later 15th century, see I S Leadam, J F Baldwin, eds, 'Select Cases before the King's Council, 1243–1482' (*Selden Soc,* vol 35, 1918).

39 I owe this insight to my good friend and colleague Professor William Doyle.

40 N Pronay, J Taylor, eds, *Parliamentary Texts of the Later Middle Ages* (Oxford, 1979), pp 39, 89–90.

41 Moore and Smith, eds, *The House of Lords,* p 107.

42 S Thurley, *The Royal Palaces of Tudor England: architecture and court life, 1460–1547* (New Haven (USA), 1993); C Platt, *The Great rebuildings of Tudor and Stuart England* (London, 1994).

43 For the Royal Navy, see D M Loades, *The Tudor Navy: an administrative, political and Military history* (Aldershot, 1992); for the new coastal forts, see H M Colvin *et al*, eds, *The History of the King's Works* (London, 8 vols, 1963–82), vol IV, pp 367–401, 415–606.

44 See p 82.

45 G Parker, *The Military Revolution: military innovation and the rise of the West, 1500–1800* (Cambridge, 1988); J Brewer, *The Sinews of Power* (London, 1989).

46 For royal revenues, see F C Dietz, *English Public Finance, 1558–1641* (New York (USA), 1933), pp 268, 284, 296, 304; C D Chandaman, *The English Public Revenue, 1660–1688* (Oxford, 1975), Appendix 2; P G M Dickson, *The Financial Revolution in England, 1689–1756* (London, 1967, repr Aldershot, 1993).

47 See pp 105, 108

48 For the new financial system, see Dickson, *The Financial Revolution in England, 1689–1756* and Brewer, *The Sinews of Power;* there is no adequate history of taxation in this period.

49 See p 116.

50 See p 119.

51 See p 118.

52 C O'Leary, *The Elimination of Corrupt Practices in British Elections, 1868–1911* (Oxford, 1962).

53 J Tomlinson, *Problems of British Economic Policy, 1870–1945* (London, 1981); R Middleton, *Towards the Managed Economy: Keynes, the Treasury and the fiscal policy debate of the 1930s* (London, 1985); G C Peden, *Keynes, the Treasury and British economic policy* (London, 1988); B P Lenman, *The eclipse of Parliament: appearance and reality in British politics since 1914* (London, 1992).

54 The re-writing of Irish economic history without nationalist prejudices and illusions began with J Mokyr, *Why Ireland starved? A quantitative and analytical history of the Irish economy, 1800–1850* (London, 1983), and has been continued especially by the work of Cormac O'Grada: *Ireland before and after the Famine: explorations in economic history, 1800–1925* (Manchester, 1988, 2nd edn, 1993); *The Great Irish Famine* (London, 1989, 2nd edn, 1993); *Ireland: a new economic history, 1780–1939* (Oxford, 1994). He has also edited *The economic development of Ireland since 1870* (Aldershot, 1994).

Chapter 1 (pages 26 - 47)

1 W Stubbs, *The Constitutional History of England in its Origin and Development,* to give the work its full title, was first published by Oxford University Press in three volumes between 1874 and 1878, and ran through many subsequent editions. The individual volumes went into new editions at different times, and three volume sets were often made up from different editions. In this chapter all references are to volume II of the fourth edition, reprinted, of 1906.

2 *Ibid,* pp 134, 235–6. Other relevant passages are on pp 248, 266, 305.

3 *Ibid,* pp 133, 236.

4 C H Jenkinson, 'The First Parliament of Edward I' (*Eng Hist Rev,* vol XXV (1910), pp 282–3). For F W Maitland, see below, 190, nn 29, 31.

5 This reaches a climax in H G Richardson, G O Sayles, 'Parliaments and Great Councils in Medieval England' (*Law Quarterly Review,* vol LXXVII (1961), pp 213–36, 401–26), repr in their *Parliaments and Great Councils in Medieval England* (London, 1961), chap XXVI, from which all subsequent quotations come.

6 For example, M Prestwich, *Edward I* (London, 1988), p 441.

7 The secondary literature on the subject is gigantic and I have made no comprehensive attempt to cite it. Particularly valuable are E Miller, *The Origins of Parliament* (London, 1960); P Spufford, *Origins of the English Parliament* (London, 1967), with translated sources; G O Sayles, *The King's Parliament of England* (London, 1975); M Prestwich, *English Politics in the Thirteenth Century* (London, 1990), chap 8, and the essays by various scholars in E B Fryde, E Miller, eds, *Historical Studies of the English Parliament. I. Origins to 1399* (Cambridge, 1970), and R G Davies, J H Denton, eds, *The English Parliament in the Middle Ages: A Tribute to J S Roskell* (Manchester, 1981). G O Sayles, *The Functions of the Medieval Parliament of England* (London, 1987), brings together a large amount of source material in translation for the years 1258 to 1348. E B Fryde, D E Greenway, S Porter, I Roy, eds, *Handbook of British Chronology* (London, 3rd end, 1986), pp 533–81, has a detailed list of parliaments and related assemblies from 1216.

8 *Curia Regis Rolls* (London, 17 vols, 1922–91), vol XV, no 2047. See H G Richardson, G O Sayles, 'The Earliest Known Official Use of the Term "Parliament"' (*Eng Hist Rev,* vol LXXXII (1967), pp 747–50).

9 *Curia Regis Rolls,* vol XV, pp lvi, n 5, lvii, n 1; H R Luard, ed, 'Matthaei Parisiensis . . . Chronica Majora' (*Rolls Ser,* vol 57, 7 pts, 1884–9), pt III, pp 380–4).

10 Some of the references are usefully brought together in W Stubbs, ed, *Select Charters* (Oxford, 9th edn, 1913), pp 328–30 (all subsequent references to *Select Charters* are to this edition, revised throughout by H W C Davis). For references to parliament in royal letters, see, eg. *Calendar of Close Rolls* [hereafter *Cal Close R*], *1237–1242,* p 447; *Cal Close R, 1247–1251,* pp 104, 107, 109; Cal Close R, 1253–4, p 43. For the 'Provisions of Oxford', see R F Treharne, I J Sanders, eds *Documents of the Baronial Movement of Reform and Rebellion* (Oxford, 1973), pp 110–11, no 21.

11 H G Richardson, 'The Origins of Parliament' (*Trans Roy Hist Soc,* 4th ser, vol XI (1928), pp 137–49).

12 H R Loyn, *The Governance of Anglo-Saxon England, 500–1087* (London, 1984), pp 100–6.

13 B Colgrave, R A B Mynors, eds, *Bede's Ecclesiastical History of the English People* (Oxford, 1969), pp 182–7.

14 H G Richardson, G O Sayles, 'The Parliaments of Edward I' (*Bull Inst Hist Res,* vol V (1927–8), p 133), reiterated in their *Parliaments and Great Councils in Medieval England* (London, 1961), chap XXVI, p 6.

15 To be fair, they completely accepted that legislation, taxation and the discussion of great affairs could take place in parliament, but they argued that, unlike the

dispensation of justice, these could equally take place in other assemblies, notably 'great councils'. Hence the dispensation of justice was parliament's 'essence' in the sense of 'distinctive quality' (*ibid,* chap XXVI, pp 6 *et seq*). It is far from clear, however, that the dispensation of justice was parliament's 'essence' in the years when the name was becoming established; see pp 26–7, 29–30, 36–41. For criticisms of Richardson and Sayles, see particularly J G Edwards, '"Justice" in Early English Parliaments' (*Bull Inst Hist Res,* vol XXVII (1954), pp 35–53), reprinted in Fryde and Miller, eds, *Historical Studies of the English Parliament, I,*

pp 279–97, to which all subsequent references in this chapter refer.

16 *Calendar of Chancery of Warrants, 1244–1326* (London, 1927), p 246; F W Maitland, ed, 'Memoranda de Parliamento. Records of the Parliament Holden at Westminster . . . 1305' (*Rolls Ser,* 98, 1893), pp 3–320).

17 N Pronay, J Taylor, eds, *Parliamentary Texts of the Later Middle Ages* (Oxford, 1979), pp 90, 114, cap XXIV. For a useful discussion of the debate surrounding the date and background of the *Modus,* see M Prestwich, 'The *"Modus Tenendi Parliamentum"'* (*Parliamentary History,* vol 1 (1982), pp 221–5). In places the tract is more a work of opinion than of fact.

18 H Rothwell, ed, *English Historical Documents, 1189–1327* (London, 1975), p 536 (cap 29).

19 H G Richardson, G O Sayles, eds, 'Fleta' (*Selden Soc,* vols 72, 89, 98 (1955, 1972, 1989, in progress), vol 72, p 109).

20 Treharne and Sanders, eds, *Documents of the Baronial Movement,* pp 102–3 (cap 6), 106–7 (cap 16).

21 J R Maddicott, 'Parliament and the Constituencies, 1272–1377', in Davies and Denton, eds, *The English Parliament in the Middle Ages,* p 62. See also Sayles, *The King's Parliament of England,* pp 76–9.

22 Edwards, '"Justice" in Early English Parliaments', p 284; *Cal Close R, 1272-79,* pp 56–7. For similar filtering measures in 1305, see *Calendar of Chancery Warrants, 1244–1326,* p 246.

23 This is very much the impression gained from reading through the answers to the petitions in Maitland, ed, 'Memoranda de Parliamento', pp 5–254.

24 Edwards, '"Justice" in Early English Parliaments', p 284; *Cal Close R, 1272–79,* pp 56–7.

25 For the 1130 revenue, see J Green, *The Government of England under Henry I* (Cambridge, 1986), pp 220–5. For the inflation, see P D A Harvey, 'The English Inflation of 1180–1220' (*Past and Present,* vol 61 (1973), pp 3–30). The comments about the revenues under King John and in 1230 I owe to forthcoming publications by Nicholas Barratt. It should be noted, however, that the pipe rolls do not present a complete picture of royal revenue and expenditure, much of which was controlled by the Chamber of the royal household and never passed through the Exchequer.

26 T D Hardy, ed, *Rotuli de Oblatibus et Finium* (London, 1835), p 459; H Hall, ed, 'The Red Book of the Exchequer' (*Rolls Ser,* vol 99, 3 pts, 1896), pt III, p 1064. See S K Mitchell, *Studies in Taxation under John and Henry III* (New Haven (USA), 1914), pp 91, 205, 218 (fundamental for taxation in this period), and for 1225 F A Cazel, 'The fifteenth of 1225' (*Bull Inst Hist Res,* vol XXXIV (1964), pp 67–81).

27 D A Carpenter, *The Minority of Henry III* (London, 1990), pp 210–11; Prestwich, *Edward I,* pp 422–5; J R Maddicott, 'The Crusade Taxation of 1268 and the development of Parliament', in P R Coss, S D Lloyd, eds, *Thirteenth-Century England, II, Proceedings of the Newcastle upon Tyne Conference, 1987* (Woodbridge, 1988), pp 97–8.

28 Luard, ed, 'Chronica Majora', pt IV, pp 185–7; Stubbs, *Select Charters,* pp 325–30.

29 Maitland, ed, 'Memoranda de Parliamento', p lxxxviii. (Maitland's introduction to the 'Memoranda de Parliamento' is party reprinted in Fryde and Miller, eds, *Historical Studies of the English Parliament,* pp 91–135.)

30 Edward had specifically called for petitions 'to be presented to the king and his council at the next parliament' (*Calendar of Chancery Warrants, 1244–1326,* p 246).

31 Maitland, ed, 'Memoranda de Parliamento', pp xxxv-xlvii, cvi-ix.

32 H R Luard, ed, 'Annales Monastici' (*Rolls Ser,* 36, 5 pts, 1864–9), pt III, pp 145–6 (where misdated). For the early history of the Council see J F Baldwin, *The King's Council in England during the Middle Ages* (Oxford, 1913), chap 2.

33 B Wilkinson, *Studies in the Constitutional History of the Thirteenth and Fourteenth Centuries* (Manchester, 1937), pp 146–50.

34 For this theme see particularly J E A Jolliffe, 'Some factors in the Beginning of Parliament' (*Trans Roy Hist Soc,* 4th ser, vol XXII (1940), pp 101–37), reprinted in Fryde and Miller, eds, *Historical Studies in the English Parliament,* pp 31–69.

35 J E Powell, K Wallis, *The House of Lords in the Middle Ages* (London, 1968), p 226.

36 *Ibid,* chap 18, but see the reservations in C Given-Wilson, *The English Nobility in the Later Middle Ages* (London, 1987), pp 58–66.

37 Pronay and Taylor, eds, *Parliamentary Texts of the Later Middle Ages,* pp 81, 104 (cap 3); Rothwell, ed, *English Historical Documents, 1189–1327,* p 925, cap 3.

38 J H Denton, 'The Clergy and Parliament in the Thirteenth and Fourteenth Centuries', in Davies and Denton, eds, *The English Parliament in the Middle Ages,* pp 88–108, is essential reading for this paragraph and the next section.

39 W Stubbs, ed, 'The Historical Works of Gervase of Canterbury' (*Rolls Ser,* 73, 2 pts, 1879–80), pt II, p 180, cap XI), translated in D C Douglas, G W Greenaway, eds, *English Historical Documents, 1042–1189* (London, 2nd edn, 1981), p 769.

40 Denton, 'The Clergy and Parliament in the Thirteenth and Fourteenth Centuries', p 91.

41 The whole question of clerical representation has been fully examined in J H Denton, J P Dooley, *Representatives of the Lower Clergy in Parliament, 1295–1340* (Woodbridge, 1987).

42 *Cal Close R, 1253–54,* pp 115–6; W E Lunt, 'The Consent of the Lower Clergy to Taxation during the reign of Henry III', in *Persecution and Liberty: Essays in Honour of George Lincoln Burr* (New York (USA), 1931), pp 142–4; Maddicott, 'The Crusade Taxation of 1268', p 117; Stubbs, ed, *Select Charters,* pp 480–1.

43 Denton, 'The Clergy and Parliament in the Thirteenth and Fourteenth Centuries', pp 103, 106–8.

44 Stubbs, ed, *Select Charters,* pp 481–2.

45 The Sheriffs were also ordered to send two citizens representing each city.

46 M McKisack, *The Parliamentary Representation of the English Boroughs during the Middle Ages* (Oxford, 1932, repr London, 1962), p 11. The number of town representatives attending fluctuated.

47 See p 36. There is very little evidence as to how town representatives were elected in the reign of Edward I (McKisack, *The Parliamentary Representation of the English Boroughs,* pp 11–16). They were likewise ordered to come with full power 'for themselves and for the community of the cities and boroughs'.

48 For what follows see particularly J C Holt, 'The Prehistory of Parliament', in Davies and Denton, eds, *The English Parliament in the Middle Ages,* pp 1–28.

49 T D Hardy, ed, *Rotuli Litterarum Clausarum* (London, 2 vols, 1833, 1844), vol I, p 132; Stubbs, ed, *Select Charters,* p 282. It is worth stressing that it was four men who were summoned from the counties in 1213, not four knights as is often stated.

50 In 1212 it is not known whether anyone was summoned to the king apart from the knights. In 1213 we do not have the original writ of summons. What survives is a supplementary writ in which the king ordered the sheriffs to cause 'all the knights' of their counties, who had been summoned, to now come armed; the barons, however, were to come unarmed. The sheriff was also to produce the four men. See Holt, 'The Prehistory of Parliament', pp 6–9.

51 Why the summons to *discretos homines* (not even free men) in 1214 rather than knights? Was John attempting to reach down to sections of society below the knights? Had he some particular task in mind unsuitable for those of knightly or even free status? Or was the writ simply loosely drafted?

52 Hardy, ed, *Rotuli Litterarum Clausarum,* vol II, pp 212b–13. The gathering of 1227 followed the cancellation of a similar summons to just nine counties the year before (*Ibid,* p 154; Stubbs, ed, *Select Charters,* p 353).

53 This is shown by the witness lists to royal charters issued in October 1227 (PRO C53/19, mm 1–2).

54 *Cal Close R, 1253–4,* pp 114–5; Stubbs, ed, *Select Charters,* pp 365–6.

55 *Cal Close R, 1253–4,* pp 15–6; Lunt, 'The Consent of the Lower Clergy to Taxation', pp 142–3.

56 For the knights representing Essex, see *Cal Close R, 1253–4,* p 42; for the writ to the sheriff of (Essex and) Hertfordshire, see Luard, ed, 'Chronica Majora', pt VI, pp 286–7.

57 Lunt, 'The Consent of the Lower Clergy to Taxation', pp 142–3. For the assembly being called a parliament in a royal letter and memorandum, see *Cal Close R, 1253–4,* p 43; *Calendar of Patent Rolls,* [hereafter *Cal Patent R*], *1247–58,* p 370.

58 Treharne and Sanders, eds, *Documents of the Baronial Movement,* pp 112–5; *Cal Patent R, 1247–58,* pp 645–9; *Cal Close R, 1256–9,* pp 332–3. See H M Cam, 'The Parliamentary Writ "de expensis" of 1258' (*Eng Hist Rev,* vol XLVI (1931), pp 630–2).

59 Treharne and Sanders, eds, *Documents of the Baronial Movement,* pp 104–5 (no 10), 110–1 (nos 5, 21–2).

60 The uncertainty arises in the period 1268 to 1270 for which see below, n 64.

61 *Cal Close R, 1261–4,* p 490; Treharne and Sanders, eds, *Documents of the Baronial Movement,* pp 246–9. For the king's assembly being called a parliament, see PRO SC 1/7, no 33, translated in Sayles, *The King's Parliament of England,* p 62.

62 Treharne and Sanders, eds, *Documents of the Baronial Movement,* pp 290–3; *Cal Patent R, 1258–66,* p 360.

63 *Cal Close R, 1264–8,* pp 84–7, 89, 96, 98–9; Treharne and Sanders, eds, *Documents of the Baronial Movement,* pp 300–9.

64 Maddicott, 'The Crusade Taxation of 1268–70', p 117. No writs of summons survive from these parliaments and their composition has to be judged from statements in chronicles and the occasional royal letter.

65 Jenkinson, 'The First Parliament of Edward I', pp 231–42. In January 1273 there was a general assembly at Westminster, attended by four knights from each county and four representatives from each city, to swear allegiance to the absent Edward I (Luard, ed, 'Annales Monastici', pt I, p 113).

66 For these figures see Fryde, Greenway, Porter and Roy, eds, *Handbook of British Chronology,* pp 545–50. I have included the gathering of January 1273 (see n 65 above) and the Northampton/York and Shrewsbury assemblies of 1281–3.

67 *Ibid,* pp 550–2.

68 Pronay and Taylor, eds, *Parliamentary Texts of the later Middle Ages,* pp 77–9, 89–91 (caps 23, 26).

69 G D G Hall, ed, *The Treatise on the laws and customs of England, commonly called Glanvill* (London, 1965), p 99.

70 Stubbs, ed, *Select Charters,* pp 295, 298, caps 18, 48.

71 Hall, ed, *The Treatise . . . called Glanvill,* p 9. There are numerous examples in the plea rolls of knights coming *pro comitatu* (*Curia Regis Rolls,* vol V, pp 16, 45, 150, 160).

72 Hardy, ed, *Rotuli Litterarum Clausarum,* vol II, pp 154, 212b–13; *Cal Close R, 1253–4,* pp 114–5; Stubbs, ed, *Select Charters,* pp 481–2.

73 For 1212 and 1213, see Holt, 'The Prehistory of Parliament', pp 5–9; for 1261 and 1264–5, see J R Maddicott, *Simon de Montfort* (Cambridge, 1994), pp 213, 285, 316–7.

74 *Cal Close R, 1259–61,* pp 246–9, 490.

75 Maddicott, 'The Crusade Taxation of 1268–70', pp 105, 117.

76 Stubbs, ed, *Select Charters,* pp 460–1.

77 W Stubbs, ed, 'Chronicles of the Reigns of Edward I and Edward II' (*Rolls Ser,* vol 76, 2 pts (1882–3), pt I, p 92).

78 Maddicott, 'The Crusade Taxation of 1268–70', pp 105, 117.

79 I am including as taxation the grant of the customs to Edward in 1275. For the role of the commons ('the communities of the realm') in making this grant, see Stubbs, ed, *Select Charters,* p 443. I am also including as one parliament the northern and southern assemblies of 1283 and the Shrewsbury assembly of the same year. None of these meetings was actually described as a parliament in

surviving records (Fryde, Greenway, Porter and Roy, eds, *Handbook of British Chronology,* pp 545–8).

80 This is including all the assemblies of this period as parliaments.

81 For what follows, see J G Edwards, 'The *"Plena Potestas"* of English Parliamentary Representatives', in Fryde and Miller, eds, *Historical Studies in the English Parliament,* pp 136–49.

82 *Ibid,* p 141: I have slightly modified the data.

83 This point is made in Prestwich, *Edward I,* pp 456–7.

84 R R Davies, *Domination and Conquest. The experience of Ireland, Scotland and Wales, 1100–1300* (Cambridge, 1990), p 74.

85 Denton, 'The clergy and parliament', pp 102–3. The revenues of the parish churches (from tithes, oblations and glebe lands) was nearly double that of the temperal revenues of the bishops, abbots and priors which were tapped by ordinary secular taxation.

86 *Cal Close R, 1253–4,* pp 115–6; see Lunt, 'The Consent of the Lower Clergy to Taxation during the Reign of Henry III', pp 142–3.

87 See, however, below, n 118.

88 For the years 1268–70, this is to accept the arguments advanced in Maddicott, 'The Crusade Taxation of 1268–70', pp 93–117.

89 Holt, 'The Prehistory of Parliament', p 26.

90 Pronay and Taylor, eds, *Parliamentary Texts of the Later Middle Ages,* pp 77, 89–90; Rothwell, ed, *English Historical Documents, 1189–1327,* pp 932–3, cap 23.

91 Eg Hardy, ed, *Rotuli Litterarum Clausarum,* vol II, p 75; *Cal Close R, 1231–34,* p 311. See Mitchell, *Studies in Taxation under John and Henry III,* pp 200–1, n 109. Likewise, according to the writ which announced it, the poll tax of 1222 for the help of the Holy Land was conceded simply 'in the presence of' lay and ecclesiastical barons and knights. On the other hand the actual agreement was said to be 'by the common will of all'. The king stressed that no-one was to be distrained to pay the tax, which effectively made it voluntary, though later arrangements for distraint were made (Hardy, ed, *Rotuli Litterarum Clausarum,* vol I, pp 516b–17, 518b, 566–66b; Mitchell, *Studies in Taxation under John and Henry III,* pp 141–2).

92 For a different perspective on what follows, see Holt, 'The Prehistory of Parliament', pp 25–6.

93 Stubbs, ed, *Select Charters,* pp 350–1.

94 *Cal Close R, 1231–34,* pp 155–6; Stubbs, ed, *Select Charters,* p 356.

95 *Cal Close R, 1231–34,* p 545; Stubbs, ed, *Select Chartres,* p 358.

96 *Cal Close R, 1234–37,* p 186. Another writ (*Ibid,* p 189, printed in Stubbs, ed, *Select Charters,* pp 357–8) states that the tax was granted by 'earls, barons and all others of all our kingdom'; I suspect that the additional phrase 'who hold from us in chief' has been accidentally omitted.

97 T Madox, *The History and Antiquities of the Exchequer* (London, 2nd edn, 2 vols, 1769), vol I, p 593, n 'f'.

98 Luard, ed, 'Chronica Majora', pt VI, p 250; *Cal Close R, 1251–53,* p 353.

99   According to the writ of 1235, after the tenants-in-chief had granted an aid to the king, it was likewise 'provided by their counsel' that they could levy a scutage of 2 marks for each of their knights' fees to pay it (*Cal Close R, 1234–37,* pp 186, 189). In 1253, the barons having conceded an aid to the king of forty shillings from each of their knights' fees, the king conceded that they might raise an equivalent amount from their tenants holding by knight service (Luard, ed, 'Chronica Majora', pt VI, pp 250–1). No consent, therefore, was needed from the under-tenants themselves. They could be obliged to pay the tax by the consent of their lords and the will of the king.

100 *Cal Close R, 1234–37,* pp 186–91.

101 T D Hardy, ed, *Rotuli Litterarum Patentium* (London, 1835), p 72; Stubbs, ed, *Select Charters,* pp 278–9. Alternatively the particulars were to be handed to the steward of the lord of the liberty in which the vill was situated.

102 *Cal Close R, 1231–34,* pp 155–6; Stubbs, ed, *Select Charters,* p 356.

103 The varying methods of assessment and collection can be followed in Mitchell, *Studies in Taxation under John and Henry III,* which surveys each tax in detail, albeit sometimes now needing correction.

104 Hardy, ed, *Rotuli Litterarum Patentium,* p 72; Stubbs, ed, *Select Charters,* pp 278–9.

105 Mitchell, *Studies in Taxation under John and Henry III,* pp 386–8.

106 Matthew Paris seems to refer to it in describing episcopal resistance to papal taxation in 1240 (Luard, ed, 'Chronica Majora', pt IV, p 37; Lunt, 'The Consent of the English Lower Clergy to Taxation', p 129; see also Luard, ed, 'Chronica Majora', pt III, p 109).

107 Rothwell, ed, *English Historical Documents, 1189–1327,* p 663, cap 46.

108 Hardy, ed, *Rotuli Litterarum Clausarum,* vol II, p 152. This writ is more informative than the one printed in F M Powicke, C R Cheney, eds, *Councils and Synods with other documents relating to the English Church, 1205–1265* (Oxford, 1964), pp 160–1. See *Ibid,* pp 158–65 for the whole episode.

109 Luard, 'Chronica Majora', pt IV, p 37; Lunt, 'The Consent of the English Lower Clergy to Taxation', p 129.

110 Powicke and Cheney, eds, *Councils and Synods,* p 506; '*maxime cum agitur de aliquo obligando, necessarius est eius expressus consensus*'.

111 The importance of looking at the representation of the lower clergy and that of the counties and towns together, and not isolating one from the other, is particularly stressed in Denton and Dooley, *Pepresentation of the Lower Clergy in Parliament, 1295–1340,* especially pp 1–3, 76–7.

112 *Cal Close R, 1234–37,* p 545. Land not belonging to churches is termed secular as opposed to spiritual property in the hands of parish clergy.

113 *Cal Close R, 1253–53,* pp 114–6.

114 W W Shirley, ed, 'Royal and Other Historical Letters Illustrative of the Reign of Henry III' (*Rolls Ser,* vol 27, 2 pts, 1862, 1866), pt II, pp 103–4).

115 F A Cazel, A P Cazel, eds, 'Rolls of the Fifteenth' (*Pipe Roll Soc,* NS, vol XLV (1977), pp ix-x).

116 Shirley, ed, 'Royal Letters', pt I, pp 151–2. The tax in 1220 was a carucage, not a tax on moveables.

117 *Ibid,* pt II, pp 103–4.

118 It should be recognized, however, as J C Holt has pointed out, that the tax envisaged in 1254 was not a general levy on the kingdom. The earls, barons and other tenants-in-chief, who were to cross personally to help the king in Gascony, were to be exempt. This division encouraged the perception that the earls and barons could or should not answer for the tax. But the perception was also strongly reinforced by the discontent in the counties to which the regents referred in their letter to the king (Shirley, ed, 'Royal Letters', pt II, pp 101–2; Holt, 'The Prehistory of Parliament' pp 26–7).

119 This follows the reconstruction in Maddicott, 'The Crusade Taxation of 1268–1270', pp 97–8, but see the reservations in Prestwich, *English Politics in the Thirteenth Century,* p 141.

120 Prestwich, *Edward I,* p 422.

121 M Prestwich, ed, 'Documents illustrating the Crisis of 1297–98 in England' (*Camden Soc,* 4th ser, vol XXIV (1980), p 110).

122 *Ibid,* pp 137–8; Rothwell, ed, *English Historical Documents, 1189–1327,* p 482.

123 Prestwich, ed, 'Documents illustrating the Crisis of 1297–98', p 151, cap I; Rothwell, ed, *English Historical Documents, 1189–1327,* p 486, cap I.

124 Prestwich, ed, 'Documents illustrating the Crisis of 1297–98' pp 27, n 157, 159, cap VI; Rothwell, ed, *English Historical Documents, 1189–1327,* p 486, cap VI.

125 Pronay and Taylor, eds, *Parliamentary Texts of the Middle Ages,* pp 77, 90 (cap 23); Rothwell, ed, *English Historical Documents, 1189–1327,* pp 932–3, cap 23.

126 Such distraint was arranged in the writs ordering the collection of scutages (*Cal Close R, 1234–37,* pp 186, 189; Luard, ed, 'Chronica Majora', pt VI, pp 250–1) and there is much evidence in the Memoranda rolls of the Exchequer for it actually taking place.

127 This point is made by Holt, 'The Prehistory of Parliament', pp 26–9.

128 D Pasquet, *Essay on the Origins of the House of Commons* (Cambridge, 1925), p 207, cited by Prestwich, *Edward I,* p 458, n 102. However, Pasquet goes on to show that in some other parliaments the proportion of deputies among the collectors was much smaller (*Ibid,* p 187).

129 Shirley, ed, 'Royal Letters', pt II, pp 101–2. For local grievances in the reign of Henry III, see J R Maddicott, 'Magna Carta and the Local Community' (*Past and Present,* vol 102 (1984), pp 25–65).

130 *Cal Patent R, 1247–58,* p 281. It was not, however, the conditions which were the main reason why no tax was granted. The emergency for which it was required, a threatened invasion of Gascony, did not materialize.

131 Treharne and Sanders, eds, *Documents of the Baronial Movement,* pp 104–7 (cap 11); Maddicott, 'The Crusade Taxation of 1268–70', pp 93–117. It should be noted that Henry III demanded a tax from the April 1258 Westminster parliament at which no representatives were present.

132 Denton, 'The Clergy and Parliament', p 106.

133 Sayles, *The King's Parliament of England,* pp 110–11, 115.

134 Stubbs, ed, *Constitutional History,* pp 133–4, 235–6.

135 *Ibid,* pp 268, 274–5.

136 *Ibid,* p 236.

137 *Ibid,* pp 235–6, 274.

138 *Ibid,* pp 133–4, 236. Another reason was his belief that the 1295 Parliament was the first to which representatives of the counties and boroughs were summoned in a single writ addressed to the sheriff of the county; previously the borough representatives had been summoned by writs sent to the individual towns. The result, Stubbs argued, was that the final process of the election took place in the county court and that 'the parliament that results contains a concentration of the persons and the powers of the shire-moot'. Thus 'the parliament of 1295 differed, so far as we know, from all that had preceded it, and was a precedent for all time to come'. Stubbs was right to inject a note of caution with his 'so far as we know', for in fact the representatives had been summoned through a single writ to the sheriffs as early as 1275 (Stubbs, ed, *Select Charters,* pp 440–2). In any case Stubbs probably exaggerated the importance of any 'concentration' which took place in the county court.

Chapter 2 (pages 48 - 69)

1 C Russell, *The Crisis of Parliaments* (Oxford, 1971), p 283.

2 G L Harriss, 'Medieval Doctrines in the Debates on Supply', in K Sharpe, ed, *Faction and Parliament* (Oxford, 1978, repr London, 1985), p 75.

3 S B Chrimes, *English Constitutional Ideas in the Fifteenth Century* (Cambridge, 1936), p 66.

4 The use of the term 'House of Commons' first appears in the early 15th century, although only in a locative sense. Not until *circa* 1540 is it found in an institutional sense, when it was employed interchangeably with the term 'lower house' (*Ibid,* pp 126–30).

5 N Pronay, J Taylor, eds, *Parliamentary Texts of the Later Middle Ages* (Oxford, 1979), pp 39, 89–90.

6 For what follows, see G L Harriss, 'War and the Emergence of the English Parliament, 1297–1360' (*Jnl of Med Hist,* vol 2 (1976), pp 45–7; J G Edwards, *The Second Century of the English Parliament* (Oxford, 1978), pp 18–24.

7 C D Ross, *Edward IV* (London, 1974), pp 348–9.

8 Harriss, 'Medieval Doctrines in the Debates on Supply', p 77.

9 For some useful comments on the law of diminishing returns in medieval taxation, see G Bernard, *War, Taxation and Rebellion in early Tudor England* (Brighton, 1986), pp 125 *et seq.*

10 For these figures, see W M Ormrod, *The Reign of Edward III* (New Haven (USA), 1990), p 207; J H Ramsay, *The Genesis of Lancaster* (Oxford, 2 vols, 1913), vol II, pp 101–2, 390–1; Ramsay, *Lancaster and York* (Oxford, 2 vols, 1892), vol I, pp 160, 321; vol II, pp 266, 471, 560; J B Gillingham, 'Crisis or Continuity? The Structure of Royal Authority in England, 1369–1422', in R Schneider, ed, *Das Spatmittelalterliche Konigtum im Europaischen Vergleich* (Sigmaringen (Germany), 1987), pp 62–3.

11 For what follows see the influential works of Harriss: 'War and the Emergence of the English Parliament', pp 35–56, and 'Medieval Doctrines in the Debates on Supply', pp 75–8, both of which summarize arguments developed at length in his *King, Parliament and Public Finance in Medieval England* (Oxford, 1975).

12 C Plummer, ed, *Sir John Fortescue's Governance of England* (Oxford, 1885), p 127, cited in Harriss, 'Medieval Doctrines in the Debates on Supply', p 84.

13 Harriss, *King, Parliament and Public Finance in Medieval England,* p 510.

14 Harriss, 'The Formation of Parliament', in R G Davies, J H Denton, eds, *The English Parliament in the Middle Ages* (Manchester, 1981), p 57. The term 'Good parliament' comes from the contemporary chronicle of Thomas Walsingham, a monk of St Albans (J Taylor, *English Historical Literature in the Fourteenth Century* (Oxford, 1987), p 199n).

15 See p 67.

16 It survives among the Colchester borough archives and is printed in Pronay and Taylor, eds, *Parliamentary Texts of the Later Middle Ages,* pp 185–9.

17 J R Maddicott, 'Parliament and the Constituencies, 1272–1377', in Davies and Denton, eds, *the English Parliament in the Middle Ages,* p 82.

18 *Ibid,* pp 81–2; Harriss, *King, Parliament and Public Finance in Medieval England,* pp 255–6.

19 Harriss, 'War and the Emergence of the English Parliament', p 42.

20 J R Maddicott, 'Poems of Social Protest in Early Fourteenth-Century England', in W M Ormrod, ed, *England in the Fourteenth Century* (Woodbridge, 1986), p 143; J Coleman, *English Literature in History, 1350–1400. Medieval Readers and Writers* (London, 1981), p 81.

21 *Calendar of Fine Rolls,* vol IV, pp 480–1.

22 Harriss, 'War and the Emergence of the English Parliament', pp 43–5.

23 Harriss, 'Medieval Doctrines in the Debates on Supply', p 88.

24 B Wilkinson, *Constitutional History of England in the Fifteenth Century* (London, 1964), p 301.

25 H G Richardson, 'The Crown and Medieval Politics' (*Trans Roy Hist Soc,* 4th ser, 28 (1946), p 28).

26 Edwards, *The Second Century of the English Parliament,* p 36. The same point is made by Gillingham, 'Crisis or Continuity?', pp 79–80.

27 *Ibid,* pp 74–6.

28 Harriss, 'Medieval Doctrines in the Debates on Supply', pp 77–8.

29 G L Harris, 'Theory and Practice in Royal Taxation: Some Observations' (*Eng Hist Rev,* vol XCVII (1982), pp 811–9).

30 M Jones, trans, *Philippe de Commines: Memoirs* (London, 1972), p 225, quoted in Harriss, 'War and the Emergence of the English Parliament', p 52.

31 *Ibid,* p 55.

32 Edwards, *The Second Century of the English Parliament,* p 29.

33 Eg the terms on which the income tax of 1404 was granted included the remarkable conditions that the conduct of the tax-collectors should not be subject to any

inquiry after the account, and that the records of the assessments should be burnt (*Calendar of Fine Rolls,* vol XII, p 253).

34 M Bush, 'Tax Reform and Rebellion in Early Tudor England' (*History,* vol 76 (1991), p 383).

35 G L Harriss, 'Political Society and the Growth of Government in Late Medieval England ' (*Past and Present,* vol 138 (1993), pp 42–3).

36 W M Ormrod, *Political Life in Medieval England, 1300–1450* (London, 1995), p 94, concludes that our period 'witnessed both the triumph and abasement of the medieval fiscal state'.

37 J R Lander, *The Limitations of English Monarchy in the Later Middle Ages* (Toronto (Canada), 1989), p 11. See also the comments of Richmond, who castigates these kings for what he sees as their failure to undertake the necessary reforms of the system of parliamentary taxation (C F Richmond, '1485 and All That, or What was Going on at the Battle of Bosworth?', in P W Hammond, ed, *Richard III: Loyalty, Lordship and Law* (London, 1986), pp 189–90).

38 G O Sayles, *The King's Parliament of England* (London, 1975), pp 119–20.

39 J G Edwards, 'Justice in Early English Parliaments', in E B Fryde, E Miller, eds, *Historical Studies of the English Parliament. I. origins to 1399* (Cambridge, 1970), pp 284–5.

40 Much of what follows is drawn from the excellent accounts in Harriss, 'The Formation of Parliament', pp 43–52, and A L Brown, *The Governance of Late Medieval England* (London, 1989), pp 215–24.

41 Maddicott, 'Parliament and the Constituencies', p 69; Richardson, 'The Commons and Medieval Politics', p 26.

42 See above pp 29, 33, 40, 43.

43 Harriss, *King, Parliament and Public Finance,* p 123.

44 Sayles, *The King's Parliament of England,* pp 115–6; Sayles, *The Functions of the Medieval Parliament of England* (London, 1987), pp 55–6. He makes the interesting point that when, in the early fifteenth century, the Inns of Court began to give their series of 'readings' on the statutes, only those enacted before 1327 were considered worthy of note.

45 Harriss, 'The Formation of Parliament', pp 45–6. On the basis of the preambles to Edward I's statutes, Cam concludes that 'Edward was to some extent permitting his subjects to suggest, if not dictate, matter for legislation' (H M Cam, 'The Legislators of Medieval England', in Fryde and Miller, eds, *Historical Studies of the English Parliament. I. Origins to 1399,* p 180).

46 *Ibid,* p 168.

47 Wilkinson, *Constitutional History of England in the Fifteenth Century,* pp 311–2; Chrimes, *English Constitutional Ideas in the Fifteenth Century,* pp 159–64.

48 Ormrod, *The Reign of Edward III,* p 67.

49 A R Myers, 'Parliament, 1422–1509', in Davies and Denton, eds, *The English Parliament in the Middle Ages,* pp 178–81; K Pickthorn, *Early Tudor Government: Henry VII* (Cambridge, 1934), pp 127–31.

50 J Loach, *Parliament under the Tudors* (Oxford, 1991), pp 61–77.

50 J Loach, *Parliament under the Tudors* (Oxford, 1991), pp 61–77.

51 For what follows, see Myers, 'Parliament, 1422–1509', pp 141–84; E B Fryde, 'Introduction', in Fryde and Miller, eds, *Historical Studies of the English Parliament. I. Origins to 1399*, pp 2–4.

52 For the private petitioner this was a most efficacious mode of proceeding: private, or singular, petitions adopted by the Commons passed to the King and Council through the clerk of the Parliament and did not face the risk of rejeciton by royal auditors.

53 The clearest account of these muddling developments is in Edwards, *The Second Century of the English Parliament*, p 65.

54 *Ibid,* p 65.

55 Myers, 'Parliament, 1422–1509', p 171; Chrimes, *English Constitutional Ideas in the Fifteenth Centuy,* pp 235, 382.

56 Brown, *The Governance of Late Medieval England,* p 223.

57 H L Gray, *The Influence of the Commons on Early Legislation* (Cambridge (USA), 1932), discusses legislation in terms of conflict. See the corrective remarks of Chrimes, *English Constitutional Ideas in the Fifteenth Century,* pp 236–49.

58 For the situation in the reign of Henry VII see the judicious remarks of Pickthorn, *Early Tudor Government: Henry VII,* p 130.

59 S J Gunn, *Early Tudor Government, 1485–1558* (London, 1995), p 184.

60 Brown, *The Governance of Late Medieval England,* pp 185–6, 206, 211.

61 J H Denton, 'The Clergy and Parliament in the Thirteenth and Fourteenth Centuries', in Davies and Denton, eds, *The English Parliament in the Middle Ages,* pp 88–108.

62 For what follows, see J S Roskell, *The Commons and their Speakers in English Parliaments,* 1376–1523 (Manchester, 1965).

63 Tiptoft has generally been seen as the leader of the opposition to the king in this parliament, but, as has recently been pointed out, it is inconceivable that a knight of the king's chamber should have played such a role (A J Pollard, 'The Lancastrian Constitutional Experiment Revisited: Henry IV, Sir John Tiptoft and the Parliament of 1406' (*Parliamentary History,* vol 14 (1995), pp 107–8).

64 J S Roskell, L Clark, C Rawcliffe, eds, *The House of Commons, 1386–1421* (Stroud, 4 vols, 1992), vol I, pp 22, 100–1.

65 J S Roskell, 'The Medieval Speakers in Parliament' (*Bull Inst Hist Res,* vol 23 (1950), p 52).

66 Roskell, *The Commons and their Speakers in English Parliaments, 1376–1523,* p 346.

67 Roskell, Clark and Rawcliffe, eds, *The House of Commons, 1386–1421,* vol I, p 55n. See also the similar cases in Sayles, *The Functions of the Medieval Parliament of England,* p 413. For the subject of parliamentary wages in general, see H M Cam, *Liberties and Communities in Medieval England* (Cambridge, 1944, repr London, 1963), pp 236–50.

68 For what follows, see S J Payling, 'The Widening Franchise – Parliamentary Elections in Lancastrian Nottinghamshire', in D Williams, ed, *England in the*

Fifteenth Century (Woodbridge, 1987), pp 167–85; Roskell, Clark and Rawcliffe, eds, *The House of Commons, 1386–1421,* vol I, pp 55–68.

69 H G Richardson, 'John of Gaunt and the Parliamentary representation of Lancashire' (*Bull John Rylands Library,* vol 22 (1938), p 201).

70 For the electoral influence of the duchy before 1399, see S Walker, *The Lancastrian Affinity, 1361–1399* (Oxford, 1990), pp 237–40; Roskell, Clark and Rawcliffe, eds, *The House of Commons, 1386–1421,* vol I, pp 329–30, 472; G L Harriss, 'The Medieval Parliament' (*Parliamentary History,* vol 13 (1994), p 221).

71 Brown's estimate of a total electorate of between 10,000 and 15,000 is probably slightly conservative (Brown, *The Governance of Late Medieval England,* p 191). There appears to have been in excess of 600 electors in mid-fifteenth-century Nottinghamshire (Payling, 'The Widening Franchise', p 178).

72 For what follows, see Roskell, Clark and Rawcliffe, eds, *The House of Commons, 1386–1421,* vol I, pp 143–60.

73 Sayles, *The King's Parliament of England,* pp 109–36; Richardson, 'The Commons and Medieval Politics', pp 21–45.

74 *Ibid,* p 37.

75 The closeness of this association is manifest in the fact that de la Mare later acted as one of the executors of March's will (Roskell, *The Commons and their Speakers in English Parliaments,* p 119). After several years in Gaunt's service, Hungerford had been appointed to the important office of chief steward of the southern parts of the duchy of Lancaster in 1375 (Roskell, Clark and Rawcliffe, eds, *The House of Commons, 1386–1421,* vol III, p 443).

76 Edwards, *The Second Century of the English Parliament,* pp 8–11.

77 Roskell, Clark and Rawcliffe, eds, *The House of Commons, 1386–1421,* vol I, Appendix C; Harriss, 'The Medieval Parliament', pp 212–3.

78 G R Elton, 'The Body of the Whole Realm: Parliament and Representation in Medieval and Tudor England', in Elton, *Studies in Tudor and Stuart Politics and Government,* vol II (Cambridge, 1974), p 22.

79 K B MacFarlane, 'Parliament and Bastard Feudalism', in MacFarlane, *England in the Fifteenth Century* (London, 1981), pp 1–21.

80 L Clark, 'Magnates and their Affinities in the Parliaments of 1386–1421', in R H Britnell, A J Pollard, eds, *The MacFarlane Legacy: Studies in Late Medieval Politics and Society* (Stroud, 1995), pp 134–6. For the relative importance of the shire and town representatives, see Roskell, Clark and Rawcliffe, eds, *The House of Commons, 1386–1421,* vol I, pp 47–54.

81 N Saul, 'The Commons and the Abolition of Badges' (*Parliamentary History,* vol 9 (1990), pp 302–15).

82 B P Wolffe, 'Acts of Resumption in the Lancastrian Parliaments', in Fryde and Miller, eds, *Historical Studies of the English Parliament,* II, pp 61–91.

83 J S Roskell, *The Impeachment of Michael de la Pole, Earl of Suffolk* (Manchester, 1984), p 154n.

84 For Suffolk's fall, see R A Griffiths, *The Reign of King Henry VI* (London, 1981), pp 676–86.

85 Sayles, *The King's Parliament of England,* p 124.

86 Brown, *The Governnance of Late Medieval England,* p 175.

87 Sayles, *The King's Parliament of England,* p 125.

88 Roskell, Clark and Rawcliffe, eds, *The House of Commons, 1386–1421,* vol I, pp 131–2.

89 B P Wolffe, *Henry VI* (London, 1981), p 217.

90 Pollard, 'The Lancastrian Constitutional Experiment Revisited', pp 103–19.

91 Ross, *Edward IV,* p 341.

92 G L Harriss, 'The Management of Parliament', in Harriss, ed, *Henry V: The Practice of Kingship* (Oxford, 1984), p 138.

93 Harriss, 'The Dimensions of Politics', in Britnell and Pollards, eds, *The MacFarlane Legacy,* p 11.

94 *Ibid,* p 14.

95 H M Cam, 'The Relation of English Members of Parliament to their Constituencies in the Fourteenth Century: a Neglected text', in her *Liberties and Communities in Medieval England,* p 232. See also the letter written by Margaret Paston to her husband John when he was sitting in the parliament of 1460: 'Ye have many good prayers of the poer pepyl that God Schuld sped yow at thys Parlement' (J Gairdner, ed, *The Paston Letters* (London, 6 vols, 1904), vol III, no 423).

96 Myers, 'Parliament, 1422–1509', p 172.

97 G R Elton, *F W Maitland* (London, 1985), p 66.

98 Harriss, 'The Management of Parliament', p 138.

99 Gillingham, 'Crisis or Continuity?', p 80; Ormrod, *The Reign of Edward III,* p 169.

100 Elton, 'The Body of the Whole Realm', p 48.

101 C Rawcliffe, 'The Place of the Commons in Medieval Parliaments', in *Las Cortes de Castilla y Leon, 1188–1988* (Valladolid (Spain), 1988), p 35.

102 P R Coss, 'The Formation of the English Gentry' (*Past and Present,* vol 147 (1995), p 52).

103 Harriss, 'Political Society and the Growth of Government in Late Medieval England', p 56.

104 Myers, 'Parliament, 1422–1509', pp 163–5; Brown, *The Governance of Late Medieval England,* pp 204–5; J S Roskell, *The Commons in the Parliament of 1422* (Manchester, 1954), pp 125–44.

Chapter 3 (pages 70 - 82)

1 W Notestein, *The Winning of the Initiative by the House of Commons* (London, 1924), p 4.

2 A F Pollard, *The Evolution of Parliament* (London, 1920, repr 1926).

3 J E Neale, *Elizabeth I and her parliaments, 1559–81* (London, 1953), p 16.

4 *Ibid,* p 21.

5 On the Commons' growing sense of 'responsibility', see D Hirst, *The Representative of the People?* (Cambridge, 1975) and the subsequent debate in *Past and Present* for 1981.

6 G R Elton, 'Parliament in the sixteenth century; functions and fortunes', in his *Studies in Tudor and Stuart Politics and Government,* vol III (Cambridge, 1983), p 157.

7 J Loach, *Parliament under the Tudors* (Oxford, 1991), pp 16–8.

8 J D Alsop, 'Parliament and Taxation', in D M Dean, N L Jones, eds, *The Parliaments of Elizabethan England* (Oxford, 1990), pp 91–116.

9 J Spedding, R L Ellis, D D Heath, eds, *Collected Works of Francis Bacon* (London, 14 vols, 1857–74), vol II, pp 85–7.

10 On this see Loach, *Parliament under the Tudors,* pp 132–8.

11 A D K Hawkyard, 'The Enfranchisement of the Constituencies, 1504–58' (*Parliamentary History,* vol 10 (1991), p 2).

12 E de Villiers, 'The Parliamentary Boroughs Restored by the House of Commons, 1621–4' (*Eng Hist Rev,* vol LXVII (1952), pp 175–202).

13 C G Cruickshank, 'The Parliamentary Representation of Tournai' (*Eng Hist Rev,* vol LXXXIII (1968), pp 775–6).

14 However, no-one was sent (A J Eagleston, *The Channel Isles under Tudor Government, 1485–1642* (Cambridge, 1949), p 34).

15 Stat 34 and 35 Henry VIII, c 13.

16 Hawkyard, 'The Enfranchisement of the Constituencies', pp 8–9. Mr Hawkyard has also drawn attention to a comment of the Tournai people regretting the loss of their accustomed resort 'en la court de parlement à Paris' (*ibid,* p 5), but it seems improbable that this comment influenced either Henry or Wolsey in their decision to give the town parliamentary representation, since both would surely have understood that what was meant by 'parlement' was a court of law rather than a representative institution.

17 *Ibid* p 14.

18 G R Elton, 'Wales in Parliament, 1542–1581', in his *Studies in Tudor and Stuart Politics and Government,* vol IV (Cambridge, 1992), pp 94–5.

19 Hawkyard, 'The Enfranchisement of the Constituencies', p 13.

20 When we discover men-of-business being returned for seats in which the Crown had some influence, we should not, then, see this as 'packing', but rather as a sensible use of crown patronage. In 1559, for example, Richard Onslow was returned for Aldborough at the nomination of the chancellor of the Duchy of Lancaster.

21 J E Neale, *The Elizabethan House of Commons* (London, 1949, repr 1963), pp 185–7.

22 D Dean, 'Patrons, clients and conferences: the workings of bicamerism in the sixteenth-century English Parliament', in H Blum, ed, *Bicamerisme* (The Hague (Netherlands), 1992), p 218.

23 Historical Manuscripts Commission, *Report on the Manuscripts of the Duke of Rutland,* vol I (London, 1888), p 117.

24 Neale, *The Elizabethan House of Commons,* p 138.

25 Dean, 'Patrons, clients and conferences', p 219.

26 J Loach, 'Parliament: A New Air', in C Coleman, D Starkey, eds, *Revolution Reassessed. Revisions in the History of Tudor Government and Administration* (Oxford, 1986), pp 119–20.

27 Neale, *The Elizabethan House of Commons,* p 136.

28 Dean, 'Patrons, clients and conferences', p 219.

29 Loach, *Parliament under the Tudors,* pp 88–96.

30 *Ibid,* p 37.

31 D M Dean, N L Jones, eds, *The Parliaments of Elizabethan England* (Oxford, 1990), p 13.

32 Neale, *The Elizabethan House of Commons,* pp 397–9.

33 P W Hasler, ed, *The House of Commons, 1558–1603* (London, 3 vols, 1981), vol I, p 243; vol II, p 171.

34 Historical Manuscripts Commission, *Seventh Report of the Commissioners* (London, 1879), Appendix, p 657.

35 Hasler, ed, *The House of Commons, 1558–1603,* vol I, p 267. The editor is grateful to Dr Felicity Heal (Jesus College, Oxford) and Dr Penry Williams (New College, Oxford) for their efforts to locate the source of this quotation.

36 B H Harvey, *Living and Dying in England, 1100–1540* (Oxford, 1993), p 131.

37 C L Kingsford, ed, *A Survey of London by John Stow* (Oxford, 2 vols, 1908), vol II, p 120.

38 R H Brodie, ed, *Calendar of the Patent Rolls, 1547–53* (London, 6 vols, 1924–9), vol IV, p 12.

39 J R Dasent *et al, Acts of the Privy Council of England* (London, 46 vols, 1890–1964), vol II, p 172.

40 V F Snow, ed, *Parliament in Elizabethan England: John Hooker's Order and Usage* (New Haven (USA), 1977), pp 163–4.

41 G Edwards, 'The Emergence of Majority Rule in the Procedure of the House of Commons' (*Trans Roy Hist Soc,* 5th ser, vol 15 (1965), pp 180–2). See also, however, J Loach, *Parliament and the Crown in the Reign of Mary Tudor* (Oxford, 1986), pp 57–9.

42 Hasler, ed, *The House of Commons, 1558–1603,* vol III, p 23.

43 The figures for the first half of the reign are taken from G R Elton, *The Parliament of England, 1559–1581* (Cambridge, 1986), and those for the second part from D Dean, 'Bills and Acts, 1584–1601' (unpublished Ph D thesis, Cambridge University, 1984). I am very grateful to Dr Dean for providing me with a copy of his thesis.

44 S D'Ewes, *A Compleat Journal* (London, 1693), p 633.

45 *Ibid,* p 640.

Chapter 4 (pages 83 - 99)

1 S Orgel, 'The royal theatre and the role of the King', in G F Lytle, S Orgel, eds, *Patronage in the Renaissance* (Princeton (USA), 1981), pp 261–73.

2 See the seminal article by C Russell, 'Parliamentary History in Perspective, 1604–29' (*History,* vol 61 (1976), pp 1–27); also K Sharpe, 'Parliamentary History, 1603–29: In or Out of Perspective?', in K Sharpe, ed, *Faction and Parliament* (Oxford, 1978, repr London, 1985), pp 1–42. But compare J S Roskell, 'Perspectives in English Parliamentary History', in E B Fryde, E Miller, eds, *Historical Studies of the English Parliament* (Cambridge, 2 vols, 1970), vol II, pp 296–323.

3 On the revealing nature of this slip, compare Russell's observation that the title of his book is often misquoted: C Russell, 'The nature of a Parliament in Early Stuart England', in H Tomlinson, ed, *Before the English Civil War* (London, 1983), p 125.

4 R Cust, A Hughes, eds, *Conflict in Early Stuart England* (London, 1989), pp 12–13; K Sharpe, P Lake, eds, *Culture and Politics in Early Stuart England* (London, 1994), pp 1–20, especially pp 4–5. The footnotes in Cust and Hughes, *Conflict in Early Stuart England,* offer a bibliographical entry to the debate over 17th century parliaments.

5 J H Hexter, 'Power Struggle, Parliament and Liberty in Early Stuart England' (*Journ of Mod Hist,* vol 50 (1978), pp 1–50); T K Rabb, 'The Role of the Commons' (*Past and Present,* vol 92 (1981), pp 55–78); G R Elton, *The Parliament of England, 1559–1581* (Cambridge, 1986); see also note 4 above.

6 T B Macaulay, *The History of England* (Harmondsworth, 1979), introduction by H R Trevor-Roper.

7 J P Kenyon, *The History Men: The Historical Profession in England since the Renaissance* (London, 1983), pp 214–22; quotation on p 220.

8 On Gardiner, see Kenyon, *The History Men;* R Usher, *A Critical Study of the Historical Method of Samuel Rawson Gardiner* (St Louis (USA), 1915); R C Richardson, *The Debates on the English Revolution Revisited* (London, 1988), pp 82–6; J S Adamson, 'Eminent Victorians: S R Gardiner and the Liberal as Hero' (*Hist Journ,* vol 33 (1990), pp 641–57); S R Gardiner, *History of England from the Accession of James I to the Outbreak of the Civil War* (London, 10 vols, 1883–4).

9 R Samuel, 'British Marxist Historians, 1880–1980' (*New Left Rev,* vol 120 (1980), pp 21–95); C Hill, *The English Revolution, 1640* (London, 1940; 2nd edn, 1949); B Manning, *The English People and the English Revolution* (London, 1976).

10 W Notestein, 'The Stuart Period: Unsolved Problems' (*Annual Report of the American Historical Association . . . for the year 1916* (Washington (USA), 1919), pp 389–99; W Notestein, *The Winning of the Initiative by the House of Commons* (London, 1924).

11 J H Hexter, 'Introduction', in J H Hexter, ed, *Parliament and Liberty from the Reign of Elizabeth to the English Civil War* (Stanford (USA), 1992), pp 1–20. This is one volume of a projected series on *The Making of Modern Freedom,* centred on English history and directed by Hexter.

12 For a review of criticism and some sharp critical observations, see J C D Clark, *Revolution and Rebellion* (Cambridge, 1986).

13 G Burgess, 'On Revisionism: an analysis of Early Stuart Historiography in the 1970s and 1980s' (*Hist Journ,* vol 33 (1990), pp 609–27).

14 We await a good study of the ideological constructions of history written in the later seventeenth and early eighteenth centuries. See, however, R Macgillivray,

Restoration Historians and the English Civil War (The Hague (Netherlands), 1974); A B Worden, ed, 'Edmund Ludlow: A Voice from the Watch Tower, 1660–1662' (*Camden Soc,* 4th ser, vol 21, 1978); J Sawday, 'Re-writing a Revolution: History, Symbol and Text in the Restoration' (*The Seventeenth Century,* vol VII (1992), pp 171–99).

15 G R Elton, 'Studying the History of Parliament', in his *Studies in Tudor and Stuart Politics and Government,* vol II (Cambridge, 1974), p 9; J P Kenyon, ed, *The Stuart Constitution, 1603–1688* (Cambridge, 1966; 2nd edn, 1986).

16 For examples, see Sharpe, *Faction and Parliament,* and C Russell, *Parliaments and English Politics, 1621–1629* (Oxford, 1979).

17 Russell, *Parliaments and English Politics;* Russell, 'Parliamentary History in Perspective'; and see now C Russell, *Unrevolutionary England, 1603–1642* (London, 1990), introduction.

18 My metaphor, but the point is well made by D Hirst, 'The Place of Principle' (*Past and Present,* vol 92 (1981), pp 79–99).

19 C Holmes, 'The County Community in Stuart Historiography' (*Journ Brit Stud,* vol 19 (1980), pp 53–73); A Hughes, 'Warwickshire on the Eve of the Civil War: a county community?' (*Midland Hist,* vol VII (1982), pp 42–72).

20 Compare D Hirst, *Authority and Conflict in England, 1603–1658* (London, 1985), p 39.

21 In the Grand Remonstrance, printed in S R Gardiner, ed, *Constitutional Documents of the Puritan Revolution, 1625–1660* (Oxford, 1899), pp 202–32.

22 G L Harriss, *King, Parliament and Public Finance in medieval England to 1369* (Oxford, 1975); G L Harriss, 'War and the emergence of the English Parliament, 1297–1360' (*Journ Med Hist,* vol 2 (1976), pp 35–56); G L Harriss, 'Medieval doctrines in the Debates on Supply', in Sharpe, *Faction and Parliament,* pp 73–103.

23 G Parker, *The Military Revolution: military innovation and the rise of the West* (Cambridge, 1988).

24 As Queen Elizabeth put it to her Commons in 1593, 'it is needful for a prince to have so much always lying in her coffers for your defence in time of need, and not to be driven to get it when she should use it.' (W Cobbett, ed, *The Parliamentary History of England* (London, 36 vols, 1806–20), vol I, p 893). Compare James I's witty remark to the 1610 Parliament 'that provision for war after its outbreak was like mustard after dinner' (E R Foster, ed, *Proceedings in Parliament, 1610* (New Haven (USA), 2 vols, 1966), vol II, p 106).

25 Russell, 'Parliamentary History in Perspective'.

26 Hampshire Record Office, Herriard MS 021; F C Dietz, *English Public Finance, 1558–1641* (Urbana (USA), 2 vols, repr London, 1964), vol II, pp 391–3; M J Braddick, 'Parliamentary lay taxation, *circa* 1590–1670: local problems of enforcement and collection with special reference to Norfolk' (unpublished Ph D thesis, Cambridge University, 1987), especially chaps 1–3.

27 Most proposals for improving royal revenue were conservative in nature. Significantly, the few radical proposals - for an excise, for example - were not adopted. See Sir Robert Cotton, 'The Manner and Means How the Kings of England have from time to time supported and repaired their estates', in

J Howell, ed, *Cottoni Posthuma* (London, 1651), pp 163–200; compare BL Cotton MS Titus F V; BL Add MS 34234, fol 169; K Sharpe, *The Personal Rule of Charles I* (London, 1992), p 13.

28 R W K Hinton, 'The Decline of Parliamentary Government under Elizabeth I and the Early Stuarts' (*Cambridge Hist Journ,* vol 13 (1957), pp 116–32, especially p 116).

29 M A R Graves, *The Tudor Parliaments* (London, 1985), pp 77–9.

30 J F Larkin, ed, *Stuart Royal Proclamations, II: Royal Proclamations of King Charles I, 1625–46* (Oxford, 1983), p xi. The average, 1603–29, was twelve a year, the same as in Mary's reign. Hinton does not discuss proclamations in his comments on extra-parliamentary government.

31 A large proportion of the bills that became statutes in Jacobean parliaments were concerned with claims to title and estates, restorations, naturalizations and marriage settlements.

32 See my introduction to *Faction and Parliament,* pp 25–8.

33 See chapter 3.

34 R C Munden, 'James I and the "growth of mutual distrust"; King, Commons and Reform, 1603–1604', in Sharpe, ed, *Faction and Parliament,* pp 46–9.

35 R E Ruigh, *The Parliament of 1624* (Cambridge (USA), 1971), p 151, for James recommending remedial legislation against monopolies and other abuses; Russell, *Parliaments and Politics,* p 191.

36 Sharpe, *Personal Rule of Charles I,* pp 1, 7–9.

37 G R Elton, 'Tudor Government: The Points of Contact: I. Parliament' (*Trans Roy Hist Soc,* 5th ser, vol XXIV (1974), pp 183–200). On James' attitude to Parliamentary advice, see W Notestein, H Simpson, eds, *Commons Debates, 1621* (New Haven (USA), 7 vols, 1935), vol II, p 4.

38 R Lockyer, *Buckingham: The Life and Political Career of George Villiers, First Duke of Buckingham* (London, 1981).

39 Sharpe, *Faction and Parliament,* pp 37–42.

40 Hill, *English Revolution;* C Hill; *Puritanism and Revolution* (London, 1958); C Hill, *Collected Essays* (Brighton, 3 vols, 1985–6); L Stone, *The Causes of the English Revolution, 1529–1642* (London, 1972); D Hirst, *The Representative of the People?* (Cambridge, 1975); R Brenner, *Merchants and Revolution: Commercial Change, Political Conflict and London's Overseas Traders, 1550–1653* (Cambridge, 1993). Despite its publication date, the last is very much old wine in new bottles.

41 M Kishlansky, *Parliamentary Selection: Social and Political Choice in Early Modern England* (Cambridge, 1986).

42 J Miller, 'The English kill their kings - from divine right to parliamentary monarchy: the Stuarts, 1603–1714', in J S Moore, R Smith, eds, *The House of Lords: a thousand years of British tradition* (London, 1994), pp 66–86.

43 V F Snow, 'The Arundel Case' (*The Historian,* vol XXVI (1964), pp 324–50); K Sharpe, 'The Earl of Arundel, His Circle and the opposition to the Duke of Buckingham, 1618–1628', in *Faction and Parliament,* pp 209–44.

44 C Roberts, 'The Earl of Bedford and the Coming of the English Revolution' (*Journ Mod Hist,* vol 49 (1977), pp 600–16); Sharpe, *Personal Rule of Charles I,* pp 946–9.

45 J S Adamson, 'The baronial context of the English Civil War' (*Trans Roy Hist Soc,* 5th ser, vol 40 (1990), pp 93–120); J S Adamson, 'Politics and the Nobility in Civil War England' (*Hist Journ,* vol 34 (1991), pp 231–55).

46 Miller, 'The English kill their kings'.

47 M Seymour, 'Pro-government propaganda in interregnum England, 1649–1660' (unpublished Ph D thesis, Cambridge University, 1987), chap 5.

48 Clark, *Revolution and Rebellion,* pp 33, 75–7; J G D Clark, *English Society, 1688–1832* (Cambridge, 1985), chap 2.

49 One about which contemporaries too were in doubt (Sharpe, *Faction and Parliament,* pp 7–8).

50 Eg C Russell, *The Fall of the British Monarchies* (Oxford, 1991).

51 J N Ball, 'The Parliamentary Career of Sir John Eliot, 1624–29' (unpublished Ph D thesis, Cambridge University, 1953); C V Wedgwood, *Thomas Wentworth, Earl of Strafford, a revaluation, 1593–1641* (London, 1961); S P Salt, 'Sir Thomas Wentworth and the Parliamentary Representation of Yorkshire, 1614–28' (*Northern History,* vol 16 (1980), pp 130–68); C Russell, 'The Parliamentary Career of John Pym', in Russell, *Unrevolutionary England,* pp 205–30.

52 P Zagorin, 'Did Strafford change sides?' (*Eng Hist Rev,* vol CI (1986), pp 149–63); *Dictionary of National Biography,* vol LX (1899), pp 268–83; compare K Sharpe, *Sir Robert Cotton* (Oxford, 1979).

53 P Collinson, 'Puritans, Men of Business and Elizabethan Parliaments' (*Parliamentary History,* vol 7 (1988), pp 187–211).

54 The history of faction added an important dimension to the study of Tudor and Stuart politics, but historians of faction have been too prone to over-schematize faction and to see political relations too narrowly in factional terms.

55 A sketch for a possible study is outlined in K Sharpe, 'Crown, parliament and locality: government and communication in early Stuart England' (*Eng Hist Rev,* vol 99 (1986), pp 321–50).

56 See above 205, n 19.

57 The *locus classicus* of this view is E M W Tillyard, *The Elizabethan World Picture* (London, 1943); compare A D Lovejoy, *The Great Chain of Being* (Cambridge, (USA), 1936, repr 1953, New York (USA), 1960).

58 Sharpe and Lake, *Culture and Politics in Early Stuart England,* pp 18–20 and *passim*; K Sharpe, *Politics and Ideas* (London, 1989), chap 1.

59 This argument will be pursued further in K Sharpe, S Zwicker, eds, *Refiguring Revolutions: Aesthetics and politics from the English revolution to the Romantic Revolution* (forthcoming).

60 See above, chaps 1–2. Elizabeth and James I often referred to these earlier periods of crisis, eg C McIlwain, ed, *The Political Works of James I* (Cambridge (USA), 1918), p 246.

61 C Haigh, *Elizabeth I* (London, 1988), chap 6; J Loach, *Parliament under the Tudors* (Oxford, 1991).

62 B Coward, *Oliver Cromwell* (London, 1991), chaps 6–7.

63 Russell points out that Sir John Fortescue began the myth 'that there was something especially English about parliaments' (Cust and Hughes, eds, *Conflict in Early Stuart England,* p 14).

64 Eg letter of Sir Arthur Hopton to Windebank, 7 February 1640: 'the Cortes do every year give more and it is strange to see how patiently the people bears being laid on by the insensible way of sisa' (Bodleian Library, Oxford, Clarendon MS 18, no 1349). Compare William Drake's observation that the French monarchy was 'the most absolute, for the king doth what he pleaseth both for making laws or laying impositions' (University College, London, Ogden MS 7, fol 66).

65 As Sir Robert Phelips put it in 1625, 'we are the last monarchy in Christendom that yet retain our original rights and constitutions' (S R Gardiner, ed, 'Debates in the House of Commons' in 1625' (*Camden Soc,* NS vol 6 (1873), pp 109–10).).

66 *Calendar of State Papers, Venetian, 1603–7,* pp 509–10.

67 G R Elton, ed, *The Tudor Constitution* (Cambridge, 1960, 2nd edn, 1982), p 270; compare James I's speech to the parliament of 1605 that parliament was 'that most honourable and fittest place for a King to be in for doing the turns most proper to his office' (McIlwain, ed, *The Political Works of James I,* p 284).

68 J Morrill, J Walter, 'Order and Disorder in the English Revolution', im A Fletcher, J Stevenson, eds, *Order and Disorder in Early Modern England* (Cambridge, 1985), pp 137–65.

69 This awaits a full investigation, but see W Kennedy, *English Taxation, 1640–1799* (London, 1913).

70 P G M Dickson, *The Financial Revolution in England, 1689–1756* (London, 1967, repr Aldershot, 1993); J Brewer, *The Sinews of Power* (London, 1989).

71 Haigh, *Elizabeth I,* pp 107–8; D H Willson, ed, *The Parliamentary Diary of Robert Bowyer* (Minneapolis (USA), 1931), p 96; *Calendar of State Papers, Domestic Series, 1623–5,* p 209.

72 D H Willson, *The Privy Councillors in the House of Commons, 1603–1629* (Minneapolis (USA), 1940, repr New York (USA), 1971); H R Trevor-Roper, 'Oliver Cromwell and his Parliaments', in his *Religion, the Reformation and Social Change* (London, 1967, 2nd edn, 1972), chap 7.

73 J H Plumb, *The Growth of Political Stability in England, 1675–1725* (London, 1967).

74 Despite the claims of J Sommerville, *Politics and Ideology in England, 1603–1640* (London, 1986). See Sharpe, *Politics and Ideas,* pp 283–9; C Russell, 'Divine Rights in the Early Seventeenth Century', in J Morrill, P Slack and D Woolf, eds, *Public Duty and Private Conscience in Seventeenth-Century England* (Oxford, 1993), pp 101–20.

75 R C Johnson, M Keeler, M Cole, eds, *Commons Debates, 1628* (New Haven (USA), 3 vols, 1977), vol III, p 189; see also R Cust, *The Forced Loan and English Politics, 1626–1628* (Oxford, 1987), pp 44, 69–71.

76 S Morrill, 'The religious context of the English civil war' (*Trans Roy Hist Soc,* 5th ser, vol 34 (1984), pp 155–78).

77 I M Green, *The Re-Establishment of the Church of England, 1660–1663* (Oxford, 1978), chap ix; J Spurr, *The Restoration Church of England, 1646–1689* (New Haven (USA), 1991), chap 3 and *passim.*

78 Compare Sharpe, *Politics and Ideas,* pp 66–71.

Chapter 5 (pages 100 - 8)

1   A Browning, ed, *English Historical Documents, 1660–1714* (London, 1953), pp 237–49.

2   G S Holmes, W A Speck, eds, *The Divided Society: Parties and Politics in England, 1694–1716* (London, 1967), pp 146–7.

3   W Coxe, *Memoirs of the life and administration of Sir Robert Walpole* (London, 4 vols, 1816), vol III, pp 135–44.

4   R Sedgwick, ed, *The History of Parliament: The Commons, 1715–1754* (London, 2 vols, 1970), vol II, p 567.

5   *The Charitable Corporation Vindicated* (London, 1745), p 13.

6   Northamptonshire Record Office L (C) 1732/1735. I owe this reference to Professor Linda Colley.

7   See especially J G A Pocock, *The Machiavellian Moment* (London, 1974, Princeton (USA), 1975).

8   A Grey, *Debates of the House of Commons from the year 1667 to the year 1694* (London, 10 vols, 1769), vol IX, p 22.

9   G Holmes, 'The Electorate and the National Will in the first Age of Party', in G Holmes, ed, *Politics, Religion and Society in England, 1679–1742* (London, 1986), p 23. The estimates of 330,000 to 340,000 provided by Holmes would not find general acceptance, but at least 300,000 men must have been enfranchised at a time when the total number of adult males cannot have been more than 1,550,000 (E A Wrigley, R S Schofield, *The Population History of England, 1541–1871* (London, 1981), pp 528–9). See Introduction, Table 2.

10 J Levin, *The Charter controversy in the City of London, 1660–1688* (London, 1969).

11 R J Sinner, 'Charles II and Local Government: the *Quo Warranto* proceedings, 1681–1685' (unpublished Ph D thesis, Rutgers University, 1976); J Miller, 'The Crown and the borough charters in the reign of Charles II' (*Eng Hist Rev,* vol C (1985), pp 53–84).

12 J R Jones, *The Revolution of 1688 in England* (London, 1972), pp 128–75.

13 B Henning, *The History of Parliament: The Commons, 1660–1689* (London, 3 vols, 1983), vol I, p 42.

14 W A Speck, *Reluctant Revolutionaries: Englishmen and the Revolution of 1688* (Oxford, 1988), p 134.

15 *A modest vindication of the petition of the Lords spiritual and temporal for the calling of a free parliament* (Exeter, 1688).

16 Jones, *The Revolution of 1688,* pp 129–30.

17 N Landau, 'Independence, Deference and voter participation: the behaviour of the electorate in early eighteenth-century Kent' (*Hist Journ,* vol 22 (1979), pp 561–83).

18 T B Macaulay, *The History of England from the Accession of James II* (London, 5 vols, repr 1986), vol IV, p 258.

19 B Worden, 'The Revolution of 1688–9 and the English Republican Tradition', in J Israel, ed, *The Anglo-Dutch Moment: Essays on the Glorious Revolution and its World impact* (Cambridge, 1991), p 266.

20 G Holmes, 'The attack on the "influence of the Crown", 1702–1716', in Holmes, ed, *Politics, Religion and Society in England, 1679–1742*, pp 41–7.

21 The best account of it is G Holmes, *The Trial of Dr Sacheverell* (London, 1973), on which these observations are based.

22 On these developments see especially G S de Krey, *A Fractured Society: the Politics of London in the first age of party, 1688–1715* (Oxford, 1985) and L Colley, *In Defiance of Oligarchy: The Tory Party, 1714–1760* (Cambridge, 1982).

23 P Langford, *A Polite and Commercial People: England, 1727–1783* (Oxford, 1989), p 32.

24 Quoted in P Langford, *The Excise Crisis* (Oxford, 1975), p 131.

Chapter 6 (pages 109 - 17)

1 F Braudel, *Civilization and Capitalism, 15th–18th Centuries: II, The Wheels of Commerce* (London, 1982), p 528.

2 I would like to thank Ian Christie, John Derry, William Gibson, and Alex Murdoch for commenting on an earlier draft of this chapter.

Chapter 7 (pages 118 - 31)

1 J A Phillips, *Electoral Behaviour in Unreformed England: Plumpers, Splitters and Straights* (Guildford, Princeton (USA), 1982).

2 P Langford, 'Property and virtual representation in eighteenth-century England' (*Hist Journ*, vol 31 (1988), pp 83–115).

3 P Fraser, 'Public petitioning and parliament before 1832' (*History*, vol 46 (1961), pp 195–211).

4 J A Roebuck, *A History of the Whig Ministry of 1830 to the Passing of the Reform Bill* (London, 2 vols, 1852), vol II, pp 291–2.

5 *Hansard*, 3rd ser, vol VIII, vols 330–31, 7 October 1831.

6 S F Woolley, 'The Personnel of the parliament of 1833' (*Eng Hist Rev*, vol LIII (1938), pp 240–62).

7 N Gash, *Politics in the Age of Peel: a study in the technique of Parliamentary Representation, 1830–1850* (London, 1953).

8 It was not until 1945, when only three seats were uncontested, that the British electorate as a whole had a real chance of exercising a choice.

9 The best studies of the passing of the 1867 act are M Cowling, *1867: Disraeli, Gladstone and Revolution. The passing of the Second Reform Act* (London, 1967) and F B Smith, *The Making of the Second Reform Bill* (Cambridge, 1966).

10 H J Hanham, *Elections and Party Management in the Age of Disraeli and Gladstone* (London, 1959, 2nd edn, Hassocks, 1978).

11 M H Port, ed, *The Houses of Parliament* (London, New Haven (USA), 1976), p 5.

12 PRO WORKS 11/1/2, vols 61–9, 6 February 1849.

13 Port, *The Houses of Parliament,* p 4.

14 *Hansard,* 3rd ser, vol CLXXIV, col 252, quoted in Port, *The Houses of Parliament,* p 227.

15 A Ramm, 'The Parliamentary Context of Cabinet Government' (*Eng Hist Rev,* vol XCIX (1984), pp 739–69).

16 H J Hanham, *The reformed Electoral System in Great Britain, 1832–1914* (London, 1971), p 24.

Chapter 8 (pages 132 - 42)

1   F W S Craig, *British Electoral Facts, 1832–1960* (Chichester, 4th edn, 1981), pp 66–8.

2   H Kearney, *The British Isles: a history of four nations* (Cambridge, 1989), pp 149–74.

3   M R G Fry, *Patronage and Principle: a political history of modern Scotland* (Aberdeen, 1987); pp 103–5.

4   K O Morgan, *Wales, the rebirth of a nation* (Oxford, 1981), pp 90–123.

5   See especially, from a vast literature, L P Curtis, *Coercion and Conciliation in Ireland, 1880–1892* (Princeton (USA), 1963), pp 158 *et seq.*

6   *Ibid,* pp 175 *et seq.*

7   The best summary is J Gallagher, R Robinson, 'The Imperialism of Free Trade' (*Econ Hist Rev,* 2nd ser, vol 6 (1953), pp 1–15).

8   J Pope, ed, *Memoirs of the Rt Hon John Alexander Macdonald* (London, 2 vols, 1894), vol I, p 312; vol II, pp 214–5.

9   O D Skelton, *The Life and Times of Sir Alexander Tilloch Galt* (Toronto (Canada), 1920), p 523.

10 P Magnus, *Gladstone* (London, 1954), pp 250 *et seq.*

11 J Wilson, *CB: a life of Sir Henry Campbell-Bannerman* (London, 1973), pp 229–99.

12 Marquess of Crewe, *Lord Rosebery* (London, 2 vols, 1931), vol I, pp 149 *et seq.*

13 Fry, *Patronage and Principle,* p 114.

14 *Ibid,* pp 115, 127–9.

15 *Ibid,* pp 120–2.

16 *Ibid,* pp 111–3.

17 J Amery, J A Garvin, *Life of Joseph Chamberlain* (London, 6 vols, 1935–69), vol V, p 255; vol VI, p 474.

18 Pope, *Memoirs of J A Macdonald,* vol II, p 220.

19 J R M Butler, *Lord Lothian* (London, 1960), pp 223–4.

20 S H Zebel, *Balfour, a political biography* (Cambridge, 1973), pp 247–9.

Chapter 9 (pages 143 - 9)

1 L Collins, *European Community Law in the United Kingdom,* (London, 4th edn, 1990), p 28; T C Hartley, *Foundations of European Community Law* (Oxford, 3rd edn, 1994), p 263.

2 European Communities Act, 1972, section 2 (4).

3 See, *eg,* Case 6/64 *Costa* v *ENEL (European Court Reports,* (1964), pp 593–4); Case C-213/89 *R* v *Secretary of State for Transport, ex parte FactorTame Ltd, et al (European Court Reports*, pt 1 (1990), p 2473).

4 Lord Bridge has stated that the effect of section 2 (4) is the same as if a section were incorporated in each subsequent Act of Parliament stating that its provisions were to be without prejudice to directly effective Community law *R* v *Secretary of State for Transport, ex parte FactorTame Ltd, et al (Appeal Cases*, pt 2 (1990), p 140).).

5 Case C-213/89 *R* v *Secretary of State for Transport, ex parte FactorTame Ltd, et al (European Court Reports*, pt 1 (1990), p 2474). See P P Craig, 'Sovereignty of the United Kingdom Parliament after *Factortame' (Yearbook of European Law,* vol II (1991), pp 221–55).

6 *Blackburn* v *Attorney General, (All England Reports,* pt 2 (1971), p 1382, *per* Lord Denning, Master of the Rolls).

7 See K Newman, 'The impact of national parliaments in the development of Community law', in F Capotorti *et al,* eds, *Du Droit international au droit de l'intégration,* (Baden-Baden, 1987) pp 481–97, and K Newman, 'Parliamentary scrutiny of European legislation' *(European Business Law Rev,* vol 2 (1991), pp 223–6). The discussion of scrutiny in this contribution is based on Newman's accounts.

8 European Community Treaty, Article 189.

9 Community law has ensured that in the case of non-implementation or incorrect implementation individuals may still take advantage, as against the State, of any rights which the directive concerned confers upon them, as long as the provisions satisfy the criteria for what is called 'direct effect'. If, however, there has been no implementation or incorrect implementation, an individual may not rely on the directive against another individual. Accordingly, if national law cannot be interpreted in accordance with the unimplemented directive, and an individual suffers loss because the failure to implement the directive means he is denied rights on which he could otherwise rely against another individual, he may look to the State to make good his loss. See, most recently, Case C-9213 /92, *Paola Faccini Diri* v *Recreb Sr (European Court Reports,* pt 1 (1994), p 3357.

10 European Communities Act, 1972 (as amended), Schedule 2, para 2 (2).

11 The rights, powers, liabilities, obligations and restrictions created by or arising under these Treaties, and remedies or procedures provided for, by, or under these Treaties are, in accordance with those Treaties, given legal effect or used in the United Kingdom without further enactment (European Communities Act, section 2(1).). Examples of such Treaties include amendments to the Treaties establishing the European Communities, decisions relating to the accession of new Member States (which of course involve adaptation of the original Treaties) and certain financial agreements.

12 Newman, 'Parliamentary Scrutiny of European Legislation', p 223.

13 Resolution of 24 October 1980 (the House of Lords has made equivalent arrangements).

14 Newman, 'Parliamentary Scrutiny of European Legislation', p 224.

15 P J G Kapteyn, P VerLoren van Themaat (L W Gormley, ed), *Introduction to the Law of the European Communities* (Deventer (Netherlands) and London, 2nd edn, (1989), p 104.

16 Cases 2 and 3/60 *Niederrheinische Bergwerkers AG et al* v *High Authority (European Court Reports* (1961), pp 146–7).

17 Case 166/78 *Italy* v *Council (European Court Reports* (1979), p 2596).

18 For outstanding descriptions of the work of the House of Lords Select Committee, see the works by Newman cited in note 7 above.

Chapter 10 (pages 150 - 60)

Chapter 11 (pages 161 - 72)

[There are no notes to chapters 10 and 11]

Chapter 12 (pages 173 - 81)

1 A Taitt, *The Right of the House of Stewart to the Crown of Scotland considered* (Edinburgh, 1746), p 20.

2 P Abercromby, *The material achievements of the Scots nation* (Edinburgh, 2 vols, 1711, 1715), vol I, pp 628–9.

3 T B Macaulay, *The History of Scotland* (London, 5 vols, 1849–61).

4 J Hill Burton, *The History of Scotland* (Edinburgh, 8 vols, 1867) vol IV, pp 90 *et seq.*

5 R Rait, *The Parliaments of Scotland* (Glasgow, 1924).

6 *The New History of Scotland* (London, 8 vols, 1981–4) and M Lynch, *Scotland: A New History* (London, 1992), and *Scotland Revisited* J Wormald, ed (London, 1991).

7 The least profitable of all these expeditions was Henry IV's in 1400, when the Scots scorched the earth of the Lothians and refused to meet the English in battle. Henry lost a significant number of his troops to disease and starvation for the sole gain of a cow on the road home.

8 *The Claim of Right* (Edinburgh, 1989) and the judgment of Lord Cooper in *McCormick v Lord Advocate, Scottish Cases,* 1953, p 396.

9 W Robertson, *History of Scotland* (Edinburgh, 2nd edn, 2 vols, 1981), vol I, pp 77 *et seq.*

10 For a further discussion, B Guenée, *States and Rulers in later Medieval Europe* (trans J Vale, Oxford, 1985), pp 172 *et seq.*

11 T Thomson & C Innes, eds, The *Acts of the Parliament of Scotland,* vol I, pp 452–3 (London, 12 vols, 1814–75).

12 Edinburgh University Library MS 207, fols 146–7.

13 Rait, *Parliaments of Scotland,* pp 258–9; *Records of the Convention of the Royal Burghs of Scotland,* ed Marwick (Edinburgh, 6 vols, 1870–90), vol I, p 371.

14 For a recent overview of the Scottish Reformation, see J Kirk, "Reformation and Revolution, Kirk and Crown", 1560–1690, in *Scotland Revisited,* J Wormald, ed, (London, 1991) pp ???

15 *Acts of the General Assembly, 1638–1842,* p 29.

16 Rait, *Parliament of Scotland,* pp 15–16.

17 *Ibid,* p 17.

18 The role of the General Assembly, in particular, and Scotland, in general, in promoting the summoning of the English Parliament and triggering the Civil War is more fully discussed in Scottish context in D Stevenson, *The Scottish Revolution,* 1637–1644 (London, 1973), and from and English standpoint in C Russell, *The Causes of the English Civil War* (Oxford, 1990).

19 J Spottiswode, *History of the Church of Scotland* (Edinburgh, 1677), p 365.

20 A Bruce, "Lairds and Blood Feuds – the Scots Nobility to the Act of Union" in J Moore and R Smith, eds, *The House of Lords, a thousand years of British tradition* (London, 1994), pp 87–97.

21 *Acts of the Parliament of Scotland,* vol II, p 15.

22 For a detailed study of the late medieval and early modern localities, see J Wormald, *Lords and Men in Scotland* (Edinburgh, 1985) and K M Brown, *Bloodfeud in Scotland 1573–1625* (Edinburgh, 1986).

23 W Ferguson, "The Electoral System in the Scottish Counties before 1832" *(Stair Society Miscellany Two,* 1984), p 264.

24 *Acts of Parliament of Scotland,* vol III, p 509.

25 Ferguson, "The Electoral System", p 267.

26 Robertson, *History of Scotland,* vol I, pp 81–2.

27 *Acts of the Parliament of Scotland,* vol VIII, p 449.

28 For a summary of the life of the Committee of Articles see Rait, *Scottish Parliament,* pp 389–91.

29 *Acts of Parliament of Scotland,* vol II, p 32.

30 *Acts of the Parliament of Scotland,* vol II, p 48.

31 *Acts of the Parliament of Scotland,* vol IX, p 38 (23).

32 Viscount Stair, *Institutes* (Edinburgh, 2nd ed, 2 vols, 1693), vol I, p 530.

33 Effectively, what the House of Lords held in *R v Secretary of State for Transport ex part Factortame* (Appeal Cases, 190, pt 2, p 85) sparked intense debate in England whether the Court had such authority. Not surprisingly, there was little negative reaction north of the border.

34 MacCormich v Lord Advocate, *Scottish Cases,* (1953), p 396 and Gibson v Lord Advocate, Scottish Law Times (1975), p 134.

35 *Dr Bonham's Case* as reported in T F Plunkett, "Bonham's Case and Judicial Review", *House of Lords Review* (1926), p 30.

36 Stair, *Institutions,* Lib 4, Tit 1.

37 Sir John Clerk of Penicuik, "History of Union of Scotland and England", *Scottish History Society,* 5th Ser, vol 6 (1993), p 164.

38 *Correspondence of George Baillie of Jerviswood,* 1702–08 *(Bannatyne Club,* 1842), p 138.

39 Sir John Clerk's observations on the present circumstances in Scotland, *Scottish History Society, Miscellany X* (1965), p 192.

40 Lynch, *Scotland: A New History,* p 314.

41 The author would like to thank Mr Michael Upton, Mrs Mary Donnelly, and the management and staff of the Quinta Bela Vista, in Madeira, for their help and assistance in the writing of this essay.

Index

Act of Settlement (1701) 105–6, 111, 180–1
Act of Union (1707) 179–81
adjournment debates 156–7
Admiralty, the 100, 105
all-party groups 152
amendments 124, 156
Andover (Hampshire) 74
Abingdon (Berkshire) 75
Anne, *Queen,* (1702–14, born 1665), vii 16, 17–18, 106, 180–1
Anson, *Sir* William Reynell (1843–1914) v; quoted vii
Appellants (Lords Appellant) 63, 64
Articles, Lords of the (Scotland) 175, 178–9
artisans 5, 67, 97, 136, 162; extension of franchise (1867) 3, 123–4, *see also* electorate;
    property qualification
Arundel, Richard Fitzalan, *Earl* of (Appellant in 1388) 63
Arundel and Surrey, Thomas Howard, *2nd Earl* of (1586–1646) 92
assemblies, royal 58, 67–8; evolution into parliaments 12, 26–7, 28, 30–1, 44, 45–6;
    and non-feudal taxes 7–8, 38–45
assize, justice of 43
attendance 78, 97, 128, 153–4, table of divisions (1861–1926° 125
Auditor General 130
Australia 134–5, 139, 140, 141
autocracy 18, 90–1, 98, 103, 116–17, *see also* Royal Prerogative
Aylesbury (Buckinghamshire) 75
backbenchers 93, 107, 155
Bacon, Francis, *Baron* Verulam of Verulam, *Viscount* St. Albans 92 quoted 71–2
Bail (Amendment) Act (1993) 157–8
Balfour, Arthur James, 1st *Earl* of Balfour 139–40
Banbury (Oxfordshire) 75, 76
Baron Court (Scotland) 175
baronage *see* nobility
Barry, *Sir* Charles (1795–1860) 126–8
Barry, Edward Middleton (1830–80) 126–8
Beaconsfield, Benjamin Disraeli, 1st *Earl* of (1804–81) 18, 126, 136, 138
Bede, the Venerable St. (c. 673–735) 27
Bedford plan 96
Berwick (Northumberland) 74, 173, 176
Beverley (Yorkshire) 75
Bigod, Roger, 5th *Earl* Norfolk (1245–1306) 42
Bill of Rights (1689) 104
bills 57–8, 110–11, 118, 130–1, 155–8, 206; debating procedures 72, 81, 89; MPs as
    agents for 119, *see also* legislation; petitions; redress before supply
Birmingham (Warwickshire) 123, 124, 139
Black, Conrad 171
Blue Books 129

Boer Wars (1881 and 1899–1902) 134, 138, 140

borough constituencies; enfranchisement 4–5, 16–17, 73–8, 103, 120–2; patronage 6, 17, 76–8, 104–5, 109–10; representation 7–10, 35–7, 63–4, 122, 124, 131; Scotland 175–6, 178; table (1295–1995) 22–3, *see also* county constituencies; elections; electorate; property qualification

Boyle, Charles, 4th *Earl* of Orrery (1676–1731), quoted 109

Bramber (Sussex) 76, 121

bribery *see* corruption

Bristol (constituency) 6, 17, 78, 110, 118, 122

Bristol, *Earls* of 92, 109

Bruce, Edward, *Lord* of Session, (late 16th c.) 177

Buckingham, *Duke* of (1727) 101

Buckingham, George Villiers, 1st *Duke* of (1592–1628) 90–1, 92

burgesses *see* borough constituencies, representation

Burghley, William Cecil, 1st *Baron* (1520–98) 15

Burke, Edmund (1729–97) 17; quoted 6, 110

Bury St. Edmunds (Suffolk) 65, 109

Bussy, *Sir* John (Speaker 1393–4, 1397, died 1399) 59, 66

Cabinet 106, 139, 156; and Commons 113, 114–15, 115–16, 130; and European Union 145–6

Calais (France) 74

Cambridge University constituency of 73

Cambridge (borough) 78

Camelford (Cornwall) 76

Campbell-Bannerman, Sir Henry (1836–1908) 137, 138

Canada 20, 134–6, 139, 141

candidates' list 150–1

Carey, George, 2nd *Baron* Hunsdon (1547–1603) 77

Carteret, John, 1st *Earl* Granville (1690–1763) 113

Cavalier Parliament (1661–79) 16, 100

Cavendish *see* Devonshire

Cecil, Robert, 1st *Earl* of Salisbury (c. 1563–1612) 77

Cecil, William, 1st *Baron* Burghley (1520–98) 15

censure, motions of 115

censuses 120–1, 124

Chaloner, *Sir* Thomas, the elder (1521–65) 76

Chamberlain, Joseph (1836–1914) 138–9, 140

Chancellor of the Exchequer 31, 64, 130

Chancery Division, High Court of Justice 12, 28

Charles I, *King* (1625–49, born 1600) vii, 16, 90–1, 93, 177

Charles II, *King* (1660–85), born 1630) 16, 100, 102–3

charters *see* enfranchisement

Chatham, William Pitt, 1st *Earl* of, ("Pitt the Elder", 1708–78) 17, 18, 109, 115–16

Cheshire 4, 5, 73, 75

Chester (Cheshire) 75

Chesterfield, Philip Dormer Stanhope, 4th *Earl* of (1694–1773) 17, 110, 115

Church of England *see* clergy; Reformation

Church of Scotland, General Assembly 174, 175, 176–7
Churchill, *Sir* Winston Leonard Spencer (1874–1965) vii, 134, 137, 153
Civil War (1642–6) 15–16, 90–1, 92–3, 95–6, 98–9
Clarendon, Constitutions of (1164) 32
clergy 6, 65, 73, 79–80; consent to taxation 32, 33, 39–43, 45, 58–9; in Scotland
    174–5, 176–7, *see also* Reformation
Clerk of the Commons 80, 154, 157
Clerk of Penicuik, *Sir* John, quoted 180
Cloakroom, Members' 126, 152
closure 131
Cobbett, William (1763–1835) 19, 128
Coke, *Sir* Edward (1552–1634) 180
Coke, *Sir* John (1563–1644) 98
commerce 112, 121, 139, 140, 180–1
Commissioners 156
committees 154, 155; accommodation 81, 126; Committee of the Whole 155; Public
    Accounts Committee 19–20, 130; Select Committee on European Legislation 144–8;
    select committees 129
Common Agricultural Policy (European Union) 166–7
common counsel 33–4, 36, 42, 90–1; Magna Carta 29, 31, 38–9, 42, 49
common law 8, 12
Commonwealth, the 20, 141
Comptroller 19, 130
computers xi–xii, 124, 159
Conservative Party 138, 139–40, 150–2; and press 161–72
constituencies *see* borough
constituencies; county constituencies; elections; electorate constitution vi–vii, 132–4,
    141–2, 143–4
Commons' assent to legislation 57, 72–3; Crown-in-Parliament 72–3, 102–4, 106,
    107–8, 111
Constitutional history of England, The (William Stubbs) 26, 45–6, 48–9, 173, 196;
    quoted 65
continental assemblies 18, 96–7, 113–14, 116–17, 175, 208
Convention of Royal Burghs (Scotland) 174, 176, 181
Copley, *Sir* Thomas 77
Cornwall, Duchy of 74, 76
coronation oath 27, 28
Corrupt Practices Act (1883) 123, 131
corruption 16–17, 51, 64, 101–2, 109–10; elections 3, 60–1, 122, 124
Council, King's 26–7, 30–1, 44, 72; Civil War 92, 94, 95–6; Great Council 12, 65;
    legislation 55, 56, 66, 144
county constituencies 17, 43–4, 68–9, 120–2, 124; representation 4–5, 8–10, 32–40,
    60–1, 93–5; of Scottish Parliament 178; table (1295–1995) 22–3, *see also* borough
    constituencies; elections; electorate
Court of King's Bench 12, 26, 31
Court of Requests 12, 126
Court of Session (Scotland) 175, 177, 178, 179
Court of Star Chamber 12

Cromwell, Oliver, (*Lord Protector* 1653–8, born 1599) 16, 93, 95, 97, 98

Cromwell, Ralph, *Baron* 64

Cromwell, Thomas, *Earl* of Essex (c. 1485–1540) 14

Cromwell, Thomas (MP 1571) 76

Crown 56–8, 64–6, 73–7, 119; cost of war 10–11, 16, 28–30, 37–8, 53–5; dependence on taxation 13–15, 36–8, 49–53, 75, 87–9; direct rule fails 90–3, 95–6, 97–8; patronage 15; 65–6, 76–7, 100, 104–7, 130; sovereignty of Crown-in-Parliament 15–17, 97–9, 102, 106–8, 111, 116–17; sovereignty of European Union 143–9, *see also* Royal Assent; Royal Prerogative; Royal Proclamations

Crypt Chapel 126

Cudlipp, Hugh 163

customs and excise 13, 15, 16, 28–30, 50–1, 88; excise 15, 18, 113; *King* John 11, 29; officials 105–6; wool subsidiary 49–50, 51, 65, *see also* taxation

Dalrymple, James, 1st *Viscount* Stair (1619–95), quoted 179, 180

Danger of mercenary parliaments, quoted 100

Davison, William (c. 1541–1608) 76

de Bohun, Humphrey, 3rd *Earl* of Hereford (d. 1298) 42

de la Mare, *Sir* Peter (Speaker, 1376) 59, 63, 200

de la Pole, Michael, *Earl* of Suffolk (c. 1330–89) 64

de la Pole, William, 4th *Earl* and 1st *Duke* of Suffolk (1396–1450) 64, 65

de Montfort, Simon, *Earl* of Leicester (c. 1208–65) 34–5, 44

De tallagio non concedendo (13th c) 42

debates 19, 49, 72, 130–1, 152–8; Reform Bills 119–20, 124–6; in St Stephen's 79–81, 154

Derby (borough) 17, 110

Derby, Edward Geoffrey Smith Stanley, 14th *Earl* of (1799–1869) 18, 124

despatch box 154

Dettingen (1743) vii, 114

Devereux, Robert, 2nd *Earl* of Essex (1566–1601) 74, 77

Devereux, Robert, 3rd *Earl* of Essex (1591–1646) 92–3

Devonshire, Cavendish family, *Dukes* of 17, 110, 122

Digby, John, 1st *Earl* of Bristol (1580–1653) 92

Digges, *Sir* Dudley (1583–1639) 94

directives (European Union) 144, 212

Disraeli, Benjamin, 1st *Earl* of Beaconsfield (1804–81) 18, 126, 136, 138

divine right 107

divisions 72, 78, 104–5, 124–6, 156; origins 80–1; table of participation (1861–1926) 125

Doncaster North 151

Dugdale, William (MP 1832) 121

Dunfermline, Treaty of (1296) 176

Durham (city and county) 4, 17, 74

East India Company 112

Edward I, *King* (1272–1307, b. 1239) 28, 29; consent to taxation established 7, 35–7, 40, 42, 47; Scotland 173; war 11, 28–9, 173

Edward II, *King,* (1307–27, b. 1284) 52, 63

Edward III, *King,* 1327–77, b. 1312) 49, 51, 52–3, 57, 79

Edward IV, *King,* 1461–83, b. 1442) 50, 59, 66, 73

Edward 'The Confessor', *King* (1042–66, b. c. 1003) 36

Edward VI, *King* (1547–53, b. 1537) 71, 73, 75, 79

elections by county court 7–8, 32–7, 60–1; corruption 98, 102–5, 122, 124, 131; frequency 108; open voting 122, 124; party machines 19, 123, 129, 131; registration of voters 122–3; uncontested 17, 109–10, 123, 210, *see also* borough constituencies; county constituencies; electorate; franchise

electorate 5–6, 74, 103, 118–19, 131, 209; forty-shilling freehold qualification (1430) 5, 14, 61, 120–1; franchise extended 6, 18, 123–4, 132; in Scotland 177–8; table (1450–1992) 24–5; urban influence 6, 9–10, *see also* borough constituencies; county constituencies; elections

Eliot, *Sir* John (1592–1632) 93

Elizabeth I, *Queen* (1558–1603, b. 1533) 70, 71; enfranchisement 73–7; monopolies 72–3; quoted 205

Elton, *Sir* Geoffrey 63, 67–8, 84, 86

empire, British 20, 112, 134–6, 141; imperial preference 139–40; parliamentary federation 137–8, 140

enfranchisement 4, 16–17, 73–7, 120–1, 122; Charles II revokes charters 103

Essex, Robert Devereux, 2nd *Earl* of (1566–1601) 74, 77

Essex, Robert Devereux, 3rd *Earl* of (1591–1646) 92–3

Essex, Thomas Cromwell, *Earl* of (c. 1485–1540) 14

European Communities Act (1972, as amended) 143, 144, 147

European Court of Justice 143, 146, 147

European Parliament 143–4, 148–9

European Parliamentary Elections Act (1978) 143–4, 145

European Union 143–9, 166–70

Ewart, William (1798–1869) 121

Exchequer 12, 28, 31, 105, 126, 130

Fiennes, William, 1st *Viscount* Saye and Sele (1582–1662) 92

fifteenths *see* tenths and fifteenths

fire (16th October, 1834) 19, 126–7

Fitzalan, Richard, *Earl* of Arundel (Appellant) 63

Fleetwood, William (c. 1535–1594) 76

Fleta (c. 1300), quoted 27

Fortescue, *Sir* John (c. 1394–c. 1476) 207–8; quoted 51

Fowey (Cornwall) 76

franchise 2, 61, 103; (1429–30) 9, 14, 66–7, 74; (1832) 120–1, 121–2; (1867) 123–4; (1884) 6–7, 131, 132; Scottish Parliament 177–8

freeholders 39, 103, 120–1; forty-shilling freehold 5, 9–10, 14, 61, 178

freemen 8, 39, 41

Galt, *Sir* Alexander Tilloch (1817–93) 135

Gardiner, Samuel Rawson 84

Gascoigne, George (c. 1525–1577) 79

Gatton (Surrey) 74, 76, 109

Gaunt (Ghent), John of, *Duke* of Lancaster (1340–99) 60, 63

General Assembly (Church of Scotland) 174, 175, 176–7

gentry 66, 68–9, 71, 112; and baronage 13–14, 62–4; and freeholders 61; local government role 43, 56

George II, *King* (1727–60, b. 1683) vii, 16, 114, 115

George III, *King* 1760–1820, b. 1738) 115

Gibbon, Edward (1737–94) 154

Gladstone, Thomas 121, 154

Gladstone, William Ewart, Liberal statesman (1809–98) 121, 122, 129, 130, 131, 136; Home Rule for Ireland 130–1, 133–4, 136, 138

Glenamara, Edward Watson Short, PC, *Baron* 111

Glorious Revolution, The (1688) 16, 85, 97, 102–8, 111, 177

Good Parliament (1376) 9, 60, 62–3, 64, 65; refusal to grant tax 51; Speaker 59, 63

Grafton, *Dukes* of 109

Grampound (Cornwall) 74, 76

Granville, John Carteret, 1st *Earl* (1690–1763) 113, 114

Greene, Thomas 127

Grey, Charles Grey, 2nd *Earl* (1764–1845), quoted 120

Guilford, Frederick North, 2nd *Earl* of, 8th *Baron* North (1732–92 114–15

guillotine (in debates) 19, 131

Gurney, *Sir* Goldsworthy (1793–1875) 128

Hales, John (d. 1571) 76

Hall, Arthur (c. 1540–1604) 81

Hansard (official record of debates) 19, 128, 159

Hansard, Thomas Curson (1776–1833, son of Luke) 128

Harwicke, Philip Yorke, 1st *Earl* of (1690–1764), quoted 1–2

Harmsworth, Vere Harold Esmond, 3rd *Viscount* Rothermere 171

Hay, William (1695–1755) 101–2

Hayter, *Sir* George 121

Hearth Tax 16

Hele, *Sir* John (c. 1543–1608) 81

Henry II, *King* (1154–1189, b. 1133) 35

Henry III, *King* 1216–72, b. 1207) 7, 26, 28, 40, 43; first monarch to ask for taxation regularly 29–30; parliaments 33–6

Henry IV, *King* (1399–1413, b. 1367) 60, 64, 66

Henry V, *King* (1413–1422, b. 1387) 53, 59, 66; quoted 57

Henry VI, *King* (1422–61 and 1470–1, b. 1421) 57, 64, 65

Henry VII, *King* (1485–1509, b. 1457) 54, 55, 65, 66, 73

Henry VIII, *King* (1509–1547, b. 1491) 57, 72; assets squandered 14, 88; enlargement of Commons 73, 75; quoted 10; rule by statute 89, 97

Hertford, Humphrey de Bohun, 3rd *Earl* (d. 1298) 42

Hertford, Edward Seymour, *Earl* of, and *Duke* of Somerset (c. 1506–52) 74

Hervey of Ickworth, John Hervey, *Baron* (1696–1743) 101

Hessians 115–16

Higham Ferrers (Northamptonshire) 75, 76

historiography 70–2, 173–4; computers 124, 125; Hanoverian 110, 119; medieval 26, 30, 45–7, 62–9; Stuart 83–7, 91–2, 94, 95–6, 97–8, 99

History of Scotland (William Robertson) 175

Hooker, *alias* Vowell, John (c. 1526–1601), quoted 80

Horsham (Sussex) 76, 122

Houldsworth, Thomas 121

hours 130–1, 153

House of Commons 10, 35–8, 62–4, 68–9, 124–6, 152–60; advice to monarch 63, 90–1;

consent to taxation 37–8, 51–8, 87–9, 113; Crown's financial dependence 10–16, 50–3, 88; fairer laws a condition 14, 51–8, 89–90, 143; procedure 57–8, 79–81, 124–6, 130–1, 152–8; representation 2–7, 32–5, 73–5, 120–1, 123–4; sovereignty and European Union 143–9, *see also* borough constituencies; constitution; county constituencies; elections; electorate; House of Lords; taxation

House of Lords 2, 62–4, 70, 92–3, 126; Crown looks beyond feudal ties 30–2, 43–4, 73, 76–7; parliamentary peerage 11, 31–2, 75, 92–3; patronage of Commons seats 14, 17, 76–7, 109, 131; reform in Commons 119–20, 122; scrutiny, procedure and tradition 1–2, 81, 140, 146, 147, 155–8, *see also* Crown; House of Commons; nobility; taxation

Howard family, *Dukes* of Norfolk 76, 77

Howard, Thomas, *2nd Earl* of Arundel and Surrey (1586–1646) 92

Hundred Years' War (1337–1453) 11, 13, 45, 52, 54

Hungerford, *Sir* Thomas (d. 1398) 63

Hunsdon, George Carey, 2nd *Baron* (1547–1603) 77

impeachment 64, 92, 107

imperial preference 20, 139–40, 141

income tax 113

India 112, 134

industrial revolution 17, 112, 137, 139

Industry and Parliament Trust 160

inflation 5, 10, 29, 88

information technology xi–xii, 124, 125, 159–60

Institutions of the law of Scotland (James Dalrymple, 1st *Viscount* Stair (1619–95), quoted 179

inter-communing 63

interest rates 18, 112

Ireland 20, 96, 110, 114, 120; Home Rule 130–1, 133–4, 136, 137–8, 140, 141–2; Union (1801) 4, 17, 126, 133–4

Isle of Wight 74, 77

Jacobites 106–7, 109, 111, 114, 115–16, 133; and throne of Scotland 173, 180–1

James I, *King* of England (1603–25, b. 1566), VI of Scotland (1567–1625), 72–3, 174, 177; quoted 48, 205; Union scheme 89, 90

James I, *King* of Scotland (1406–37, b. 1394) 177–8

James II of England, VII of Scotland, *King* b. 1633, reigned 1685–8, d. 1701) 15–16, 102, 103–4, 173, 180

Jenkins, Simon, quoted, p vii

Jersey (Channel Islands) 74

John Balliol, *King* of Scotland (1292–96, b. circa 1250) 173

John of Gaunt, *Duke* of Lancaster (1340–99) 60, 63

John, *King* 1199–1216, b. 1167) 11, 29, 33, 56; quoted 40

Journal, House of Commons' 81, 83, 128

justice 104; county courts 7, 9, 33, 35–6, 43, 68; parliamentary petitions 12, 27–8, 55–7; royal law courts 8, 23, 31

justices of the peace 68

justiciars 28, 43–4

Kennedy, George Penrose 127

Knaresborough (Yorkshire) 76

knights 7–10, 32–40, 60–1, 76, 79; tax collectors 40, 43, 54–5, *see also* county constituencies

Labour Party 7, 136, 137, 151, 152 and press 161, 162, 163, 167

Lamb, *Sir* Albert (Larry) 161–2

Lancaster (Lancashire) 76

Lancaster, Duchy of 15, 60, 76, 88

Lancaster, John of Gaunt, *Duke* of (1340–99) 60, 63

le Scrope, Richard, *Archbishop* of York (c. 1350–1405) 60

legislation 51–8, 64, 155–8; delegated 19, 130–1, 144; and membership of European Union 143–9; and Royal Prerogative 13–14, 57–8, 65–6, 72–3, 89–90, 143; of Scottish Parliament 179–80

Leicester, Simon de Montfort, *Earl* of (c. 1208–65) 34–5, 44

Liberal Party (Liberal Democrats) 20, 124, 129, 132–42

lighting 128

Liverpool (borough) 74, 76, 112, 121

livery badges 64

Lloyd-George of Dwyfor, David Lloyd George, 1st *Earl* (1863–1945) 20, 133

loans 29, 112, 113

lobbies *see* divisions

lobbyists 159

local government 43–5, 55–6, 68–9, 103–4, 110–11; *see also* enfranchisement; justice

London season 79, 94

Long Parliament (1406) 59, 65, 66; petition about sheriffs 60–1

Looe, East (Cornwall) 76

Lords Appellant 63, 64

Lords of the Articles (Scotland) 175, 178–9

Lothian, Philip Kerr, *Marquess* of 140

Luce, *Sir* Richard Napier, PC 151

Lucy, *Sir* Henry 128

Lynn, King's (Norfolk) 76

Maastricht, Treaty of (1993) 148, 165, 169

Macaulay, Thomas Babington Macaulay, 1st *Baron* (1800–59) 84; quoted 105

Macdonald, *Sir* John Alexander (1815–91) 135, 140

McGurk, Anna 157

MacKenzie, Kelvin 162–3

Magna Carta (1215) 12, 31–2, 42, 49; consent to taxation 29, 38–9, 43–4; election of knights 33, 35; individual summonses 31–2

maiden speeches 154

Major, *The Rt. Hon.* John, PC, MP, Prime Minister (1990–) 166–71

majorities 115, 131

Mary Tudor, *Queen* 1553–8, b. 1516) 70, 72, 73, 75

May, Baptist (1629–98) 100

Members of Parliament 58–9, 65–6, 78–9, 91–3, 101–2, 105; advice to monarch 29–30, 90–1; constituency role 37, 52, 66–7, 131, 153, 158–9; contemporary 150–60; knights and burgesses 7–10, 13, 37–8, 71, 78; London's attractiveness 79, 94

Merciless Parliament (1388) February 60, 63; September 64

Miles, Philip 122

Modus tenendi parliamentum (14th c.) 13, 27, 31, 35; feudal magnates no longer representatives 38, 42, 49

Mompesson, *Sir* Giles (1584–c. 1651) 92

Monmouthshire 4, 5, 74

monopolies 72–3, 88, 89, 176

Montfort, Simon de, *Earl* of Leicester (c. 1208–65) 34–5, 44

Murdoch, (Keith) Rupert, (1931–) 161–72

Namier, *Sir* Lewis Bernstein (1888–1960) 110

National Debt 18, 97, 112

navy 14, 112, 114, 115, 160

Neale, *Sir* John, quoted 70–1, 77

necessity 51–5, 65, 71

New Palace of Westminster (1848–51) 126–8

New Zealand 134–5, 139, 140, 141

Newark (Nottinghamshire) 17, 77, 103

Newcastle, Thomas Pelham Holles, *Duke* of (1693–1768) 102, 109, 113, 115, 116

Newcastle under Lyne (Staffordshire) 79

nobility 11, 28–30, 37–43, 49–51, parliamentary peerage 30–2, 56, 62–4, 92–3, 109–10, 119–20; Scottish 177–8

Norfolk, *Dukes* of, Howard family 76, 77

Norfolk, Roger Bigod, 5th *Earl* (1245–1306) 42

North, Frederick North, 8th *Baron* and 2nd *Earl* of Guilford (1732–92) 114–15

Northampton, Treaty of (1328) 173

Notestein, Wallace 70–1, 85, 89

Noy, William (1577–1634) 94

obstruction 1–2, 130, 131, 133, 140

Old Sarum (Wiltshire) 74, 76, 109

Oldhall, *Sir* William (c. 1390–c. 1466) 59

Ordinances (1311) 27

Orford, *Sir* Robert Walpole, 1st *Earl* of (1676–1745) 100–1, 108, 113

Orrery, Charles Boyle, 4th *Earl* of, (1676–1731), quoted 109

Oxford, University constituency of 73

packing 75–6, 100, 102–5

Painted Chamber 126

pairing 156

Palmerston, Henry John Temple, 3rd *Viscount* (1784–1865) 128

Parliament Act (1911) 1, 140

Parliament (United Kingdom) 30–2, 44–7, 55–6, 90–1; and European Union 143–9; judicial role 26–8; law-making 55–8; Scottish Parliament (1296–1707) 173–81; sovereignty of Crown-in-Parliament 16–17, 48–9, 58, 91–3, 102–4, 106–8; taxation 28–30, 38–40, 49–50; two houses 1–2, 12–14, 35–8, 62–4, 92–3, *see also* Crown; House of Commons; House of Lords

Parnell, Charles Stewart (1846–91) 130–1; *see also* Ireland, Home Rule

parties 18, 19, 96; constituency organisations 19, 124, 129, 130–1, 150–2; court and country 97, 105–6, 108, 114–15, *see also* Conservative Party; Labour Party; Liberal Party (Liberal Democrats); Tories; Whigs

patents 89, 92

patronage; crown 65–6, 72, 76, 91, 97, 104–7; nobility 76–7, 92, 94, 109–10

Peasants' Revolt (1381) 9

peerage *see* nobility, parliamentary peerage

Pelham, Henry (c. 1695–1754) 115

Pelham, Thomas Pelham Holles, *Duke* of Newcastle (1693–1768) 102, 109, 113, 115, 116

Pembroke, *Earls* of (16th c.) 77–8, 79

Pepys, Samuel (1633–1703) 100

Percy, *Dr* John 128

Peterborough (Northamptonshire) 75

Petition of Right (1628) 90, 92

petitions 12, 27–8, 45, 55–8, 89–90, 130; (1429–30) 60–1, *see also* bills; redress before supply; taxation

Petty, William, 2nd *Earl* of Shelburne (1737–1805) 115

Pilgrimage of Grace (1536–7) 75

Pitt, William, 1st *Earl* of Chatham, ("Pitt the Elder", 1708–78) 17, 18, 109, 115–16

placemen 100–2, 104–6; *see also* corruption; patronage

Police and magistrates' courts bill (enacted 1994) 155–6

political reform associations 118

poll books 3, 122, 124

population 4–5, 8–10, 123–4, 139; no link to representation 3–6, 74, 103, 118, 178

Portillo, *The Rt. Hon.* Michael, PC, MP 170

press, the 21, 118, 128–9, 161–72

pressure groups 112, 129, 135–6, 159

Preston (Lancashire) 76

Primrose, Archibald Philip, 5th *Earl* of Rosebery (1847–1929) 137–8

Primrose League 129

Private Members' Bills 156–7

privilege 62, 78–9

property qualification 43–4, 61, 74, 97, 103; forty-shilling freehold 5–6, 9–10, 61, 103; reform 120–1, 123–4

prospective parliamentary candidates 151–2

Provisions of Oxford (1258) 26, 34, 44

Pugin, Augustus Welby Northmore (1812–52) 126–8

Pym, John (1584–1643) 87, 93, 94

questions 130, 154–5

quorum 97–8

radicals 119–20, 122–3, 129, 131, 136–7

Ragman's Roll, the 173

Redistribution of Seats Act (1885) 122, 124, 131

redress before supply 10–13, 51–8, 130–1

Reform Act (1832) 3–7, 18–19, 118–23

Reform Act (1867) 3–7, 18–19, 123–4, 129

Reform Act (1884) 3, 6, 132, 133

Reformation, the 70, 88, 89, 94–5, 97, 98–9 chantries 79, 80; James II 103–4; monasteries 10, 14, 75, 177; Reformation Parliament 77; Scotland 174, 176–7, 178–9, 180–1, *see also* clergy

Regency Act (1706) 106–7

registers, of electors 6–7, 122–3, 124, 129, 132; to Scottish Parliament 178

Reid, David Boswell (1805–63) 127–8

report stage 156, 158

Representation of the People Act (1884) 131

residential qualification 78, 123–4

Restoration (1660) 5, 102

Retford, East (Nottinghamshire) 77

returning officer 60–1

returns, blank 76, 77

Richard I, *King* (statue) 126

Richard II, *King* (1367–1400, reigned 1377–99) 57, 60, 63, 64

Richmond (Yorkshire) 75

Ripon (Yorkshire) 76

Rising, Castle (Norfolk) 77

Robert I (the Bruce), *King* of Scotland (1306–29, b. 1274) 173

Robertson, William (*History of Scotland*) 175

Roebuck, John Arthur, quoted 119–20

Roman law 7, 8, 40, 175, 184

Rome, Treaties of (1957) 143, 147

Rosebery, Archibald Philip Primrose, 5th *Earl* of (1847–1929) 137–8

Rothermere, Vere Harold Esmond Harmsworth, 3rd *Viscount* 171

Roxburghe, John Ker, 5th *Earl* and 1st *Duke* of (cr. 1707) quoted 180

Royal Assent vi–vii, 1, 13, 14, 156

Royal Prerogative 2, 12, 53; borough charters 73–7, 102–3; and European Union 143, 144; monopolies 72–3, 88, 89

Royal Proclamations 19, 33, 89

Russell, Conrad Sebastian Robert Russell, 5th *Earl* (historian) 84, 86–7, 88, 89, 91, 99

Russell family 122

Rutland, *Earls* of (16th c.) 77

Sacheverell, Henry (c. 1674–1724) 107

Sadler, *Sir* Ralph (1507–87) 76

St. Albans (Hertfordshire) 75

St. Albans, *Viscount see* Bacon, Francis Salisbury, Robert Cecil, 1st *Earl* of (c. 1563–1612) 77

Saye and Sele, William Fiennes, 1st *Viscount* 1582–1662) 92

Scotland 96, 120, 132, 173–81; and France iii, 176, 180; Home Rule viii, 20, 132–3, 136, 137–8, 141–2; Parliament of (1296–1707) 173–81; Union (1707) 5, 17, 148, 179–81; Union scheme, James I and VI 89; 90

Scrope, Richard *Archbishop* (c. 1350–1405) 60

scutage, 39–41, 43, 193–4

Seasonable argument, a (1677), quoted 100

seats *see* borough constituencies; county constituencies

second reading 155–6

secret ballot 3, 123, 124, 130, 131

serfs 8–9, 11

sessions, 19, 114, 128, 130–1, 155

Seymour, Edward, 1st *Duke* of Somerset (c. 1506–1552) 74

Seymour of Sudeley, Thomas Seymour, 1st *Baron* (c. 1508–1549) 77

Shelburne, William Petty, 2nd *Earl* of (1737–1805) 115

sheriffs 33–5, 38, 41, 42, 60–1; tax collection 40, 43

Shoreham, New (Sussex) 76

Short, Edward Watson, PC, *Baron* Glenamara 111

Shrewsbury 36, 37, 192

sifting 145–8

sittings 128, 130–1, 153, 156

Skinner, Dennis, MP, quoted 152

smoking room 153

Somerset, Edward Seymour, 1st *Duke* of (c. 1506–1552) 74

South Africa 134, 138, 139, 140

Speaker 14, 59–60, 63, 72, 78, 101; adjournment debates 156–7

speeches 80, 81, 93, 153, 154

Stair, James Dalrymple, 1st *Viscount* 1619–95), quoted 179, 180

Stamp Act (1765) 113

Stanhope, Philip Dormer, 4th *Earl* of Chesterfield (1694–1773) 17, 110, 115

Stewart, *Prince* Charles Edward Louis; Philip Casimir (1720–88) 114, 115–16; *see also* Jacobites

Stewart, *Prince* James Francis Edward, the "Old Pretender" (1688–1766) 180–1; *see also* Jacobites

Stockbridge (Hampshire) 76

Strafford, Thomas Wentworth, 1st *Earl* of (1593–1641) 93, 94

Strangers' Gallery 152

Stubbs, William (*The constitutional history of England*) 26, 45–6, 48–9, 173, 196; quoted 65

subsidiarity 147

Sudbury (Suffolk) 76

Sudeley, Thomas Seymour, 1st *Baron* Seymour of (c. 1508–1549) 77

Suffolk, Michael de la Pole, *Earl* of (c. 1330–89) 64

Suffolk, William de la Pole, 4th *Earl* and 1st *Duke* of (1396–1450) 64, 65

summons, writs of 30–2, 35–6, 38, 184, 191, 196; election returns 60–1; parliament unable to meet unless summoned 16, 65, 102, 107

Sun, The (newspaper) 161–72

supply 130, 131; *see also* common counsel; redress before supply; taxation

Sutton, *Sir* Robert 101

swords 152

Szostak, Rick (historian) 111

Table Office 154

taxation 13, 28–30, 37–43, 54–5, 139; assessments 13, 15, 52, 54, 88–9; collection 40, 42, 43, 52, 54–5; consent 51–6, 71–2, 112; 113, 130; Scottish monarch 174; yield 15, 16, 50–1, 54, 88, *see also* tenths and fifteenths

Tea Room, Members' 153

Temple, Henry John, 3rd *Viscount* Palmerston (1784–1865) 128

ten minute rule 157–8

tenths and fifteenths 15, 53–5, 65, 75; fixed rate 50–1; a tax on moveables 11, 13, 29–30, 39

Thames (river) 128, 130

Thatcher, Margaret Hilda Thatcher, OM, PC, FRS, *Baroness* 7, 139, 161–2, 165, 166

Thetford (Norfolk) 76

third reading 156

Thirsk (Yorkshire) 76

Times, The 165, 167–9, 171

Tiptoft, John Tipftoft or Tibetot, *Baron* (c. 1375–1443) 59, 199

Toland, John (1670–1722), quoted 106

Toleration Act (1689) 99

Tories 100–1, 106–8, 120–1, 122, 124, 138; *see also* Conservative Party

Tournai (France) 74, 202

Tower of London 36

towers 127

towns *see* borough constituencies

Townshend Act (1767) 113

Treasury 19–20, 105, 112

Trevor, *Sir* John (c. 1637–1717) 101

Triennial Act (1694) 107

unanimity (in European Union decisions) 146

United States of America viii, 85, 106, 159; War of American Independence (1775–83) 18, 112, 113, 114–15, 135

universities, ancient 4, 73, 103

Vane or Fane, *Sir* Ralph (d. 1552) 80

ventilation system 127–8

Verulam, *Baron see* Bacon, Francis

villeins 8–9, 39, 40

Villiers, George, 1st *Duke* of Buckingham (1592–1628) 90–1, 92

votes *see* divisions; elections; franchise

Wales 132; conquest 36, 37, 38; Home Rule 20, 133, 136, 137, 148; seats in Commons 4, 5, 73, 74, 75, 120

Walpole, *Sir* Robert, 1st *Earl* of Orford (1676–1745) 100–1, 108, 113

war 28–30, 51–5, 71–2, 87–8, 97; of American Independence (1775–83) 18, 112, 113, 114–15, 135; continental 65, 90–1, 111–12, 115–16; costs 10–11, 18, 112, 130; South African wars (1881 and 1899–1902) 138, 140

Ward, John (expelled 1727) 101

Wars of the Roses (1455–85) 72, 87–8, 92–3

Wenlock, Much (Shropshire) 73

Wentworth, Thomas, 1st *Earl* of Strafford (1593–1641) 93, 94

Westminster Abbey 36, 79

Westminster (Middlesex) (constituency) 75

Westminster Hall 126

Westminster, Palace of 12, 79–81, 126–8

Whigs 18, 19, 103, 106–8, 118–21, 173; *see also* Liberal Party (Liberal Democrats)

Whips 20–1, 125, 131, 156

Wigan, (Lancashire) 76

Wilkes, John (1727–97) 119

William III, *King* (1689–1702, b. 1650) vii, 85, 97, 104, 111, 177

William IV, *King* (1830–7, b. 1765) 119

Williams, *Sir* Thomas 100
Wilton (Wiltshire) 76
Wolsey, Thomas, *Cardinal* (c. 1475–1530) 77
women 6, 7, 19, 131, 132, 157
wool subsidy 49–50, 51, 65
Worcester (merchant vessel) 181
Wortley, James 121
Yarmouth, Great (Norfolk) 76
yeomen 9, 67
Yonge, *Sir* William (d. 1755) 101
York (Yorkshire) 75
Yorke, Philip, 1st *Earl* of Hardwicke (1690–1764), quoted 1–2